Carol Tosone
Editor

Shared Trauma, Shared Resilience During a Pandemic

Social Work in the Time of COVID-19

Foreword by Charles R. Figley

 Springer

Editor
Carol Tosone
Silver School of Social Work
New York University
New York, NY, USA

ISSN 2520-162X   ISSN 2520-1611   (electronic)
Essential Clinical Social Work Series
ISBN 978-3-030-61441-6   ISBN 978-3-030-61442-3   (eBook)
https://doi.org/10.1007/978-3-030-61442-3

This Springer imprint is published by the registered company Springer Nature Switzerland AG
The registered company address is: Gewerbestrasse 11, 6330 Cham, Switzerland

This book is dedicated to YOU and all social workers, whether starting or seasoned, who practice bravely in a COVID-19 world.

Foreword[1]

Joe Boscarino, who grew up in New Jersey, had just started his new job at the New York Academy of Medicine (NYAM) on Fifth Avenue and 103rd Street in Manhattan. On the morning of September 11, his Port Authority Trans-Hudson train from Hoboken was one of the last to enter the basement of the World Trade Center. Joe remembers going up the escalators from the basement to the crowded main mezzanine level. He recalls heading to the subway tunnels at the end of the mezzanine and walking into the entrance to the C train, northbound to 96th Street. At 8:46 a.m. and about 50 meters inside the C train tunnel, he heard a very loud metallic noise and felt a deep tremor on the subway platform. Joe suspected a train derailment and thoughts of the 1993 World Trade Center attack ran through his mind as he entered his uptown-bounded train.

About 15 min or so later, when Joe emerged from the subway tunnel at 96th Street and Central Park West, there was no hint of an attack. The word on 96th Street was that a plane had flown into one of the Twin Towers. A plane? he thought. Arriving at work about 10 min later, Jose, the elevator operator, announced excitedly that a second plane had flown into the Twin Towers. Joe knew exactly what that meant. He arrived at his office. But after a few minutes of thought, he knew what to do. He needed to find his way out of Manhattan that morning and to call me. That was the start of a long collaboration.

When Joe called me that day, I knew we had important work to do. First, I needed to attend to Joe and help him process the day. Then we talked about work matters and our plans to study New Yorkers' mental health in the wake of the attacks. We completed and published our findings, and we continued our discussions about the shock of the attack on a great city and how the City has responded. We understood that the dark nights of shared trauma were gradually overcome by the light of shared resilience.

---

[1] The author wishes to thank his colleague and wife, Dr. Kathleen Regan Figley, for her editing assistance.

Shared trauma has emerged as one of the most important constructs in understanding the mental health consequences for mental health experts working with trauma survivors. Like burnout, compassion fatigue, secondary trauma, and vicarious trauma, the concept of shared trauma provides an important framework for practitioners' understanding of the consequences of their work with those who have been traumatized. Shared resilience is the desired outcome and the focus of trauma processing for practitioner and client. The shared trauma and shared resilience lessons learned from the September 11 attack paved the way for understanding and coping with today's shared traumas.

This is an important book with the concept of Shared Trauma as its unifying and descriptive reference point. What will distinguish it from other books, however, is highlighting the desired result of shared trauma consequences by embracing the concept of shared resilience as we all struggle to thrive (not just survive) in the time of COVID-19 and the World Pandemic of 2020.

Who could have imagined that the year 2020 would present practitioners with multiple experiences of shared trauma? We wonder as individuals: Where will the COVID-19 World Pandemic take us? Will we survive? Will our lives be changed as a result of debilitating symptoms that take hold after being ill? As practitioners, we face these fears as we address the fears of our clients. Add to that the ongoing collective traumas of today's real-life struggles with racism, the declining health of many Americans, the troubling economic and social divides, and the toxic national discourse and disgust felt across our country. When will our lives return to normal? And how do we address our own health and safety while caring for our clients who experience similar problems?

The term Shared Trauma was introduced by the practitioners' narrative accounts of their exposure to the same collective trauma as their clients after our country was attacked on September 11 (Altman and Davies 2002; Saakvitne 2002; Tosone and Bialkin 2003; Tosone et al. 2003; Tosone 2006). Baum's (2010) shared trauma was traced back to Schmideberg's (1942) work during the Second World War and the London blitz and the impact on clinical work with patients. She notes that much later (during the 1991 Gulf War) the shared traumatic reality and the concept of "shared reality" emerged. Today, faced with these choices, Shared Trauma is the more commonly employed term used to describe the impact of single catastrophic events in relation to individual client-provider situations.

Shared Trauma is a term most suited to clinicians and their practice and life experiences when living and practicing in toxic, trauma-saturated environments. Competing constructs do not consider the direct clinician exposure factor. Shared Trauma is the response of professionals who experience both primary and secondary exposure to the same traumatic stressors as their clients. Both the client and the practitioner are survivors of the same traumatic event. There are significant psychosocial consequences from this sharing that can lead to permanent alterations in the clinician's worldviews and the views through their mental schema. So, this question must be addressed: How long can the clinician be exposed to the trauma first-hand and retain their professional responsibilities?

As with vicarious traumatization, these reactions have the potential to lead to permanent alterations in the clinician's existing mental schema and worldviews due to having a shared trauma exposure. As a result, both client and practitioner are potentially more susceptible to trauma symptoms such as the symptoms related to posttraumatic stress. Obviously, the blurring of professional and personal boundaries creates challenges for the practitioner, such as increased self-disclosure for both client and practitioner. Clients as well as clinicians may both experience common symptoms associated with shared trauma, compassion fatigue, and secondary trauma, particularly the frequently cited symptoms of overall exhaustion, depletion of empathy, and identification with others experiencing trauma (Tosone, 2012).

Based on this backdrop, Carol Tosone, as long-time editor-in-chief of the *Clinical Social Work Journal,* has produced this new and important book. Perhaps more than any other work, this book provides considerable insight into the stress and strains of trauma practitioners who both witness a traumatic event and provide support and therapy for survivors of the same event who witnessed it as well.

Because Shared Trauma is a phenomenon born out of a traumatic event, be it an individual or collective trauma, that is experienced at all levels – worldwide / multinational, societal, community, interpersonal, intrapsychic – practitioners must be prepared to share the clinical decisions within the Shared Trauma paradigm. It is the nature of the clinical context that Shared Trauma be communicated between practitioner and client, that a more intimate and more transparent client-practitioner context be worked out.

The assessment and psychometric strategies not only take into account the clients and practitioners most at risk in working with fellow survivors; additional factors also must be considered which indicate an increased exposure risk among those who will be at greater risk of post-traumatic reactions and psychopathology. Clients and practitioners will require more patience and time if they: (a) were in close proximity to the traumatic events; (b) had a history of exposure to similar high-stress situations with high disaster exposure; (c) developed insecure attachment; (d) were highly empathic; (e) perceived social support from friends, colleagues, and family is limited; and (e) are inexperienced practitioners with little psychotherapy practice. Practitioners may also require more interpersonal support and supervision. This is in addition to being aware of countertransference, the need for clearly marked work boundaries, supportive clinical settings, work-life balance, and the need for self-care and a comprehensive plan to maintain it. This also includes support for practitioners who wish to take a break from their role as long as it takes, and includes a clearly articulated plan for successful recovery. All available and appropriate resources for the treatment of shared trauma should be available to practitioners.

Shared Trauma of the practitioner, then, is a particular type of collective trauma that transforms practitioners and survivors in different ways. Both are exposed to powerful and personal experiences they share together in their respective individual ways. Practitioners and their clients co-create their clinical experiences that eventually conclude on a positive and productive note. What practitioners retain from these sessions is savored as a source of wisdom and inspiration they can disburse throughout their career.

In Tosone's 2012 contribution to the *Encyclopedia of Trauma*, she notes the clinical implications and applications of Shared Trauma as consonant with the relational approach to psychotherapy. Here the emphasis is on the mutuality of influence in the clinical dyad as well as affect regulation, that the clinical dyad exists in a unique, intersubjective context linked to this dyad and their background matter of histories, current interpersonal context, among other conditions created by this rich clinical context. Blurring of boundaries separating client and therapist is especially challenging for both. This situation can lead the practitioner to become emotionally absorbed in their clients' challenges because frequently it is a shared experience.

The next-to-last chapter (Chap. 36) seems to speak to me more directly because it contains the voices of the future: students from Professor Tosone's class this summer who were forced to take their trauma course online. Their shared COVID-19 trauma was contrasted with that of another NYU class back in 2001 (Tosone, et al. 2003). Focusing on the class members in her 2020 class, she is again co-authoring a report of shared trauma with her class toward their separate journeys toward trauma resilience. Some of these students struggled personally with what they saw and experienced while sheltered with their Zoom software. Social isolation has been a signature stressor for many practicing self-isolation, despite living with a spouse, a partner or parents, not to mention children. Yet many students report counteractive factors of remote learning, teletherapy, and free time which offset the challenges of self-quarantine. As one student noted: "Isolation is empowering in some ways, in that the more isolated I am, the more I know I am doing my part to help stop the spread [of COVID-19]."

Joe has worked through the challenges of September 11 and beyond, as evidenced by his sense of humor, sense of self, and scholarly productivity. The same can be said about the editor of this book and the author of this foreword.

Paul Henry Kurzwerg Distinguished Chair   Charles R. Figley, PhD
in Disaster Mental Health, Traumatology
Institute Chair and Distinguished Professor,
School of Social Work
Tulane University,
New Orleans, LA, USA

References

Altman, N., & Davies, J. M. (2002). Out of the blue: Reflections on a shared trauma out of the blue: Reflections on a shared trauma. *Psychoanalytic Dialogues, 12*(3), 359–360.

Baum, N. (2010). Shared traumatic reality in communal disasters: Toward a conceptualization. *Psychotherapy Theory, Research, Practice, 47*(2), 249–259.

Saakvitne, K. W. (2002). Shared trauma: The therapist's increased vulnerability. *Psychoanalytic Dialogues, 12*(3), 443–449.

Schmideberg, M. (1942). Some observations on individual reactions to air raids. *International Journal of Psycho-Analysis, 23*, 146–176.

Tosone, C. (2006). Therapeutic intimacy: A post-9/11 perspective. *Smith College Studies in Social Work, 76*(4), 89–98.

Tosone, C., & Bialkin, L. (2003). The impact of mass violence and secondary Trauma in clinical practice. In L. A. Straussner & N. Phillips (Eds.), *Social work with victims of mass violence* (pp. 157–167). Jossey-Bass.

Tosone, C., Lee, M., Bialkin, L., Martinez, A., Campbell, M., Martinez, M. M., et al. (2003). Shared trauma: Group reflections on the September 11th disaster. *Psychoanalytic Social Work, 10*(1), 57–77.

Endorsement

"*Shared Trauma, Shared Resilience During a Pandemic: Social Work in the Time of COVID-19* is a goldmine for social work practitioners, educators, and students. Carol Tosone, herself a treasure, has done the impossible – put together a volume about the pandemic DURING the pandemic. Carol might be the only person who has the editorial skills and depth of clinical knowledge to create a volume that validates the experiences of frontline workers and educates the reader about shared trauma in the dual pandemics of racism and COVID-19. Educators and students at the undergraduate and graduate levels will appreciate the breadth of populations, problems, and settings covered in the text."

–Jonathan B. Singer, PhD, LCSW, *Associate Professor, School of Social Work, Loyola University Chicago; Founder and Host of the Social Work Podcast*

Acknowledgments

Any book is a labor of love, not only for the person writing it but also for those who sacrificed precious time with the author(s) so that they could complete the project. In this instance, there are 68 contributing authors and countless loved ones who made this book possible. These authors generously shared their expertise and passion for the populations they serve, so a warm thank you to each of you, your families, and loved ones. Thank you to Janet Kim, Senior Editor for Springer, for your heartfelt belief in the project and prioritization of its publication. Every suggestion was an excellent one and enhanced the scholarship and value of the work. Thank you to Jack Osea for your availability (nearly 24/7), professional interaction with the contributors, stellar editorial support, good nature, and great sense of humor that made every aspect of the work enjoyable. Lastly, a big shout-out to my family, friends, and even "Lovey" (my dog) who only heard "no" to all invitations for the past 2 months so that this time-sensitive book could be brought to fruition.

With deep appreciation to all,
Carol

Contents

1   **Introduction**.   1
Carol Tosone

Part I   On the Front Lines of the COVID-19 Pandemic

2   **Repurposed, Reassigned, Redeployed**.   15
Patricia Hecht

3   **COVID-19 and Moral Distress/Moral Anguish Therapeutic
Support for Healthcare Workers in Acute Care: Our Voice**.   21
Victoria L. Cerone

4   **On the Front Lines of the Fight Against the COVID-19 Pandemic:
Meaning-Making and Shared Trauma**.   33
Sophia Tsesmelis Piccolino

5   **Supervising Psychiatry Residents in a COVID-19-Only
Hospital: A Hall of Mirrors**.   39
Leslie Cummins

Part II   Specialty Populations Impacted by the COVID-19 Pandemic

6   **Staying True to Our Core Social Work Values During
the COVID-19 Pandemic**.   53
David Kamnitzer, Elisa Chow, and Jeanine D. Costley

7   **Safety Planning with Survivors of Domestic Violence:
How COVID-19 Shifts the Focus**.   61
Catherine Hodes

8   **Reflections on COVID-19, Domestic Violence,
and Shared Trauma**.   69
Shari Bloomberg

9   COVID-19 and Sheltering in Place: The Experiences
    of Coercive Control for College Students Returning Home   79
    Christine M. Cocchiola

10 Treating Eating Disorders During COVID-19: Clinician
    Resiliency Amid Uncharted Shared Trauma   93
    Cassandra Lenza

11 Shared Trauma and Harm Reduction in the Time of COVID-19 . . .   101
    Anna Wilking

12 Job Loss and Shared Trauma During the COVID-19 Pandemic:
    Helping Clients and the Impact on the Clinician.   107
    Howard Leifman

13 Considerations in Working with Veterans During COVID-19:
    When the Battle Is at Home.   115
    Jillian Tucker

14 Reflections on the HIV/AIDS Crisis, COVID-19, and Resilience
    in Gay Men: Ghosts of Our Past, Demons of Our Present   127
    Nicholas Santo

15 School Social Workers Responding to the COVID-19 Pandemic:
    Experiences in Traditional, Charter, and Agency-Based
    Community School Agency Settings   135
    Dayna Sedillo-Hamann, Jessica Chock-Goldman,
    and Marina A. Badillo

16 Transition to Teletherapy with Adolescents in the Wake
    of the COVID-19 Pandemic: The Holding Environment
    Approach   145
    Cierra Osei-Buapim

17 Autism in the COVID-19 Pandemic: Reflecting on Loss
    and Resilience   157
    Samantha Fuld

Part III Practice Perspectives, Innovations, and Impact
          on Social Work Practice

18 The Impact of the COVID-19 Pandemic on the Relational World
    of the Patient-Clinician Dyad: Obstacles and Opportunities   167
    Constance Catrone

19 Wholeheartedness in the Treatment of Shared Trauma:
    Special Considerations During the COVID-19 Pandemic.   179
    Jill Zalayet

20 Reflections on the Impact of Remote Counseling: Friendship
    in a New Therapeutic Space................................. 187
    Meredith Hemphill Ruden

21 The Natural World: The Role of Ecosocial Work During
    the COVID-19 Pandemic 193
    Michelle Willoughby

22 Building the Capacity of Neighborhoods and the Resilience
    of Neighbors to Respond to COVID-19: The Neighbor
    to Neighbor Volunteer Corps................................. 205
    Stacey Gordon, Ernest Gonzales, and Jillian Hinton

23 The Importance of Pets During a Global Pandemic:
    See Spot Play 213
    Katherine Compitus

24 Dialectical Behavior Therapy and the COVID-19 Pandemic:
    Building a Life Worth Living in the Face of an Unrelenting Crisis . . 219
    Madelaine Ellberger

25 Reflections on Providing Virtual Eye Movement Desensitization
    and Reprocessing Therapy in the Wake of COVID-19:
    Survival Through Adaptation 235
    Gillian O'Shea Brown

26 Shared Traumatic Stress and the Impact of COVID-19
    on Public Child Welfare Workers 249
    Deirdre S. Williams

27 How COVID-19 Exposed an Inadequate Approach
    to Burnout: Moving Beyond Self-Care................................. 259
    Julian Cohen-Serrins

Part IV Convergence with Racism Pandemic

28 The Pandemic Within the Pandemic of 2020: A Spiritual
    Perspective................................. 271
    Terry S. Audate

29 Black Lives, Mass Incarceration, and the Perpetuity of Trauma
    in the Era of COVID-19: The Road to Abolition Social Work 281
    Kirk Jae James

30 COVID-19 and the Injustice System: Reshaping Clinical Practice
    for Children and Families Impacted by Hyper-Incarceration 291
    Anna Morgan-Mullane

31 An Intimate Portrait of Shared Trauma Amid COVID-19
    and Racial Unrest Between a Black Cisgender Femme Sex
    Worker and Her Black Cisgender Femme Therapist   303
    Raashida M. Edwards

32 COVID-19 as Post-Migration Stress: Exploring the Impact
    of a Pandemic on Latinx Transgender Individuals
    in Immigration Detention.   313
    Diana Franco

Part V   Social Work Education

33 Teaching Social Work Practice in the Shared Trauma
    of a Global Pandemic   323
    Beth Sapiro

34 Reconceptualizing Service-Learning During the COVID-19
    Pandemic: Reflections and Recommendations   331
    Peggy Morton and Dina Rosenfeld

35 Grief Lessons of the Apocalypse: Self-care Is a Joyful Jab
    in the Arm   341
    Abigail Nathanson

36 Shared Trauma: Group Reflections on the COVID-19 Pandemic . . .   347
    Carol Tosone, Evelyn Solomon, Raquel Barry, Elisha Beinart,
    Kathryn K. Bellas, Emily Carlotte Blaker, Natalie Capasse,
    Moorea Diane Colby, Martha Corcoran, Amanda Delaney,
    Kylee Doyle, Stacie Elfo, Tyler-Ann Patricia Gilzene,
    Armina Kadriovski, Ray Kim, Madison Lavoie, Robin Lempel,
    Carly Iliza Linn, Catherine Yin Heung Liu, Kelly Felix Machado,
    Jennifer Maldonado, Alaphia Robinson, Alicia Denise Ross,
    Valerie Russell, Alexandra Skinder, and Zhaojie Wei

Part VI   Clinician Self-Care During the COVID-19 Pandemic

37 The COVID-19 Self-Care Survival Guide: A Framework
    for Clinicians to Categorize and Utilize Self-Care Strategies
    and Practices   357
    Julian Cohen-Serrins

Index.   369

About the Editor and Contributors

Editor

Carol Tosone, PhD, LCSW, is Professor and Director of the DSW Program in Clinical Social Work at New York University Silver School of Social Work, recipient of the NYU Distinguished Teaching Award and Medal, and a distinguished scholar in social work in the National Academies of Practice in Washington, D.C. Dr. Tosone also served as a Fulbright scholar at Hanoi University of Education in Vietnam, and as a distinguished visiting Lydia Rappaport professor at Smith College in Massachusetts. Dr. Tosone received her certification in psychoanalysis and psychotherapy from the Postgraduate Center for Mental Health, where she was the recipient of the Postgraduate Memorial Award. She is editor-in-chief of the *Clinical Social Work Journal*, editor for the *Essential Clinical Social Work* book series, co-editor of four books, author of numerous professional articles and book chapters, and executive producer of community service and educational media. Dr. Tosone is in private practice in New York City. Her area of research is shared trauma and she has studied Manhattan clinicians post 9/11, New Orleans clinicians post Hurricane Katrina, and, most recently, completed a study on the long-term impact of the troubles on clinicians living and working in Northern Ireland. She has lectured or served as a consultant on shared trauma in Afghanistan, China, Indonesia, Southern Israel, and the United Arab Emirates. She was recently interviewed for a podcast on shared trauma and the coronavirus pandemic, which was downloaded more than 40,000 times in its first 3 months of posting. It is available at http://socialworkpodcast.blogspot.com/2020/05/covid19.html

Contributors

Terry S. Audate, LCSW-R, is an adjunct lecturer and a DSW Candidate at NYU Silver School of Social Work in New York City. Her studies focus on a concentration in Spirituality and Clinical Social Work. She is a licensed clinical worker and is the founding owner of Autesh Therapy Services in Queens, New York.

Marina A. Badillo, LCSW, is a counseling director at a Transfer Charter High School in Brooklyn, New York. She is currently a doctoral candidate at NYU Silver School of Social Work focusing on school social work practice in charter schools and ethics.

Raquel Barry, MSW, is an MSW graduate from NYU Silver School of Social Work in New York City.

Elisha Beinart, MSW, works with clients who are under parole supervision at CSEDNY in Brooklyn. Elisha's practice focuses on trauma, anger management, domestic violence, and substance abuse counseling. Her clinical areas of interest include trauma and emotionally focused therapy. She strives to awaken awareness and advocate action.

Kathryn K. Bellas, LMSW, MFA, is a psychotherapist who lives and works in New York. She holds a BA from Duke University in North Carolina, an MFA from Brooklyn College in New York City, and an MSW from New York University's Silver School of Social Work. She is currently a candidate in the Psychoanalysis Program and the Psychoanalytic Psychotherapy Study Center.

Emily Carlotte Blaker, MSW, is an MSW graduate from NYU Silver School of Social Work in New York City.

Shari Bloomberg, LCSW, is a doctoral student in the Silver School of Social Work at New York University. She is also the Clinical Director of Rachel Coalition, a New Jersey-based domestic violence program, and maintains a private practice.

Natalie Capasse, LMSW, currently practices with children, adolescents, and adults at a mental health clinic in upstate New York. She received her MSW from New York University (NYU) in 2020. Prior to this, she completed her BA at NYU in 2016 and post-baccalaureate certificate in Psychology from Columbia University in New York City in 2018.

Constance Catrone, MA, LCSW, is an experienced clinician, supervisor, and teacher in private practice in the New Haven, Connecticut area. She is an adjunct faculty member at Southern Connecticut State University's Social Work Department and a candidate for a Doctorate in Social Welfare at New York University.

Victoria L. Cerone, DSW, LCSW, is a social worker at NYU Langone Medical Center. Her article, "A Brief Psychodynamic and Person-Centered Approach to Address Anticipatory Loss in Acute Care Settings" was recognized as the *Journal of Social Work in End-of-Life and Palliative Care* Editor's Choice Best Journal Article for 2019.

Jessica Chock-Goldman, LCSW, is the school social worker at Stuyvesant High School in New York City. She is currently a doctoral candidate at NYU Silver School of Social Work focusing on restructuring how mental health and suicidal ideation are managed within the Department of Education (DOE).

Elisa Chow, PhD, is Vice President at the Institute for Community Living (ICL) and adjunct assistant professor at NYU Silver School of Social Work in New York City.

Christine M. Cocchiola, LCSW, is a doctoral student in social work at New York University. She is a full-time college professor in social work studies at a Connecticut community college and has spent much of her career creating programming and educating on the topic of intimate partner violence and sexual assault.

Julian Cohen-Serrins, LCSW, is a PhD student at New York University's Silver School of Social Work. He received his MSW from the University of Pennsylvania's School of Social Policy and Practice. Julian's research focuses on discerning and implementing optimal burnout reduction interventions in acute-care settings.

Moorea Diane Colby, MSW, is an MSW graduate from NYU Silver School of Social Work in New York City.

Katherine Compitus, DSW, LCSW, MSEd, MA, is a bilingual licensed clinical social worker, educator, animal behaviorist, and applied anthrozoologist. She is the founder of Surrey Hills Sanctuary, a nonprofit organization providing trauma-informed animal-assisted therapy. She teaches as adjunct faculty at New York University, Columbia University, and Fordham University in New York.

Martha Corcoran, MA, received her MA in Counseling for Mental Health and Wellness from NYU Steinhardt School of Culture, Education, and Human Development in New York City.

Jeanine D. Costley, DSW, is senior vice president at the Institute for Community Living (ICL) and adjunct lecturer at NYU Silver School of Social Work in New York City.

Leslie Cummins, DSW, LCSW, is a psychoanalyst in private practice in New York City, working with adults, adolescents, and couples. She is an adjunct clinical assistant professor at SUNY Downstate Medical Center in Brooklyn and clinical instructor at NYU Langone School of Medicine, where she supervises psychiatry residents.

Amanda Delaney, MSW, earned her MSW in 2020 from New York University Silver School of Social Work. She is currently a multisystemic prevention therapist at the New York Foundling working with children and families. Her passion is working with individuals as an alternative to incarceration.

Kylee Doyle, MSW, is an MSW graduate from NYU Silver School of Social Work in New York City.

Raashida M. Edwards, DSW, is a recent graduate of the Silver School of Social Work at New York University. She graduated from the Columbia University School of Social Work in New York City in 2011 with a Masters in Science. She received post-graduate training at the Institute for Contemporary Psychotherapy in New York City. Her clinical practice focuses on working with the ambivalence in mature cisgendered women career sex workers who are considering transitioning out of the adult industry.

Stacie Elfo, MSW, is an MSW graduate from NYU Silver School of Social Work in New York City.

Madelaine Ellberger, LCSW, MSEd, is a licensed clinical social worker and senior staff clinician at the Center for Cognitive and Dialectical Behavior Therapy in New York, specializing in providing DBT and CBT for transdiagnostic personality, mood, anxiety, and trauma disorders. She also holds an adjunct professor position at New York University Silver School of Social Work.

Charles R. Figley, PhD, is the Paul Henry Kurzweg, MD Distinguished Chair in Disaster Mental Health. He is the Tulane University Traumatology Institute director and a full professor in the School of Social Work at Tulane University in New Orleans. He has published more than 185 refereed journal articles and 29 books.

Diana Franco, DSW, LCSW, serves as MSW Field Education Associate and DSW Core Faculty at Capella University, School of Public Service Leadership, Department of Social Work in Minneapolis, Minnesota. She obtained a DSW from New York University's Silver School of Social Work in 2018. Dr. Franco's area of research focuses on migration trauma.

Samantha Fuld, DSW, is a clinical assistant professor at the University of Maryland School of Social Work in Baltimore. Her work focuses on the impact of trauma and stigma on mental health in people with developmental disabilities and promoting a critical social model of understanding disability in social work practice and education.

Tyler-Ann Patricia Gilzene, MSW, is an MSW graduate from NYU Silver School of Social Work in New York City.

Ernest Gonzales, PhD, MSSW, is an associate professor at New York University's Silver School of Social Work. He is a scholar in the areas of productive aging, health equity, discrimination, and social policy. His research advances our understanding on the relationships between healthy aging, social determinants of health, productive activities, and intergenerational contexts.

Stacey Gordon, LMSW, is currently a DSW student at the Silver School of Social Work at New York University. She also serves as the Program Director of Next Phase Caregiving and Retirement at the New York University Office of Work Life.

Patricia Hecht, DSW, LCSW, CASAC-T, received her doctorate in Advanced Clinical Social Work from Rutgers University in New Brunswick, New Jersey. She completed her psychoanalytic training from the Postgraduate Center in New York City and is currently a supervisor and training analyst at the Institute for Contemporary Psychotherapy. She has a private practice in New York City and Westchester County in New York.

Jill Hinton is pursuing a BA in Psychology at CUNY-Brooklyn College in New York City and is completing an internship through the Center of Health and Aging Research, Policy, and Practice at NYU Silver School of Social Work. She is especially interested in geriatric mental health.

Catherine Hodes, LICSW, LCSW, is the Community Program Director at Safe Passage in Northampton, Massachusetts, overseeing the provision of crisis intervention, counselling, safety planning, and advocacy for survivors of domestic violence. She was formerly the program director at Safe Homes Project in Brooklyn, New York.

Kirk " Jae" James, DSW, is a social worker and a Clinical Assistant Professor at NYU Silver School of Social Work in New York City. He is formerly incarcerated and has dedicated his life to creating liberatory spaces to heal and dismantle systems of oppression—for all people.

Armina Kadriovski, MSW, graduated from New York University. She is a Functional Family Therapy interventionist with The Jewish Board, where she provides counseling to low-risk families. She is also a former case management intern of the Ali Forney Center, where she provided services to LGBT+ youth experiencing homelessness.

David Kamnitzer, LCSW-R, is chief clinical officer at Institute for Community Living (ICL) and adjunct associate professor at NYU Silver School of Social Work in New York City.

Ray Kim, MSW, is an MSW graduate from NYU Silver School of Social Work in New York City.

Madison Lavoie, MSW, is an MSW graduate from NYU Silver School of Social Work in New York City.

Howard Leifman, PhD, MBA, is an internationally recognized expert in the area of human development. He specializes in advisement and consultation with corporate clients, consulting firms, not-for-profit agencies/organizations, and individuals on executive coaching, career development, change management, counselling, diversity, psychotherapy, trauma, human resources, out-placement, training, recruitment, staffing, and time management.

Robin Lempel, MSW, is an LMSW in New York City. She received her MSW from NYU and BA from Oberlin in Ohio. She has experience in professional development and healthcare settings and with assault survivors. She is passionate about health equity and justice, which has only been strengthened by the pandemic.

Cassandra Lenza, DSW, LCSW, is the owner of Healing on Hudson, a private practice specializing in eating disorders and body image issues in New Jersey. She received her Doctorate of Social Work from New York University and is a Certified Eating Disorder Specialist (CEDS) through the International Association of Eating Disorder Professionals (IAEDP).

Carly Iliza Linn, MSW, is an MSW graduate from NYU Silver School of Social Work in New York City.

Catherine Yin Heung Liu, MSW, is an alumna of NYU Silver School of Social Work in New York City. She has 2 years of experience in mental and behavioral health with specialized community, suicide prevention program, and training. She spent 5 years in administration and fundraising for nonprofit organizations and holds a degree in business management.

Kelly Felix Machado, LMSW, graduated from New York University. She has primarily worked with clients who are domestic violence and abuse survivors. Kelly's practice has focused on trauma-informed approaches, strengths-based interventions, and cognitive restructuring strategies. Her clinical areas of interest include early adulthood and trauma.

Jennifer Maldonado, MSW, is a first-generation graduate student from New York University Silver School of Social Work. During her graduate studies, she specialized in trauma-informed clinical social work.

Anna Morgan-Mullane, DSW, LCSW-R, serves as vice president of Mental Health Services for Children of Promise, New York City (CPNYC), a not-for-profit that provides anti-oppressive trauma-responsive services to children impacted by parental incarceration. She is also an adjunct lecturer at the Silver School of Social Work at New York University.

Peggy Morton, DSW, is a clinical associate professor at NYU Silver School of Social Work in New York City. She teaches service-learning and other undergraduate social work courses at Silver and is field instructor to interns in the New York Public Library system, a partnership that she created. Her social work interests include service-learning, library social work, and gerontology.

Abigail Nathanson, LCSW, DSW, APHSW-C, ACS, is a board-certified palliative social worker in New York. She received both her master's and doctorate in clinical social work from New York University, where she continues as an adjunct faculty member. She works in program management at an academic medical center in New York City.

Gillian O'Shea Brown, LCSW, is a psychotherapist, EMDR-certified practitioner, and complex trauma specialist. She serves as adjunct faculty at NYU Silver School of Social Work and has previously served as a clinical affiliate of the Integrative Trauma Program at the National Institute for the Psychotherapies in New York City. She is the author of the forthcoming Springer book *Healing Complex Posttraumatic Stress Disorder – A Clinician's Guide* and has a special interest in the research of relational trauma. She maintains a private practice in Manhattan.

Cierra Osei-Buapim, DSW, has over 10 years of clinical experience working with adolescents with social, emotional, and behavioral difficulties. She is also an adjunct instructor and held positions as a field instructor/supervisor to BSW student interns. Her most recent accomplishment includes earning a Doctorate in Social Welfare from New York University.

Sophia Tsesmelis Piccolino, LCSW, OSC-C, is a doctoral student in the Silver School of Social Work at New York University. She is a Program Coordinator at Mount Sinai Hospital's Cancer Centers in New York City, overseeing psycho-oncology programming, the leadership of psychosocial cancer center standards, and supervising oncology social workers.

Alaphia Robinson is an MSW candidate at NYU Silver School of Social Work in New York City.

Dina Rosenfeld, DSW, is a clinical associate professor at NYU Silver School of Social Work in New York City. She teaches in the undergraduate and MSW programs and coordinates minors and Undergraduate Service-Learning. She is lead teacher for Practice I and II. Her social work interests include adoption, social work and spirituality, prison education, hospice care, refugees, and Holocaust survivors.

Alicia Denise Ross, MSW, is an MSW graduate from NYU Silver School of Social Work in New York City.

Meredith Hemphill Ruden, DSW, LCSW, works as a Clinical Director at City Center Psychotherapy in New York City. She also acts as the executive director of The Feather Foundation, a non-profit organization for parents who have cancer. She teaches at New York University as an adjunct professor within its social work program.

Valerie Russell, MSW, is a licensed master social worker in New York City. She received a Master of Social Work and a Bachelor of Arts in Psychology from New York University. Valerie works with children and families, and has experience in educational, health, and mental health settings.

Nicholas Santo, LCSW-R, is a licensed clinical social worker working in private practice in New York City. Nicholas works with individuals and couples. His practice has a focus on LGBTQ people and trauma. His doctoral work at New York University focuses on treatment of trauma from a self-psychological perspective.

Beth Sapiro, LCSW, PhD, is an assistant professor in the Department of Social Work and Child Advocacy at Montclair State University in New Jersey. She has a small private practice and researches the intersection of healing and marginalization in interpersonal relationships. She teaches social work practice to undergraduate and graduate students.

Dayna Sedillo-Hamann, LMSW, is a licensed social worker in New York City, where she works as a Community School Director for the Henry Street Settlement. She earned her MSW from the Silberman School of Social Work at Hunter College in New York City and is a current doctoral candidate in the DSW program at NYU Silver School of Social Work.

Alexandra Skinder, MSW, is an MSW graduate from NYU Silver School of Social Work in New York City.

Evelyn Solomon, LMSW, is a graduate of NYU Silver School of Social Work in New York City. She is a trauma-focused CBT-certified clinician who has worked with children and families that have experienced domestic violence, sexual abuse, and other complex traumas. Evelyn currently works for E Wellness Therapy, a private psychotherapy practice in New York.

Carol Tosone, PhD, LCSW, is professor and director of the DSW Program in Clinical Social Work at NYU Silver School of Social Work in New York City, recipient of the NYU Distinguished Teaching Award and Medal, Distinguished Scholar in Social Work in the National Academies of Practice in Washington, D.C., and editor-in-chief of the *Clinical Social Work Journal.*

Jillian Tucker, DSW, received her doctorate in clinical social work from New York University and a bachelor's degree from Brown University in Providence, Rhode Island. She works with combat veterans through the Headstrong Project and is an EMDR International Association-certified clinician. Dr. Tucker teaches at New York University and Columbia University in New York City.

Zhaojie Wei, MA, received her MA in Counseling for Mental Health and Wellness from NYU Steinhardt School of Culture, Education, and Human Development in New York City.

Anna Wilking, PhD, LMSW, holds a PhD in Cultural Anthropology and LMSW from New York University (NYU). She works as a bilingual psychotherapist at the Puerto Rican Family Institute in New York City. Her treatment interests include substance use, sexuality and gender issues, and trauma. She is an adjunct professor of anthropology at NYU and Brooklyn College.

Deirdre S. Williams, DSW, LCSW, SIFI, holds a Doctor of Social Welfare with a concentration in social work from New York University. She is a skilled clinical and forensic social worker with a specialty in working with court-involved individuals. She employs mindfulness and respect to all individuals she serves.

Michelle Willoughby, LCSW, ACM, is a doctoral student in social work at New York University. She has more than 10 years of experience as a hospital social worker in New York City. One of Michelle's professional goals is incorporating the notion of biophilia into social work practice.

Jill Zalayet, LCSW-R, DSW, received her doctorate in clinical social work from New York University and is a certified psychoanalyst from the American Institute for Psychoanalysis. She has a private practice in Manhattan and specializes in the treatment of trauma. Jill is also an instructor at Columbia University and New York University.

Chapter 1
Introduction

Carol Tosone

It seemed to happen overnight or at least over the course of a week. Even though these events occurred during 1 week in March, it feels like a lifetime ago when I was at a Rangers game in Madison Square Garden, dining at a packed, near impossible-to-get-reservations Manhattan restaurant; running a race; seeing a Broadway play; and meeting with clients and students face-to-face. The following week, coinciding with the first day of spring, I was sheltering in place with a friend in his rural Pennsylvania farmhouse, the nearest neighbor a mile away, wondering if I should prepare my will in the event that I had already contracted COVID-19.

I miss my old life. For this die-hard New Yorker and those of my ilk, the COVID-19 pandemic has many of the features of a traumatic event: sudden, unexpected, and potentially life-threatening (van der Kolk 2014). While a persuasive argument could be made contradicting these factors—COVID-19 was a known entity anticipated to impact the United States, and only a fraction of those who contract the illness die—subjectively, it *felt* traumatic. And as we know, trauma is a subjective experience, such that what one person perceives as traumatic may not be construed the same by another (Herman 2015).

C. Tosone (✉)
Silver School of Social Work, New York University, New York, NY, USA
e-mail: ct2@nyu.edu

© The Author(s), under exclusive license to Springer Nature Switzerland
AG 2021
C. Tosone (ed.), *Shared Trauma, Shared Resilience During a Pandemic*,
Essential Clinical Social Work Series,
https://doi.org/10.1007/978-3-030-61442-3_1

1

Theoretical and Research Contributions to the Understanding of Shared Trauma

My experience, coupled with a steady diet of hearing the fears, anxieties, and major adjustments that my clients are undergoing, lends itself to the development of shared trauma. *Shared trauma*, defined previously, is the "affective, behavioral, cognitive, spiritual, and multimodal responses that mental health professionals experience as a result of primary and secondary exposure to the same collective trauma as their clients" (Tosone 2012, p. 625). Experienced on multiple levels—intrapsychic, interpersonal, community, and societal—shared trauma can impact the clinician personally and professionally in a myriad of ways (Tosone et al. 2012). Shared trauma has sometimes been misunderstood as the clinician and client having the same experience in relation to collective trauma (Kaplan 2020) or as "emotional contagion" from the client's affective state to that of the clinician, such that the clinician understands exactly what the client is feeling (Seeley 2008). In fact, the clinician may be projecting their reactions onto the client; the emotional contagion may be bidirectional if the client and clinician are both sufficiently anxious and the boundaries between them are permeable.

Rather, the dual nature of the clinician's trauma—primarily as citizen of a traumatological environment and secondarily through exposure to the trauma narratives of one's clients—does not imply that the clinician's response is identical to that of the client. Deprived of the clinical distance usually afforded them by having a different set of external experiences from their clients, clinicians may overidentify with a particular client, self-disclose, or offer an interpretation better suited to themselves, potentially traumatizing the client further. Clinicians and clients can be variably affected by the same catastrophic event, and given the potential blurring of boundaries, it behooves the clinician not to assume that their experience is the same as that of the client.

Although the term was initially used in response to the September 11th disaster by psychoanalysts (Saakvitne 2002; Altman and Davies 2002) and social work educators (Tosone et al. 2003; Tosone and Bialkin 2003), it is important to note that, while not named as such, the phenomenon may have begun with Freud as he was known to treat patients during World War I (Zilcosky 2018). Baum (2010) traces the phenomenon to a brief report by Schmidenberg, a psychoanalyst, writing about her experience treating patients during the World War II London Blitz. Schmidenberg (1942) described the impact that the prolonged bombing had on her personally and on her psychoanalytic work. In other parts of the world, notably Israel, the same phenomenon is referred to as *shared reality* and *shared traumatic reality* (e.g., Dekel and Baum 2009) as the terms are believed to better capture the chronic nature of a traumatogenic, terrorist-prone environment rather than a single terrorist event, such as 9/11, or any number of natural disasters, most recently Hurricane Laura.

Shared trauma differs from existing clinician-based trauma concepts such as *compassion fatigue*, *secondary trauma*, and *vicarious traumatization* in that these latter terms individually and collectively describe the deleterious effects of working with trauma survivors, but do not consider the dual impact of the traumatic experience. Following 9/11, there was a call to develop a construct that adequately captures the ramifications of the clinicians' direct and indirect exposure to collective trauma (Eidelson et al. 2003). And while the reactions may be similar to those associated with the secondary trauma constructs—such as an enduring alteration of one's self-perception or world view, or symptoms that mirror those of the client—shared trauma suggests that the responses are attributed to the dual nature of the traumatic exposure. That is, as a result of interacting directly in a traumatogenic environment and serving as witness to the trauma narratives of their clients, these clinicians are potentially more susceptible to the blurring of professional and personal boundaries, increased self-disclosure with clients, and the development of posttraumatic stress.

I have written about my own 9/11 experience (Tosone 2002; Tosone et al. 2003) and its influence on my practice (Tosone 2006) and research (Tosone 2011). Suffice it to say that my experience sitting with a client as the first plane flew over the building on route to crash into the North Tower of the World Trade Center changed my personal and professional life in profound ways. The experience spawned my curiosity as to how other Manhattan clinicians dealt with the potentially traumatizing event. Did the experience increase clinician self-disclosure and/or increase therapeutic intimacy? What are the personal and professional characteristics of clinicians who fared better post 9/11?

My quest to answer these questions began in earnest as I undertook the *Post 9/11 Quality of Professional Practice Survey (PQPPS)* which examined the long-term impact of 9/11 on 481 Manhattan social workers living and working in Manhattan at the time of the disaster. The PQPPS consisted of several established measures for PTSD, compassion fatigue/secondary trauma, compassion satisfaction, resiliency, and adult attachment styles, as well as demographic, practice, supervisory, training, and 9/11-related professional and personal experience questions. Secure attachment was found to serve as a protective factor against the development of compassion fatigue and as an enhancement to resiliency; fostering secure attachment in agency settings through identification of vulnerable workers, and provision of peer supervision and self-care, might help to decrease the development of compassion fatigue (Tosone et al. 2010).

While an important start, compassion fatigue alone did not address the primary nature of exposure to the trauma, thereby necessitating the development of a measure for *shared traumatic stress*. The construct was operationalized by the mean scores for the PTSD and compassion fatigue/secondary traumatic stress, rescaled to give equal weight to both components. Risk factors for shared traumatic stress include insecure attachment styles, exposure to potentially traumatic life events, and enduring stress attributed to the events of 9/11. These findings underscore the relational nature of trauma in that clinicians may attribute their traumatic responses to direct exposure, work with clients, or both (Tosone, McTighe, Bauwens, & Naturale, 2011). A noteworthy finding from a thematic analysis of open-ended questions on the PQPPS was that respondents described *professional posttraumatic growth* following the 9/11 disaster. Specifically, they noted having a greater ability and urgency to care for themselves (e.g., reduce number of patient hours, take on fewer trauma cases), as well as a renewed appreciation for the profession. These are aspects of posttraumatic growth (Tedeschi and Calhoun 2004) but focus on the nature and context of practice. Other themes emerged consistent with their dual exposure to the disaster, including (1) an increased sense of vulnerability and living in fear of another terrorist attack; (2) past traumas served as either preparation for or complicating recovery from 9/11; (3) traumatic reactions persisted long after September 11; and (4) blurred client-clinician roles, increased clinician self-disclosure, and a sense of a shared traumatic experience with their clients (Bauwens and Tosone 2010).

Would shared trauma manifest similarly in a natural disaster as it did in the September 11th terrorist attack? The *Post Hurricane Katrina Quality of Professional Practice Survey* (PKQPPS) replicated the PQPPS, with the addition of an instrument to measure posttraumatic growth. Findings from this study of 244 social workers from New Orleans indicated that insecure attachment, greater exposure to potentially traumatic life events in general, and distress related to the events surrounding Hurricane Katrina specifically were predictive of higher levels of shared traumatic stress (Tosone et al. 2015). The *Shared Traumatic and Professional Posttraumatic Growth Inventory* (STPPG), a 14-item, Likert-type scale composed of three subscales (Technique-Specific Shared Trauma, Personal Trauma, and Professional Posttraumatic Growth), developed as a result of this study to further understand the nuances and nature of clinicians' dual trauma exposure (Tosone et al. 2014). The STPPG correlates well to existing measures for posttraumatic stress and secondary trauma and supports the reciprocal nature of shared trauma, such that personal traumatic experience can impact professional practice and client trauma narratives can influence one's personal trauma responses.

Others (Faust et al. 2008; Boulanger 2013) have applied the concept of shared trauma to the understanding of the dual impact of Hurricane Katrina on psychotherapists living and working in New Orleans and more recently to psychiatric residents in New York City during Hurricane Sandy (Rao and Mehra 2015). Increased self-disclosure and the blurring of professional and personal boundaries were also found in these reports. Shared trauma has been studied in counselors working on campus during the Virginia Tech shootings, with results indicating the need for counselors to practice self-care to better help their clients, in addition to the blurring of boundaries between the counselors and clients (Day et al. 2017). Bell and Robinson (2013) note that when exposed to the same collective disaster as their clients, counselors are at an increased risk for retraumatization, as well as decreased objectivity, empathy, and professional engagement. In examination of the long-term impact of the Troubles on social workers living and working in Northern Ireland during the 30-year period of sectarian violence, Duffy et al. (2019) found themes of increased therapeutic intimacy and self-disclosure and a renewed appreciation for the social work profession.

Shared Trauma and the COVID-19 Pandemic

By contrast to the other collective disasters, both natural and man-made, which have been restricted by location, the COVID-19 pandemic is worldwide and negatively impacting nearly all aspects of everyday life for everyone, clinicians included. We, along with our clients, have had to contend with quarantining, isolation, social distancing, fears of contagion, possible or actual loss of loved ones to COVID-19, disruption to work and transition to teletherapy, and remote learning/teaching/working. In trying to make sense of the impact of the COVID-19 pandemic on their personal and professional lives, some clinicians considered the literature on shared trauma. I received numerous calls for virtual speaking engagements from local, national, and international professional organizations; there was curiosity for the research of those working in the area. As an example, a podcast on shared trauma and the COVID-19 pandemic received over 40,000 downloads in 3 months (Singer 2020).

Shared Trauma, Shared Resilience During a Pandemic: Social Work in the Time of COVID-19 came to fruition as a result of the renewed interest garnered by the coronavirus pandemic. Importantly, shared trauma needs to be discussed in relation to shared resilience, a term coined by Nuttman-Shwartz (2014) to describe the positive experiences that clinicians derive from exposure to traumatic events, both directly and through their work with clients; the term suggests a reciprocal mutual aid that can take place between client and clinician. Throughout this volume there is an emphasis on shared trauma, but it would be remiss not to acknowledge the silver lining of shared trauma, and many of the chapters do discuss positive attitudes, experiences, and sentiments that result from interactions with clients exposed to the same collective trauma as themselves. Shared resilience differs from vicarious resilience (Hernandez et al. 2007) and compassion satisfaction (Figley 2002) in that the resilience and satisfaction derive respectively from work with clients and the clinicians and clients are "not in the same boat" (Nuttman-Shwartz 2014, p.467) as with shared resilience.

Understanding the Impact of the COVID-19 Pandemic on Practice: An Outline

Many of the contributors to the book are members of the New York University Silver School of Social Work community—full-time or adjunct faculty, students, and graduates—who write courageously about their clinical work with clients, including the adjustments they have made and the innovations they have undertaken during the pandemic to maintain the continuity of the therapeutic process and an ethic of care. They write openly about their experiences related to the pandemic, including several contributors who contracted COVID-19 and had to contend with the illness, along with the fears and reactions of their clients. As an editor, I didn't want to impose too much structure to the content of the chapters. Rather, I wanted the contributors' voices to be clear, strong, conversant in their areas of specialization, and as if you are in conversation with them. The resulting 36 chapters are an embarrassment of riches in the populations and topics covered, especially the intersection of the COVID-19 and racism pandemics. The number of hospitalizations and deaths related to COVID-19 among Black and brown persons is disproportionate to that of their white counterparts and confirms the racism inherent in access to and utilization of health care in the United States.

The book is organized into six parts, beginning with reports from those on the front line of health care during the COVID-19 pandemic, followed by chapters pertaining to special populations impacted by the pandemic—such as intimate partner violence (IPV)/domestic violence (DV), eating disorders, addiction, veterans, LGBTQ, autism, adolescents in school settings, and job loss. Part III includes reflections and practice perspectives from seasoned clinicians on theories, adaptations to teletherapy, innovative therapeutic techniques, and the necessity for self-care. Part IV addresses the convergence of the COVID-19 and racism pandemics; Part V includes reports from social work educators, followed by Part VI, a guide for self-care practices consistent with the Centers for Disease Control and Prevention (CDC) guidelines for social distancing.

More specifically, Part I begins with an intimate interaction between a therapist, Patricia Hecht, and her patient, a hospital nurse on the front line of the COVID-19 pandemic. We next hear from a clinical social worker and supervisor, Victoria L. Cerrone, who in the midst of mourning the loss of a loved one discusses the moral distress and anguish experienced by patients and their families, many of whom did not have the opportunity to say goodbye before the patients' deaths. Sophia Tsesmelis Piccolino addresses the critical role that healthcare social workers play in supporting patients and families, while she herself confronted COVID-19 directly. As a leader in social work health care, she discusses the importance of meaning-making for both the workers and patients. Lastly, Leslie Cummins offers candid reflections as a psychoanalytic supervisor to residents who are working in hospitals that were converted into COVID-only facilities.

Part II considers the populations most disrupted by the pandemic, beginning with the severely mentally ill. David Kamnitzer, Elisa Chow, and Jeanine D. Costley examine our profession's Code of Ethics and the applicability of its six core values at a nonprofit human service organization delivering mental health and supportive services remotely during the pandemic. Three chapters address the increase in intimate partner and domestic violence as a result of the COVID-19 pandemic: Catherine Hodes discusses the role of advocates in providing safety options other than leaving for survivors of intimate partner abuse and their families, especially those living with, or in close contact with, an abuser. Shari Bloomberg reflects on both shared trauma and shared resilience in her work with survivors of domestic violence and the innovative ways she found to communicate with clients as they were forced to shelter in place with their abusers. Christine M. Cocchiola also addresses sheltering in place, but from the standpoint of college students returning home and the coercive control that may intensify in post-separation abuse. She argues that these young adults are primary, not secondary, victims of intimate partner violence, alongside their victimized parent. In addition to IPV, concerns also have been raised about the exacerbation of addictions during the pandemic. Cassandra Lenza examines the social norms about gaining weight and using food to control one's anxieties or for comfort, as clinicians navigate their own experience of pandemic life while providing known and novel resources and interventions to their eating disorder clients. Anna Wilking draws on her own experiences to help clients deal with addictive behaviors during the pandemic and argues for harm reduction rather than abstinence. For her, shared trauma provided an opportunity to deepen client relationships and help her to accept and heal her own behaviors. Howard Leifman discusses his work coaching increasing numbers of unemployed clients to find jobs during the coronavirus pandemic while helping them increase their sense of agency and self-worth. Jillian Tucker discusses her clinical work with veterans and how their crisis response military skills (e.g., social isolation and long-term separation from loved ones) can help manage aspects of COVID-19; on the other hand, veterans also can experience a reactivation of posttraumatic stress symptoms, survivor's guilt, and moral injuries. Nicholas Santo also addresses reactivation, but as it applies to LGBTQ individuals who lived through the AIDS epidemic. Also included in this part are two chapters on school social work, one by Dayna Sedillo-Hamann, Jessica Chock-Goldman, and Marina A. Badillo comparing their experiences in different school settings and the other by Cierra Osei-Buapim describing the challenges of transitioning to teletherapy with adolescents previously seen in a residential school setting and the importance of maintaining a holding environment in the virtual space. The final chapter in this part by Samantha Fuld argues that shared experiences of loss associated with the COVID-19 pandemic may foster greater empathy and awareness for clinicians working with autistic clients.

Continuing the discourse on practice, Part III offers perspectives that speak to a more general discussion of therapeutic work and inclusive of theoretical applications, case material, innovative approaches, and the need for self-care and reflective practice. With rich case illustrations, Constance Catrone invites us into the intersubjective sphere of the therapeutic relationship and holding environment with clients deeply impacted by the racial disparities revealed through the COVID-19 pandemic. Jill Zalayet, also working from a relational frame, reminds us of the value of applying Karen Horney's theory of wholeheartedness to an understanding of the mutual anxiety generated by the coronavirus, and the need for clinicians to be fully present for patients, while attending to our own fears and conflicts. Similarly, Meredith Hemphill Ruden applies Irvin Yalom's concept of friendship in therapy to the virtual realm, noting its potential to foster strong therapeutic engagement and positive outcomes in a new, co-created therapeutic space. Next in this part are three chapters that offer innovative approaches to enhancing connection and decreasing anxiety during the COVID-19 pandemic. Starting with Michelle Willoughby's ecosocial work approach to practice, she asserts that the natural world is part of human development and an expansion of the "person-in-environment" perspective, one which places the natural environment at the heart of anti-oppressive practice and environmental justice. Following which, Stacey Gordon, Ernest Gonzales, and Jillian

Hinton describe the development of the Neighbor to Neighbor Volunteer Corps as a civic engagement program to assist neighbors with basic needs, mental health, and social isolation during the pandemic while building resilience among neighbors and enhancing productive aging on a community level. Next, Katherine Compitus, a COVID- 19 survivor, clinician, and director of a nonprofit animal sanctuary, discusses the value of animal-assisted therapy (AAT) adapted to conform to the current CDC guidelines for social distancing, as well as how to adapt AAT when working remotely with clients. These chapters are followed by two that address adaptation to teletherapy for Dialectical Behavior Therapy (DBT) and Eye Movement Desensitization and Reprocessing (EMDR), respectively. First, Madelaine Ellberger ponders the challenges of providing DBT remotely to patients at potential risk for suicide during the pandemic and emphasizes the importance of the treatment team and peer supervision to mitigate the impact of shared trauma. Then through a composite case, Gillian O'Shea Brown discusses adapting to the use of mobile health applications in virtual EMDR. The final two chapters in the part address the impact of trauma on clinicians and the important role that organizations can play to mitigate the development of shared trauma and burnout. Deirdre S. Williams posits the need to provide institutional support to public child welfare workers who face cases complicated by pandemic-specific stressors, such as quarantine and economic instability that can heighten the risk of abuse for children in precarious situations. In the final chapter of the part, Julian Cohen-Serrins suggests that the COVID-19 pandemic has underscored the limitations of self-care; he shifts the primary responsibility for reduction of burnout and shared trauma from the individual worker to the organization.

As mentioned previously, the coronavirus pandemic has highlighted the disparities in health care for African-Americans and Latinx. This, coupled with the brutal and hate-filled murder of George Floyd by a police officer, has ignited awareness of the racism hiding in plain sight in the United States. This book would not be complete without addressing the convergence of these two pandemics. Part IV begins with a spiritual perspective on the "pandemic within the pandemic of 2020" by Terry S. Audate who proffers a spiritual framework to provide meaning and purpose to these specific events and to one's life in general. Kirk "Jae" James offers an *Abolition Social Work* framework to combat the perpetuity of Black trauma evident in overrepresentation in the carceral system and COVID-19 pandemic hospitalization and death rates. Adopting such a framework, he asserts, is an actualization of social work's core values. Relatedly, Anna Morgan-Mullane addresses the impact of parental hyper-incarceration on children and adolescents amid the COVID-19 pandemic and lays the groundwork for the implementation of Relational Cultural and Attachment Theory to treat this population in community-based settings. Raashida M. Edwards describes the emotional impact of shared cultural trauma in the psychotherapeutic interaction between Dana, a Black cisgender female sex worker and her therapist, also a Black cisgender female. Because of the clandestine nature of the sex industry, voices such as Dana's have been largely absent in the professional literature to date; shifts in the sociopolitical climate are creating spaces for persons of color engaged in sex work to procure appropriate representation, protection, access to resources, and support. This part concludes with a chapter by Diana Franco, who addresses the negative impact of the COVID-19 pandemic on the lives of Latinx transgender migrants in detention, including the challenges they face in accessing mental health care and establishing credible fear in seeking asylum.

Turning to the future of the social work profession, Part V offers four chapters describing the experience and strategies of teaching in the midst of the coronavirus pandemic. Beginning with Beth Sapiro, who offers an intimate account of shared trauma with her students, keeping in mind that trauma is not shared proportionately in environments of persistent racial and economic inequality, she emphasizes the importance of self-care and administrative support in the context of shared trauma teaching environments. Peggy Morton and Dina Rosenfeld describe the shift in emphasis for service-learning courses necessitated by the suspension of in-person service, such that learning went from "SERVICE-learning" to "service-LEARNING" depending upon which goals are primary, with the hyphen symbolizing the process of reflection. Abigail Nathanson presents an intimate account of navigating shifts in multiple roles: doctoral student, professor, social worker, and COVID-19 patient. Themes of shared trauma, object relations, grief, and parallel process are described from a first-person narrative of the first few months of quarantine. My students and I conclude the part with a chapter describing our personal and professional reflections on the coronavirus pandemic, touching on the challenges of both social isolation and living with others, the role of social media, the uncertainty of the future, and the need for the social work profession to focus more on macro-level issues of social injustice and racial inequality highlighted by the COVID-19 pandemic.

No book on trauma would be complete without a chapter devoted to clinician self-care. While in a previous chapter Julian Cohen-Serrins argues cogently that the primary responsibility for the infrastructure to support self-care strategies resides within the organizations employing mental health practitioners, in this chapter he acknowledges the state of practice administration and the limited resources available in most social service agencies. He offers a guide for workers to access self-care procedures that are relevant now and consistent with CDC guidelines for social distancing, including various forms of mindfulness-based practices. While it does not inoculate clinicians from the effects of the COVID-19 pandemic, it helps clinicians to sustain their crucial services in the absence of structural resources.

Conclusion

It is difficult to conclude an introduction, especially about shared trauma when in the midst of a global pandemic and without any clear-cut remedy in sight. I applaud the authors whose work I describe in this chapter for recognizing the need to add their voices to the discourse on social work practice during the COVID-19 pandemic. You, the reader, have your own shared trauma narratives to tell, and we encourage you to add your voices to this discourse. The paradox of shared trauma, particularly now, is that in the isolation of quarantine and life in the virtual world, we are building a strong sense of community, shared resiliency, and promise of a future with more intimacy, both personally and professionally.

References

Altman, N., & Davies, J. M. (2002). Out of the blue: Reflections on shared trauma. *Psychoanalytic Dialogues, 12*(3), 359–360.

Baum, N. (2010). Shared traumatic reality in communal disasters: Toward a conceptualization. *Psychotherapy Theory, Research, and Practice, 47*(2), 249–259.

Bauwens, J., & Tosone, C. (2010). Professional posttraumatic growth after a shared traumatic experience: Manhattan clinicians' perspectives on post 9/11 practice. *Journal of Loss and Trauma, 15*(6), 498–517.

Bell, C., & Robinson, C. (2013). Shared trauma in counseling: Information and implications for counselors. *Journal of Mental Health Counseling, 35*(4), 310–323.

Boulanger, G. (2013). Fearful symmetry: Shared trauma in New Orleans after hurricane Katrina. *Psychoanalytic Dialogues, 23*(1), 33–41.

Day, K., Lawson, G., & Burge, P. (2017). Clinicians' experiences of shared trauma after the shootings at Virginia Tech. *Journal of Counseling and Development, 95*, 269–278.

Dekel, R., & Baum, N. (2009). Intervention in a shared traumatic reality: A new challenge for social workers. *British Journal of Social Work, 40*(6), 1927–1944.

Duffy, J., Campbell, J., & Tosone, C. (2019). *Voices of social work through the Troubles. British Association of Social Workers, Northern Ireland and Northern Ireland Social Care Council.* Belfast: BASWNI and NISCC.

Eidelson, R. J., D'Alessio, G. R., & Eidelson, J. I. (2003). The impact of September 11 on psychologists. *Professional Psychology: Research and Practice, 34*(2), 144–150.

Faust, D., Black, F., Abrahams, J., & Warner, M. (2008). After the storm: Katrina's impact on psychological practice in New Orleans. *Professional Psychology: Research and Practice, 39*(1), 1–6.

Figley, C. R. (2002). *Treating compassion fatigue.* New York: Brunner/Routledge.

Herman, J. (2015). *Trauma and recovery: The aftermath of violence—From domestic abuse to political terror.* New York: Basic Books.

Hernandez, P., Gangsei, D., & Engstrom, D. (2007). Vicarious resilience: A new concept in work with those who survive trauma. *Family Process, 46*, 229–241.

Kaplan, R. (2020). Not all is shared trauma – The impact of COVID and anti-Black violence. *Psychoanalysis today.* Retrieved from https://psychoanalysis.today/en-GB/PT-Covid-19/Not-All-is-Shared-Trauma-The-Impact-of-COVID-and-A.asp

Nuttman-Shwartz, O. (2014). Shared resilience in a traumatic reality: A new concept for trauma workers exposed personally and professionally to collective disaster. *Trauma, Violence, and Abuse, 16*(4), 466–475.

Rao, N., & Mehra, A. (2015). Hurricane Sandy: Shared trauma and therapist self-disclosure. *Psychiatry, 78*(1), 65–74.

Saakvitne, K. W. (2002). Shared trauma: The therapist's increased vulnerability. *Psychoanalytic Dialogues, 12*(3), 443–449.

Schmideberg, M. (1942). Some observations on individual reactions to air raids. *International Journal of Psycho-Analysis, 23*, 146–176.

Seeley, K. (2008). *Therapy after terror: 9/11, psychotherapists, and mental health.* Cambridge University Press.

Singer, J. B. (Producer). (2020, May 9). #126 – Shared Trauma in the COVID19 Pandemic: Interview with Carol Tosone, Ph.D. [Audio Podcast]. Social Work Podcast. Retrieved from http://www.socialworkpodcast.com/2020/05/covid19.html

Tedeschi, R. G., & Calhoun, L. G. (2004). The posttraumatic growth: Conceptual foundations and empirical evidence. *Psychological Inquiry, 15*, 1–18.

Tosone, C. (2002, Fall). On the eve of 9/11: Reflections from a New York colleague. *Newsletter of the National Membership Committee on Psychoanalysis in Clinical Social Work.*

Tosone, C. (2006). Therapeutic intimacy: A post-9/11 perspective. *Smith College Studies in Social Work, 76*(4), 89–98.

Tosone, C. (2011). The legacy of September 11: Shared trauma, therapeutic intimacy, and professional posttraumatic growth. *Traumatology, 17*(3), 25–29.

Tosone, C. (2012). Shared trauma. In C. R. Figley (Ed.), *Encyclopedia of trauma: An interdisciplinary guide* (pp. 625–628). Sage.

Tosone, C., & Bialkin, L. (2003). The impact of mass violence and secondary trauma in clinical practice. In L. A. Straussner & N. K. Phillips (Eds.), *Understanding mass violence: A social work perspective* (pp. 157–167). Boston: Allyn & Bacon.

Tosone, C., Bialkin, L., Campbell, M., Charters, M., Gieri, K., Gross, S., et al. (2003). Shared trauma: Group reflections on the September 11th disaster. *Psychoanalytic Social Work, 10*(1), 57–77.

Tosone, C., Bettmann, J., Minami, T., & Jasperson, R. (2010). New York City social workers after 9/11: Their attachment, resiliency, and compassion fatigue. *International Journal of Emergency Mental Health, 12*(2), 103–116.

Tosone, C., Nuttman-Shwartz, O., & Stephens, T. (2012). Shared trauma: When the professional is personal. *Clinical Social Work Journal, 40*(2), 231–239.

Tosone, C., Bauwens, J., & Glassman, M. (2014). Measuring shared trauma and professional posttraumatic growth: A preliminary study. *Research on Social Work Practice.*

Tosone, C., McTighe, J., & Bauwens, J. (2015). Shared traumatic stress among clinicians in the aftermath of Hurricane Katrina. *British Journal of Social Work, 45*(4), 1313–1329.

van der Kolk, B. A. (2014). *The body keeps the score: Brain, mind, and body in the healing of trauma.* New York: Viking.

Zilcosky, J. (2018). The times in which we live: Freud's *the uncanny,* World War I, and the trauma of contagion. *Psychoanalysis and History, 20*(2), 165–190.

Part I
On the Front Lines of the COVID-19 Pandemic

Chapter 2
Repurposed, Reassigned, Redeployed

Patricia Hecht

"They've repurposed me!" This was the barely audible voice of my patient, an OR nurse who had been reassigned to the intensive care unit (ICU). "My God, I can't work a ventilator!"

We first met a year ago when Thea[1] and her husband were referred for help managing one of their sons who was struggling. I was struck then by their commitment to their own family as well as to others. They were quick studies in gaining new tools to address their son's struggle. It was with the virus and the "lockdown" that they returned.

All three sons had returned to quarantine in the family home, two with girlfriends in tow. "We've got our own WE WORK situation at home." With her usual good humor, Thea described the division of labor in the house as everyone managed their own workspace and dinner get-togethers at the end of each day. That all changed when Thea was reassigned to the ICU.

Thea has been the chief operating room (OR) nurse in a local suburban hospital for more than 30 years. She was able to set up an operating room for a complicated surgery with her eyes closed. But all elective, non-emergent surgeries had been cancelled. Nearly the entire hospital had been converted into critical care units – every floor. Every nurse redeployed as an ICU nurse.

Each ICU nurse is in charge of four ventilated patients, unheard of in normal times. Thea panics wondering how she can possibly be of help. Many of her OR colleagues have left, quit in terror. After several coworkers tested positive for the virus, they all fear that there have been others that they haven't been told about. When Thea's manager tests positive, Thea rushes to be at her bedside, changing her

---

[1]The client's name and other personal identifiers have been changed to protect privacy and confidentiality.

P. Hecht (✉)
Institute for Contemporary Psychotherapy, New York, NY, USA

© The Author(s), under exclusive license to Springer Nature Switzerland AG 2021
C. Tosone (ed.), *Shared Trauma, Shared Resilience During a Pandemic*,
Essential Clinical Social Work Series,
https://doi.org/10.1007/978-3-030-61442-3_2

bed sheets and bedclothes and hoping the same would be done for her should she be diagnosed. Meanwhile her colleagues continue to disappear, not from illness but from fear. "What's killing me is that nobody thinks it's their duty. We need to do the right thing. We're nurses and that's the meat of who we are." Nursing is more than Thea's job; it's her duty.

There is an almost daily changing of rules, procedures, policies, and guidelines. There is the "donning" and "doffing" of personal protective equipment (PPE), the mask, the hair covering, the face shield, and the hazmat jumpsuit and repeat, the horrible headaches from all the protective gear, and washing hands 50–60 times a day until they're dry, sore, and chapped.

The nightly news reports were comparing this viral pandemic to the AIDS crisis of the 1970s and 1980s, no cure, lives lost with staff standing by helpless. Voices over the hospital intercom announced "codes" for dying patients. Staff was terrified, terrified of getting sick, terrified of not being able to do their jobs. It created a palpable sense of anxiety within the hospital walls. The anxiety rivaled the virus for airtime. "We're all on edge. Our patients are the virus that inhabits them. They are both our enemies and our charges."

In addition to reinventing herself as a critical care nurse, Thea is struggling with moral injury in the context of a trauma (Jones 2020, pp. 127–128). This is a term that originated in the military and describes the violation of a person's deepest and most closely held values and moral standards. Thea and her coworkers have lost trust in their boss and become suspicious of her unwillingness to tell them whether other staff members have tested positive for the virus. The boss denies that she knows of any testing results but Thea knows that can't be true. She also knows that her boss is working with the pressure of only a skeletal staff and fears that with spiking test results others will flee.

There is a "cultural dissonance" that allows moral injury to develop. Often this dissonance develops within a specific culture. For veterans it is the military culture, the culture of war. For these nurses it is the hospital culture that has now turned into a battle zone. Working in an environment where both leadership and staff put their own fears above their responsibilities to patients can induce a sense of powerlessness and hopelessness, gateway feelings to depression. The entire country is struggling with toxic leadership, caregivers, and caretakers. Those who stay at the hospital could soon be patients, too, as could Thea. The stress increases exponentially.

Much of this work feels so familiar to me from my days working with the American Red Cross disaster mental health team. We worked with families who lost loved ones in air disasters, fires, and of course the Twin Towers. We were instructed, in fact required, to debrief one another every day, reviewing our experiences, our feelings, and what lay in store for us as we returned home; what were our responsibilities, our worries, and our supports? Listening to Thea revived my own memories and complex emotions from those days.

It wasn't hard to identify with Thea's experience; in fact, identification was inescapable. In the early part of my career, I worked nearly 10 years in both psychiatric emergency and inpatient psychiatry units. Seeing 300 patients a day in the emergency room of a midtown NYC hospital was often harrowing. Families of victims of gunshot wounds and knifings, heart attacks, and strokes were more often than not inconsolable. Memories of one particular day working with five different families of dead on arrival (DOA) had sent my autonomic nervous system spiraling. My neck and chest were covered with hives. After passing my boss in the hallway, I was sent home to recover, taken out of the line of fire. But Thea couldn't just be sent home or walk away to recover. Exhausted, she had to remain fighting.

We clearly had a context in common and likewise the panoply of responses that go with the territory of being immersed in an emergency universe. We were experiencing a shared trauma (Tosone et al. 2012). We'd both been exposed to the same collective trauma – the viral pandemic that had overtaken our world. We were both being impacted by the same event but were working differently with our patients. Thea tended to their physical, medical, and psychological needs. I envied her. My work was limited to my patients' psychological narratives. I coveted Thea's ability to work with the practical and tangible and see immediate results, often relief. My "do-over" wishes to go to medical school to train as a neurosurgeon were manifestly revived and dashed instantaneously; I'm too old for do-overs.

Tosone et al. (2012) describe shared trauma as a term first used after 9/11, but note that the phenomenon was described in the psychoanalytic literature in 1942 after the London Blitz. They describe how shared trauma can heighten and strengthen as well as blur the boundaries of the intimacy of the therapeutic connection. I am reminded of a dear friend and colleague's experience with her patient in an Israeli bomb shelter. She was treating a male patient when suddenly the emergency sirens blared and everyone was instructed to go into their shelter and don their gas masks. My colleague struggled with hers as her patient reached over and reassuringly detangled it and gently placed it on her face, sweetly brushing back her hair off her cheek in the process. That experience provided fodder for many sessions to come.

My therapy with Thea involved listening about her days in the ICU, warding off trauma, and reframing her distorted ideas of herself as inadequate and useless. She was being hailed as a hero but felt like an imposter. "I'm posing as a nurse, anyone can change bed linens." She hadn't learned "vent settings" and didn't know how to record medications in the hospital computer system. She felt ill prepared. "Thirty years as an OR nurse and I'm not ready to be thrown into the ICU."

Thea used our sessions as debriefings, an apt metaphor as she compared her job to being in a war zone. Military analogies seemed to be everywhere. She described in detail what it was like to treat patients who were dying and who knew they were dying but whose families could not be with them. She reminded herself what she *could* do. It is with the families that she found her sense of value. She FaceTimed from patients' bedsides with the husbands, the wives, the children, and the grandchildren. She had the therapeutic touch.

She was repurposed in those moments as a pastor, as a giver of hope when she looked into her patients' eyes at the scariest moments of their lives, and acted as the center of calm. She acts as the transitional object (Winnicott 1953) for the families as they say goodbye. She embodies and channels individual family members and absorbs all of their feelings. She is their container, their vessel to move their feelings to their loved ones.

Her low-tech handholding has given her a purpose in her repurposed position. "I am the conduit and I hold everyone's feelings. I come home and stand naked in the shower letting the steaming hot water wash away the day's poison and pain. This is when I realize what my body has absorbed all day. I am the patient's husband, their wife, their child, even God help me – their dog, all crying and pleading for them to pull through. An hour in the shower goes by without my being aware of the constant ticker tape of feelings circling my psyche."

According to a recent article (Lai et al. 2020), referencing 34 Chinese hospitals, the psychological impact on healthcare workers fell most heavily on the female nursing staff. They worried about contaminating family members and trying to balance their responsibility to family with their responsibility to their patients. Thea knows this feeling all too well, the terror of bringing this virus home to the five millennials who are quarantining with her as well as her husband.

But while she can call me to "debrief," so many of her colleagues don't have therapists and rely solely on any programs their hospitals provide. So much of trauma can be headed off with programs in place – "oasis rooms," meditation breaks, complimentary massages, and even staff dancing breaks to boost morale and discharge the stress. Alcoholics Anonymous's (AA) *move a muscle; change a thought* never seemed so true. One hospital instituted a program called *Check You, Check Two*, urging staff to tend to their own needs and then touch base with two colleagues daily (Hoffman 2020).

The terror of bringing this virus home drove her to a nightly ritual of stripping off her scrubs, socks, underwear, and even her jacket, bagging them, and tossing them into the washing machine even before she entered the main house. She looked forward to the reprieve of the hot shower, hoping the steaming water would cleanse her of any remnants of virus and keep her family safe. "Every day I'm faced with the responsibility I have towards my patients and their families, and my own family, but there is truly nowhere I'd rather be."

Thea's courage moved her from a sense of not being enough to being "good enough" (Winnicott 1953). Thea is a nurse, woman, wife, and mother person who believes deeply in giving back. She "drags" (her word) her husband and three sons twice a year to a struggling third-world country to help with building housing and infrastructure. She hopes it will build in her children a sense of compassion and empathy for others. But, here, now, she is fighting an unseen, unkillable enemy with small gestures of usefulness and kindness. She learns to "prone" patients, flip them on their stomachs, which relieves pressure on their lungs. Nurses not trained with ventilators can help do this and actually save lives. She hands medications to PPE-clad nurses from outside patients' rooms, saving them the trips outside and having to re-gown with all new PPE. That began to feel like enough. The work required a complete subjugation of her ego. As a senior nurse, she was performing tasks she hadn't done since graduation decades before. She was learning to live with being repurposed.

Everyone is evolving in order to survive. Homes have become WE WORK organizations, little corporate worlds with no one paying rent. Five-star hotels house
healthcare workers. They become mini-hospital settings where their occupants have
their temperatures taken as they enter, mitigating infection. Parents become teachers, camp counselors, and feeders of their adult children who have boomeranged
home to wait out the quarantine. Dating morphs into walks in the park 6 feet apart.
All people become DIYers (do it yourselfers); artists and dentists make face shields
from 3D printers, and mothers form sewing clubs to make masks for their
communities.

We all have shifting identities, myself included. Without my daily commute into
the office, I've reconnected to my kitchen, finding joy and meditation in recipes I
can make for my family. I've become a parent who has dinner with her children,
after decades of working late into the evening. We can all become creative with our
changing characters.

Everyone's been reassigned. Adult children become ambulance drivers to elderly
parents who have tested positive and need a hospital where they won't linger in a
hallway for hours. Grocery workers, mail deliverers, and drivers have all become
our new emergency essential workers. If we are separated and living apart from
loved ones, we find ways to have sex across state lines. TV personalities use makeshift crews often comprised of their own family members. Even the old family
bookcase adopts a patina of authority to give anchors and reporters stuck at home a
grab at credibility; a gesture toward intellectual depth normally manifests in their
book- and diploma-laden offices.

We all reach for some respectability in the midst of our vulnerability. Those navigating sobriety attend virtual AA meetings, making something familiar out of something virtual. Families become animal shelters, adopting "pandemic puppies."
We've developed new routines and new habits. We've become bridge learners,
online learners, and virtual museumgoers. We plant gardens when we're not garden-
ers and turn ourselves into techno Zoomers and day traders. Professors teach from
their cars to maintain some sense of privacy. We become sleuths to find free and,
most of all, reliable Internet. We find hot spots near libraries and schools to cope
with an overburdened circuitry.

This pandemic divides the real from the faux. The experts are the new influencers. "Influencers" find themselves with less "influence" as the real medical advice
comes from those who have actually earned their influence through hard work,
study, research, and education. We ward off the manifestations of grief that come
from a collapse of civilization as we've known it. We innovate and become activists,
even when we're not. We reinvent, rediscover, and reorganize ourselves, all in the
service of survival. We tap into our creativity to survive and to stay sane, healthy,
and valuable when we feel just the opposite. We take inventory of our relationship
with ourselves and with others. We reorganize our priorities in the service of controlling what we can. Hopefully, like with Thea, our breakdowns become break-
throughs. When a crisis like this pandemic reshuffles our deck, we use it as an
opportunity for change. All the research tells us that when we engage in generous
and altruistic behavior, we activate circuits in the brain that dictate well-being.

We use humor to dilute the intensity, but not the importance. Thea's husband did just that when he interrupted his wife's most recent tele-session with me. After handing her a cold glass of water, he said, "hey honey, ask the Doc why we're not having more sex!"

References

Hoffman, J. (2020, May 17). I can't turn my brain off. *The New York Times,* p. 8.

Jones, E. (2020). Moral injury in a context of trauma. *British Journal of Psychiatry, 216*(3), 127–128.

Lai, J., Ma, S., Wang, Y., et al. (2020). Factors associated with mental health outcomes among health care workers exposed to coronavirus disease 2019. *Journal of the American Medical Association Psychiatry, 3*(3), e203976.

Tosone, C., Nuttman-Shwartz, O., & Stephens, T. (2012). Shared trauma: When the professional is personal. *Clinical Social Work Journal, 40*, 1–10.

Winnicott, D. W. (1953). Transitional objects and transitional phenomena: A study of the first not-me possessions. *International Journal of Psychoanalysis, 34*, 89–97.

Chapter 3
COVID-19 and Moral Distress/Moral Anguish Therapeutic Support for Healthcare Workers in Acute Care: Our Voice

Victoria L. Cerone

Introduction

In the midst of the novel coronavirus disease (COVID-19) pandemic (WHO 2020), healthcare workers (HWs) worldwide are at the forefront of a war against the viral enemy. As with all wars, the COVID-19 battle has claimed mass casualties. Reported by the Johns Hopkins Coronavirus Resource Center (2020), as of July 18, 2020, there were 14,107,052 confirmed cases worldwide and 602,657 deaths. In the United States, there were 3,677,453 confirmed cases and 140,888 deaths. HWs in hospital facilities' acute care areas—including physicians, nurses, social workers, dieticians, chaplains, pharmacists, physical and occupational therapists, and varied support workers—are caring for the medical needs of these patients against the backdrop of their own fear of exposure. Also, with the increase of people presenting to acute care, HWs are concerned about having adequate resources to treat COVID-19 patients and those with other conditions (Moench 2020; White and Lo 2020). Thus, the COVID-19 crisis is a time of acute shared trauma for HWs and the communities they serve.

Where HWs treat patients undergoing life-altering events, the HWs are commonly at risk for traumatic workplace experiences of moral distress and moral anguish (MDA). Jameton (1984) offered the first definition of moral distress in the nursing literature. He described moral distress as occurring when a nurse experiences a painful feeling of knowing the right thing to do but encountering constraints (e.g., organizational policies) that make this course nearly impossible to pursue. In Corley (2002) the effect of MDA on nurses is examined as to how it correlates with organizational support or lack thereof. Unlike moral distress, which refers more

V. L. Cerone (✉)
NYU Langone Medical Center, New York, NY, USA
e-mail: victoria.cerone@nyu.edu

© The Author(s), under exclusive license to Springer Nature Switzerland AG 2021
C. Tosone (ed.), *Shared Trauma, Shared Resilience During a Pandemic*, Essential Clinical Social Work Series, https://doi.org/10.1007/978-3-030-61442-3_3

narrowly to an individual's emotions in response to institutional constraints, moral anguish encompasses interpersonal reactions to a specific patient interaction. Included in MDA are one's own value-laden standards of behavior or beliefs concerning what is and is not acceptable to do and the emotional and existential conflict that can occur in attempting to reconcile these standards with organizational guidelines of patient care.

The potential is high for the COVID-19 pandemic to increase MDA among HWs. They are working during an enormously stressful time, enduring high mortality rates alongside unusual isolation, as acute facilities have restricted social interaction between colleagues and visitors for patients in an effort to contain the spread of the virus. This chapter examines how MDA is being experienced by HWs since the arrival of COVID-19. It highlights therapeutic approaches that may serve to mitigate their distress and build resilience, allowing them to continue the work.

Moral Distress and Moral Anguish

Figley (1995) describes a parallel phenomenon in which a clinician experiences secondary trauma when treating traumatized people. The emotional stress on the clinician may manifest in symptoms of "compassion fatigue," including the responses "sadness, depression, sleeplessness, and gen anxiety..." (pg. 16). MDA encompasses emotional responses common to compassion fatigue and other syndromes: burnout and post-traumatic stress disorder (Hamric 2014). MDA responses include physical exhaustion, gastrointestinal issues, headaches, insomnia, nightmares, anger, frustration, anxiety, depression, depersonalization, and loss of personal fulfillment (Dalmolin et al. 2012). HWs working in the high-stress environment of a pandemic are at high risk for psychological distress with responses in accord with MDA, including fight or flight response, anxiety, panic attacks, post-traumatic stress, depression, and others (Cai et al. 2020; Mecca 2017; U.S. Department of Veterans Affairs National Center for PTSD- NCPTSD 2020). Dr. Spoorthy (2020) of the Department of Psychiatry at Jawaharlal Nehru Medical College, Wardha, India, conducted a review of six current studies (Cai et al. 2020; Kang et al. 2020; Lai et al. 2020; Liang et al. 2020; Mohindra et al. 2020; Xiao et al. 2020) looking at mental health problems HWs may confront during the COVID-19 pandemic. All six studies found data which suggest health sector work during COVID-19 could be an independent risk factor for disturbances of emotional stress (e.g., depression, anxiety, and insomnia). The participants of the studies were identified as physicians, nurses, and other/allied healthcare workers. Although social workers were not specifically identified as research participants, in acute care, they are included as primary members of the medical teams providing care. Therefore, social workers working with patients with COVID-19 are subject to the same risk of moral distress as their colleagues. Also, where work involves such physical and emotional distress, social workers, as all HWs, may feel a loss of job satisfaction, making them more likely to abandon the job and the profession (Nathaniel 2002). Significant rates of attrition may result in lower standards of care and other possible issues related to the care and safety of patients (Corley 2002).

MDA occurs across health professions but can occur for different reasons and to different degrees depending on circumstances. At an 825-bed medical center in Virginia, Whitehead et al. (2015) found evidence of moral distress among many healthcare professionals (n = 592): nurses, social workers, physicians, dieticians, chaplains, pharmacists, and physical and occupational therapists. The study utilized the 21-item Moral Distress Scale-Revised (MDS-R) (Hamric et al. 2012) and a shortened measure of Olson's Hospital Ethical Climate Survey (HECS-S) (Olson 1998). Findings from the study showed that nurses had the highest levels of MD. Further, Whitehead et al. (2015) found that "watching patient care suffer due to lack of provider continuity" (p. 117) was a top cause of moral distress across the professions. Pressure from insurers to reduce costs was often reported as a root cause for moral distress by non-ICU workers but less so by ICU workers. Whitehead et al. (2015) further noted that "continuing to care for a hopelessly ill patient when no one will make a decision to withdraw support" (p. 122) was a common source of moral distress for ICU workers.

Dalmolin et al. (2012) synthesized scientific literature over the prior 10 years and looked at moral distress in nurses and the similarities between this phenomenon and burnout. The review found that signs/symptoms of moral distress experienced by nurses included physical and emotional dimensions which affected their lives and the lives of those they cared for in their organizations.

What Does MDA Look Like During the COVID-19 Crisis?

Ms. M[1] is an 84-year-old female who was admitted to the hospital intensive care unit (ICU) for fever and shortness of breath. While in the ICU, she tested positive for COVID-19 and her symptoms worsened. Her course was complicated by pneumonia, cardiac arrhythmia, persistent fevers, and ventilator dependency. Years prior to admission, Ms. M had been diagnosed with sugar diabetes which she controlled with medication. She was an active person, living alone since the death of her spouse 10 years prior. She enjoyed spending time with her three adult children and several grandchildren. During her 35-day course of treatment, her medical status improved, which included being weaned off the ventilator, supported by a high level of oxygen via a nasal cannulation. The HWs, an interdisciplinary team including physicians, social workers, and RNs, and her family were cautiously optimistic her condition would continue to improve. Unfortunately, while Ms. M remained in hospital, her eldest daughter was stricken with COVID-19 and admitted to another acute facility. Sadly, Ms. M's daughter passed away from the virus. The family struggled with

---

[1]All names and other personal identifiers of this case have been changed to protect privacy and confidentiality.

whether to tell Ms. M, concerned that doing so would risk her relapsing. Ms. M had noticed her eldest child missing from video chats, however, and eventually the family, unable to hide their overwhelming grief, told her. With this news the family's worst fears were realized: Ms. M's medical status declined. She seemed to lose the will to live, and within days of the news, she died.

MDA Challenges

The HWs treating Ms. M faced several MDA challenges as a result of the organization's no visitation policy. Every day during normal circumstances, HWs witness how the power of touch, in something as simple as a hug from a caring person at the bedside, addresses the patient's need for human connection and soothing. Winnicott (1953) believed that as babies, humans have transitional self-regulating abilities directed toward finding objects to meet their needs, e.g., a mother's voice for soothing. Bowlby (1969) developed attachment theory, which deepened the understanding of the need for people to feel and stay connected to others. The presence of family caregivers at the bedside often reinforces a feeling of caring human connection, which in turn may strengthen a patient's resilience to endure often laborious or agonizing treatments and their chances of survival and return to normal life.

To help cope with Ms. M's and her family's feelings of isolation, the social worker and RNs treating her implemented video chats with a cell phone and laptop. This was difficult for the patient as she was not familiar with screen chat and just wanted to see her children in person. It was extremely difficult for the family, who wanted to be with her. The situation was stressful and MDA inducing for the HWs, who understood the organization's reasoning in forbidding visitors to help curb the spread of the virus but felt helpless to provide the time and level of support needed by Ms. M and all of their patients.

It is a primary social work tenet that a person's self-determination and autonomy should be facilitated wherever possible. However, as has been the case with many patients stricken with this sudden and debilitating illness, prior to COVID, Ms. M had not discussed with her family her wishes regarding her medical care should she become critically ill. As her symptoms worsened, she deferred to her family to discuss with the HWs her goals of care and treatment plan. The HWs struggled with identifying via video chats the family's physical cues to facilitate a comfort level in such discussions. For example, during in-person discussions, the social worker may respond to moments of apparent distress by pausing, touching a shoulder, or providing other simple gestures of comfort and understanding. These can make discussions much smoother when serious concerns are being addressed, such as the futility of sustained treatments in which the burdens may outweigh the benefits (e.g., painful tests, prolonged intubation, tube feeding). During video discussions such gestures were difficult or impossible. Meanwhile, the family and the HWs struggled with wanting Ms. M to recover, while understanding her poor prognosis and seemingly diminished wishes to prolong her life after the death of her child. After several meetings the family began to accept her poor prognosis, eventually transitioning to comfort care.

The HWs felt Ms. M and her family were robbed of their time to be physically together to support and comfort each other during the most sorrowful time of their lives. The social worker L consoled the patient and family, working to bear witness to, and therapeutically hold, their fear and anxiety. L facilitated between the medical team and family a person-centered experience that involved empathic listening and validation of their feelings as they processed their anticipatory grief. After Ms. M died, the family thanked all of the HWs for their care. They were most grateful to L for her frequent calls to listen to their concerns and update them as to how Ms. M was physically and emotionally enduring.

The HWs shared their compassion and distress with the process. Each from their own perspectives, members of this interdisciplinary group struggled with MDA; their compassion caused them distress in witnessing Ms. M's hospitalization, grief, and death and the grief of her family. Due to the intense needs of all their patients coping with the challenges of treatment, they had minimal time to discuss their distress among themselves. L questioned her role in the process, wondering how, or even whether, SWs can effectively intervene and assist in the processing of anticipatory loss/grief in a setting of isolation. She noted that isolation was a factor not only for patients separated from their families but also for HWs who felt deprived of normal levels of support from colleagues, since all were guarded with masks, gowns, gloves, and social distancing policies. For her own self-care and to soothe her distress, L listened to classical music from her country of origin. The music, which her mother used to play for her, reminded her of happier times as a child, and this brought comfort to her and strengthened her resolve to continue the work. However, it was also bittersweet, as her mother had died years earlier and the comforting music reignited L's grief.

Professional Perspectives and MDA Challenges

HWs are collectively taught and work from a perspective of historical knowledge within mission-driven organizations. Physicians, social workers, nurses, and other hospital HWs practice with a medicalized lens of themselves and their patients. The disciplines work as teams in a structured fashion, a collective body working to stabilize symptoms and discharge patients. Structured methodology is practiced to reduce suffering and to make room for the next patient. It gives universality to the discipline, in effect saying "We are all in this together, aware of what others are doing for a focused outcome." The structure normalizes events which are not everyday occurrences in an individual's life. Under normal circumstances, this allows HWs to proceed with a semblance of certainty and regularity, even when patients and their families are feeling disoriented and unsure.

However, with the advent of COVID-19, I and my fellow HWs have been reminded of how wildly unpredictable illness can be. In contrast with everyday illnesses, a pandemic is largely unknown to HWs as it is to the general population, and they must often improvise and learn how to respond as they go along, all while facing a surging number of cases. It is thus a powerful lesson in how life and death do not always follow a delineated path. The story of COVID-19 is more than the numbers, and it is not finished. It is still being created in narratives being authored and shared by all involved, especially the HWs, patients, and their loved ones. It is not sanitized but messy with tears of regret and thoughts for the future.

In the midst of caring for patients with COVID-19, HWs are enduring a shared trauma, or "experiences of clinicians exposed to the same community trauma as their clients" (Tosone et al. 2012, p. 231). I, along with my colleagues, the patients, and their caregivers, fear the virus and suffer isolation from loved ones because of it. Patients and caregivers are unable to physically be with each other; when HWs go home, many are isolated as they practice social distancing from spouses, children, parents, and friends out of fear of spreading the virus. Many have sent their families away to less affected areas. Others who live alone are unable to see their parents, sisters, brothers, nieces, and nephews because their work in the hospital makes them high-risk visitors. Many are making life and death decisions for their own loved ones with COVID-19 or other critical illness while caring for patients. They, too, are being robbed of precious time with their loved ones due to no-visitor policies.

This tragic chapter in history must be explored and understood in terms of shared trauma (Tosone 2011). In its dual reality of isolation and universality, it facilitates a particular way of understanding the human experience. During the COVID-19 crisis, I have worked with varied medical services and with both patients and caregivers, all undergoing their unique experiences but all experiencing forms of loss. All long for the chance to be with their loved ones, rest, administer self-care, and inform themselves while and contemplating medical goals of care and treatment options. During this time, I lost a loved one from an illness unrelated to COVID-19. The organizational policy of no visitors heightened my feelings of moral distress as it robbed us of our time together. After a few days of prohibited visitation, I was allowed to visit and was thankful for this. But, as was the case for my patients, visitors were restricted to one, so I was alone with no friends or family support at bedside.

My loved one died, and although my grief is at times unbearable, I find some comfort in being part of a new shared reality which many in the world will have to overcome and in the knowledge that, with my colleagues, I am being forced to forge a new reality. I question: How am I going to do my work? How will I and my work be different because of the pandemic and its protocols? Will I be able to provide a holding environment, especially when I don't even know what I have left to give? How do I keep my personal experiences and feelings separate from my patients'? How do I share my experience, adding life and practice wisdom but not blurring the lines between my experience and those of my patients?

I do this work with benevolent intentions of helping others. However, there is a reciprocity in provider-patient interactions, a natural back-and-forth that must be managed. When I am feeling I might share too much, I return to early-learned social work basics: start where the client is; and if in doubt, ask yourself why. I find these basics give me some distance, a moment to pause, and reestablish focus on the work at hand. The following section of this chapter outlines therapeutic strategies which have helped me as a medical social worker to maintain this focus and address clients' needs and can be applied to HWs in general, to mitigate the distress of the work and build resilience in battling MDA. The reflective and transformative models lend themselves to "post-traumatic growth" regarded as "positive psychological change" to help cope with our feelings of MDA (Tedeschi and Calhoun 2004, p.1). This experience can also illustrate "shared resilience in a traumatic reality" (Nuttman-Shwartz 2014, p. 1) in that both HWs, patients, and their family members can undergo positive transformations and interpret their experiences through a different lens.

The model of reflective learning cycle (Gibbs 1988) can be implemented in a group process or one on one. The cycle includes processing an event in terms of description, feelings, evaluation, conclusion, and action. This sequencing enables reflection and critical thought about incidents and occurrences in order to learn from them. For example, a registered nurse (RN) was experiencing MDA as a result of their uncertainty about how to respond to a patient saying, "I think I am going to die today." The RNs found themselves trying to ease the patient's fears by saying "It's going to be OK. We are here to help you." The RN was hopeful and focused on the patient recovering. Unfortunately, however, the patient died, and the RN in retrospect felt their response to the patient, meant with great empathy, had been inadequate and unprepared; looking forward, the RN feared dealing with any similar situations with future patients.

The reflective model facilitates a reevaluation of what occurred and possible future responses should it occur again. It helped the RN to envision processing the patient's fears from a stance of not fixing the situation but instead just being and bearing witness. Should a patient state they are dying in the future, the RN might respond with "I hear you" and/or "Do you want to talk about what you are feeling?" During COVID-19, social workers as well as all HWs are treating an unprecedented number of critically ill patients fearful they are going to die. Many of the patients prior to contracting the quickly debilitating virus were healthy. The reflective model offers HWs a quick, agile tool to recalibrate one's thoughts and personal reactions to the fear of death, allowing them to continue the work feeling more prepared for situations as they unfold. I carry a copy of the model in my work papers. It helps me not to dwell endlessly on self-doubt over what I feel I might have done wrong. Instead I can acknowledge the issue and critically develop alternative responses.

Another approach, transformative learning (Mezirow 1990), seeks transformation in regard to psychological subjective responses, beliefs/values, and behavioral knee-jerk reactions. It describes a planned course of action which includes acquiring knowledge and skills for the purpose of understanding and validating clinical practice, with a focus on questioning how we know versus what we know. For example, an HW may experience an MDA conflict around questions of treatment benefits versus burdens for the patient and the patient's family. One HW experienced MDA witnessing the volume of pain management medications administered to a patient, medications which controlled physical pain but left the patient unable to communicate with their family due to sedation. The HW understood it is humane to have the patient comfortable and without pain; however, they also expressed sadness watching how the medication limited the patient's communication with loved ones. In another example, the HW had the opposite experience: the patient's family wanted only a minimal dose of sedation, even though the patient was uncomfortable, and their pain level was not properly addressed. The HW felt powerless. In both cases, education and critical thinking regarding the efficacy or futility of treatments may help HWs clarify the situation in their own minds and, possibly, in communication with patients' family members going forward. Treating COVID-19 is especially a challenging time when HWs need guidance on how to be kind to ourselves while responsive to the needs of our patients, caregivers, and colleges. The reflective and transformative models lend themselves to "post-traumatic growth" regarded as "positive psychological change" to help understand and cope with our feelings of MDA (Tedeschi and Calhoun 2004, p.1).

Witnessing the substantial level of MDA among HWs involved in such agonizing situations, one question becomes poignantly obvious: How do HWs care for themselves? A crucial first step in helping HWs deal with MDA is acknowledging the existence of MDA and their struggles with it. MDA is inevitable for most HWs, a matter of when, not if. HWs must set aside the notion that MDA is a sign of emotional or physical weakness and acknowledge their strengths, while assessing their coping abilities and resources for resilience. Resilience influences how an event is appraised (Fletcher and Sarkar 2013). Resilience is "not just an attribute or capacity"; it is a "process to harness resources to sustain well-being" (Panter-Brick and Leckman 2013, p.334). COVID-19 has facilitated a shared resilience (Nuttman-Shwartz 2014) as HWs battle the virus in emergency departments, intensive care, and other hospital units. The feeling is we are stronger in numbers and we will adjust to what is needed fighting this horrific virus together.

To aid HWs' recovery and maintaining personal wellness, organizational policies and therapeutic practices must be directed toward acknowledging, understanding, and addressing their feelings of moral distress and moral anguish. Hamric and Epstein (2017) described three well-recognized approaches to addressing healthcare workers' moral distress: a direct approach (e.g., journaling, retreats, systematic reflection), an indirect approach (e.g., education, ethics conversations discussing examples and different views), and a general approach (e.g., policies that target institutional restraints and interprofessional relationships) (p. 128).

Many institutions pre-COVID-19 developed wellness collaboratives to address MDA. For example, Schwartz Center Rounds is a group forum organized for case reflection, along with psycho-education projects, interactive competency workshops, and systematic rapid/ongoing response teams. With regard to maintaining social distancing, many Internet resources are available, e.g., Social Work Hospice and Palliative Care Network (SWHPN) and Center to Advance Palliative Care (CAPC). HWs themselves often take responsibility for identifying MDA issues and searching for solutions in a grassroots fashion. The self-determination to do so initiates the self-care process, heightening autonomy and ownership of one's welfare.

Conclusion

Acute care requires critical thought and moral courage to underpin engagement with difficult biopsychosocial circumstances. This challenging work requires management of time, tempo, and negotiating and maintaining boundaries, while dealing with the complexities of detachment, commitment, desensitization, and compassion (Breaden et al. 2012). HWs must be engaged in self-care and understand the potential for MDA to arise, as well as interventions available to lessen its effects. The implementation of educational programs has proven to mitigate moral distress in acute care settings (Brandon et al. 2014; Rogers et al. 2008). However, such resources and accommodations are not always offered by organizations. The insights of this chapter come from case examples exploring circumstances, determinants, and therapeutic modalities related to understanding and addressing MDA in a time of COVID-19. The case vignettes provided are brief narratives of representative experiences of MDA, which have affected HWs across disciplines during the most challenging of times in acute care. The therapeutic approaches Gibbs' reflective cycle and Mezirow's transformative learning warrant consideration as interventions to understand and facilitate a strengthening of the self amid the ever-evolving situation unfolding around treatment of COVID-19.

This chapter identifies shared trauma inflicted by the surge of COVID-19 on social workers and those they treat in hospital settings and demonstrates helpful therapeutic approaches to address MDA among HWs practicing in acute care settings. It is a privilege to be a social worker and care for patients and their caregivers during the most challenging of times. I find the work coincides with sadness, bittersweet expression, and often, outstandingly courageous events. Never has this been truer than during the COVID-19 crisis and its particular brand of shared trauma. I make moral sense of the work guided by professional ethics and personal values. Prior to the pandemic, I experienced a greater separation from patients' experiences. Now, however, we all share a collective experience of loss, fear, and uncertainty. COVID-19 has impacted all of our lives. We are living a shared trauma which has yet to fully unveil the biopsychological toll it will have on humanity, but certainly that toll will be unfolding for decades to come.

While this crisis has underscored the reality of shared trauma, I have long contemplated that social workers are foremost humans sharing in the experience of their clients. Upon coming home from work some years ago, I would routinely be asked by Anne, my 93-year-old mother-in-law, "How are you?" and would routinely reply, "I'm fine." On one occasion, Anne answered, "Sure, Miss Fine, you work in the hospital all day with sick and dying patients and you are fine" (Cerone 2005). Her comment was said with concern and realism. To set aside and rationalize feelings of MDA fall under the "Miss Fine philosophy," which works in the short term but is not sustainable over time. At this time, I especially remember her words and have learned from my personal and professional experience with COVID-19 that it is OK to be vulnerable and seek the support of my colleagues. In fact, it is imperative to do so to maintain a semblance of normality in a time of which is not normal.

Going forward by acknowledging, working to understand, and addressing our shared challenges of MDA in this time of COVID-19, I hope to ease our distress, build our resilience, and bolster our courage to carry on our truly compassionate work.

References

Bowlby, J. (1969). *Attachment and loss*. New York: Basic Books.

Brandon, D., Ryan, D., Sloane, R., & Docherty, S. L. (2014). Impact of a pediatric quality of life program on providers' moral distress. *Maternal Child Nursing, 39*(3), 189–197.

Breaden, K., Hegarty, M., Swetenham, K., & Grbich, C. (2012). Negotiating uncertain terrain: A qualitative analysis of clinicians' experiences of refractory suffering. *Journal of Palliative Medicine, 15*(8), 896–901.

Cai, H., Tu, B., Ma, J., Chen, L., Fu, L., Jiang, Y., & Zhuang, Q. (2020). *Psychological impact and coping strategies of frontline medical staff in Hunan between January and March 2020 during the outbreak of coronavirus disease 2019 (COVID-19) in Hubei, China.*

Cerone, A. (2005). *Direct quote.*

Corley, M. (2002). Nurse moral distress: A proposed theory and research agenda. *Nursing Ethics, 9*(6), 636–650.

Dalmolin, G. L., Lundardi, V. L., Barlem, E. L., & Silveira, R. S. (2012). Implications of moral distress on nurses and its similarities with burnout. *SciELO Analytics Texto context- enfern, 21*(1) Florianopolis.

Figley, C. R. (Ed.). (1995). *Compassion fatigue: Coping with secondary traumatic stress disorder in those who treat the traumatized*. New York: Brunner Mazel.

Fletcher, D., & Sarkar, M. (2013). Psychological resilience a review and critique of definitions, concepts, and theory. *European Psychologist, 18*(1), 12–23.

Gibbs, G. (1988). *Learning by doing: A guide to teaching and learning methods*. Oxford: Further Educational Unit, Oxford Polytechnic.

Hamric, A. B. (2014). A case study of moral distress. *Journal of Hospice & Palliative Nursing, 16*(8), 457. Retrieved January 18, 2019 from http://www.jhpn.com.

Hamric, A. B., & Epstein, E. G. (2017). *A health system-wide moral distress consultation service: Development and evaluation*. Dordrecht: Springer Science+Business Media. https://doi.org/10.1007/s10730-016-9315-y.

Hamric, A. B., Brochers, C. T., & Epstein, E. G. (2012). Development and testing of an instrument to measure moral distress in healthcare professionals. *AJOB Primary Research, 3*(2), 1–9. https://doi.org/10.1080/21507716.2011.652337.

Jameton, A. A. (1984). *Nursing practice: The ethical issues*. Upper Saddle River: Prentice Hall.

Johns Hopkins Coronavirus Resource Center. (2020). *Coronavirus COVID-19 global cases by the Center for Systems Science and Engineering (CSSE) at Johns Hopkins University (JHU)*. Retrieved June 8, 2020 from https://coronavirus.jhu.edu/map.html

Kang, L., Li, Y., Hu, S., Chen, M., Yang, C., Yang, B.X., Wang, Y., Hu, J., Lai, J., Ma, X., Chen, J., Guan, L., Wang, G., Ma, H., & Liu, Z. (2020). The mental health of medical workers in Wuhan, China dealing with the 2019 novel coronavirus. *Lancet Psychiatry, 7*, e14. 017. Retrieved June 1, 2020 from https://pubmed.ncbi.nlm.nih.gov/32035030/

Lai, J., Ma, S., Wang, Y., Cai, Z., Hu, J., Wei, N., Wu, J., Du, H., Chen, T., Li, R., Tan, H., Kang, L., Yao, L., Huang, M., Wang, H., Wang, G., Liu, Z., & Hu, S. (2020). Factors associated with mental health outcomes among health care workers exposed to coronavirus disease 2019. *JAMA Network Open, 3*, e203976. https://doi.org/10.1001/jamanetworkopen.2020.3976.

Liang, Y., Chen, M., Zheng, X., & Liu, J. (2020). Screening for Chinese medical staff mental health by SDS and SAS during the outbreak of COVID-19. *Journal of Psychosomatic Research, 133*, 1101–1102. Mahase, E., 2020. https://doi.org/10.1016/j.jpsychores.2020.110102.

Mecca, S. (2017). *The gift of crisis: Finding your best self in the worst of times*. Dallas: Soul Circle.

Mezirow, J., & Associates (Eds.). (1990). *Fostering critical reflection in adulthood*. San Francisco, CA: Jossey-Bass.

Moench, S. (2020). *The COVID-19 Pandemic: ASCO addresses ethical considerations for the allocation of scarce resources to patients with cancer*. CancerTherapyAdvisor.com. Retrieved May 15, 2020 from https://www.cancertherapyadvisor.com/home/cancer-topics/general-oncology/covid19-coronavirus-pandemic-asco-addresses-cancer-patient-resource-scarcity/. https://www.cancertherapyadvisor.com/home/cancer-topics/general-oncology/covid19-coronavirus-pandemic-asco-addresses-cancer-patient-resource-scarcity/

Mohindra, R., Ravaki, R., Suri, V., Bhalla, A., & Singh, S. M. (2020). Issues relevant to mental health promotion in frontline health care providers managing quarantined/isolated COVID19 patients. *Asian Journal of Psychiatry, 51*, 102084. https://doi.org/10.1016/j.ajp.2020.102084.

Nathaniel, A. (2002). Moral distress among nurses. *The American Nursing Association Ethics and Hum Rights Issues Updates, 1*(3). [online]. [Acessed 12 Nov 2005]; Retrieved September 17, 2018 from http://www.nursingworld.org/MainMenueCategories/EthicsStandards/Resources/IssuesUpdate/UrIssuesUpdateSpring2002/MoralDistress.aspx [Links].

Nuttman-Shwartz, O. (2014). Shared resilience in a traumatic reality: A new concept for trauma workers exposed personally and professionally to collective disaster. *Trauma, Violence, and Abuse*, 1–10. https://doi.org/10.1177/1524838014557287.

Olson, L. L. (1998). Hospital nurses' perspectives of the ethical climate of their work setting. *Journal of Nursing Scholarship, 30*(4), 345–349.

Panter-Brick, C., & Leckman, J. F. (2013). Editorial commentary: Resilience in child development-interconnected pathways to wellbeing. *The Journal of Child Psychology and Psychiatry, 54*, 333–336. https://doi.org/10.1111/jcpp.12057. [PubMed] [Cross Ref].

Rogers, S., Babgi, A., & Gomez, C. (2008). Educational interventions in end-of-life care: Part I: An educational intervention responding to moral distress of NICU nurses provided by an ethics consultation team. *Advances in Neonatal Care, 8*(1), 56–65.

Spoorthy, M. S. (2020). Mental health problems faced by healthcare workers due to the COVID-19 pandemic- A review. *Asian Journal of Psychiatry, 51*, 102119. https://doi.org/10.1016/j.ajp.2020.102119. [Epub ahead of print].

Tedeschi, R. G., & Calhoun, L. G. (2004). The posttraumatic growth: Conceptual foundations and empirical evidence. *Psychological Inquiry, 15*, 1–18.

Tosone, C. (2011). The legacy of September 11th: Shared trauma, therapeutic intimacy and professional posttraumatic growth. *Traumatology, 17*(3), 25–29.

Tosone, C., Nuttman-Shwartz, O., & Stephens, T. (2012). Shared trauma: When the professional is personal. *Clinical Social Work Journal, 40*, 231–239. https://doi.org/10.1007/s10615-012-0395-0.

U. S. Department of Veterans Affairs National Center for PTSD (NCPTSD). (2020). *For mental health providers: Working with patients affected by the coronavirus (COVID-19) outbreak*. Retrieved May 10, 2020, from https://www.ptsd.va.gov/

White, D. B., & Lo, B. (2020). A framework for rationing ventilators and critical care beds during the COVID-19 pandemic. *JAMA* [published online March 27, 2020], https://doi.org/10.1001/jama.2020.5046.

Whitehead, P. B., Herbertson, R. K., Hamric, A. B., Epstein, E. G., & Fisher, J. M. (2015). Moral distress among healthcare professionals: Report of an institution-wide survey. *Nursing Scholarship, 47*(2), 117–125.

Winnicott, D. W. (1953). Transitional objects and transitional phenomena: A study of the first not-me possession. *The International Journal of Psych-Analysis, 34*, 39–97.

World Health Organization (WHO). (2020). *Coronavirus – World Health Organization*. Retrieved May 10, 2020 from https://www.who.int/health-topics/coronavirus

Xiao, H., Zhang, Y., Kong, D., Li, S., & Yang, N. (2020). The effects of social support on sleep quality of medical staff treating patients with coronavirus disease 2019 (COVID-19) in January and February 2020 in China. *Medical Science Monitor, 26*, e923549. https://doi.org/10.12659/MSM.923549.

Chapter 4
On the Front Lines of the Fight Against the COVID-19 Pandemic: Meaning-Making and Shared Trauma

Sophia Tsesmelis Piccolino

The COVID-19 pandemic has become known as the greatest crisis of our lifetime, affecting us individually and collectively, creating bonds and severing connections, bringing unity and exacerbating difference, extending compassion, and pronouncing intolerance. These reflections come following several months of living through the COVID-19 pandemic leading oncology social workers within a large NYC hospital system, the once national epicenter of the novel coronavirus. Social workers support the psychological and emotional needs of people, while simultaneously enduring the trauma, loss, suffering, and uncertainty of this pandemic. Our resilience and sources of hope and meaning are explored through the existential distress of this shared trauma (McTighe and Tosone 2015).

As social workers, we are trained to support complex trauma, agony, tragedy, and loss, but what happens when, in parallel, we are grappling through the same pain, uncertainty, anxieties, and fears? As a New Yorker, when I think of shared trauma, the attacks of September 11 come to my mind, the deadliest single terror attack in US history. On 9/11, I was not yet a professional clinician, but I can now envision the complexity and challenge for social workers at that time in supporting individuals' mental health needs, providing support for the financial, spiritual, practical, and social impact of this devastating day that rippled for days, months, and years to come, while simultaneously dealing with the impact of the trauma. At the onset of this pandemic, COVID-19 was being compared to wars, and as a medical social worker, a warzone painfully depicts the images imprinted in my mind of the hospital that once brought me comfort and symbolized caretaking. The intangibility of the pandemic's oppressor and its ongoing nature align its suffering to the effects of a

S. T. Piccolino (✉)
Department of Social Work Services, The Mount Sinai Hospital, New York, NY, USA

Silver School of Social Work, New York University, New York, NY, USA
e-mail: sophia.piccolino@mountsinai.org

© The Author(s), under exclusive license to Springer Nature Switzerland AG 2021
C. Tosone (ed.), *Shared Trauma, Shared Resilience During a Pandemic*,
Essential Clinical Social Work Series,
https://doi.org/10.1007/978-3-030-61442-3_4

natural disaster, while its seeming incontrollable and endless attack signals a unique trauma incomparable to others in our lifetime. The long-term effects of the impact of COVID-19 on our nation and the world will be for later writings and future reflections, research, and exploration. Presently, I write to share the experiences in the here and now, living and surviving through COVID. The suffering through COVID has pressed for exploring sources of hope, strength, comfort, and peace. Inquiries around meaning and purpose in suffering leave me wondering what I hold onto during difficult times and what do those around me hold on to.

The search for meaning and hope has been central to my work as a clinical social worker. I have experienced pain, suffering, and loss, searching and holding onto hope and meaning through the lens of oncology and palliative care. Searching for meaning has helped me persevere in the field of oncology and palliative care and given me fuel to understand that above all else, we are all human, in need of love, kindness, and hope. Whether it is hope for cure, hope for the end of suffering, hope to see loved ones a final time, or a hope for a peaceful departure from this world, through the pain and suffering, hope has felt tangible. Undoubtedly, these concepts have been at the forefront of my mind through what many are referring to as the collective trauma of the COVID-19 pandemic. Navigating this societal upheaval as a social work manager in a large urban medical center in New York City has been arduous. Certainly, collective trauma, despite its name, creates varying degrees of psychological and emotional distress across individuals and communities. It is not the individual suffering and loss but the very breakdown of the fabric of our communities and society that may inevitably lead to the effects of COVID-19 being a collective trauma (Hirschberger 2018).

In a moment's time, cancer can change everything about what we know our life to be. Cancer brings about psychologically distressing issues related to feelings of loss, especially around certainty in life and finances, changes in self-identity, body image, issues and changes around sexuality/fertility, loss of meaning and purpose, unstable emotions, and fears and thoughts about mortality (Holland 2002). These psychologically distressing issues among many others may be present at one or several stages of the cancer trajectory: diagnosis, treatment, recurrence, survivorship, and end of life (Grassi et al. 2017). In my clinical experience in oncology and palliative care, issues around existential distress, meaning, purpose, and spirituality have resonated throughout the myriad of distressing stages that patients and I have faced.

In a moment's time, COVID-19 changed everything about what we knew our life to be. For some cancer patients, the pandemic brought about a greater acceptance of their cancer diagnosis, as their experience of isolation and alienation from others was minimized and their distress became normalized by family, friends, and the community. The distress of illness, infection, isolation, financial worry, job insecurity and loss, and mortality have become communal struggles. In some instances, social workers have shared a stronger level of connection and understanding to their patient's distress than ever before. In other instances, social workers' own fears, anxieties, and stressors around the pandemic led to greater boundaries and less emotional availability for patients. As I individually and we collectively in our communities, nationally, and globally face the COVID-19 pandemic, I cannot help but think of the impact of the existential distress and search for meaning in the suffering, loss, and pain. I walk through this pandemic as a clinical social work supervisor, my years in direct care having left scars of suffering, memories of love and hope, and humbling lessons of gratitude. As a supervisor, I walk along my team, and I walk along our patients, along my family and friends, as we face the suffering and loss uniquely and collectively.

Loss, trauma, and tragedy have pressed me to question my understanding of life, my perceptions of suffering, and how to find hope professionally and personally. I have looked for a way to redefine the pain and find some peace amidst the chaos. The work of Viktor Frankl comes to the forefront, a psychiatrist, neurologist, and Holocaust survivor whose work was on the basis that life can have meaning even in the most difficult circumstances and under the greatest suffering (Frankl 1946), following his own suffering in concentration camps during the Holocaust and the loss of his family members. Frankl brought to the surface that we cannot escape suffering and loss of life and not only can we find meaning in suffering, it also can, in fact, allow for suffering to be more bearable and enable an individual to be more resilient, having profound insight. As Frankl (1946) suggests, we have the power to choose how we respond to our most challenging situations and control how we react in the face of adversity. In fact, that power is a human responsibility.

Finding meaning through the crises of this pandemic and searching for understanding of the suffering and uncertainty and its rippling effect in our community and our nation have created the holding space I have needed, grounding me, allowing for a calm in the storm, the space to dissipate the feelings of uncertainty, anger, anxiety, and fear. Searching for meaning and purpose in suffering is not the cliché of a "silver lining" – finding the positive within a negative. Four months after the onset of the New York "pause," 4 months following COVID-19 spreading through our nation, more than 30,000 New Yorkers and 140,000 Americans have lost their life (Centers for Disease Control and Prevention 2020). These facts are not the positive within the negative. They are the devastating truth of the pain and loss. Suffering is an inescapable part of life. Within it we can choose a path to find meaning despite the pain, trauma, and loss. Facing adversity does not elicit growth in us; the active attempt to choose how we respond is where that transpires.

Being in a leadership role throughout this crisis has felt like the culmination of great privilege and strain. The tasks of balancing the well-being and needs of our social workers and supporting patients, healthcare staff, and the institution through a pandemic that has brought unmeasurable strain on our healthcare system and essential workers have been stormy uncharted waters. Decisions, rules, regulations, and systematic needs are in constant clash, seemingly impossible to bring the safety and relief that all social workers needed and expected, as they faced the same crisis, often with fears, anxieties, gratitude, worries, and hope along the way. I walked alongside with them processing my role in supporting them, while faced with supporting my family, providing security and safety to my children, and fighting physically through being infected with the virus itself. I longed for ways to create a safe and secure holding environment (Winnicott 1960) for my supervisees, for my children, and for my family, a holding environment to create space for conflicting feelings around the social work role within an institution occupied by infection, fear, sickness, and loss of life. I wondered if we could find a way to continue to best support our patients, provide care to our hospital and our team members, create a safe emotional and physical space for our staff, preserve our role as medical social workers, and uphold the values of the social work profession.

The social work profession has a crucial role in the COVID-19 crisis to provide psychosocial support to individuals struggling with the emotional and psychological impact of this pandemic, while uniquely in tune to social determinants of health to help address the pandemic's disproportionate negative impact on racial and ethnic minorities and individuals of lower socioeconomic status. For social workers and other healthcare professionals, there is dual exposure to the coronavirus pandemic, both in their personal lives and in bearing witness to their clients' and patients' experiences. Supervisors, social workers, patients, clients, parents, spouses, and children are all walking in parallel, coping and managing a shared trauma (Tosone et al. 2003).

A prevalent theme that has arisen is the role of an essential worker amidst the COVID-19 crisis and how social workers define ourselves professionally and within our institutions. To be an essential worker may mean you have been on the front line, exposed, in closer proximity to the virus, at greater risk for your own health (United States Department of Labor 2020). It may mean you have had the responsibility to protect, help, and save in a more visible way. It may mean you have had the privilege to leave your home, to have greater social connection to others, and to feel less isolated. It may mean you have had job security, salary increases, or hazard pay. For some professions and workers, there has been no choice in the category they have been placed; as a social worker, within a large hospital system, the question of who constitutes an essential worker was more significant than I could have envisioned. In essence, do I have the physical safety and security to work remote in my role, as I navigate the emotional and psychological burden of supporting our patients through a mutual crisis that I simultaneously am navigating? Do I have the clearance and authority to be present in the hospital, to provide critical in-person support to patients at the end of their life and to clinical team members battling through long shifts and fear and fatigue as they fight for our patients and their own survival?

We did not expect what happened. We were not prepared. Our nation, our cities, our communities, our neighbors, our families, and ourselves, we were not prepared for the societal upheaval, the extreme suffering and loss, the fear and uncertainly, the politics that would persist and exacerbate the crisis, and the division and mistrust. Take a moment to pause and consider your thoughts, feelings, reactions, and fears and the culmination of how you have responded to this pandemic personally and professionally, from your closest family and friends to unknown individuals walking 6 feet apart from you. Could you have predicted how you have reacted to the upheaval and the dismantling of the fabric of our society, to the loss and suffering, and does it align with your world thinking, history of loss, and prior exposure to suffering and trauma? Can you find meaning and purpose in this suffering, and have you been able to do so before? Its significance is understanding the role of meaning, transcendence, and resilience in existential distress.

The COVID-19 pandemic has brought waves of psychological, physical, and social distress to our nation and the world. In the social work role within health care, our close proximity to the suffering and distress of this crisis through our own struggles has been unique and challenging. Social workers are familiar with responding and supporting people in distress and doing so with humility. This shared trauma is unscripted, but together, through reflecting on our experiences, sharing our knowledge, and learning from one another, we can create greater understanding for this trauma.

References

Centers for Disease Control and Prevention. (2020, July 22). *Covid data tracker.* https://www.cdc. gov/covid-data-tracker/

Frankl, V. E. (1946). *Man's search for meaning, an introduction to logo-therapy.* Boston: Beacon Press.

Grassi, L., Spiegel, D., & Riba, M. (2017). Advancing psychosocial care in cancer patients. *F1000Research, 6,* 2083. https://doi.org/10.12688/f1000research.11902.1.

Hirschberger, G. (2018). Collective trauma and the social construction of meaning. *Frontiers in Psychology, 9,* 1441.

Holland, J. C. (2002). History of psycho-oncology: Overcoming attitudinal and conceptual barriers. *PsychosomaticMedicine,64*(2),206–221.https://doi.org/10.1097/00006842-200203000-00004.

McTighe, J., & Tosone, C. (2015). In the long shadow of 9/11: Narratives of Manhattan clinicians' efforts to make meaning of a shared trauma. *Social Work in Mental Health, 13*(4), 299–317.

Tosone, C., et al. (2003). Shared trauma: Group reflections on the September 11th disaster. *Psychoanalytic Social Work, 10*(1), 57–77.

United States Department of Labor. (2020, July 27). *Covid-19 control and prevention; Healthcare workers and employers.* https://www.osha.gov/SLTC/covid-19/healthcare-workers.html

Winnicott, D. W. (1960). The theory of the parent-child relationship. *International Journal of Psychoanalysis, 41,* 585–595.

Chapter 5
Supervising Psychiatry Residents in a COVID-19-Only Hospital: A Hall of Mirrors

Leslie Cummins

Discussions about supervision have often revolved around the role of the supervisor, its contrast to that of the psychotherapist, the boundaries between them, the potential pitfalls, and what constitutes effective educational process. Although literature exists on supervision in a shared trauma experience, little has been written about the supervisor's experience when they, the trainee, and the patient experience simultaneously a global incident affecting themselves, their families, colleagues, and organization, as well as the supervisor's own patients. Supervisees and supervisors can become ill; the supervised case may contract the disease or become a treating provider; the roles can suddenly shift, and the caretaker can quickly become the one in need of care. In a medical facility, trainees may be put into other roles of which the supervisor has little knowledge. Previous tensions between institution and supervisee may be exacerbated, and the supervisor as representative of the institution/employer may test the relationship. Such has been my experience supervising psychiatry residents in an outpatient clinic at a hospital that was designated a "COVID-19-only" hospital in New York City.

The shared trauma of a global pandemic could multiply this phenomenon to vertiginous effect; the treatment and supervision can feel like a funhouse mirror in which each relationship contains and reflects the other, and reverse subject and

L. Cummins (✉)
Department of Psychiatry, SUNY Downstate Medical Center, Brooklyn, NY, USA

Department of Psychiatry, New York University Langone Medical Center,
New York, NY, USA

Psychoanalytic Association of New York, New York, NY, USA

Metropolitan Institute for Training in Psychoanalytic Psychotherapy, New York, NY, USA

Editorial Board, Smith College Studies in Social Work, Northampton, MA, USA
e-mail: lb2038@nyu.edu

© The Author(s), under exclusive license to Springer Nature Switzerland
AG 2021
C. Tosone (ed.), *Shared Trauma, Shared Resilience During a Pandemic*,
Essential Clinical Social Work Series,
https://doi.org/10.1007/978-3-030-61442-3_5

object; the roles can duplicate, repeat, and distort. The supervisee can overidentify with the patient, the patient with the supervisee, the supervisor with the supervisee and with the patient, the patient with the institution and their patients, and so on in a dizzying array of challenging possibilities. As Arlow (1963) writes, "[t]he phenomenon of transient identification with the patient... is also important in the supervisory experience" (p. 579). The supervisor empathizes with the student and their patient, but, as in ordinary times, the identification must be short-lived to avoid becoming unhelpful or even detrimental.

The topic not only addresses the current pandemic but also touches upon what may occur when supervisor and supervisee share similar crises and experiences and highlights the importance of maintaining the supervisory relationship in the face of enormous stressors. However, a situation such as the current one tests all the boundaries. The supervisee needs support, as do the supervisor, the supervisor's patients, the supervisee's patients, and the institution; all as private relationships may be stressed by illness, absence, living situations, and/or relationships. The supervisor may be called upon for more support than usual, perhaps even advocacy, but the role of therapist is still best left to the supervisees' own process and peer groups or other institutional supports. However, the isolation posed by COVID-19 amplifies both the need for and obstacles to this assistance. The supervisor can also, of course, be caught between evaluator and educator status (Knight and Borders 2018; Scharff 2014a, b), which can pose additional difficulties for both parties. The supervisor may act as confidant but also as reporter to the employing organization; the supervisee needs to discuss openly their difficulties with a case and to show the best work they can. These balances become even more delicate in such an environment.

There exists no perfect analog to our current situation, neither is there a perfect blueprint for supervision or treatment. Other fields offer resemblances. Studies of combat trauma usually refer to post-traumatic stress disorder, by the DSM-5 definition requiring 1 month following the event to develop (as opposed to acute stress disorder, a diagnosis that can be made immediately). Disaster psychiatry often requires mental health workers to travel to the location of a circumscribed, discrete trauma. Our current situation has elements of these but doesn't fit neatly in either category. The pandemic is protracted; the enemy is protean, somewhat random, invisible, and inescapable – experienced literally by the entire world. The closest situation may be to mental health care in countries that have suffered years of war and random violence, such as Northern Ireland and Israel. Much of the recent research on trauma treatment comes out of those experiences as well as post-hurricane and other disasters, including the World Trade Center incident on 9/11 (Ursano et al. 2007).

The past 20 years has seen a burgeoning literature on trauma studies, with an attendant growth of categories and nomenclature. Trauma, stated simply, is the overwhelming of the ego by a powerful event or experience (Herman 2015). Largely growing out of disaster psychiatry, war-torn and refugee states, and terrorist attacks, various delineations have been made of trauma's effects on patients and providers. Burnout, compassion fatigue, vicarious trauma, and secondary traumatic stress are all terms that have been used to capture these effects. According to Halpern and

Vermeulen (2017), vicarious trauma is a trauma reaction by a therapist (or other helper) due to exposure to a client's traumatic experience. Its roots can lie in therapist empathy. This means the very quality required for good psychotherapy may predispose practitioners to a traumatic response themselves. These authors define secondary traumatic stress as more pervasive and pernicious, with a direct relationship to post-traumatic stress. In the current situation, there may exist few differences between stress reactions of direct and secondary exposure. For the purpose of this chapter, I will use the term vicarious trauma more broadly to include both definitions.

More germane to the current situation is another concept: shared trauma. For Tosone et al. (2012), the term adds to those listed above, to "describe the entirety of the clinician's experience when living and practicing in traumatogenic environments" (p. 231). Shared trauma refers to the therapist and patient experiencing the same overwhelming events simultaneously. It is important to delineate the differences in the current situation to those giving rise to most of the literature cited. This is not to increase or decrease the significance or magnitude of any of these experiences; it is merely to help further the discussion of similarities and differences in the various types in order to enrich the discussion of the challenges and needed supports in such a fluctuating situation.

A brief word about the particularities of psychiatry training in regard to psychotherapy is in order. Psychiatry residents often do not begin outpatient work until their third year of study and therefore have had exposure to complex cases not always found with the beginning psychotherapist or even postgraduate training program candidate. By third year, most have been the audience to significant trauma histories, particularly those working in urban settings. They therefore may not need more "guidance and instruction" (Knight and Borders 2018, p. 25) when treating trauma. They usually do, however, have little exposure to dynamic therapy. In my experience, this can vary from one setting to another, but most dynamic exposure to this point has been through didactics and/or the supervisee's own psychotherapy. Even in hospitals that value insight-oriented therapy, the residency consists of students with varied interests and future plans. (In fact, one might take exception to the idea of "trauma-informed care" as an entire category, when psychoanalytic psychotherapy is founded upon treatment of *all* types of trauma.) The principal program in which I work offers dynamic supervision in an evening clinic that is utilized by both the academic community and the community at large. It is a well-utilized service that cares for people across the diagnostic spectrum. In addition, the psychiatry department began another hospital-wide volunteer service for more focused and short-term help to address the growing mental health needs of medical workers during the pandemic. The department provided its own faculty and students with increased meetings and support groups.

At the end of March 2020, at the height of the pandemic, New York Governor Andrew Cuomo appointed the hospital as treating only COVID-19 patients. At the time, more than half (30,000 of 52,000) of the COVID-19 cases in New York state were in New York City. Also at the time, the medical education that could be conducted remotely was moved online. Residents in all specialties were being slated to be deployed to COVID-19 or other floors; psychiatry residents were required to shift their patients to remote treatment. Also occurring were travel bans, quarantine and isolation directives, confusion about signs and symptoms, and the consequent overburdening of all systems at all levels. Stressors were magnified at a residency program that includes many international medical graduates (IMGs). The preexisting potential for high stress of IMGs (loneliness, family concerns, immigration and visa status, language and cultural adjustments, and others) was now magnified exponentially by a pandemic and by a political situation that threatened to isolate them from their countries and families of origin even further (Kramer 2015). Two physician couples faced the added strain of potentially isolating from their partners or, worse, isolating from and caring for ill partners. Anxiety levels about contracting the disease were high, particularly as the picture of the virus, possible treatments, and preventive measures were rapidly changing. By the end of April, two medical-worker suicides occurred in other New York City-area hospitals, further compounding anxieties among the student practitioners and faculty.

Some examples will illustrate the complexity of supervising within the context of shared trauma. A young psychiatry resident has been working for a few months with a resident from another specialty, now transferred to a COVID-19 floor. The treatment had been going well. The resident is a conscientious and talented clinician. He prepares well for supervision, is attentive to the patient's presenting problem, and is attuned and warm, and, pre-pandemic, the patient's initial symptoms of anxiety have lessened and been reframed dynamically, that is, something to be understood, interpreted, and worked through. The resident is adept and interested in the dynamic approach and therefore interested in his own feelings as potentially meaningful about his patient. As can be imagined, the identification that the supervisee has with his patient, another resident sharing some attributes, is potentially complicated, offering opportunity for empathy but also for overidentification and disruptive countertransference.

Due to the patient's deployment to a COVID setting, accommodations to his schedule were needed. This, of course, was consented to without consideration or further discussion. I think here we can see the easy slippage between potential overidentification with a patient, between the needed attention to external reality and internal conflict, and between supervision and therapy. Although minor, this became a pattern that soon had to be addressed. The patient requested many changes and additional sessions and grew irritated when they could not be granted, and this understandably resulted in feelings of resentment by the supervisee. To the student's credit, he did not seek the same of the supervisor. What did become obvious, however, were the feelings of inadequacy being induced in the therapist when he could not meet the demands, a reaction possibly sought by his perfectionistic and highly competitive patient. This example brings up two other issues: one is the nature of the helping professional, perhaps especially physicians, and the other is the tendency of the neophyte to underestimate pre- and unconscious pressure.

To address the second point first, it was a common question of trainees to understand the necessity for and utility of addressing more long-standing and/or less-than-conscious behaviors and symptoms of their patients. Often a dilemma for students who are new to dynamic therapy or who are more interested in biological and/or behavioral approaches, the question may have taken on added meaning for even those students who were psychoanalytically inclined: it became a place of rest and resistance. Learning a new approach, its underlying theory, and listening on several levels, in addition to the new stress of teletherapy and pandemic anxieties, became overwhelming. As with the students, I also found myself drawn to a more supportive stance with several of my own patients. (In fact, it was a patient's complaint that I seemed to be talking more than was quite helpful in this realization.) The third-year resident has not yet gained the conviction of the experienced practitioner of insight-oriented psychotherapy that helps maintain the stance of curiosity and exploration. But even the more seasoned clinician could find themselves leaning on supportive techniques to bolster one's own sense of security.

The first point is also important and can be intertwined with the second – physicians often have what can become a debilitating Achilles' heel: their difficulty seeking treatment. In his book on physician suicide, Myers (2017) discusses these risk factors. As with other healthcare workers discussed previously, the positive attributes doctors need to be successful and professional, such as drive, high expectations, exacting standards, sensitivity, and altruism, can, under the wrong circumstances, tip into self-destruction. Myers also cites the medical culture of "the special club" and the marginalization of women and minorities as other possible contributors to distress and/or suicide. Perhaps more so than in other mental health disciplines, the stigma of becoming a patient and its perceived (or real) negative effects on records, career advancement, and liability may preclude seeking help. Additionally, the competitive and demanding nature of residency may dovetail negatively with the psychiatry resident's sacrificing, perhaps even masochistic, nature to be exploited by an overburdened system that may abet residents' "unconscious need for martyrdom" (Hashmonay 2020, p. 471). As Figley (1995) observes, however, there may be a cost to caring, a cost that at times can be tragically high.

As with my own patients and like other residents who were now seeking flexibility, I found myself wavering between yielding to the trainees' pressures and the need to maintain the structure and mission of supervision. Complementary to this, I remembered my own experience as a psychoanalytic trainee after 9/11: classes were held by my institute the same week, and I attended in disbelief and anger. At the time, reeling from a close family member's near-miss and my close exposure to the day's events, it seemed to me the epitome of classical psychoanalysis' failure to recognize reality. As with any trauma, it was easy to reexperience that feeling, and I was aware of wanting to demonstrate to the residents that I would not fail in the same way. However, I needed to refind my supervisory footing and remember all I had learned since – that there are many realities and privileging one may come at the expense of others.

Some of the same personal difficulties plaguing the supervisee and his patient were experienced by me as well: worries about and separation from family, concerns about my and others' health, and concerns about my practice and my patients. Supervisees and patients did become ill, and I worried about my contact with them before transitioning to remote work. Several patients were medical professionals who were experiencing the same exposure as my supervisees and their patients; the call to support family, patients, and supervisees while experiencing the same anxieties could be daunting. Early on, I felt a fleeting sense of hopelessness and uselessness: what could I do for anyone in this situation so outside of our control? Aside from partially stale bromides, what did I have to offer? As Herman (2015) writes, "[p]sychological trauma is an affliction of the powerless" (p. 33). A regression to helplessness could be dangerously seductive.

As carrying on business as usual was critical, there nonetheless needed to be an acknowledgment of a terrifying reality that required at times a more directly supportive stance, with all of whom I worked. Modifications had to be made, particularly with young trainees who not only were new to outpatient and psychodynamic work but also were being put into unknown situations professionally and personally, sometimes without clear guidelines or lines of support. Concurrently, I was working in a way I had previously used sporadically in temporary, sometimes transitional situations. Simultaneously, my practice was also moving online and to telephone, a practice previously held, and valued, in person. This was not only true of work with patients but also with supervisees as well. Walking the line between supervisor, advocate, and therapist threatened to become more complex.

This resident's case took on more intense feelings of competition and potential belittlement. The patient, initially presenting with anxiety that was a thin veneer for disappointment with a family that focused on other family members' difficulties, found great solace in her new role as essential healthcare worker. The veiled charges of psychiatry as a lesser medical profession were rife, and my supervisee was sensitive to them. Simultaneously, as a licensed clinical social worker, my role could be seen as even lower on the hierarchy. My psychoanalytic training and supervision experience are the qualifications for my role, but being a clinical social worker in a medical setting could have the potential to fuel feelings of inadequacy in an increasingly dire situation.

In another case, a young woman had begun treatment with a resident for intrusive thoughts and separation-individuation issues revolving around romantic and family relationships. Herself the child of a physician, the young woman was struggling against identifications with and the shadow of her parent, while choosing a specialty and training program. The treatment was proceeding well. The therapist and patient had made a good connection, the patient was beginning to see her "intrusive thoughts" as perhaps meaning something true about her relationship, and she began questioning her previously unexamined career choice that had been contributing to her anxiety.

COVID hits. The patient's stable and strong physician-father struggled mightily; he was debilitated by a severe depression. As the patient's father, previously seen as an incorruptible model of success and fortitude, became further incapacitated, the patient became increasingly anxious and demanding of the supervisee. My earlier 9/11 memories of the debilitation and destabilization of loved ones resurfaced. The supervisee's world was similarly shaken, as he was put into new situations as was his physician-wife. The patient's situation potentially had too many similarities to those of the treating resident's not to pull on the trainee's insecurities and inexperience: they were of similar age, had comparable family backgrounds and constellations, faced stressors on their relationships, and were enlisted to help struggling family members. A significant difference for the supervisee was that he was now learning and treating in a completely remade landscape, with new demands on and by his partner and her patients. The similarities and difficulties among all involved demanded vigilance.

With both these and other medical workers under my supervision, new demands for support and flexibility arose that had been more easily navigated prior to the pandemic. The few previous reschedulings, latenesses, and poor preparation threatened to become the norm. What could more easily be addressed as possible parallel processes, and in light of the supervisee's own educational level, were now overly tinged with reality factors that could blur the treatment and supervision processes. I, too, needed to shift things in my own schedule to accommodate patients' growing treatment needs. It became more difficult to know what accommodations actually needed to be made for residents and how much was coming from anxiety, resentment, overload, and/or true need. Never a martinet in my approach, I found myself bending more than usual; the stressors in my own life sometimes could make it easier to allow for cancellations and rescheduling, possibly threatening the supervisory frame.

Further reverberations. Concurrently, I was volunteering to treat healthcare workers across New York state. As this progressed, I found myself further identified with my supervisees as I engaged with healthcare workers in my practice and others now deployed to COVID-19 settings across New York City. Listening to one physician and emergency responder after another recount overwhelming stories of illness, death, family management, frustration, and lack of guidance was overly close to supervisees' experiences at times, as the level of distress and uncertainty was unprecedented. Speaking to patients and supervisees could exacerbate the feelings of helplessness and futility, threatening my own equilibrium.

One doctor whom I was seeing pro bono tapped into my own deepest fears when discussing deaths of several young people in his hospital. My own children were similarly aged and, as such, had been more casual and possibly more exposed. Attending to the details of horrifying experiences could become numbing, and I reminded myself more than once that these were not my children, nor were the elderly patients my parents. It was not only heartbreaking to attend to the stories of cellphones held up to a dying patient's ear, of efforts at FaceTime with families of those intubated, and of scrambling to find ways of communication for families with little or limited knowledge of English and/or technology, but it was also frightening. And counseling residents and patients who were now explaining potential death, life-threatening illness, and advanced directives was sad and, at times, angering. Young students, many of whom were not training in critical or emergency care, were struggling with anxieties that resembled my own. Moral injury, not a disorder but can cause negative thoughts about self, others, and institutions and may result in shame and guilt, was everywhere. A treasured colleague passed away, but, aside from peripheral acquaintances, I had not yet suffered the loss or illness of anyone close to me. But having worked at the hospital into the start of the pandemic, seeing several patients who had recently traveled overseas, frequent mass transit use, and other factors combined to increase the anxiety I was treating and supervising in others.

There is a growing literature on what has come be known as "trauma-informed supervision." Berger and Quiros (2014), for example, quoting Etherington (2009), write that "trauma-informed supervision combines knowledge about trauma and supervision, and focuses on the characteristics of the interrelationship between the trauma, the practitioner, the helping relationship, and the context in which the work is offered." These writers discuss trauma-informed supervision as mitigating against vicarious trauma. They describe the essentials of effective supervision in these cases as bearing the same hallmarks of trauma-informed care: "safety, trustworthiness, choice, collaboration, and empowerment" (p. 298.).

Historically, psychotherapy supervision has not been taught. Learning has been akin to that of a guild in which apprentices (trainees) are assumed or hoped to gain enough knowledge and proficiency to practice the skill themselves. Being a competent clinician has presumed competence as a supervisor. It has been argued by many (e.g., Cabaniss et al. 2014; Courtois 2018; Kolar 2020; Scharff 2014a, b) that there be formalized guidelines for training supervisors of psychodynamic psychotherapy. The competencies required of residents and candidates in other training programs should be required in teaching of supervision as well. I believe this may be an important change for several reasons: the efficacy and relevance of the method could be made more evident; the possible lack of structure reinforces ideas of lack of structure of psychodynamic therapy and social work; and it may improve learning outcomes and help with trainee confidence and conviction. The methods suggested by these and other writers are outside the interests of this chapter, but how we become supervisors is relevant in the current climate insomuch as a structured approach may provide important goalposts in an ever-shifting landscape. When a supervisee may be overwhelmed by a patient, particularly one with whom it may be difficult to empathize, I often point them toward the literature that may explain the genesis and possible meanings of the person's behavior. It might be helpful, when the ground is moving beneath everyone's feet, for the supervisor also to have guidelines and educational material to consult.

Although of various magnitudes and specifics, we are all having a shared traumatic experience. Add in the varieties of experience, individuals, histories, personalities, identities, and the many permutations of how this pandemic may be experienced, the possible supervision complexities become clear. A young doctor comes to the resident service for symptoms of sleeplessness and irritability. This doctor may match the student's educational status and may be close in age, gender, and background. They are going through the same pandemic, which means they will also be socially distancing, if not quarantining. The supervisor is caring for similar patients, supervising the students, and in the same situation. This scenario can elicit strong feelings in all of us and present temptation to cross the boundary into familiarity, casualness, and over-involvement, if it does not affect us traumatically, as well.

Group meetings with academic and professional colleagues were key to maintaining the conviction that even, perhaps especially, in an unknowable situation, I could be of help. Volunteering to offer counseling through various organizations and institutions was also beneficial. A large supportive family hedged against threatening despair. Maintaining as much stability for myself, patients, and supervisees was essential; and remaining as true as possible to the frames of these relationships was more important than ever. Training as a social worker and psychoanalyst, which could be seen as obstacles in postgraduate medical education, equipped me with balancing the roles as teacher, advocate, confidante, and support of the residents under my supervision. Flexibility and understanding were key as residents were deployed to medicine units or scheduling challenges arose. As I and supervisees faced the shift to remote treatment, we became students, together, of a method somewhat new to all of us. Listening actively, not only to the content being presented in supervision but also to the supervisee's experience, is vital. Social worker training is concerned not only with the patient but also with the supervisee within their environment.

As some residents became ill or suspected they were, they became cut off from their families, either domestically or internationally, and were moved to units they had little or distant experience with, all the while attending to their psychiatric duties. This called up a strong maternal feeling for each of them. As with any reaction, I had to understand my responses as understanding something but also as a potential for inhibiting other responses, such as resentment or hostility. Further, I could not let external forces foster dependence or prevent the residents' own "theory of mind" from developing as an unfortunate and unforeseen consequence. Psychoanalytic training privileged the emerging affects and unconscious expression in the supervision. I held the belief that adherence to theoretical constructs steadied me, as I simultaneously had to consider its defensive aspect. Both taught me the importance of tending to the roles of provider/providee, which were consistently challenged, knotted, reflected, and refracted.

Supervisor and the supervision need to mesh and complement each other during such a time. Prescriptions to one's patients need also to be made to oneself and one's students. These could include the usual recommendations such as meditation, mindfulness, journaling, and/or any of a host of customary behavioral interventions. However, some of the same suggestions could not be instituted – contact with loved ones could only be virtual (or not at all), helpful routines had to be abandoned, and formerly communal and spiritual activities could only be practiced alone. The effectiveness of cognitive restructuring appeared to have limitations in the face of the reality of the unknown and unknowable, when news could worsen from day to day. Scheduling, short-term projects, and virtual socialization were added to the arsenal of self-care.

As a therapist and as a supervisor, however, one is obligated not to relinquish their roles nor their theoretical underpinnings. Perhaps regardless of theoretical approach, it is essential to adhere to the principles that one teaches at any time, to any trainee. Good psychotherapy supervision aids the resident in understanding the patient and the content presented; this requires theoretical grounding and a similar formulizing ear to the supervisee's material that models for them their way of listening to their own patients. The material the patient is presenting remains the focus of supervision, and students are helped in learning how to reframe and think of the patient, their difficulties, themes, conflicts, and other presenting material in terms of the theory and practice being taught (Shanfield et al. 1993).

However, it may never be possible to steer clear completely of supervisees' personal dilemmas, perhaps impossible during a shared trauma. Indeed, I would argue it would not be indicated. According to some (e.g., Jacobs 2016; Scharff 2014a, b), the limitation may be neither simple nor in order. It is incumbent upon the supervisor to point out blind spots and consistent technical missteps to the supervisee: they owe it to the student *and* the patient. The current situation may call upon the supervisor to share their own experience in an effort at normalizing or empathizing with the trainee's experience. As with a patient, it is my experience that considering self-disclosure occurs proportionally to the gravity of the event or affect and, as such, should be weighed significantly before undertaking. And, as with a patient, self-disclosure in supervision should be done *only* toward a clinical end. Generally, I confine the definition of self-disclosure as being useful when it is of one's own reaction to the patient in an attempt to shed light on relational or defensive patterns and amplify the patient's sense of themselves and their inner and outer worlds. In supervising during the time of COVID-19, some sharing of the challenges to the role of the therapist has been in order with students. They have needed to see, while also being reassured and modeled for, that there is a recognition of our new reality.

The supervisory situation is complex (Jacobs 2016). It needs to move between roles within the relationship. As such, the supervisor must be aware of the special educational and sometimes personal needs of the student. There is an overlap here that cannot be avoided. In an organization, the supervisor may be a representative of the educational body, while also encouraging the student to grow through didactic processes, studied introspection, and self-knowledge. During a time of shared trauma, the supervisor also needs support, perhaps from the same body as the student, in addition to their own systems and loved ones. The containment function of supervision (Pisano 2014) may become even more pronounced, but it needs to be for the supervisee, not for the dyad nor the supervisor. As per Arlow (1963), "in therapy, the patient oscillates between experiencing and reporting, while the therapist oscillates between identifying with the patient and observing him. During supervision, the therapist recapitulates this oscillation of roles" (p. 581). In the potentially disorientating oscillations of a global pandemic, technical and theoretical grounding is paramount to maintaining the stability of the supervisory situation.

References

Arlow, J. A. (1963). The supervisory situation. *Journal of the American Psychoanalytic Association, 11*, 576–594.

Berger, R., & Quiros, L. (2014). Supervision for trauma-informed practice. *Traumatology, 20*(4), 296–301.

Cabaniss, D. L., Arbuckle, M. R., & Moga, D. E. (2014). Using learning objectives for psychotherapy supervision. *American Journal of Psychotherapy, 68*(2), 163–176.

Courtois, C. A. (2018). Trauma-informed supervision and consultation: Personal reflections. *The Clinical Supervisor, 37*(1), 38–63.

Etherington, K. (2009). Supervising helpers who work with the trauma of sexual abuse. *British Journal of Guidance & Counselling, 37*(2), 179–194.

Figley, C. R. (1995). Compassion fatigue: Toward a new understanding of the costs of caring. In B. H. Stamm (Ed.), *Secondary traumatic stress: Self-care issues for clinicians, researchers, and educators*. Derwood: The Sidran Press.

Halpern, J., & Vermeulen, K. (2017). *Disaster mental health interventions: Core principles and practices*. New York: Routledge.

Hashmonay, G. (2020). On masochism: A resident's conflict between sacrifice and self-preservation during the COVID-19 pandemic. *Journal of the American Psychoanalytic Association, 68*(3), 471–473.

Herman, J. (2015). *Trauma and recovery*. New York: Basic Books.

Jacobs, D. (2016). Review: Clinical supervision of psychoanalytic psychotherapy. *Journal of the American Psychoanalytic Association, 64*(2), 431–434.

Knight, C., & Borders, L. D. (2018). Trauma-informed supervision: Core components and unique dynamics in varied practice contexts. *The Clinical Supervisor, 37*(1), 1–6.

Kolar, D. (2020). Psychotherapy supervision for psychiatry residents. *European Psychiatry, 30*(S1), 1.

Kramer, M. (2015). Training international medical graduates in psychiatry: A cultural adventure. *Transcultural Psychiatry, 52*(2), 280–282.

Myers, M. (2017). *Why physicians die by suicide*. Middletown: Delaware Ophthalmology Consultants.

Pisano, M. J. (2014). Supervision as a model of containment for a turbulent patient. In *Clinical supervision of psychoanalytic psychotherapy* (pp. 33–42). Washington, DC: American Psychiatric Press.

Scharff, D. E. (2014a). Supervision of the therapist's resonance with her patient. In *Clinical supervision of psychoanalytic psychotherapy* (pp. 139–146). Washington, DC: American Psychiatric Press.

Scharff, J. S. (2014b). Theory of psychoanalytic psychotherapy supervision. In *Clinical supervision of psychoanalytic psychotherapy* (pp. 13–23). Washington, DC: American Psychiatric Press.

Shanfield, S. B., Matthews, K. L., & Hetherly, V. (1993). What do excellent supervisors do? *American Journal of Psychiatry, 150*(7), 1081–1084.

Tosone, C., Nuttman-Shwartz, O., & Stephens, T. (2012). Shared trauma: When the professional is personal. *Clinical Social Work Journal, 40*, 231–239.

Ursano, R. J., et al. (Eds.). (2007). *Textbook of disaster psychiatry*. New York: Cambridge University Press.

Part II
Specialty Populations Impacted by the COVID-19 Pandemic

Chapter 6
Staying True to Our Core Social Work Values During the COVID-19 Pandemic

David Kamnitzer, Elisa Chow, and Jeanine D. Costley

Introduction

The COVID-19 pandemic has impacted the lives of individuals, families, and communities around the world. These past few months have given social workers a new perspective and appreciation of the NASW Code of Ethics, the foundation from which all social workers operate. Working in a nonprofit human service agency providing services to vulnerable populations living in impoverished communities in New York City, social workers were the unspoken essential workers grappling to provide mental health and supportive services as usual. During these unprecedented times, the six core values and principles that support the NASW Code of Ethics – service, social justice, dignity and worth of the person, importance of human relationships, integrity, and competence (National Association of Social Workers [NASW] 2015) – brought hope, guidance, and a reminder of what social workers strive to do.

Service

Service is the first core value of the NASW Code of Ethics (NASW 2015). Social workers' primary goal is to help people in need and to address social problems (NASW 2015). It reminds us that individuals who generally go into the social work

D. Kamnitzer · E. Chow (✉) · J. D. Costley
Institute for Community Living (ICL), New York, NY, USA

New York University Silver School of Social Work, New York, NY, USA
e-mail: echow@iclinc.net

© The Author(s), under exclusive license to Springer Nature Switzerland
AG 2021
C. Tosone (ed.), *Shared Trauma, Shared Resilience During a Pandemic*,
Essential Clinical Social Work Series,
https://doi.org/10.1007/978-3-030-61442-3_6

field have a genuine desire to help others, contribute to the larger community, and personally grow from these experiences (Bent-Goodley 2017).

The core value of service was notable during the height of the COVID-19 pandemic. At our agency, with the uncertainty surrounding transmission, protection, and treatment, social workers carried on to identify gaps and render solutions. Social workers continued to provide mental health treatment and supportive services, met and admitted new individuals for services, and completed regulatory treatment plans and required assessments on health and family relations. We put aside our own worries and fears so that we could remain empathic, present, and supportive to our clients. We heard and allayed clients' uncertainties through telephonic or videoconference sessions, connected them to food and medications when they could not leave their homes, and comforted them when someone they knew died from COVID-19. Social workers taking part in providing direct supportive care of individuals living in our housing programs, homeless shelters, and group homes promoted the idea of physical distancing rather than social distancing. To counter social isolation during this time of self-quarantine, social workers helped set up videoconferencing with their primary care providers, family, and friends.

Social Justice

Social justice is a core value rooted in our profession. Our training asks us to pursue social change, particularly with and on behalf of vulnerable and oppressed individuals and populations. During the COVID-19 pandemic, as a nation, we witnessed the striking disparities in access to health care and the risk factors facing racial and ethnic minority groups in impoverished communities (Artiga et al. 2020). The consequences of these differences have resulted in disproportionate levels of infection and death in black and brown individuals (Richardson et al. 2020).

Historically these disparities have been ever present; however, the inequities during the COVID-19 pandemic brought this to the forefront. The early days of the COVID-19 pandemic evoked public and scientific reactions to the staggering disparities about unknown genes that would make communities of color more vulnerable to the virus rather than a focus on the devastating biological consequences of systemic inequality and oppression. The racial impact of the virus is deeply rooted in historic and ongoing social and economic injustices.

Individuals experiencing unstable housing, living in dorm-style shelter arrangements, and residing in congregate care and nursing facilities often found it difficult to safely social distance from others. Housing availability and stability are an area where some of the largest disparities can be found. The distribution of wealth and obtaining affordable and appropriate housing stemming from racism have resulted in the crisis of homelessness, housing instability, and vulnerability to COVID infection for many of our clients.

Individuals who are also essential workers may not have the option to work from home, which increases their vulnerability to COVID-19. They may be in a position where they do not have the benefits of sick or personal time that would allow them to care for their children who are out of school due to COVID-19 or to care for loved ones who may be ill. Another added stressor is the loss of employment. Many individuals who are low-wage workers tend to be the first to lose their job and last to be hired back (Smith 2020).

Diseases like diabetes, hypertension, obesity, and asthma disproportionately affect minority populations, which increases vulnerability to transmission. These also take significant tolls on their mental health. Inequities in health outcomes, healthcare access, and benefits result in our nation's response to preventing and mitigating its harms that are not equally felt in every community.

In challenging social injustice, it's important that we recognize the social construction of race, power, privilege, and racial supremacy as core foundations of oppression in our country, made more evident with the COVID-19 pandemic.

Dignity and Worth of the Individual

In honoring the dignity and worth of our clients throughout this pandemic, social workers have advocated for safer environments, increased opportunities for social distancing, and identified safe resources for individuals experiencing homelessness. This advocacy reflects our attention to anti-oppressive practices with an ambition to challenge inequality, marginalization, and oppression at structural levels by using structural understandings of social problems (Mattsson 2014). As social workers engage in anti-oppressive practices, it's important to listen carefully for oppressive language when assessing client's needs. These assessments highlight the intersections of our clients' identities and help in advocating for the best resources to facilitate change.

When clients living in dorm-style shelter environments were not able to adequately social distance or protect themselves from COVID-19 transmission, it was community organizations, advocacy groups, social workers, and coalitions that demanded a resolve until safer solutions were presented. Although our position as social workers connote power differentials within a larger system, this partnership within the community and advocacy groups invokes change, as it makes the client the narrator of his or her own experiences (Sakamoto and Pitner 2005). This change manifested into the mayoral initiative to increase social distancing and lessen the opportunity for transmission of COVID-19 in homeless shelters by relocating all clients living in single adult dorm-style shelters to hotels. These moves enhanced safety and security and demonstrated our dedication to individual value and worth. Clients were furnished with single or double rooms and private bathrooms.

Social worker's partnerships with coalition and advocacy groups focused on dignity, worth, and value of each person, a core principle. This ongoing advocacy in our social service agencies spawned the movement for personal protective equipment (PPE) to be distributed to each client living in New York City's continuum of housing. PPE was also provided for all essential staff each day in these 24-hour facilities.

Large shipments of masks, gloves, and hand sanitizers were obtained on a monthly basis, and case managers ensured that each client had access to medical care, psychiatric care, and medications for chronic physical and mental health issues. Most importantly, staff ensured that clients could access remote services by researching providers who would continue to serve clients during the COVID-19 pandemic.

Importance of Human Relationships

The importance of human relationships is perhaps the most sacrosanct of values inherent in social work practice. At the core of our profession is the fundamental belief in the capacity for change, and for this to occur, social workers must be keenly attuned to the connection between themselves and the individuals served in practice. The COVID-19 pandemic challenged our profession to think about new ways of connecting with our clients. We pondered how to sustain trust in the relationship and how to be flexible and available to our clients, and we recognized the importance of self-reflection among other traits. During any pandemic there is prone to be a myriad of reactions and feelings. As there were so many unknowns about the COVID-19 virus and the dangers in the environment, many social workers found themselves encountering individuals engaged in a fight-or-flight experience. There was tremendous fear, sadness, and even anger all around us, and this triggered many people to run away to a safe place (Chery and Gans 2019). Yet social workers did not run. We were part of a group called essential workers. We were called to task, and we needed to fulfill our mission to strengthen relationships and enhance the well-being of families, social groups, organizations, and communities (NASW 2015).

Many individuals enter our programs straight from institutional settings including state hospitals and prisons. They arrive to us after many years of street homelessness and experiencing trauma and oppression, and far too many have been ostracized and shunned by their own families. It is the role of the social worker at our agency to understand their trauma, use recovery-oriented principles, focus on integrated health care, and instill notions of hope and self-determination. Hence, these overarching themes are tantamount in one's quest for solid attachments and the corrective recapitulation of one's primary family experience (Yalom 1995). It requires an understanding of micro-, mezzo-, and macro-views of social work practice for all of these elements to converge. As an agency we remained steadfast in our commitment that none of these critical components of social work would be compromised during the COVID-19 pandemic.

Engagement, a term widely known in the social work literature, is often the beginning of forming human relationships. For many individuals living with a chronic mental health condition such as schizophrenia and major depression, establishing trust, a fundamental role in engagement, can be a long and complex process. The face-to-face encounter that often begins the engagement process presented a clear barrier during the pandemic. Many clinics and day programs stopped in-person sessions and were forced to reimagine a new way of building rapport and sustaining healthy relationships. During the COVID-19 pandemic, social workers were faced with new challenges; as clinics closed due to safety reasons, how would these important relationships be sustained? As social workers, one might say we were "called to action." Indeed, we pondered the benefits of fostering a place where individuals felt less isolated and where there was a sense of mutual aid (Yalom 1995). At a time when social isolation is occurring in unprecedented ways, the role of groups as a protective factor was something we needed to consider. The importance of preserving social worker-client relationships during times when clients are forced to quarantine during the COVID-19 pandemic became abundantly clear. In these instances, social workers played a key role in helping clients reduce feelings of isolation. As Zoom and GoToMeetings became ever more popular, it was the recognition that online groups also may offer social workers an efficient and effective way to support the mental health and decrease feelings of isolation of the larger community during the COVID-19 pandemic (Whittingham and Martin 2020).

Integrity

It is noteworthy to recognize the sense of integrity that is also essential to our profession and inherent in social work practice. There is no code of ethics specific to supervision. However, it could easily be argued that nearly all aspects of our practice apply to the supervisory relationship, since a contemporary view in social work is that supervision is actually a form of social work practice and mutual aid (Brashears 1995). During the COVID-19 pandemic, social work supervisors played essential roles in the accountability department. As agencies had to confront complex decisions in the face of COVID-19, we needed to ensure that those individuals who had been so used to being served in-person were still receiving care with a sense of dignity and clinical integrity. Our profession has always placed great importance on the value of supervision. Social workers would need to get used to a new paradigm shift that called into question the very importance of the value of delivering services with integrity and purpose for all.

On an agency level, there exists a culture that reinforces our profession's core principles. Integrity is inherent in all of our departments. We practiced due diligence by immediately forming a multidisciplinary task force. The group met daily to address clinical excellence, system issues, and ongoing communications with key stakeholders including staff, clients, and key regulators.

Competence

Competence, another core value, emphasizes the importance of continuous learning for social workers to grow personally and professionally. Social workers recognize the importance of competent practice and that good intentions, along with having the knowledge and skills, are what is needed to be effective in practice (Bent-Goodley 2017; Reamer 2017).

The onset of the COVID-19 pandemic significantly impacted the way social workers and staff delivered care. Routine procedures and traditional practices were deferred in order to protect clients and staff from exposure to infection. Social distancing and wearing PPE were the norm. In many states, including New York state, mental health providers responded to the COVID-19 pandemic with rapid and widespread conversion to telehealth services, supported by relief from the former regulatory and legislative barriers (NYS Office of Mental Health 2020). This was a movement toward the right direction within the continuity of services. However, this was an awakening for agencies and staff alike who believed telehealth services would take place sometime in the far future. For agencies, they had to quickly take inventory of their existing systems. Were there enough smartphones and laptops to distribute to staff across the agency? Did we have enough bandwidth? Do we need to upgrade our firewall? How do we ensure HIPAA compliance with staff working remotely (US Department of Health and Human Services 1996)? Which platform, Zoom or GoToMeeting, would best fit our staff and client needs? Hence, for many social workers, incorporating digital clinical tools as a means to remain connected with clients, provide services, and complete documentation remotely had a new set of essential competencies and ethical guidelines to adhere to (NASW 2017; Reamer 2017). At the same time, the use of digital technology created new ways and opportunities for social workers to interact and communicate with clients.

Conclusion

The COVID-19 pandemic will have long-lasting global effects. It is evident that social workers are needed now more than ever. Social workers are one of the largest providers of mental health services in the country with the knowledge and skills to operate on micro-, mezzo-, and macro-levels (Council of Social Work Education 2014). The NASW Code of Ethics keeps social workers grounded and focused in today's constantly changing environment. While the code of ethics has adapted and changed over the years, its core values and principles remain the same – serving as a guide in delivering services with fairness and respect. Our mission to serve others in need, advocate for social justice, honor the dignity and worth of each unique individual, understand the importance of human relationships, practice with integrity, and continue to enhance our competence makes social work stand apart from other mental health professions.

References

Artiga, S., Orgera, K., Pham, O., & Corallo, B. (2020, April 21). *Growing data underscore that communities of color are being harder hit by COVID-19.* Kaiser Family Foundation. https://www.kff.org/coronavirus-policy-watch/growing-data-underscore-communities-color-harder-hit-covid-19/

Bent-Goodley, T. B. (2017). Living our core values. *Social Work, 62*(4), 293–295. https://doi.org/10.1093/sw/swx046.

Brashears, F. (1995). Supervision as a social work practice: A reconceptualization. *Social Work, 40*(5), 692–699. https://doi.org/10.1093/sw/40.5.692.

Chery, K., & Gans, S. (2019, August 18). *How the flight or fight response works.* Very Well Mind. https://www.verywellmind.com/what-is-the-fight-or-flight-response-2795194#:~:text=What%20Happens%20During%20the%20Fight,which%20include%20adrenaline%20and%20noradrenaline

Council on Social Work Education. (2014, October). *The role of social work in mental and behavioral health care principles for public policy.* https://www.cswe.org/getattachment/Advocacy-Policy/RoleofSWinMentalandBehavorialHealthCare-January2015-FINAL.pdf.aspx

Mattsson, T. (2014). Intersectionality as a useful tool: Anti-oppressive social work and critical reflection. *Affila: Journal of Women and Social Work, 29*(1), 8–17. https://doi.org/10.1177/0886109913510659.

National Association of Social Workers. (2015). *Code of ethics of the National Association of Social Workers.* https://www.socialworkers.org/About/Ethics/Code-of-Ethics/Code-of-Ethics-English

National Association of Social Workers. (2017). *NASW, ASWB, CSWE, & CSWA Standards for technology in social work practice.* https://www.socialworkers.org/LinkClick.aspx?fileticket=lcTcdsHUcng%3d&portalid=0

NYS Office of Mental Health. (2020, March 30). *Use of telephone and two-way video technology by OMH-licensed, funded or designated providers and clients affected by the COVID-19 pandemic.* https://omh.ny.gov/omhweb/guidance/covid-19-consolidated-telemental-health-guidance.pdf

Reamer, F. G. (2017). Evolving ethical standards in the digital age. *Australian Social Work, 70*(2), 148–159. https://doi.org/10.1080/0312407X.2016.1146314.

Richardson, S., Hirsch, J. S., Narasimhan, M., Crawford, J. M., McGinn, T., Davidson, K. W., & Northwell COVID-19 Research Consortium. (2020, April 22). Presenting characteristics, comorbidities, and outcomes among 5700 patients hospitalized with COVID-19 in the New York City area. *JAMA.* https://doi.org/10.1001/jama.2020.6775.

Sakamoto, I., & Pitner, R. O. (2005). Use of critical consciousness in anti-oppressive social work practice: Disentangling power dynamics at personal and structural levels. *British Journal of Social Work, 35,* 435–452. https://doi.org/10.1093/bjsw/bch190.

Smith, N. (2020). *Six ways the coronavirus will make inequality worse.* Bloomberg Opinion. https://www.bloomberg.com/opinion/articles/2020-5-13/six-ways-coronavirus-will-make-u-s-inequality-worse

U.S. Department of Health & Human Services. (1996). *Health Insurance Portability and Accountability Act of 1996.* https://aspe.hhs.gov/report/health-insurance-portability-and-accountability-act-1996

Whittingham, M., & Martin, J. (2020, April 10). *How to do group therapy using telehealth.* American Psychological Association Services, Inc. https://www.apaservices.org/practice/legal/technology/group-therapy-telehealth-COVID-19

Yalom, I. D. (1995). *The theory and practice of group psychotherapy* (4th ed.). New York: Basic Books.

Chapter 7
Safety Planning with Survivors of Domestic Violence: How COVID-19 Shifts the Focus

Catherine Hodes

Intimate Partner Abuse and COVID-19

Not long after the world began to shut down due to COVID-19, there were conflicting reports about domestic violence calls to police and hotlines. In some places calls to police dropped, while in others calls to hotlines and providers surged (Southall 2020). The data was difficult to interpret, but after 30 years of working with survivors, it made sense to me. Abusers are intent on controlling their partners, and when families are restricted from going to work or school, visiting friends and relatives, or socializing, it is easier to maintain control. Physical violence, understood as a crime, becomes less necessary, hence reduced calls to police. Less understood is the fact that abuse is not primarily about acts of physical violence. Isolation, manipulation, monitoring, and threats may not rise to the level of criminal behavior, but they are enough to instill fear and maintain control. Increased calls to hotlines and service providers may indicate that survivors locked down at home are seeking connection, support, and ways to navigate and lower risk.

There was skyrocketing anxiety among advocates supporting survivors of domestic violence as we watched relied-upon responses slow and resources shrink. In the early days of shutdowns, we met virtually through state and local task forces, and while efforts focused on bringing resources back online, there were also searching conversations about the nature and reality of safety for survivors. This chapter reflects some of what emerged from those discussions and, importantly, from the knowledge and experiences of survivors themselves.

C. Hodes (✉)
Safe Passage, Northampton, MA, USA
e-mail: catherineh@safepass.org

© The Author(s), under exclusive license to Springer Nature Switzerland AG 2021
C. Tosone (ed.), *Shared Trauma, Shared Resilience During a Pandemic*,
Essential Clinical Social Work Series,
https://doi.org/10.1007/978-3-030-61442-3_7

Managing Stress and Conflict

Living with the fear and uncertainty of a global pandemic is traumatizing, and many people will experience states of emotional withdrawal, panic, defensiveness, over- or under-functioning, and despair. Such responses are normal in adverse circumstances but can put couples and families at risk of heightened conflict. Where people are struggling with increased tension and conflict at home, improved communication skills, boundary setting, and de-escalation tools can help mitigate relational stress. Such tools have become increasingly available via webinars and online trainings intended to assist with coping during the COVID-19 crisis (e.g., see Impact Boston). As we dealt with the realities of lockdown, advocates wondered if strategies of avoidance, de-escalation, and conflict management might also hold potential for survivors of abuse trying to maintain equilibrium under the increased stress and changes associated with the pandemic.

When discussing accountability, we rightly draw bright lines between the abuser's choices and behaviors and those of their target. Understandably, no advocate wants to imply that a survivor has caused or should manage an abuser's behavior, much less put them at risk from the abuser (or from law enforcement), by employing confrontational strategies. Yet managing daily, low-level, and chronic risk is more the hallmark of abusive relationships than acute crises. Could de-escalation and stress management strategies assist survivors in close proximity to their abusers? These nuanced tools include creating zones of safety such as:

- Scheduling time in different parts of the home
- Walks, exercise, or running errands separately from one's partner
- Keeping a schedule for children's meals, wake-up, learning, and bedtime
- Creating as much calm at home as possible, using television, games, puzzles, or music that family members can do on their own or together

Also important is identifying points of access that already exist in the survivor's circle or the possibility of developing new ones. These might include:

- Arranging for a trusted neighbor, friend, or family member to call and check in regularly
- Connecting to someone the abuser trusts, like a relative, friend, or faith leader who also cares about safety, having them stay in close touch with the abuser
- Creating a safe "pod" of neighbors/family/friends who are managing the pandemic in mutually agreed-upon ways, in order to share childcare, homeschooling, errands, and so on

These de-escalation and stress management strategies can offer a measure of control, and many survivors already employ such tools, though we often do not acknowledge them as safety plans. The advent of COVID-19 has provided advocates with a moment to pause and look more deeply, and with humility, at the ways in which survivors understand and employ safety strategies.

Survivor-Focused Safety Planning

Jill Davies (2017) defines "survivor-centered advocacy" as that which privileges the needs and priorities determined by survivors. Advocates have worked to become expert at helping survivors plan for safety but have conflated that expertise with being in control of survivor safety. Under COVID-19, we are reminded that safety planning is not about advocate expertise or control; it's about options that make sense for the survivor, assisting them to assess their own resources and making unique safety determinations in the present moment. No safety plan was ever a guarantee of safety or a permanent solution to danger or abuse. By definition, safety plans are temporary, dynamic, and relevant to context. Instead of offering solutions, advocates can use their relational skills, such as open-ended questions, to help explore and expand the survivor's narrative around options for safety. Such questions include:

- How have you been navigating safety at home so far?
- What has worked, what isn't working, and what's changing?
- What's your biggest safety worry at the moment?
- What are your thoughts about how this situation could improve?
- What might create more space and reduce tension for everyone?
- Do you have access to any social supports ("quaran-teams," pods, mutual aid)?
- Do you have access to home computers, tablets, or smartphones, as well as Internet connection for all family members?

In the following scenario, an advocate talks with D, a Latinx woman living in a midsize town, locked down at home with her partner who has been explosive and abusive in the past. D has been laid off from her job at a retail store, and her two children, ages 7 and 10, are attending school virtually a few hours per day. Both children use an old family desktop computer in the living room, while their father works as a warehouse inventory manager on an employer-issued laptop in the bedroom. D stepped out onto the front stoop to speak with the advocate (A) by phone, while her partner was working and the children were eating lunch in the kitchen and watching TV.

D: It's pretty tense around here now. The kids are going crazy, and he's getting a temper on him.

A: How are things feeling less safe as this drags on?

D: We're cooped up, I'm out of work, money is tighter, I'm feeling worried.

A: What's your biggest worry?

D: The kids. I can't keep them calm enough. They're just kids, this is hard on them, too, so they run around and start fighting. At a certain point he's going to blame me.

A: Do any ideas come to mind that might help create some more space for all of you, help reduce the tensions of being cooped up at home?

D: Well, actually, my mom and sister offered to get the kids their own tablets. I said they didn't need that; I didn't want to impose, but maybe…

A: That would be something new to help keep them occupied.

D: And my downstairs neighbor might be willing to watch them a few hours a week. I just didn't want to risk it with social distancing.

A: Yes, that's understandable. We're all trying to figure that out.

D: I know she's staying home, too, so I think it's pretty low-risk. Maybe a few hours a week would help? I could shop or bake for her in exchange.

A: It sounds worth exploring. Tablets at home, some childcare help; those small things can reduce the stress and increase safety for now. Let's try to stay in touch regularly.

Here the focus was on immediate needs and strategies, how to maintain equilibrium, and think through points of access D already has. With mainstream safety tools less operational under COVID-19 restrictions, the advocate needed to trust D's own assessment of her safety and options. They could not take control of the situation and offer solutions but could listen actively and closely and support D in identifying self-generated options. The lesson here is in the listening, the ability to empower survivors as resources. This is the kind of empowerment Davies (2017) discusses and to which we have long paid lip service but lost touch with as the field institutionalized. Though it may feel like "doing less," witnessing, listening deeply, maintaining contact, and partnering with survivors in exploring their unique circumstances on their own terms are the definition of survivor empowerment.

Technology and Connection

We often think of technology negatively, as a means for abusers to stalk or monitor their targets, but there are important ways that technology can keep survivors connected and reduce isolation. As we move away from in-person contact, being able to talk and text with survivors via phone is an important option for safe communication. Safe technology access, including stable Wi-Fi, encrypted platforms that meet privacy and confidentiality standards, low-cost or free tablets or smartphones, and clear information about tech safety, including how to log out of sites, delete history, and protect passwords, might well be the most crucial safety tools we can develop during the pandemic (Hodes 2020).

It's a heavy lift, but the reality is that the domestic violence field is behind the curve in terms of supporting survivors in gaining access to technology and related safety skills. Domestic violence shelters struggle with residents having cell phones and computer access due to confidentiality violations and fears of being located. Some shelters still restrict cell phone use or refuse to provide Internet access. Instead of avoiding technology, the field must recognize these tools as having the potential to contribute to survivor empowerment and autonomy. Partnering with organizations, such as the National Network to End Domestic Violence (see Technology Safety Toolkit), to better understand safe technology and educate survivors in its use is an area for ongoing advocacy post-COVID-19.

Self-Protection

In some cases, survivors may wish to learn skills to set assertive boundaries and even physically protect themselves from abuse. These are controversial topics. The concern that confronting an abuser might result in escalation and the fact that self-defense may not be recognized by law enforcement mean these protective measures come with risk but so does living with an abuser. Many of us have been taught that the way to stay safe when being threatened is to cooperate with the attacker. Many targets of abuse do that, only to find that compliance can cause anger and retaliation as well. One survivor I worked with shared that their abuser hit them for "daring" to make eye contact and then later hit them for "refusing" to make eye contact. There is no single abuser profile, and it will always be hard to predict the outcome of any safety strategy. That is why it's important to understand that the failure of a safety plan is never the fault of the target or the advocate but always the fault of the perpetrator.

In this time of increased isolation and reduced options, we cannot withhold information about strategies and skills that might make a difference to any survivor managing contact with an abuser. Organizations that offer training in empowerment self-defense, such as verbal boundary setting, evasive tactics, blocking blows, and striking primary bodily targets, have put extensive information and demonstrations online in virtual workshops (see Center for Anti-Violence Education, Brooklyn, New York). Gaining access to such information can be fundamentally empowering when providers communicate unequivocally that survivors have as much right to protect themselves as anybody else. After viewing such a workshop on a smartphone in their car (out of earshot of their partner), one survivor said, "I don't know if I'd ever do anything like that. I hope I don't have to, but it's inspiring to know about."

Messaging to Abusers

In the midst of a global pandemic, public messaging to those who might abuse could be key to reducing harm (Areán and Strodthoff 2020). Historically, intervention with abusers has been tied to court systems, mandated, and fee-based. With such systems less operational, nonpunitive, non-mandated, and free supports made widely available for anyone who felt at risk of overcontrolling, threatening, or hurting their partner seem obvious, yet these strategies are missing.

Organizations could partner with domestic violence advocates as well as those who have developed abuser education and intervention to craft messaging and supports for those who might abuse. Points of entry could include faith communities, many of which have gone remote, as well as health, mental health, and other community-based programs. Noninstitutional and nonsectarian organizations, such as "She Is Not Your Rehab" in New Zealand, have social media presence and approach violence prevention from a community and cultural standpoint, encouraging those at risk of causing harm to seek support and learn new ways of coping and having safer, healthy relationships, (e.g., see She is Not Your Rehab). Other relational and culturally informed models, including those that offer alternatives to traditional masculinity/control paradigms, have demonstrated success in providing the kind of support and empathic accountability many abusers need to shift their behavior and thus prevent violence (Almeida and Lockard 2005). When accessible resources for those at risk of abusing increases while the stigma of seeking support decreases, there may be a rise in survivors' ability to access supports as well, reducing isolation and increasing safety for everyone. This challenging time is also an opportunity to apply efforts to researching such responses more deeply.

Conclusion

The COVID-19 pandemic has impacted many institutional safety options for survivors of domestic violence, including obtaining court orders of protection, attending in-person support services, or entering a shelter. As a result, advocates have had to explore new avenues and messages in preventing and addressing abuse, increasing safety, and intervening with survivors. Maintaining contact is central in this time of isolation and distance. Connecting survivors to smartphones, netbooks, or tablets, which are portable and more easily concealed, will allow them greater access to workshops, support groups, and information they desperately need. Access for children in the form of child-friendly tablets would support their safety by occupying them at home and increasing their engagement with the outside world. One domestic violence program is considering using COVID-19-related funding to build a tech access project for survivors, including the purchase of devices for distribution and the creation of a user-friendly safety skills manual. For many poor and rural communities, advocacy will be needed in order to make low-cost and free Internet service connection available.

Survivor-focused advocacy, in which the knowledge, needs, and experiences of each survivor is prioritized over what advocates may be most familiar with, is vital in this unprecedented and difficult time. Communication skills, boundary setting, conflict management, avoidance and de-escalation strategies, and information about self-defense are being made more widely available through remote access, and while they may not be appropriate or possible for all survivors, they may well be worthwhile and empowering options for many. In the interest of increasing resources and options for families struggling under lockdown, we must also advocate for options to be available to perpetrators of abuse. While we may not be the ones to provide these services directly, we can partner with and vet those who do or those who are willing.

As advocates, we experience fear on behalf of those we work with, and shared trauma (Tosone 2012) is inevitable, as we all cope with the COVID-19 reality. But in spite of the loss of familiar tools, we do not need to be paralyzed or despairing around planning for safety with survivors. There are options and ideas worth exploring, some that return us to our roots of empowerment and activism and others that focus on community involvement and accountability, all of which will likely serve us well beyond this moment.

References

Almeida, R., & Lockard, J. (2005). The cultural context model. In N. J. Sokoloff (Ed.), *Domestic violence at the margins: Readings at the intersection of race, class, gender & culture* (pp. 301–320). New Brunswick: Rutgers University Press.

Areán, J. C., & Strodthoff, T. (2020). *The other side of domestic violence: helping survivors by working with their abusive partners*. https://medium.com/@FuturesWithoutViolence/the-other-side-of-domestic-violence-helping-survivors-by-working-with-their-abusive-partners-8916c9ac72cb

Davies, J. (2017, January). Victim-defined safety planning: A summary. *National Resource Center on Domestic Violence (NRCDV)*. https://vawnet.org/sites/default/files/assets/files/2018-07/Victim-Defined-Safety-Planning.1-17.pdf

Hodes, C. (2020). *To become safer amid pandemic we must explore our response to buse more deeply*. https://truthout.org/articles/to-become-safer-amid-pandemic-we-must-explore-our-responses-to-abuse-more-deeply/?eType=EmailBlastContent&eId=c7559ba3-e4d3-4901-9fe6-ff2ac5981ba6

Southall, A. (2020). *Why a drop in domestic violence reports may not be a good sign*. https://www.nytimes.com/2020/04/17/nyregion/new-york-city-domestic-violence-coronavirus.html

Tosone, C. (2012). Shared trauma. In C. Figley (Ed.), *Encyclopedia of trauma*. New York: Sage Publishers.

Chapter 8
Reflections on COVID-19, Domestic Violence, and Shared Trauma

Shari Bloomberg

When I first heard about COVID-19 and the devastation that occurred in China and Europe, it seemed implausible that we could face a similar situation and shutdown in the United States. After all, we had faced threatening illnesses in the past 50 years including AIDS, SARS, and West Nile virus, and the country, while living in a more heightened state of fear, had not shutdown. Even in the context of our natural and man-made catastrophes such as Hurricane Katrina, Superstorm Sandy, and September 11, while the regions directly impacted were crippled for a period of recovery, the rest of the country, after a period of shock and empathy, resumed usual activity. Thus, when my counseling agency announced mid-March that we would move to work-from-home on a telehealth platform, I imagined the severity of the illness would pass, and we would be back in the office within a few weeks, limiting our interruption to client services. As I write this, 4 months later, with the pandemic resurging in most of the country and no visible return to our pre-COVID life, I cannot help but consider and reflect on the way our profession has shifted to accommodate the new stressors of our clients, new ways of communicating with them, and the shared trauma experienced between clients and professionals.

As a specialist working with domestic violence victims, the "stay-at-home" orders, intended to keep the general population safe, created new avenues of danger for victims. Financial stressors due to job loss and inability to work, children attending classes from home, and constant exposure to the abuser severely limited her options to leave or seek help. The goal of this chapter is to explore the impact the

S. Bloomberg (✉)
Rachel Coalition, Livingston, NJ, USA

Silver School of Social Work, New York University, New York, NY, USA
e-mail: st732@nyu.edu

© The Author(s), under exclusive license to Springer Nature Switzerland
AG 2021
C. Tosone (ed.), *Shared Trauma, Shared Resilience During a Pandemic*,
Essential Clinical Social Work Series,
https://doi.org/10.1007/978-3-030-61442-3_8

69

pandemic has had on victims of domestic violence, the programs that serve them, and the nature of the changed relationship between providers and clients due to shared trauma.

The Nature of Domestic Violence

The Centers for Disease Control and Prevention (CDC) defines intimate partner violence (IPV) or domestic violence (DV) as physical violence, sexual violence, stalking, or psychological aggression (including coercive acts) by a former or current intimate partner. Considered a major social and public health epidemic across the globe, there is often a struggle to understand the underlying theories behind domestic violence. Even though victims of domestic violence can be of any gender and that domestic violence can also be seen in LGBTQ+ relationships, at equal proportions to the rest of society, the chapter will focus on violence against women given its wide prevalence. Accordingly, in a study by the US Bureau of Justice Statistics, from 2003 to 2012, 82 percent of domestic, dating, and sexual violence was committed against women and 18 percent against men (Truman and Morgan 2014). More recently, Ali and Naylor (2013) discuss some of the recognized theories of domestic violence as violence against women, including feminist theory and the sociological perspective, both of which exist within the patriarchal framework and elucidate the perpetuation of women as a marginalized population.

The feminist perspective views domestic violence not as a private or family matter but as a deeply embedded social problem that needs to be addressed through social change (Gondolf 1990). Violence against women, in general, is considered to be a social phenomenon determined by the patriarchal structure of most societies that forces women to remain in a submissive state through the use of physical, psychological, economic, and control tactics and permits coercive behavior such as prostitution and forced sex. These theorists maintain that until society sees women as more than subservient, compliant victims, little will change (Ali and Naylor 2013). Tools such as the "cycle of violence" and the "power and control wheel" along with ideas such as "learned helplessness" explain the continuation of abuse against women. The power and control wheel, specifically, addresses male dominance by having a category dedicated to male privilege. Learned helplessness, as explained by Lenore Walker (1977), suggests that IPV negatively affects a woman's cognitive ability to perceive a successful outcome and enforces the belief that her actions cannot make a meaningful difference. Therefore, she stays in the relationship as she believes there are no other options available (Walker 1977). Restrictions placed on society due to COVID-19 have limited options even further.

Overlaying a Global Pandemic on the Epidemic of Domestic Violence

Early reports of the pandemic spreading focused on China and then Europe. Eager to slow the spread of the virus, many countries initiated lockdowns resulting in people forced to stay at home. Within weeks, reported incidents of domestic violence grew considerably as victims sought relief from the abuse. The Hubei province of China noted a tripling of domestic violence during February 2020, from 47 victims to 162 victims. Both Cyprus and Singapore found calls to police increased by one-third each. France also noted an increase of 30%, and while Italy noted that their calls to police had dropped, they were being flooded with desperate texts and emails from victims who could not safely use the phone. The United Kingdom's largest abuse charity, Refuge, noted a 700% increase in calls in a single day (Bradbury-Jones and Isham 2020; Taub 2020; Usher et al. 2020). Several months later, an article in the *New York Times* noted that at least 26 women and girls in the United Kingdom had been killed by their abusers during the COVID-19 pandemic. Sixteen of them were killed during the first month of the lockdown, more than triple the number of domestic violence homicides from the previous year (Taub and Bradley 2020).

According to the World Health Organization, during times of crisis—such as natural disasters, wars, and epidemics—the risk of gender-based violence tends to rise (Bradbury-Jones and Isham 2020). Programs across the country enacted emergency plans as they had as many staff working from home as possible. Reported increases became part of the news cycle nationwide. In Portland, Oregon, after their mid-March stay-at-home orders were put in place, there was an increase of 22% in domestic violence incidents. In San Antonio, Texas, there was an increase of 18% in emergency calls between March of 2020 and March of 2019. In Jefferson County, Alabama, there was a reported increase of 27% more calls in March of 2020 than in March of 2019 (Boserup et al. 2020). Locally, at a recent Family Justice Center meeting, the Newark (NJ) Police Department shared that they had a 21% increase in calls from March 2020 to May 2020.

With such an increase in those seeking help for domestic violence, I believed that our programs would become flooded with help seekers. I was very wrong. Instead, the hotline, shelters, and outreach centers remained eerily silent. During weekly meetings at the New Jersey Coalition to End Domestic Violence, program heads from around the state discussed the trends that they were witnessing. Collectively and in line with the literature reported above, we discussed the challenge of clients being safely able to reach out for help. Many reported situations where perpetrators and/or victims had lost their jobs causing perpetrators to spend more time at home and victims to have less ability to leave. In some cases, victims who had left were forced to return due to financial constraints or, due to COVID-19, no longer having a place to stay. Victims were reluctant to call shelters or go to the emergency rooms for medical help, as they were unsure if they would be medically compromising themselves by doing so. The pandemic provided new items to withhold where perpetrators were hiding masks, sanitizer, and gloves, thus forcing her to stay at home. Perpetrators threatened to expose her to the virus, to force her to leave, or to force her to work in risky environments. Threats to take the kids away increased, especially with the knowledge that the courts were closed and she would have minimal recourse. Her experience, more than ever, was truly one of intimate terrorism and coercive control (Stark 2009). More than ever I felt powerless to support my clients and was restricted by the same collective trauma.

COVID-19 as a Collective Trauma

COVID-19 was a traumatic incident different from any that had been experienced in many decades. Often, traumatic work focuses on an individual or family who have experienced something out of the norm. In Judith Herman's words, "Traumatic events are extraordinary, not because they occur rarely, but rather because they overwhelm the ordinary human adaptations to life" (Herman 1992, p. 33). Psychological trauma, such as domestic violence, is a type of damage that violates the familiar ideas and expectations about the world of an individual, plunging them into a state of extreme confusion and uncertainty (Aydin 2017). However, collective trauma refers to the psychological upheaval that is shared by a group of people who all experience an event. This type of trauma can affect groups of people of any size, including entire nations or societies (Cherry 2020). As opposed to natural or unintended events such as hurricanes and wildfires, which are regional and limited in scope, or deliberate events such as 9/11, which also more heavily impacted New York City and Washington DC, the COVID-19 pandemic is a new type of mass or collective trauma. The pandemic is truly global, affecting the entire world and infiltrating every part of society. Despite the virus affecting everyone, there is clear discrimination and inequity as to who receives assistance and who is more at risk. Media coverage, both through established sources and social media, has demonstrated a level of unprecedented documentation. Other differences included a focus on isolation for traumatic incidents; we banded together as a society to help and support one another (Horesh and Brown 2020).

With COVID-19, there is a new level of anticipatory anxiety. After other traumatic events, within a week or so after the trauma, healing and rebuilding begin. With COVID-19, there is ongoing uncertainty (Horesh and Brown 2020). It has been over 4 months, at the time of this writing, since the initial stay-at-home order was issued, and there remain more questions than answers about reopening, the lasting impact on jobs and the economy, and a possible second wave of the illness. In many states, the number of people contracting the disease is growing, and there are talks of possibly returning to a lockdown. This would re-endanger victims of domestic violence who are slowly trying to emerge from their abusive strongholds.

In times of trauma, peoples' nervous systems can become overwhelmed trying to process the experience. In the current pandemic, people are often existing in extreme hypervigilance where they are facing total isolation by staying at home, fearing their death or the death of loved ones, dreading making a "wrong move," and grieving the loss of the world as they knew it (Horesh and Brown 2020). If the community at large is struggling with these issues, how much harder is it for those also dealing with home as an unsafe place? How difficult is it for the clinicians that work with them?

Redefining Boundaries

As my agency mandated the staff to work from home and moved to a telehealth platform, I began a parallel process with my clients, learning how to best use the technology. Despite the best efforts, technology has its challenges. Wi-Fi would fail, sound would not be working properly, or the next-door neighbor would be loudly mowing his lawn. Some of our clients faced challenges in not having the technology to use telehealth or not having a safe, private way to have telehealth sessions. "Offices are the physical containers of treatment, the familiar places where patients find sanctuary … free from constraints of reality" (Boulanger 2013). No longer able to use our offices as a safe and contained holding space, where clients were free from interruptions and able to focus on themselves, improvisation was necessary. Clients currently participate in therapy from bedrooms, bathrooms (with the shower running), hallways, laundry rooms (while folding laundry), on walks, in parking lots, in their cars, and at times when they knew their partners would be out grocery shopping or in another meeting. Safety, as always, remains the priority.

In addition to the physical boundaries changing, clients appear less formal. I noticed they dress more casually, no longer apply makeup, and will at times engage in a comforting activity or continue with an activity that started before the session. I was taken aback during a pivotal moment in a session when I heard a timer ring and my client rose from her seat, found her oven mitts, and took a chicken out of the oven. Boundaries have also loosened as I have seen the inside of my clients' houses (except for one client, a self-proclaimed hoarder, who will not use telehealth and will only speak to me by phone). At times, sessions have been visited by pets, interrupted by a young child, or occurred while eating lunch or having a cigarette. While these moments have been addressed, the loosened expectations have become part of the new therapeutic experience.

As with many shared traumatic experiences, not only was the client more vulnerable, but as a therapist, I was in a similar position. Trained in a setting where the therapist was to remain a blank slate and the work was done in the office, I needed to exercise my own flexibility and adapt. It felt inauthentic and intolerable to maintain the usual therapy stance (Tosone 2011). Through telehealth, clients saw the inside of my house, heard my doorbell ring, and witnessed my struggles with technology. A colleague shared how her cat had leapt on to her mid-session, startling her, and causing her to scream and jump up (the client laughed, and the cat now spends the day in the bedroom).

I have also redefined the hours I consider my "workday." As my clients try to safely navigate this new reality, I have tried to accommodate them as much as possible, while still being mindful of my own work-life balance. Many of my morning clients needed to shift to afternoon sessions as mornings were prime virtual schooling time and they needed to help their children. Together we also developed code words to maintain safety. If one client suddenly gave me the pre-arranged message of "talk to you soon," it meant she was no longer able to safely speak, as her partner had returned. Providing or reviewing safety planning also presented a challenge and a learning curve to master, as steadfast resources such as the courts had closed and protocols for shelters and other services had changed due to the pandemic.

Shared Trauma

Shared trauma is a situation where helping professionals live and/or work in the same community as the people they serve and are exposed to the same traumatic and threatening experiences as their clients (Nuttman-Shwartz 2016; Tosone 2020). This speaks to the dual nature of the traumatic experience, also referred to as a shared traumatic reality by other authors (Baum 2013; Bauwens and Tosone 2010; Dekel and Baum 2009; Dekel et al. 2016; Tosone 2012). Shared trauma is defined as the affective behavioral, cognitive, spiritual, and multimodal responses that clinicians see as a result of the same collective trauma as their clients (Tosone 2012). Colloquially, it can be considered as "we are all in this together" or, as Dekel and Nuttman-Shwartz proffered, we are "in the same boat" (Dekel and Nuttman-Shwartz 2009).

In my recent experience, I have noted that my clients have become very concerned about my well-being and the well-being of my family. They are also curious as to how I am managing emotionally through the pandemic and if I can relate to their challenges. In my initial struggles with the level of disclosure, I conceded that the "rules against self-disclosure become difficult to enforce when the asymmetrical nature of the therapeutic relationship was forcibly re-calibrated by the shared trauma" (Boulanger 2013, p. 35). As time continued, I concurred with Tosone's sentiment where "I found myself engaging on a deeper level and revealing more than usual" (Tosone 2011, p. 26). I think I was also fortunate that, until this point, my clients had all been in treatment with me for at least a year. While the boundaries have been more flexible, the established therapeutic relationship permitted room for growth and change. Still, as I carefully and selectively contemplate what information I am willing to share, I am mindful to ensure that the motivation for the disclosure is for the client's best interest and not my own personal need (Tosone 2012).

Sharing a traumatic event or reality can become an equaling experience. Tosone noted that the shared experience of September 11 made it difficult to maintain any stance or emotional distance (Tosone 2006). The changing and blurring of roles and norms that were noted in working with victims of terrorist attacks in Israel apply to the current situation as well. Both the familiar work setting and the walls where we complete this work are gone for now. There has also been a changing and blurring of roles as my clients' needs have shifted. Many are now facing financial stressors and job losses, problems that lack straightforward solutions, and are looking to me for concrete suggestions and direction (Baum 2013). The blurring of professional and personal boundaries can also become confusing, as I previously mentioned regarding accommodating clients.

One idea that has resonated with me is the differences seen between individuals who have varying levels of responsibility in my agency. As observed by Tosone (2012) in her comparison between student clinicians and supervisors, the latter had added stressors of extra job responsibilities. One of the challenges for me has been not only worrying about my clients but the clients of the people I supervise, my supervisees themselves, and the program. I wonder about the extra stress I am experiencing in the many roles I serve agency-wide and how that may affect my *professional posttraumatic growth*, a term coined by Bauwens and Tosone (2010).

Posttraumatic Growth

Posttraumatic growth is defined as a positive psychological change experienced as a result of this trouble with highly challenging circumstances (Tedeschi and Calhoun 2004). It has a quality of transformation or a qualitative change in functioning unlike the apparently similar concepts of resilience, sense of coherence optimism, and hardiness (Tedeschi and Calhoun 1996). Clinicians working with trauma survivors reported positive consequences such as increased self-confidence, independence resilience, emotional expressiveness, sensitivity, compassion, and deepened spirituality. Bauwens and Tosone (2010), in their study of Manhattan clinicians post-9/11, similarly found that participants attributed the trauma of 9/11 as the impetus for enhancing self-care, changing clinical modalities, forging new skills, and enhancing compassion and connection in the therapeutic relationship.

Relatedly, shared resilience in traumatic reality allows the therapist to have increased bonding, empathy, and compassion due to the shared experience (Nuttman-Shwartz 2014). As I proceed with my clients and colleagues through this pandemic, I can already see the changes in the therapeutic relationship I have with my clients, as well as with my professional relationships with colleagues. Although I already had positive working relationships with all of them, this shared experience has furthered our connection and therapeutic bond. There is a different ease with our interactions, a different mutual understanding, and room for continued growth.

Conclusion

It is difficult to make overall comments about my experience through the COVID-19 pandemic as I believe we are still fully in the midst of its grip. Anticipatory anxiety and uncertainty as to the immediate future remain. I can see the benefits and challenges that have occurred in my therapeutic work with my clients. Over the next few months, I hope to continue to consider the role of boundaries, shared trauma, professional posttraumatic growth, and the evolving needs of my clients. One cannot yet predict the long-term effects of this global pandemic on the future of the social work profession and the clients we serve.

References

Ali, P. A., & Naylor, P. B. (2013). Intimate partner violence: A narrative review of the feminist, social, and ecological explanations for its causation. *Aggression and Violent Behavior, 18*(6), 611–619. https://doi.org/10.1016/j.avb.2013.07.009.

Aydin, C. (2017). How to forget the unforgettable? On collective trauma, cultural identity, and mnemotechnologies. *Identity, 17*(3), 125–137. https://doi.org/10.1080/15283488.2017.1340160.

Baum, N. (2013). Professionals' double exposure in the shared traumatic reality of wartime: Contributions to professional growth and stress. *British Journal of Social Work, 44*, 2113–2134. https://doi.org/10.1093/bjsw/bct085.

Bauwens, J., & Tosone, C. (2010). Professional posttraumatic growth after a shared traumatic experience: Manhattan clinicians' perspectives on post 9/11 practice. *Journal of Loss and Trauma, 15*(6), 498–517.

Boserup, B., Mckenney, M., & Elkbuli, A. (2020). Alarming trends in US domestic violence during the COVID-19 pandemic. *American Journal of Emergency Medicine.* https://doi.org/10.1016/j.ajem.2020.04.077.

Boulanger, G. (2013). Fearful symmetry: Shared trauma in New Orleans after hurricane Katrina. *Psychoanalytic Dialogues, 23*(1), 31–44. https://doi.org/10.1080/10481885.2013.752700.

Bradbury-Jones, C., & Isham, L. (2020). The pandemic paradox: The consequences of COVID-19 on domestic violence. *Journal of Clinical Nursing, 29*(13–14), 2047–2049. https://doi.org/10.1111/jocn.15296.

Cherry, K. (2020, May 22). *Collective trauma from COVID-19.* Retrieved July 24, 2020, from https://www.verywellmind.com/collective-trauma-from-covid-19-4844357

Dekel, R., & Baum, N. (2009). Intervention in a shared traumatic reality: A new challenge for social workers. *British Journal of Social Work, 40*(6), 1927–1944. https://doi.org/10.1093/bjsw/bcp137.

Dekel, R., & Nuttman-Shwartz, O. (2009). PTSD and PTG following Qassam attacks: Correlations and contributors among development town and kibbutz residents. *Health and Social Work, 34*, 87–96.

Dekel, R., Nuttman-Schwartz, O., & Lavi, T. (2016). Shared traumatic reality and boundary theory: How mental health professionals cope with the home/work conflict during continuous security threats. *Journal of Couple and Relationship Therapy, 15*(2), 121–134. https://doi.org/10.1080/15332691.2015.1068251.

Gondolf, E. W. (1990). *Battered women as survivors: An alternative to treating learned helplessness.* Lexington: Lexington Books.

Herman, J. (1992). *Trauma and recovery.* New York: Basic Books.

Horesh, D., & Brown, A. D. (2020). Traumatic stress in the age of COVID-19: A call to close critical gaps and adapt to new realities. *Psychological Trauma: Theory, Research, Practice, and Policy, 12*(4), 331–335. https://doi.org/10.1037/tra0000592.

Nuttman-Shwartz, O. (2014). Shared resilience in a traumatic reality. *Trauma, Violence, & Abuse, 16*(4), 466–475. https://doi.org/10.1177/1524838014557287.

Nuttman-Shwartz, O. (2016). Research in a shared traumatic reality: Researchers in a disaster context. *Journal of Loss and Trauma, 21*(3), 179–191. https://doi.org/10.1080/15325024.2015.1084856.

Stark, E. (2009). *Coercive control: How men entrap women in personal life.* New York: Oxford University Press.

Taub, A. (2020, April 6). A new COVID-19 crisis: Domestic abuses rises worldwide. *The New York Times.*

Taub, A., & Bradley, J. (2020, July 2). As domestic abuse rises, U.K. failings leave victims in peril. *New York Times.*

Tedeschi, R. G., & Calhoun, L. G. (1996). The posttraumatic growth inventory: Measuring the positive legacy of trauma. *Journal of Traumatic Stress, 9*(3), 455–471. https://doi.org/10.1002/jts.2490090305.

Tedeschi, R. G., & Calhoun, L. G. (2004). TARGET ARTICLE: "Posttraumatic growth: Conceptual foundations and empirical evidence". *Psychological Inquiry, 15*(1), 1–18. https://doi.org/10.1207/s15327965pli1501_01.

Tosone, C. (2006). Therapeutic intimacy: A post-9/11 perspective. *Smith College Studies in Social Work, 76*(4), 89–98.

Tosone, C. (2011). The legacy of September 11: Shared trauma, therapeutic intimacy, and professional posttraumatic growth. *Traumatology, 17*(3), 25–29. https://doi.org/10.1177/1534765611421963.

Tosone, C. (2012). Shared trauma. In C. R. Figley (Author), *Encyclopedia of trauma: An interdisciplinary guide* (pp. 625–628). Thousand Oaks, CA: SAGE.

Tosone, C. (2020). Shared trauma and social work practice in communal disasters. In J. Duffy, J. J. Campbell, & C. Tosone (Eds.), *International perspectives on social work and political conflict* (pp. 50–64). New York: Routledge.

Truman, J. L., & Morgan, R. E. (2014, April). *Nonfatal domestic violence, 2003–2012.* Retrieved July 30, 2020, from https://www.bjs.gov/content/pub/pdf/ndv0312.pdf

Usher, K., Bhullar, N., Durkin, J., Gyamfi, N., & Jackson, D. (2020). Family violence and COVID-19: Increased vulnerability and reduced options for support. *International Journal of Mental Health Nursing, 29*(4), 549–552. https://doi.org/10.1111/inm.12735.

Walker, L. E. (1977). Battered women and learned helplessness. *Victimology, 2*(3–4), 525–534.

Chapter 9
COVID-19 and Sheltering in Place: The Experiences of Coercive Control for College Students Returning Home

Christine M. Cocchiola

Introduction

"The safest place you can be right now is at home." We have all heard this statement in recent months from public health officials and our own community leaders as we attempt to slow the spread of the novel coronavirus (COVID-19), and for most of us, this is true. Yet what if the home you have returned to—more specifically, the home of one of your parents—is not a haven, but a place where one parent uses you as a "pawn" to harm your other parent? This parental alienation, a form of psychological abuse, and an aspect of coercive control usually becomes evident at the time of parental separation and refers to persistent, unwarranted denigration of one parent by the other, in an attempt to alienate the child from the other parent (Gardner 1998).

According to the US Department of Justice, Juvenile Justice Bulletin, about 1 in 15 children are exposed to intimate partner violence each year, and 90% of these children are eyewitnesses to this violence (Hamby et al. 2011). There is much research on the impact of physical IPV, but very little agreement on the impact of coercive control on children, and the subsequent alienation that often occurs during the time following the separation of the partnership. The negative implications of IPV on child victims, specifically as it affects the young adult child prematurely returning home due to the pandemic, are vital to understanding and implementing support for this population. Their stage in development and their abrupt loss of independence due to the novel coronavirus, along with trauma they have experienced as witnesses and victims of coercive control, make this population extremely

Doctorate in Social Welfare Candidate, 2022

C. M. Cocchiola (✉)
Silver School of Social Work, New York University, New York, NY, USA
e-mail: cmc1316@nyu.edu

© The Author(s), under exclusive license to Springer Nature Switzerland AG 2021
C. Tosone (ed.), *Shared Trauma, Shared Resilience During a Pandemic*, Essential Clinical Social Work Series, https://doi.org/10.1007/978-3-030-61442-3_9

vulnerable. Home indefinitely due to COVID-19, these young adults are taking up residence between two parents, one of whom has been a victim of coercive control, and the other an offender. This chapter will explore how these young adults are affected by coercive control and how they can be better supported by research and best practices of clinicians.

IPV, Psychological Abuse, and Coercive Control

The Centers for Disease Control and Prevention (CDC) (2019) defines psychological abuse as an **aggression that uses** communication, verbal and non-verbal, with intent to harm another emotionally or mentally, and/or to exert control over another. The WHO uses the term "violence" rather than abuse and describes psychological violence as including such things as insults, belittling, constant humiliation, intimidation (e.g. destroying things), threats of harm, and threats to take away children. Controlling behavior is defined as isolating a person from family and friends; monitoring their movements; and restricting access to financial resources, employment, education, or medical care (World Health Organization 2012).

IPV, inclusive of psychological abuse, is a serious public health problem, having significant mental health ramifications, and a legal and social justice problem, shrouded in secrecy and shame. It is motivated by a need for control on the part of the perpetrator, and need to exert "power over" is part of a much larger systemic, cultural, and geo-historical problem of dominance (Price 2014). Physical abuse, the abuse recognized by our criminal justice system and known as the "violent incident model" (Stark 2012, p. 7), leaves a bruise and is horrifying, often requiring medical intervention. However, covert abuses related to the offender's need for control do not require medical intervention. Psychological in nature, these abuses are more easily hidden and insidious, as well as more difficult to define or explain. Evan Stark uses the term "liberty crime" for abuse intended to undermine a person's autonomy, freedom, and integrity (Stark 2007). A non-physical abuse, coercive control is prevalent in most IPV situations and oftentimes is a precursor to physical abuse, encompassing psychological, emotional, and financial abuse, along with "use of the children" and parental alienation. Sometimes called "intimate terrorism," coercive control involves "tactics deployed to hurt and intimidate victims (coercion) and to isolate and regulate [victims] (control)" (Stark 2012).

Stark, the founder of one of the first battered women's shelters in the United States, explains that these insidious patterns of coercively controlling another are often invisible to outsiders and due to the manipulated loss of autonomy, victims are often unaware of their victim status. Due to the ambiguity of defining psychological and emotional abuse, and the manipulation used by offenders, including portraying themselves as victims, the victim "becomes captive in an unreal world created by the abuser, entrapped in a world of confusion, contradiction and fear" (Women's Aid, n.d., para. 4). Additionally, Stark states, coercive control is an abuse that is a "strategic course of oppressive behavior," meaning it is rational, premeditated behavior and not a loss of (the offender's) control. It is "ongoing" rather than episodic, and based on multiple tactics like violence, intimidation, degradation, isolation, and control (Stark, personal communication, 2018, Aug 16). There is little that will prevent a perpetrator from continuing abusive behaviors, even if it means using and thereby harming "shared" (either legally or otherwise) children in the process.

Post-separation Abuse

Only recently we have recognized a specific form of coercive control occurring in the context of separation and divorce, known as Post-Separation Abuse (PSA). The time of exiting the relationship is the time when the victim is most at risk for injury or death (Sharp-Jeffs et al. 2017) and is when PSA occurs through coercive control. Sharps-Jeff et al. found that leaving the relationship was only the first step of the process of ending the abuse, and "over 90 percent [of victims] experienced post-separation abuse" (2017, p. 182). At this time the coercively controlling behaviors escalate, and where children are involved, the abuse is inclusive of "using the children" and parental alienation, making them also the victims of this PSA. According to Kelly et al. (2014), women make up 95% of those who experience coercive control. The National Domestic Violence Hotline (2013) reports that it takes a victim of IPV approximately seven attempts to leave the relationship (The National Domestic Violence Hotline 2013), and it can be assumed that each time is a risk to the victim's well-being. According to the Domestic Violence Shelter, Inc., of domestic violence homicides, 75% occurred when the victims attempted to leave the relationship or after the relationship had ended (n.d.). A study by Adhia, Austin, Fitzmaurice, and Hemenway found that 20% of child homicides were related to IPV (2019), and research suggests there is an association between child domestic homicide and adult domestic violence, since child domestic homicide is often preceded by adult domestic violence (Bourget et al. 2007).

Coercive Control and Subsequent Parental Alienation

The impact of witnessing coercive control perpetrated by one parent against another, and experiencing these controlling behaviors through the role of a "pawn" for the perpetrator, creates a victimization not readily explained. This use of the children as "pawns" is central to PSA; however, research on this aspect of coercive control is focused on children as minors and in relation to custody disputes, not on how young adults are used in this manner, as custody is not typically an issue. These young adults are often going off to live on their own and/or to college, partially escaping an abusive situation but coming home to the same circumstances on school breaks or weekends. With the COVID-19 pandemic, these young adults have returned home unexpectedly, and because of quarantining, do not have a choice about the extent of time spent under these conditions, with little opportunity for reprieve. These intensified circumstances have given perpetrators carte blanche to exert their control.

In coercive control scenarios, parental alienation occurs when the perpetrator or "alienating parent" (AP) intensifies his behaviors at the time that his partner, the "targeted parent" (TP), exits the relationship and the AP realizes the extent to which he has lost control. This typically occurs against the backdrop of relationship dissolution and heightened risk that adult victims and their children enter child custody proceedings (Jeffries 2016, p. 3). The AP sets their sights on the child(ren) to exert control and to terrorize the TP, "weaponizing the children" and turning the coercively controlling behavior on to the children (Jeffries 2016). The parental alienation appears to have three basic narratives: the abuser's need for control, the abuser's need to "win," and the abuser's desire to hurt or punish the TP.

Parental alienation syndrome (PAS) refers to one possible outcome of experiencing PA, and refers to a condition in which a child has been successfully indoctrinated and controlled by an AP, resulting in unwarranted fear, hatred, and rejection of the TP. The psychological foundation of parental alienation, "lack of empathy and inability to tolerate the child's separate needs and perceptions – is also the foundation of psychological maltreatment" (Baker and Ben-Ami 2011, p. 473). This psychological maltreatment, inclusive of manipulation, has often started well before the separation of the parents through "splitting" (Bernet et al. 2017). Splitting is the attempts of the AP to engage the children in the rejection of the TP through the psychological abuse tactic of gaslighting, whereby the person in a position of power undermines an individual's sense of self in an attempt to confuse and distort a person's reality (in this case, a child's) such that the individual must accept the imposed reality in place of their own (Sweet 2019). The TP may be portrayed as "evil, dangerous, or not worthy of love" (Bernet et al. 2017, p. 777).

Parental alienation comes in covert ways, such as monitoring behaviors in ways that intrude upon children's thoughts and feelings, and implementing manipulative parenting techniques, such as guilt-induction, shaming, and love withdrawal (Barber, 1996 as quoted by Soenens and Vansteenkiste 2009). This "psychological control" can also be assumed to inhibit children's development of a secure sense of self, as we know psychological control is a form of psychological maltreatment. Children inducted into parental alienation dynamics are not allowed the freedom to develop an autonomous emotional life (Ben-Ami and Baker 2012), with the AP demanding obedience and threatening retaliation, much as the child may have already witnessed against the TP.

The AP will go to great lengths to destroy the relationship between the child and the TP. In extreme cases, any mention of the other parent is forbidden within the family or any mention of the other parent must be one of extreme negativity (Kelly and Johnston 2001). Clinical observations have been corroborated by qualitative research carried out by Baker (2005), whose study involved adults who had experienced parental alienation as children. Baker identified 33 alienating strategies used by alienating parents, such as regularly speaking about the other parent in a negative manner, limiting contacts with the other parent, becoming angry or demonstrating less affection for the child if the child acts positively toward the other parent, and telling the child that the other parent does not love him or her.

The Impact of Coercive Control and Parental Alienation

As Baker and Ben-Ami found in their research (2011), "to turn a child against a parent is to turn a child against himself" (p. 472), and there is a correlation between parental alienation and low self-esteem, higher rates of depression, insecure attachment styles, and self-medication, i.e., substance abuse. Additionally, parents utilizing parental alienation tactics can be considered to be psychologically maltreating their children because the strategies result directly in children feeling "worthless, flawed, unloved, endangered, or only of value in meeting other's needs" (Binggeli et al. 2001, p. 6). The consistent negative feedback, insidious or otherwise, that children receive in such situations, leads to feelings of despair, confusion, sadness, and a profound sense of loneliness that may together manifest as depression (Lammers et al. 2005).

Until recently, conceptualizing children living in households with IPV as "witnesses" rather than as "victims" has been the norm. A study by Callaghan et al. (2015), however, determined that child victims (ages 8–18) of coercive control are direct victims, not passive "witnesses" or "collateral damage," since their experiences can be described as victimization using abusive control (p. 1551). Harman, Kruk, and Hines stress the importance of seeing coercive control in the form of parental alienation as a type of family violence which specifically impacts children in the form of psychological abuse (2018). They cite parental alienating behaviors "an unacknowledged form of family violence" (p. 1275).

Paramount to our understanding the impact of children being coercively controlled is the recognition of coercive control as a form of child maltreatment. Indirect experiences, such as seeing or hearing violent episodes, or being used as a "pawn" to hurt a parent, result in direct damage to the child. We know that there are significant long-term psychological associations in the lives of adults who experienced parental alienation as children, with vulnerabilities different from those experienced by children in non-PSA situations. Nathanson, Shore, Tyrone, and Rhatigan's research (2012) found that psychological abuse is a predictor of post-traumatic stress disorder (PTSD). Additionally, children exposed to IPV are at a greater risk of both attachment insecurity and internalizing/externalizing problems (Levendosky et al. 2012). Studies suggest that the risk of IPV (victimization or perpetration) may be carried intergenerationally (Caron et al. 2018). Exposure to IPV may lead to a child's inability to regulate emotions to higher rates of aggression with adverse impact on mental health and development, particularly as violence exposure becomes more extensive and as stressors in the family increase (Graham-Bermann et al. 2012), as one might experience in PSA. Studies of long-term effects have shown that childhood exposure to IPV is associated with increased risk for delinquency, greater mental health problems, and the potential for intergenerational violence in dating and intimate partner relationships (Cater et al. 2015). Loue (2005) describes psychological maltreatment as "the most elusive and damaging of all types of maltreatment for a child" and represents "the core issue and most destructive factor across all types of child abuse and neglect" (p. 311).

Post-separation Abuse and College Students Returning Home Due to COVID-19

Events that provoke stress, including natural disasters, pandemics, and economic downturns, can increase the number of IPV incidences, with experiences of violence after disasters appearing to be gendered, in that women experience increased rates of violence when compared to men (Bell and Folkerth 2016). A study completed by Josie Serrata (2019) concluded that families affected by Hurricane Harvey who had already experienced IPV had higher rates of both IPV, including child abuse, during and after the hurricane. She also notes additional research with a similar pattern of increased IPV after disasters, citing a study completed by Lauve-Moon and Ferreira (2017) that found that those directly impacted by the Deepwater Horizon oil spill in the Gulf of Mexico were more than twice as likely to experience physical and emotional IPV. Hurricane Katrina post-disaster saw an increase in IPV from 33.6% to 45.2% victimization rate for women, and 36.7–43.1% for men (Schumacher et al. 2010). Specifically looking at young people, a study of 2000 adolescents who experienced tornadoes in Tuscaloosa, Alabama, and Joplin, Missouri, in 2011 found that they had significantly higher rates of suicidal ideation post-disaster when they had experienced IPV in their homes pre-disaster (Zuromski et al. 2018), and research by Sallouma et al. (2011) suggests that exposure to prior trauma is related to increased distress post-disaster. This finding demonstrates how an already vulnerable population may be at greater risk of developing mental health issues post-disaster than children who have no exposure to trauma.

Serrata affirms that we are seeing increases in IPV and mental health issues with the pandemic, similar to those seen in the wake of other major disasters and crises. In addition, many of the resources usually available to victims are no longer available during the pandemic, leaving victims trapped in an escalating cycle of tension, power, and control. Pre-pandemic solutions, including the ability to flee a violent situation by staying with a family member, going to a shelter, or having access to the judicial system to file a protective order, are less available (Abramson 2020). Victims who have been able to acknowledge their abuse and seek support, or who are preparing to seek support, are in a potentially dangerous situation by living with their abusers, and this was true even without considering the current lockdown protocols. The worst-case scenario has materialized (Fetters and Khazan 2020).

When people feel powerless in one area of their lives, such as the AP does, and it is compounded by the stressors of the current pandemic, they often seek to establish more power over other areas of their lives. This is particularly dangerous in situations where coercive control is the dominant pattern, since at its core coercive control is an effort by one to dominate and establish psychological, emotional, physical, and sexual control over another (Wagers 2020). IPV-perpetrating fathers may use opportunities that present themselves to victimize children post-separation, such as physical custody arrangements or parenting time (Hardesty and Ganong 2006), which may include increased time during this pandemic.

Anecdotal evidence and early studies and reports from the United States, China, Brazil, and Australia indicate an increase in IPV and child abuse due to isolation and quarantine. France reported a 32–36% increase in domestic abuse complaints following the implementation of self-isolation and quarantine measures (Reuters News Agency 2020). China, the first country to impose mass quarantine, saw reported domestic abuse incidents rise threefold in February 2020 compared to the previous year (Allen-Ebrahimian 2020). As Europe imposed quarantine measures, the Italian government began commissioning hotels to provide shelter to the increasing number of people fleeing abusive situations (Davies and Batha 2020). In the United States, IPV rate increases due to COVID-19 have been 21–35% (Wagers 2020).

Holt and Elliffe (2020) note, "Covid-19 respects no boundaries" and suggest that perhaps being in school, with possible exposure to the virus, is less dangerous for this population than staying at home. School provides safety, and at least a temporary escape from the reality of problems at home. Due to quarantine, many children are also missing the buffering effect of extended family and the inability to spend time with people outside the household who are positive influences in the child's life. Even friends may be off limits, as well as employment; those who are working or going to school may be doing so from home, which creates further entrapment. During isolation, there are fewer opportunities for people living with family violence to call for help. Isolation also helps to keep the abuse hidden with physical or emotional signs of family violence and abuse less visible to others (Stark 2009). Finally, for some young adults already reticent about seeking out support, telehealth, like online learning, are "not the same," and without school counseling services, there have been fewer interventions and support (Holt and Elliffe 2020).

As Callaghan et al. (2015) observe, similar to adult victims, children victimized by coercive control have a sense of constraint imposed on their lives, both prior to and post-separation, and they learn early on to monitor their speech and their space, remaining ever "vigilant" and aware of the perpetrator's mood. Children describe constant fear as a regular feature of their lives. During the COVID-19 pandemic, traumatizing symptoms may occur simply with the knowledge of needing to quarantine in a coercively controlling environment. As one college student and anonymous blogger for the *Atlanta Journal-Constitution* writes:

> Home is not that way [happy and with unconditional love] for me. Home is the place where I first learned fear, pain, and heartbreak. It is the place I have suffered a great deal of lovelessness, violence, and trauma. It is where I feel manipulated, hopeless, and resigned to deep depression and suicidal thoughts. Home is dark for me. (Downey 2020)

In an IPV situation, and with children contending with PSA, typical support services are minimal or entirely absent (Gramigna 2020), and college students have their own set of unique circumstances. The uncertainties surrounding COVID-19 heighten the risk of anxiety (Gramigna 2020) and contending with IPV will add to these stressors. Suicide risk is higher for those who have experienced violence, including child abuse, bullying, or sexual violence. Feelings of isolation, depression, anxiety, and other emotional or financial stresses are known to raise the risk for suicide also (Centers for Disease Control and Prevention 2015).

Sheltering in place in a coercively controlling relationship, inclusive of PSA, may only exacerbate these risk factors. Feelings of hopelessness are aggravated by lack of contact with the outside world, lack of activity, and the increased rumination that tends to accompany long days at home (Conrad et al. 2020). van Gelder et al. (2020) describe how the "perfect storm" has been created to instigate more family violence: the combination of isolation with psychological and economic stressors, along with the potential increases in negative coping mechanisms (e.g. substance abuse).

Due to COVID-19, college students can no longer access mental health services confidentially, as they could have on campus (Zhai and Du 2020). This lack of support may exacerbate their psychological symptoms and increase some students' risk for suicide and substance abuse. These safety nets and safe zones have been removed during this lockdown period, and according to Campbell (2020), the loss of these institutions is devastating, since they provided critical emotional support and a reprieve from abusive home environments.

Due to this intense period of "sheltering in place," it can be assumed that many of these young people, forced to acknowledge the coercive control by one parent against another, and/or re-experience the coercive control that they were able to flee from by going off to college (or summer internships, employment, etc.), will experience a compounded impact on their overall mental health and well-being, this trauma, the main outcome of IPV. When traumatic events have occurred repeatedly and/or chronically, then a complex form of post-traumatic stress disorder is diagnosed, complex post-traumatic stress disorder (C-PTSD). The incidences of this occurring may increase among this population, with victims in a state of captivity, under the control of perpetrators (Lewis-Herman 1992).

COVID-19, Coercive Control, and Clinical Implications

Not "sheltering in place" with an abusive parent may mean making a choice to have no relationship with that parenting. When the child chooses to create boundaries with the unhealthy parent by sheltering instead with the TP (or elsewhere), the AP's loss of control over the child will manifest with psychologically abusive tactics such as verbal assaults, stonewalling (complete ignoring of the child) or worse, discard, the same tactics used with the TP. Research on the emotional maltreatment and/or psychological abuse of children tends to focus on minor children; there is very little research specific to young adults who have witnessed the coercive control of one parent, have become aware of their own victimization (coercive control) by the offending parent, and have come to terms with the recognition of the tactics used. Katz (2016) acknowledges that much research on children's experiences with domestic violence focuses on physical abuse rather than on experiences contending with a coercively controlling parent. In a study of 30 participants, including 15 children under the age of 15 years, Katz found that coercively controlling tactics perpetrated by fathers/father-figures against mothers cause many of the same consequences on the children as the adult victimized partner. If it takes an adult victim of IPV seven attempts to leave an abusive relationship, then one can only imagine the difficulty in doing so as the child victim of the perpetrator. For this reason, and for the many particular pressures the COVID-19 pandemic has imposed on families and college students returned home, the time is ripe for addressing how to help victims of college-aged children who are victims of coercive control within their families.

From the state level to the international level, including the World Health Organization, authorities have provided information to support victims of IPV during COVID-19. The Battered Women's Justice Project (2020) discusses how skilled abusers find ways to use crises to their advantage by confining family members at home, for example, interfering with children's visitation with the other parent using COVID-19 as an excuse. This is helpful information, but again, not specific to the young adult victim who is sheltering in place with a coercively controlling abuser. No longer eligible for child welfare services, this victim also lacks access to campus support services, nor any direct support that is focused on his/her population, and is grieving the loss of independent living that college affords. Now isolated, the burden of contending with this abusive behavior and being "used as a weapon" against the TP wreaks havoc on the mental health of this young adult.

To maintain control and punish ex-partners post-separation, perpetrators/fathers often manipulate both children and professionals. Thiara and Gill (2012) highlight fathers manipulating children by buying them expensive presents and blaming mothers for all the problems in the family. Monk (2017) and Bancroft et al. (2011) show how some professionals inadvertently assist and collude with perpetrators/fathers owing to the perpetrators'/fathers' skill at "lying, threatening, charming, playing the victim or the hero" (Monk, 2017, p. 18).

It is apparent that, like COVID-19, IPV respects no boundaries—whether of geography, religion, class, or culture. Some of the research on IPV and COVID-19 recommends that victims do not leave unless it comes to a crisis point, referencing the risk factors when a woman decides to leave. Instead, IPV supportive websites ask victims to reach out to support personnel before making the decision to leave during this time (Victim Support 2020). Such recommendations are quite startling, to say the least, and clinicians working with adult clients who have had experiences of coercive control need to be aware of the best practices being utilized to support victims, such as the advice aforementioned about leaving the situation during this quarantine time.

Clinicians also need to be cognizant of the client's children being victimized. The heightened use of the children and alienation that may occur due to PSA must be addressed and anticipated. Educating coercive control victims on how their own experiences of this abuse may be replicated in their children is imperative to ensure that this insidious abuse is not missed. As the research illustrates, children who experience these abuses are victims, and as such may not recognize their abuse. This may leave them unable to process how long-standing psychological abuse inclusive of controlling behaviors was used against them. Their C-PTSD will manifest in maladaptive coping schemas unless these children are given a safe environment in which to process their experiences. Having a mentally stable, healthy parent who is patient and consistent, providing unconditional positive regard, is of primary importance yet difficult after possible parental alienation and rejection. Educating and supporting the "healthy" parent on how best to support the child(ren) and heal herself offers the best hope for mitigating significant traumatic experiences.

Conclusion

It will be some time before we understand the impact of the pandemic on the rates and nature of IPV, but it is critical to acknowledge the experiences of the young adults who are victims of coercive control, seen all too often in PSA. As Miller-Graff explains (2020), the pandemic has brought to the forefront the many gaps in our support services for victims of IPV, specifically, the lack of resources and research to support the young adult victims of this abuse. Further research to help understand and address the very toxic circumstances of children being "used as pawns" for the sake of an abusive parent is paramount. A greater awareness of coercive control and how children of all ages are often targeted is necessary, as is making resources readily available for this marginalized population, during COVID-19, post-COVID-19, and into the future.

References

Abramson, A. (2020, April 18). *How COVID-19 may increase domestic violence and child abuse.* Retrieved from https://www.apa.org/topics/covid-19/domestic-violence-child-abuse.

Adhia, A., Austin, B. S., Fitzmaurice, G. M., & Hemenway, D. (2019, January). The role of intimate partner violence in homicides of children aged 2-14 years. *American Journal of Preventive Medicine, 56*(1), 38–46. https://doi.org/10.1016/j.amepre.2018.08.028.

Allen-Ebrahimian, B. (2020). *China's domestic violence epidemic.* Axios. Retrieved from https://www.axios.com/china-domestic-violencecoronavirus-quarantine-7b00c3ba-35bc-4d16-afdd-b76ecfb28882.html.

Baker, A. (2005, January). Parental alienation strategies: A qualitative study of adults who experienced parental alienation as a child. *American Journal of Forensic Psychology, 23*(4), 41–63.

Baker, A. J., & Ben-Ami, N. (2011, October 27). To turn a child against a parent is to turn a child against himself: The direct and indirect effects of exposure to parental alienation strategies on self-esteem and Well-being. *Divorce and Remarriage, 52*(7), 427–489. https://doi.org/10.1080/10502556.2011.609424.

Battered Women's Justice Project. (2020, May 13). *COVID-19, coercive control, and shared parenting*. Retrieved from https://www.bwjp.org/news/covid-coercive-control-shared-parenting.html

Bancroft, L., Silverman, J. G., & Ritchie, D. (2011). *The batterer as parent: Addressing the impact of domestic violence on family dynamics*. Sage publications.

Bell, S. A., & Folkerth, L. A. (2016). Women's mental health and intimate partner violence following natural disaster: A scoping review. *Prehospital and Disaster Medicine, 31*(6), 648–657. https://doi.org/10.1017/S1049023X16000911.

Ben-Ami, N., & Baker, A. J. L. (2012). The long-term correlates of childhood exposure to parental alienation on adult self-sufficiency and well-being. *The American Journal of Family Therapy, 40*(2), 169–183. https://doi.org/10.1080/01926187.2011.601206.

Bernet, W., Gregory, N., Reay, K., & Rohner, R. (2017, August). An objective measure of splitting in parental alienation: The parental acceptance-rejection questionnaire. *Journal of Forensic Sciences, 63*(3). https://doi.org/10.1111/1556-4029.13625.

Binggeli, N., Hart, S., & Brassard, M. (2001). *Psychological maltreatment of children*. Thousand Oaks: Sage Publishing.

Bourget, D., Grace, J., & Laurie, W. (2007). A review of maternal and paternal filicide. *American Academy of Psychiatry Law, 35*(1), 74–82.

Callighan, J. E., Alexander, J. H., Sixsmith, J., & Chiara, F. L. (2015, December 10). Beyond "Witnessing": Children's experiences of coercive control in domestic violence and abuse. *Interpersonal Violence, 33*(1), 1551–1581. https://doi.org/10.1177/0886260515618946.

Campbell, A. M. (2020, December 2). An increasing risk of family violence during the Covid-19 pandemic: Strengthening community collaborations to save lives. *Forensic Science International: Reports, 2*. https://doi.org/10.1016/j.fsir.2020.100089.

Caron, A., Lafontaine, M.-F., & Bureau, J.-F. (2018). Exploring the relationship between child maltreatment, intimate partner violence victimization, and self-injurious thoughts and behaviors. *Aggression, Maltreatment & Trauma, 27*(7), 759–776. https://doi.org/10.1080/10926771.2017.1410746.

Cater, A. K., Miller, L. E., Howell, K. H., & Graham-Bermann, S. A. (2015, April). Childhood exposure to intimate partner violence and adult mental health problems: Relationships with gender and age of exposure. *Family Violence, 30*, 875–886. https://doi.org/10.1007/s10896-015-9703-0.

Centers for Disease Control and Prevention. (2015). *The National intimate partner and sexual violence survey: 2015 Date brief – Updated Release*. Retrieved from https://www.cdc.gov/violenceprevention/pdf/2015data-brief508.pdf.

Centers for Disease Control and Prevention. (2019). *Preventing intimate partner violence* [fact sheet]. Retrieved from https://www.cdc.gov/violenceprevention/intimatepartnerviolence/fastfact/html.

Conrad, R., Rayala, H., Menon, M., & Vora, K. (2020, March 23). Universities' Response to Supporting Mental Health of College Students During the COVID-19 Pandemic. *The Psychiatric Times*. Retrieved from https://www.psychiatrictimes.com/view/universities-response-supporting-mental-health-college-students-during-covid-19-pandemic.

Davies, S., & Batha, E. (2020). Europe braces for domestic abuse 'perfect storm' amid coronavirus lockdown. *Thomas Reuters Foundation News*. Retrieved from https://news.trust.org/item/20200326160316-7l0uf.

Domestic Abuse Shelter, Inc. (n.d.). *Definition of Domestic Violence*. Retrieved from https://domesticabuseshelter.org/domestic-violence/

Downey, M. (2020, March 25). *The Atlanta Journal-Constitution. Getting Schooled Blog:* Campuses sent students home for their safety, but some are returning to family violence rather than family support. (Anonymous blogger). Retrieved from https://www.ajc.com/blog/get-schooled/coronavirus-closings-when-college-students-must-back-abusive-homes/1oSNzpzWPP6Qoe12BcBXAN/.

Fetters, A., & Khazan, O. (2020, May 8). The Worst Situation Imaginable for Family Violence. All over the United States, adults and children have been quarantined for weeks with people who hurt them. *The Atlantic*. Retrieved from https://www.theatlantic.com/family/archive/2020/05/challenge-helping-abuse-victims-during-quarantine/611272/.

Gardner, R. A. (1998). Recommendations for dealing with parents who induce a parental alienation syndrome in their children. *Journal of Divorce & Remarriage, 28*, 1–21.

Graham-Bermann, S. A., Castor, L., Miller, L. E., & Howell, K. H. (2012). The impact of additional traumatic events to trauma symptoms and PTSD in children exposed to intimate partner violence (IPV). *Traumatic Stress, 25*(4), 393–400. https://doi.org/10.1002/jts.21724.

Gramigna, J. (2020, April 8). *COVID-19's mental health effects by age group: Children, college students, working-age adults, and older adults*. Retrieved from https://www.healio.com/news/psychiatry/20200408/covid19s-mental-health-effects-by-age-group-children-college-students-workingage-adults-and-older-ad

Hamby, S., Finkelhor, D., Turner, H., & Ormond, R. (2011, October). Children's exposure to intimate partner violence and other family violence. [Juvenile Justice Bulletin]. *Office of Justice Programs*. Retrieved from https://www.ncjrs.gov/pdffiles1/ojjdp/232272.pdf.

Hardesty, J. L., & Ganong, L. H. (2006). How women make custody decisions and manage co-parenting with abusive former husbands. *Social and Personal Relationships, 23*(4), 543–563.

Harman, J. J., Kruk, E., & Hines, D. A. (2018). Parental alienating behaviors: An unacknowledged form of family violence. *Psychological Bulletin, 144*(12), 1275–1299. https://doi.org/10.1037/bul0000175.

Holt, S., & Elliffe, R. (2020, June 2). *Like COVID-19, child domestic abuse respects no boundaries*. Retrieved from https://www.tcd.ie/news_events/articles/like-covid-19-child-domestic-abuse-respects-no-boundaries/

Jeffries, S. (2016, March 10). Review. *In the best interests of the abuser: Coercive control, child custody proceedings, and the "expert" assessments that guide judicial determinations*. School of Criminology and Criminal Justice, Griffith Institute of Criminology, Griffith University, Australia.

Katz, E. (2016). Beyond the physical incident model: How children living with domestic violence are harmed by and resist regimes of coercive control. *Child Abuse Review*. https://doi.org/10.1002/car.2422.

Kelly, J. B., & Johnston, J. R. (2001, July). The alienated child: A reformulation of parental alienation syndrome. *Family Court Review*. https://doi.org/10.1111/j.174-1617.2001.tb00609.x.

Kelly, L., Sharp-Jeffs, N., & Klein, R. (2014). *Finding the costs of freedom: How women and their children rebuild their lives after domestic violence*. London, England: Child and Woman Abuse Studies Unit and Solace Women's Aid. Retrieved from http://solacewomensaid.org/wp-content/uploads/2014/06/SWA-Finding-Costs-of-Freedom-Report.pdf.

Lammers, M., Ritchie, J., & Robertson, N. (2005). Women's experience of emotional abuse in intimate relationships: A qualitative study. *Journal of Emotional Abuse, 5*(1), 29–64. https://doi.org/10.1300/J135v05n01_02.

Lauve-Moon, K., & Ferreira, R. J. (2017). An exploratory investigation: Post-disaster predictors of intimate partner violence. *Clinical Social Work Journal, 45*, 124–135. https://doi.org/10.1007/s10615-015-0572-z.

Levendosky, A., Lannert, B., & Yalch, M. (2012). The effects of intimate partner violence on women and child survivors: An attachment perspective. *Psychodynamic Psychiatry, 40*(3), 397–433. https://doi.org/10.1521/pdps.2012.40.3.397.

Lewis-Herman, J. (1992, July). Complex PTSD: A syndrome in survivors of prolonged and repeated trauma. *Traumatic Stress, 5*(3), 377–391. https://doi.org/10.1002/jts.2490050305.

Loue, S. J. D. (2005). Redefining the emotional and psychological abuse and maltreatment of children. *Journal of Legal Medicine, 26*(3), 311–337. https://doi.org/10.1080/01947640500218315.

Miller-Graff, L. (2020, June 2). *Intimate partner violence: COVID-19 and our collective, ongoing responsibility to families*. Dignity & Development. Retrieved from https://keough.nd.edu/intimate-partner-violence-covid-19-and-our-collective-ongoing-responsibility-to-families/.

Monk, L. M. (2017). *Improving Professionals' Responses to Mothers who Become, or are at Risk of Becoming, Separated from their Children, in Contexts of Violence and Abuse* (Doctoral dissertation, Coventry University).

Nathanson, A. M., Shorey, R. C., Tirone, V., & Rhatigan, D. L. (2012). The prevalence of mental health disorders in a community sample of female victims of intimate partner violence. *Journal of Partner Abuse, 3*(1), 59–75. https://doi.org/10.1891/1946-6560.3.1.59.

Price, L. (2014). Critical realist versus mainstream interdisciplinary. *Critical Realism, 13*(1), 52–76. https://doi.org/10.1179/1476743013Z.00000000019.

Reuters News Agency (2020, April 7). *As domestic abuse rises in lockdown, France to fund hotel rooms.* Aljazeera. Retrieved from https://www.aljazeera.com/news/2020/03/domestic-abuse-rises-lockdown-france-fund-hotel-rooms-200331074110199.html.

Sallouma, A., Carter, P., Burch, B., Garfinkel, A., & Overstreet, S. (2011). Impact of exposure to community violence, hurricane Katrina, and hurricane Gustav on post-traumatic stress and depressive symptoms among school age children. *Anxiety, Stress, & Coping, 24*(1), 27–42. https://doi.org/10.1080/10615801003703193.

Schumacher, J. A., Coffey, S. F., Norris, F. H., Tracy, M., Clements, K., & Galea, S. (2010). Intimate partner violence and hurricane Katrina: Predictors and associated mental health outcomes. *Violence and Victims, 25*(5), 588–603. https://doi.org/10.1891/0886-6708.25.5.588.

Serrata, J., & Hurtado Alvarado, G. (2019, August 23). Texas Council on Family Violence. *Understanding the impact of Hurricane Harvey on family violence survivors in Texas and those who serve them.* Retrieved from https://tcfv.org/wp-content/uploads/2019/08/Hurricane-Harvey-Report-FINAL-and-APPROVED-as-of-060619.pdf.

Sharp-Jeffs, N., Kelly, L., & Klein, R. (2017, February 2). Long journeys toward freedom: The relationship between coercive control and space for action—Measurement and emerging evidence. *Violence Against Women, 24*(2), 163–185. https://doi.org/10.1177/1077801216686199.

Soenens, B., & Vansteenkiste, M. (2009, March 23). A theoretical upgrade of the concept of parental psychological control: Proposing new insights on the basis of self-determination theory. *Developmental Review, 30*, 74–99.

Stark, E. (2007). *Coercive control: How men entrap women in personal life.* Oxford: Oxford University Press.

Stark, Evan. (2009, October). Rethinking coercive control. *Violence Against Women, 15*, 1509–1525. https://doi.org/10.1177/1077801209347452. p. 1510.

Stark, E. (2012). *Re-presenting battered women: Coercive control and the defense of liberty.* [Paper Presentation]. Violence Against Women: Complex Realities and New Issues in a Changing World. Les Presses de l'Université du Québec. Rutgers School of Public Affairs and Administration. Retrieved from https://www.stopvaw.org/uploads/evan_stark_article_final_100812.pdf.

Stark, E. (2018). *Personal interview with New York State Office for the Prevention of Domestic Violence.* Retrieved from https://opdv.ny.gov/professionals/abusers/coercivecontrol.html.

Sweet, P. L. (2019). The sociology of gaslighting. *American Sociological Review, 84*(5), 851–875. https://doi.org/10.1177/0003122419874843.

The National Domestic Violence Hotline. (2013, June 10). *50 obstacles to leaving.* Retrieved from https://www.thehotline.org/2013/06/10/50-obstacles-to-leaving-1-10/.

Thiara, R., & Gill, A. (2012). Domestic violence, child contact, post-separation violence: Experiences of South Asian and African-Caribbean women and children, executive summary. *London: NSPCC.*

van Gelder, N., Peterman, A., Potts, A., O'Donnell, M., Thompson, K., Shah, N., & Oertelt-Prigione, S. (2020, April 19). COVID-19: Reducing the risk of infection might increase the risk of intimate partner violence. *EClinicalMedicine.* https://doi.org/10.1016/j.eclinm.2020.100348.

Victim Support. (2020, April 3). *Domestic abuse or coercive control during Covid-19.* Retrieved from https://www.victimsupport.org.uk/crime-info/types-crime/domestic-abuse/living-domestic-abuse-or-coercive-control-during-coronavirus.

Wagers, S. (2020). Domestic violence growing in wake of coronavirus outbreak. *The Conversation*. Retrieved from: https://theconversation.com/domestic-violence-growing-in-wake-of-coronavirus-outbreak-135598.

Women's Aid. (n.d.) *What is coercive control?* Retrieved from https://www.womensaid.org.uk//information-support/what-is-domestic-abuse/coercive-control/. *Violence*, 28:547–560. https://doi.org/10.1007/s10896-013-9528-7.

World Health Organization. (2012). *Understanding and addressing violence against women*. Retrieved from: http://apps.who.int/iris/bitstream/handle/10665/77432/.WHO_RHR_12.36_eng.pdf?sequence=1.

Zhai, Y., & Du, X. (2020, June). Addressing collegiate mental health amid COVID-19 pandemic. *Journal of Psychiatry Research, 288*, 113003. https://doi.org/10.1016/j.psychres.2020.113003.

Zuromski, K. L., Resnick, H., Price, M., Gala, S., Kilpatrick, D. G., & Ruggiero, K. (2018). Suicidal ideation among adolescents following natural disaster: The role of prior interpersonal violence. *Psychological Trauma: Theory, Research, Practice, and Policy*, 1–5. Retrieved from https://doi.org/10.1037/tra0000365.

Chapter 10
Treating Eating Disorders During COVID-19: Clinician Resiliency Amid Uncharted Shared Trauma

Cassandra Lenza

Introduction

The emergence of the novel coronavirus has brought unparalleled fear, worries, and mental-health struggles to the forefront of the clinical landscape. The human race has been plighted with individual experiences of loss, fear, and grief. As clinicians, the experience of shared trauma is extremely relevant. Shared trauma is defined as a community trauma that is completely and wholeheartedly experienced with aspects of primary and secondary trauma by both clinician and client (Tosone et al. 2012). COVID-19 has presented a paradoxical challenge for clinicians who treat eating disorders (EDs), whereby their clients were told to shelter-in-place with food. Used for nourishment, security, and safety for most, food often becomes a method of self-punishment, control, and self-loathing for those with the diagnosed eating disorder. Food serves as a way to navigate the uncertainties and unfamiliarities of this crisis, while also moonlights as a coping mechanism, a self-soothing yet self-hatred agent, and a voyeuristic form of escapism.

While numbing one's emotions with television, wine, and online shopping has become socially acceptable, ED clients suffer deeper isolation, shame, and feelings of failure. Furthermore, risks to the population include "food insecurity, fat-phobic messaging, and restricted healthcare access" (Cooper et al. 2020, p. 1).

COVID-19 has halted the lives of many, but a particularly vulnerable client is one whose recovery hangs in the unfamiliarity between pre-pandemic and the "new normal." This chapter will serve to describe the setbacks in the clinical landscape as a result of COVID-19, and how clinicians can tap into their own experiences of

C. Lenza (✉)
Healing on Hudson, Hoboken, NJ, USA

Silver School of Social Work, New York University, New York, NY, USA

© The Author(s), under exclusive license to Springer Nature Switzerland AG 2021
C. Tosone (ed.), *Shared Trauma, Shared Resilience During a Pandemic*,
Essential Clinical Social Work Series,
https://doi.org/10.1007/978-3-030-61442-3_10

trauma, find clinical resiliency, and effectively treat eating disorders with their struggling clients.

Clinical Landscape and Developing Risk Factors

Structure in the Absence of Routine

In times of uncertainty or strife, it is common human behavior to engage in routine and structure. "Highlighted as being crucial for patients as a way of coping with change and preventing boredom...[routines and structures] often led to increased ED preoccupations" (Fernandez-Aranda et al. 2020, p. 241). During the COVID-19 pandemic, the absence of the normal routine allows individuals to relapse into ED behaviors. "Self-regulation" or "coping" takes the shape of becoming hyper-focused and rigid about routines designed around food and exercise. Coping skills can mimic escapism for some such as those suffering with bulimia nervosa (BN) or binge eating disorder (BED). Routine can also take the shape of denial of bodily needs and appetite, such as in anorexia nervosa (AN). *For the ED client, to do either is normal.* The quarantine, and the pandemic itself, has posed a great risk to the population.

Clinicians should be reminded that EDs are brain based and eating behaviors can be reinforced by continued symptom-use. Recovery is often aimed at decreasing symptoms, first and foremost, as a way to interrupt the patterns in emotion regulation and the "positive" albeit detrimental effects that eating pathology provides. During the COVID-19 pandemic, it is a tremendous challenge to extinguish symptoms that are designed specifically for mechanisms of control and security in times of unknown. How can we expect our ailing clients to commit to decreasing symptoms when they know symptom-use can aid in emotional stability and feelings of safety in a crisis?

Specifically, the health risk correlating COVID-19 and symptomatic AN clients is not yet known. There is evidence that those with AN enter a vicious cycle whereby calorie restriction spurs lapses in typical dysphoric feelings. Sufferers find that the food-restrictive behaviors provide relief from an otherwise depressed mood (Kaye 2008). AN clients are aware that they feel better if they restrict their food intake, often citing that restriction numbs their emotions. "Very low weight people with anorexia nervosa may be particularly vulnerable to COVID-19 because of emaciation and their compromised physical health, although it isn't clear that the degree that this applies to those less physically compromised" (Touyz et al. 2020, p. 19).

BN and BED sufferers are also struggling with symptomatic difficulties. Touyz et al. (2020) write that "many people with bulimia nervosa and binge eating disorder are now at home for 24 hours a day seven days per week. There is no escape from distancing oneself from food at home and there are limited opportunities to leave home to buy food. Bingeing on the family's food when restocking is problematic, may lead to further family conflict, heightened emotional arousal, depression and anxiety as well as the likelihood of increased self- harm or even suicidality" (p. 19). The risk factors of increased symptom-use for these clients during the pandemic are prevalent and warrant further research as the pandemic continues.

Lack of Available Interventions for Symptom-Use

Eating disorders are typically understood as manifestations of deeper anxieties, and fears, which bubble to the surface as control and preoccupation with food, shape, and/or one's appearance (Fairburn 2008). EDs are considered serious physical diseases whereby one's food pathology and manipulation creates cognitive impairment, emotional instability, and affects the daily life activities of sufferers. Furthermore, EDs, and anorexia nervosa specifically, are some of the most deadly psychiatric disorders (Klump et al. 2009). The juxtaposition between the trauma of the COVID-19 pandemic and those previously diagnosed with EDs is profound. Clients with concurrent EDs and a history of trauma have more severe eating pathology, more psychosocial impairment, and more psychiatric comorbidity of depression and anxiety than eating disordered patients without a history of trauma (Backholm et al. 2013). Since trauma, anxiety, depression, and eating disorders are linked with eating pathology and psychosocial impairment, it is estimated that social distancing and stay-at-home orders in the midst of a global trauma have posed greater risks.

Pre-COVID treatment interventions are challenging to implement in the age of COVID-19. Some interventions, such as employing "opposite action" – whereby clients would seek social inclusion when urged to self-isolate – have become impossible due to the stay-at-home orders. A therapist might suggest signing on to social media or the use of phone or virtual communication platforms to combat isolation. In actuality, both methods tend to be risky for the ED client, whereby bodily appearance and self-image are intertwined with both methods of communication. Studies reflect "a strong correlation between social media use and body dissatisfaction, as well as symptoms congruent with eating disorder pathology"; thus, social media often poses as a trigger for many when they engage with it (Lenza 2020, p. 47). The use of phone or virtual tele-therapy is not always comforting. Clients have found it feels less supportive than in-person treatment (Fernandez-Aranda et al. 2020). This creates a cycle of social isolation with little relief, paving way for the urge to isolate.

A preliminary study on the effects of COVID-19 in the ED unit of a Spanish hospital demonstrated that clients were distressed by phone or virtual tele-health, and felt increased bodily awareness as a result of moving to virtual tele-therapy models (Fernandez-Aranda et al. 2020). Researchers correlated their lack of clinical engagement due to body image dissatisfaction, which is an emotional experience that often triggers ED symptom-use.

There are many emerging fears regarding symptom-use during the COVID-19 pandemic and the lack of assurance in the tele-therapy modality. As a provider, it has become increasingly difficult to track the progress, or lack thereof, of clients on their recovery journey. Without this vital knowledge, ED clients have been able to use symptoms, "under the radar," overeating or undereating without the direct confrontation of tangible data.

First, it is near impossible for ED clinicians (therapists, dietitians, and ED physicians) to assess stability through the form of taking a client's weight or vitals. Without access to a scale in-session, along with the shutdown of many primary care offices, it is not feasible to capture weight or vitals as a snapshot of a client's overall health and recovery. Second, seeing clients face to face is undeniably more beneficial; the point of contact gives clinicians the general sense of how a client is faring. In-person sessions provide clinicians with some basic markers of the client's health, such as personal hygiene or cleanliness, fullness of the cheeks and the face, coloring in the face, or the general experience of the client as *looking healthy on the whole,* a phenomenon lost in the tele-therapy model where one typically sees the client's face. Clinicians have suggested finding an ally in the client's recovery, such as a caregiver or loved one, to assist in obtaining "blind weights" (e.g., taking the weight of a client without them witnessing the number on the scale) for clinicians who need more physical measurements of progress (Waller et al. 2020). This puts additional burden on the caregiver.

Ultimately, it is crucial diagnostic criteria if the clinician is fearful of someone's declining physical health. It may be important to explore with the client a higher level of care, such as a day treatment program, whereby their weight and symptom-use can be monitored more closely. Even so, recommending a client to attend an in-person day program poses its own health risks; "because of physical distancing and the mantra around the globe of 'staying at home' the running of face to face programs becomes at the least challenging" (Touyz et al. 2020, p. 19).

Such setbacks to recovery do not come without consequence. It is a common experience for clients to experience immense feelings of failure and self-hatred for losing their grips on their recoveries and for struggling with the battle against their EDs. Clinicians must remind themselves of the characterological traits inherent to those who suffer with eating pathology. Relapses or slips in recovery may ignite feelings of failure, self-loathing, and general ambivalence toward recovery in the future. Such as in the case of a BED client, "body dissatisfaction leads to pathological overeating, which then results in being overweight…people are then more likely to experience further symptoms of depression and body image distress, entering a repetitive cycle in which they use their eating pathology to self-regulate" (Lenza 2020, p. 47). When working with clients, it is disheartening to navigate the true despair that clients face when experiencing their recovery efforts as thwarted by a global pandemic. Self-loathing, self-hatred, and clinical ambivalence due to these obstacles have emerged as thematic norms.

The Physicality of the Fridge

The lack of readily available therapeutic interventions when paradoxically food has become increasingly available is a pain point for clinicians. As human beings who all thrive under behavioral intervention models, we have conditioned ourselves to remove the stimulus of food, when snacking or emotional eating is not appropriate. This has been rather difficult during the pandemic, especially in the early days of the crisis, when individuals and families began stocking their pantries and filling their fridges in response to sheltering-at-home.

Food delivery, snacking, and "putting on the quarantine 15" are social norms during the age of quarantine; social media has highlighted the reality of weight gain for many in the pandemic (Yu 2020). While the physicality of the fridge is now known to us all, those with eating disorders experience stocked cabinets, full fridges, and pandemic preparations as direct threats to their recoveries, challenging all they know as safe and comfortable. For the average individual, food-stocked homes have provided a sense of security in the pandemic. However, clinicians lack proper interventions for this new reality as food-in-bulk is often a behavior trigger for ED clients. The normal therapeutic routes, such as suggesting to "take a walk outside," "get a pre-packaged meal from the grocery store," or even "step completely away from food and try the movie theater" do not apply here. Clinicians are now tasked with getting inventive with their therapeutic interventions, which often rely heavily on removing the stimulus, the physicality of the fridge, rather than coping alongside it.

A group-think of clinicians who treat EDs was compiled for preliminary research exploring adaptation of ED treatment for tele-health modalities. Examples of available interventions include the use of virtual social eating opportunities (e.g., book dates with friends to eat on a webcam, or catch up over coffee and a snack) and the use of therapy session as an opportunity to conduct food exposure activities (Waller et al. 2020). Another helpful idea is assisting BED clients to break free from the notion that social isolation must then spiral into eating-in-secret, "given the tendency for binge-eating episodes to occur in social isolation, stress to the patient that the current social climate is an opportune time to utilize cue exposure to break the association between social isolation and binge eating" (Waller et al. 2020, p. 1132). These interventions help clients create appropriate distance from the fridge and their urges to eat; instead, they motivate the client to create new pathways of eating that are much healthier.

Clinician Resiliency Amid Uncharted Shared Trauma

Clinicians have now been tasked with altering and adapting to the new treatment environment, a promising byproduct. Clinicians are extremely resilient and will be able to integrate new knowledge while adapting treatments and interventions. It may be crucial to first connect with the experience of shared trauma, and work with one's own pandemic experience to further understand and empathize with clients in crisis.

Clinicians should first acknowledge their own experience in the pandemic; this could present itself as symptoms of shared trauma or one's own countertransference regarding maladaptive food patterns and/or behaviors. Systematic review of countertransference in eating disorder treatment reveals that therapists often demonstrate negative attitudes toward their ED clients (Forget et al. 2011). Future research should focus on whether countertransference effects have increased in the age of coronavirus. Still, if a clinician is struggling with their own relationship to food, with their bodies, or with exercise, it is certainly the time to be mindful of how one's challenges may skew the clinical work at hand. A clinician should be especially wary of prescribing a diet mentality out of one's own personal parallel, such as pandemic weight gain. It is not the clinician's job to help suss out weight gain or weight loss, to give advice, or to provide solutions to the client regarding their weight and appearance issues. Clinicians can altogether remain authentic, however, and emphasize to clients that clinicians, too, are experiencing their own discomforts in this traumatic environment.

Resiliency Through Adaptation of Known Methods

Clinicians can assert shared resiliency, a phenomenon whereby clinicians experience increased personal resiliency, confidence, and self-growth with clients by demonstrating adaptation of the interventions that they are trained to use in-person (Nuttman-Shwartz 2015). Effective treatments in tele-therapy may take trial-and-error and an individualized approach, and clinicians are encouraged to remain innovative and exploratory. For closer monitoring of client symptoms and engagement in recovery, use a Health Insurance Portability and Accountability Act (HIPAA)-compliant phone application, such as "Recovery Record," whereby clients can regulate eating by food monitoring, a key principle of Cognitive Behavioral Therapy (CBT) for EDs. An explanation of the application is as follows:

> Building on the foundation of paper-based CBT self-monitoring forms, a central meal-monitoring feature was built into the application. This feature digitized the original question set and also included a range of optional additional questions to accommodate the diverse symptoms and experiences of eating disorder patients. Because regular eating is the foundation on which other changes in eating are built. Reminders were added to the application, prompting users to eat and log their meals six times per day by default. To enable flexibility and personalization, options to change the default reminder times, sounds, and messages were included (Tregarthen et al. 2015, p. 974).

Preliminary research of the efficacy of this application demonstrated that users benefitted from the application (Tregarthen et al. 2019; Cooper et al. 2020). By participating together in the smartphone application, clients and clinicians feel as though they are maintaining accountability and focus in recovery, even when in-person therapy is not an option. "Recovery Record" can also link other treatment providers; that is, clients can have their doctors, dietitians, or coaches on the application, also tracking their progress in real-time.

"Road-mapping," a new clinical intervention developed out of Acceptance and Commitment Therapy (ACT; Hayes 2004), can help clients combat feelings of failure when they succumb to their ED urges. ACT is a known effective therapeutic intervention for eating disorders (Lenza 2020). To properly implement ACT, the conceptualization should be that "while most clients come into therapy hoping the therapist will help them decrease whatever emotion they are experiencing...ACT is about living a vital life, and sometimes that means living that life with difficult emotions." A client who desires perfect and uninterrupted control can be understood as taking a "detour that never gets back to the main highway" (Hayes and Twohig, 2008, p. 22). Road-mapping encourages the client to seek self-compassion and self-understanding that their treatment journey resembles a road that is winding and confusing, and not altogether straight and simple to navigate. Reviewing the "highway" analogy is helpful. Hayes (2004) demonstrates that when individuals live in accordance with one's true values, such as self-worth, then one is actually moving on their version of the ACT highway, not on the detour.

By way of road-mapping, clients can begin to provide themselves with self-compassion. Self-compassion is known to be helpful for clients to navigate distress and body image issues in their recoveries (Cooper et al. 2020). Clients can come to understand that their recovery mindset can remain a positive one even if there are struggles, obstacles, or detours. By simply desiring recovery and by engaging with their own motivations, exploring available treatments, and attending their teletherapy appointments, they are indeed moving in the right direction toward recovery. Clinicians may be accustomed to the motivational reflection that "progress is not linear," and this can serve as a reminder when implementing this notion of self-compassion as a direct clinical intervention.

Future Practice

As clinicians navigate next steps, and researchers continue to determine the lasting consequences of the COVID-19 crisis, exploring and comprehending the parallel processes of shared trauma and shared resiliency remain beneficial. Especially in ED treatment, clients have indeed become adaptive to tele-therapy and non-traditional support. It is now the responsibility of the clinician to do the same, challenging the notion that their own therapeutic work is less successful when not conducted face to face. Eating disorder professionals, who have dedicated their careers to treating these life-threatening diseases, must remain hopeful. By exemplifying the notion of shared resiliency, or rather, the clinician's authentic desire to forge ahead despite their own traumatic response, the client/clinician relationship will survive this untraveled "highway," that is the new pandemic reality.

References

Backholm, K., Isomaa, R., & Birgegård, A. (2013). The prevalence and impact of trauma history in eating disorder patients. *European Journal of Psychotraumatology, 4,* 10.

Cooper, M., Reilly, E. E., Siegel, J. A., Coniglio, K., Sadeh-Sharvit, S., Pisetsky, E. M., & Anderson, L. A. (2020). Eating disorders during the COVID-19 pandemic and quarantine: An overview of risks and recommendations for treatment and early intervention. *Eating Disorders.* https://doi.org/10.1080/10640266.2020.1790271.

Fairburn, C. G. (2008). Eating disorders: The transdiagnostic view and the cognitive behavioral theory. In C. G. Fairburn (Ed.), *Cognitive behavior therapy and eating disorders* (pp. 7–22). New York: Guilford.

Fernández-Aranda, F., Casas, M., Claes, L., Bryan, D. C., Favaro, A., Granero, R., Gudiol, C., Jiménez-Murcia, S., Karwautz, A., Le Grange, D., Menchón, J. M., Tchanturia, K., & Treasure, J. (2020). COVID – 19 and implications for eating disorders. *European Eating Disorders Review, 28,* 239–245.

Forget, K., Marussi, D. R., & Le Corff, Y. (2011). Le contre-transfert dans le traitement des troubles alimentaires: recension systématique des écrits. [Counter-transference in eating disorder treatment: A systematic review]. *Canadian Journal of Psychiatry, 56*(5), 303–310.

Hayes, S. C. (2004). Acceptance and commitment therapy, relational frame theory, and the third wave of behavior therapy. *Behavior Therapy, 35,* 639–665.

Hayes, S. C., & Twohig, M. P. (2008). *ACT Verbatim for depression and anxiety* (pp. 18–22). Oakland, CA: New Harbinger.

Kaye, W. (2008). Neurobiology of anorexia and bulimia nervosa. *Physiology & Behavior, 94*(1), 121–135.

Klump, K. L., Bulik, C. M., Kaye, W. H., Treasure, J., & Tyson, E. (2009). Academy for eating disorders position paper: Eating disorders are serious mental illnesses. *International Journal of Eating Disorders, 42*(2), 97–103.

Lenza, C. (2020). Eating disorders in "millennials": Risk factors and treatment strategies in the digital age. *Clinical Social Work Journal, 48*(1), 46–53.

Nuttman-Shwartz, O. (2015). Shared resilience in a traumatic reality: A new concept for trauma workers exposed personally and professionally to collective disaster. *Trauma, Violence, & Abuse, 16*(4), 466–475.

Tosone, C., Nuttman-Schwartz, O., & Stephens, T. (2012). Shared trauma: When the professional is personal. *Clinical Social Work Journal, 40*(2), 231–239.

Touyz, S., Lacey, H., & Hay, P. (2020). Eating disorders in the time of COVID-19. *Journal of Eating Disorders, 8,* 19.

Tregarthen, J. P., Lock, J., & Darcy, A. M. (2015). Development of a smartphone application for eating disorder self-monitoring. *International Journal of Eating Disorders, 48,* 972–982.

Tregarthen, J., Paik, K. J., Sadeh-Sharvit, S., Neri, E., Welch, H., & Lock, J. (2019). Comparing a tailored self-help mobile app with a standard self-monitoring app for the treatment of eating disorder symptoms: Randomized controlled trial. *JMIR Mental Health, 6*(11). Retrieved from https://mental.jmir.org/2019/11/e14972/.

Waller, G., Pugh, M., Mulkens, S., et al. (2020). Cognitive-behavioral therapy in the time of coronavirus: Clinician tips for working with eating disorders via telehealth when face-to-face meetings are not possible. *International Journal of Eating Disorders, 53,* 1132–1141.

Yu, B. (2020, July 10). The reality of eating disorders during quarantine; Bridget believes some lesser known truths about supporting our struggling loved ones. *The Daily Pennsylvanian.* Retrieved from https://www.thedp.com/.

Chapter 11
Shared Trauma and Harm Reduction in the Time of COVID-19

Anna Wilking

None of us knew how COVID-19 would affect our patients or our treatment of them. It is hard slipping into a world of uncertainty as we sit by and watch helplessly as deaths mount. It is difficult being a practitioner during this time, in which our own fears may match our patients', as we struggle together. Perhaps not since 9/11 have therapists had the opportunity to share such an experience—a shared trauma—in which we can so readily identify with our patients' doubts and anxieties on this scale. Tosone, Nuttman-Shwartz, and Stephens (2012) describe shared trauma as the "affective, behavioral, cognitive, spiritual, and multi-modal responses that clinicians experience as a result of dual exposure to the same collective trauma as their clients" (p.233). As clinicians, our complex and multilayered response to the COVID-19 pandemic inevitably affects how we treat our patients during this time.

It goes without saying that my patients are struggling during quarantine. This was especially true during the early, dark days of the pandemic when people's lives were turned upside down overnight. Suddenly, my patients lost their jobs or had to make speedy transitions to working from home, adjust to new household dynamics, and become accustomed to staying put. Some have been trying to balance home-schooling their children and work, all the while trying to cultivate a sense of normalcy and stability in their home. Many have lost structure to their days, and their sleep patterns have been disrupted.

As their therapist, I could relate, as I was in an identical process, trying to adjust to the "new normal." As I sought the best treatment modalities for my patients during this extraordinary time, I realized that I would need to turn inward in order to better understand my own reactions. Tosone (2012) points out that clinicians experiencing shared trauma "are potentially more susceptible to posttraumatic stress, the

A. Wilking (✉)
Puerto Rican Family Institute, New York, NY, USA
e-mail: avw202@nyu.edu

© The Author(s), under exclusive license to Springer Nature Switzerland AG 2021
C. Tosone (ed.), *Shared Trauma, Shared Resilience During a Pandemic*,
Essential Clinical Social Work Series,
https://doi.org/10.1007/978-3-030-61442-3_11

blurring of professional and personal boundaries, and increased self-disclosure in the therapeutic encounter" (p. 625). Indeed, the first thing I noticed was the abrupt disappearance of the typical distance I usually maintain during my therapeutic encounters. I had to utilize this sense of increased intimacy to enhance the therapeutic alliance while simultaneously maintaining appropriate boundaries and navigating the complexities of self-disclosure. I felt self-disclosure would be an inevitable part of treatment during COVID-19.

Given my own struggles with food and alcohol, I have been particularly attuned to my shared experiences with patients who have tendencies towards compulsive behaviors. Quarantine has been a cruel test of our coping skills. As I have experienced my own tests during COVID-19, I have also observed some patients slip back into addictive behaviors or experience a surge in their compulsions. One patient started smoking again, after years without a cigarette, while another has gained 15 pounds due to her uncontrollable binges. Another patient has started pulling at her hair nonstop, while another has become a daily marijuana smoker. A patient who used to drink exclusively on weekends has become a daily drinker. One of my teenage patients has developed crippling insomnia, falling asleep at 6 am every morning due to her compulsive checking of social media. Another patient is experiencing an uptick in her self-harm cutting behavior. The list goes on and on.

It is no mystery what is happening here. My patients are turning to these comforting behaviors to help them through our current crisis. Like me, they are revisiting "old friends," as they watch opportunities disappear to put into practice other healthier coping mechanisms. No more going to the gym or yoga classes, no more connecting with friends, no more breaks from their loved ones or for those that live alone, no visits with loved ones, no more nights out on the town, no more escape to the office, no movies, theater, or museums. Indeed, in the early days of quarantine, such was the feeling of alarm and panic that some people did not even leave their apartments for grocery shopping. Stripped of our typical adaptive strategies to self-regulate and process emotions, it is no surprise that I have seen resurgence in my patients' self-destructive habits.

Another interesting factor that plays a role in the re-emergence of these maladaptive mechanisms is the concept of time and the idea that the COVID-19 pandemic has a specific trajectory, which includes a beginning, middle, and potential end, when a vaccine emerges. It is significant that my patients use the temporal arc of quarantine and COVID-19 to rationalize and justify their behavior. Patients tell themselves (and me) that they have regressed back to whatever habit, "just during quarantine", and once "quarantine is over" they will stop. A lot of individuals use crises to relapse or self-indulge, and indeed, the bell curve of COVID-19 facilitates this behavior as patients see an external marker of when they will stop. They think that they can briefly revisit self-destructive behavior because they tell themselves that it will only be temporary. On more than one occasion, I have had patients tell me their "quit date" is when COVID-19 ends. However, it remains a risky proposition. As I know from personal experience, sometimes it is difficult to stick to quit dates once back deep into compulsive behavior. Furthermore, it looks increasingly like the coronavirus pandemic will not have a clear end, so these potential quit dates have become muddled and unreliable. They no longer work as behavioral cues.

In my treatment of patients during COVID-19, I have found that harm reduction strategies have been a useful clinical approach. Starting initially as a public health approach, harm reduction is typically utilized in the substance use field, in which providers help decrease the negative consequences experienced by drug and alcohol consumers and the communities within which they live (Marlatt & Tatarsky, 2010). It includes a set of policies and practices that advocate for the dignity and empowerment of substance users, recognizing them as individuals with agency who can make choices without fear of facing discrimination or stigma based on their substance use (Marlatt & Tatarsky, 2010). Harm reduction steps away from criminalization and moves towards treatment of substance use. It challenges views that label these individuals as "evil" or "morally compromised" (Seiger, 2014). It recognizes the complex social factors that affect individuals' consumption patterns, their history of use, and their future potential trajectory of use, taking into consideration the challenges they might face due to positions of class, race, gender, sex, educational level, housing and food access, social supports, and myriad other issues. In the spirit of "meeting individuals where they are," the idea is to broaden the framework of assisting substance users beyond the strict confines of abstinence. Although abstinence can be part of harm reduction, it is recognized that abstinence might not be the goal for every substance user (Seiger, 2014). As a public health model, harm reduction was perceived as a radical intervention that might not stop individuals from using altogether but could save lives in the long run, by making consumption safer. Hence, in the 1990s during the AIDS crisis, the distribution of clean needles became a successful harm reduction strategy that gained national force to help stop spreading the epidemic (Heller et al. 2009).

Why is this approach particularly suited to COVID-19? As explored above, I had to first recognize that during the current COVID-19 crisis, my patients do not have access to many of their typical adaptive coping strategies, like socializing or going to the gym, and, as such, will turn to self-soothing by any means necessary. Maladaptive coping mechanisms are still coping mechanisms, even if they can be self-destructive in nature. It is not my job to strip my patients of the only ways they know to cope through crisis. It *is* my job to guide my patients in developing skills that will promote their well-being and mental health. However, I recognize the need to approach the emergence of maladaptive behavior with the therapeutic tool of acceptance. Indeed, at the core of any harm reduction strategy is the notion of acceptance and a withholding of judgment in order to prevent patients from falling into cycles of shame.

Shame is often the engine fueling addiction. Flanagan (2013) points out that "shame is partly constitutive of addiction…[the addict] is appalled by the twin normative failures from which he suffers, and shame is the appropriate, respectful, humane, first-person response to these failure" (p. 8). Substance users fail to adhere to not only their own moral code but also the social norms set by wider society. None of my patients who have reverted back to self-destructive compulsions are proud of their slips backwards. Often they are frightened by their behavior and feel out of control. I can relate to such fears. They do not reveal their behaviors to me immediately, and some have only recently mentioned them as desperate confessions because they do not want to slide backwards further. In all of my cases, the overwhelming feeling that comes forth again and again is shame. They view their compulsions as the darkest part of themselves, often buried beneath layers of secrets and deception. They are ashamed because they know they are hurting themselves, despite "knowing better." They are just as baffled as their loved ones are as to why they continue their self-destructive behavior. As they continue to act against their values and moral code, they feel greater and greater shame. But that is the nature of compulsion and addiction more widely—the continuation of use despite mounting negative consequences. According to Flanagan, the cycle of addiction can only be broken by "overcoming shame" (2013, p. 8).

I argue that one way to overcome shame is through acceptance. Countless treatment strategies have incorporated ideas of acceptance into their toolbox, including various behavioral therapies, mindfulness, and perhaps the most widely known—as the cornerstone of 12-step programs like Alcoholics Anonymous. Acceptance in 12-step programs is best illustrated by the Serenity Prayer in which participants "accept the things they cannot change." The power of acceptance rests in its reframe, in which we surrender to our reality instead of resisting or fighting it. Such surrender often pushes us to seek help outside of ourselves, as we can finally admit that we cannot stop our insane behavior alone. Acceptance removes judgment and allows for clarity and, ultimately, a path forward.

As therapists, it is our job to accept our patients as they are. They might come to us broken and emotionally fragile. We recognize their innate value as humans and empower them to help reframe cognitive distortions and make self-serving decisions to improve their lives. When patients finally work up the courage to share their concern about the re-emergence of a self-destructive habit, it is imperative that I refrain from alarm or "scolding" and provide the gentle reminder that it's ok, that they are doing the best under the current crisis, and that it is only natural that they are revisiting practices that they once found so comforting. Indeed, I would be highly surprised by any therapist who would take a punitive approach towards their patients after they have shared such vulnerability. Furthermore, my patients have only been able to share their compulsions with me because we have already established a therapeutic alliance based on trust and security. Just the fact that they can divulge their darkest secrets is a testament to the strength of our relationship.

The power of acceptance lies in the validation of my patients' worth. It is a powerful antidote to the self-loathing that accompanies compulsion. Once a patient can move into acceptance of the behavior—guided by *my* acceptance first—the overwhelming feelings of shame can be minimized in order to allow other coping mechanisms to emerge. It is a relief that often a simple reassurance to my patients that they are ok—that a slip during the COVID-19 crisis does not mean a lifetime of imprisonment—acts to open up the necessary dialogue to examine the behavior more closely and to do the work to prevent it from continuing. Patients want to know that they are ok at their core and that they have value and are loveable regardless of their slips.

Once acceptance has been established, I next work with my patients to apply the practical principles of harm reduction on a case-by-case scenario. I do not push for complete abstinence of their behavior overnight, but rather set gradual goals to ease the transition from maladaptive thoughts and practices into healthier ones. This works to empower my patients in order for them to see improvement in their behavior to open the door to further recovery. For instance, in the case of my patient who has started smoking again, we have established a plan that simply reduces her number of daily cigarettes. My patient who struggles with binge eating is stocking her fridge with healthy options. She is also reducing the number of hours of Netflix she watches at night, as that is a major trigger. My patient who pulls out her hair is trying to reduce the practice to a certain restricted time, instead of feeling the urge to pull all day. The daily marijuana smoker is reducing the days he smokes and the daily amount. My patient whose drinking has escalated is not drinking hard liquor and must interrupt his rapid consumption by involving himself in another activity between drinks. My teenage patient who is addicted to social media has her parents take away her phone a half hour earlier each night to reduce her access. My patient who engages in self-harm uses other things to replicate the results and sensation of cutting—she snaps a rubber band on her wrist often to the point of dire pain, but yet she has put down her sharp objects. These tactics have prevented patients from feeling the sudden panic of removing their deeply comforting coping skills. It creates a gentle transition in which they see the slow reduction of the behavior, which in turn empowers them to continue on an upward trajectory.

I experience the shared trauma of COVID-19 with my patients. However, I was not expecting to share the trauma of dipping back into battles of compulsion. More than ever before, I identify with these patients' struggles. Although I have refrained from sharing specifics, I have found that self-discourse about experiencing "slips" into compulsive behaviors has been deeply soothing to my patients. I do not have to share the details of my story; anyone "in the know" can immediately identify that I am "one of them" simply by the language I use to describe the emotional turmoil of addiction. They are relieved that I understand and rejoice in knowing that their therapist is a flawed human as well. Self-disclosure becomes another tool in breaking down the wall of shame, as they can now connect to someone who knows addiction/compulsion intimately.

The silver lining of COVID-19 is that I have learned to connect to many of my patients in a new way. I had anticipated that we would share similar anxieties about the trajectory of the virus or adapting to new routines, but it had not occurred to me that I would face parallel battles against compulsive behaviors. This type of shared trauma creates a unique intimacy that has strengthened and deepened my client relationships. I know that in my own transition back to self-regulation, I must apply my own advice. Little do my patients know that when they are able to accept their behaviors, I am better able to accept my own.

References

Flanagan, O. (2013). The shame of addiction. *Frontiers in Psychiatry, 4*(120), 1–11.

Heller, D., Paone, D., Siegler, A., & Karparti, A. (2009). The syringe gap: An assessment of sterile syringe need and acquisition among syringe exchange program participants in New York City. *Harm Reduction Journal, 6*(1), 1–8.

Marlatt, G. A., & Tatarsky, A. (2010). State of the art in harm reduction psychotherapy: An emerging treatment for substance misuse. *Addictive Behaviors, 27*, 867–886.

Seiger, B. (2014). The clinical practice of harm reduction psychotherapy. In S. L. A. Straussner (Ed.), *Clinical work with substance-abusing clients* (pp. 165–178). New York: The Guilford Press.

Tosone, C. (2012). Shared trauma. In C. R. Figley (Ed.), *Encyclopedia of trauma: An interdisciplinary guide* (pp. 625–628). Thousand Oaks: Sage.

Tosone, C., Nuttman-Shwartz, O., & Stephens, T. (2012). Shared trauma: When the professional is personal. *Clinical Social Work Journal, 40*, 231–239.

Chapter 12
Job Loss and Shared Trauma During the COVID-19 Pandemic: Helping Clients and the Impact on the Clinician

Howard Leifman

Introduction

As a social work clinician and trained psychotherapist, I work with adults on issues surrounding anxiety, trauma, and the daily grind of living in New York City. As a coach serving outplacement firms and private clients, I work with individuals who have lost their jobs and assist them with decision-making and tools for their job search. At times, it is tricky to have both professional hats, especially when a client arrives looking for job placement assistance, and our conversation reveals the existence of personal issues that, if addressed, could assist the client in both their professional and personal life. If the client is not interested in exploring those deeper issues, it can be frustrating for me to witness.

The loss of one's job under "normal circumstances" is often fraught with fear, anxiety, and trauma. Add the current pandemic and it is a recipe for an exacerbation of those symptoms, as well as shared trauma for the clinician (Tosone 2012). As human beings we associate our identity, our worth, and our status with our jobs. The loss of a professional role can leave an individual feeling lost, powerless, and worthless, and during the pandemic, these feelings are coinciding with other experiences of confusion and helplessness related to the virus and its repercussions.

The pandemic also aggravates the impact of job loss in the sense that, amid the widespread unemployment and recession related to COVID-19, it is taking longer on average for people to find jobs. With drawn-out periods of unemployment, I see more depression and more anxiety in my clients, along with more revelation of childhood trauma related to feelings of inadequacy. Individuals who may have been able to bury feelings of worthlessness because they were "always successful on their job" find themselves confronting such feelings once they face continued

H. Leifman (✉)
Silver School of Social Work, New York University, New York, NY, USA

© The Author(s), under exclusive license to Springer Nature Switzerland AG 2021
C. Tosone (ed.), *Shared Trauma, Shared Resilience During a Pandemic*, Essential Clinical Social Work Series, https://doi.org/10.1007/978-3-030-61442-3_12

unemployment; they begin to tell themselves, "I'll never get a job; I'm a failure; how can I even support my family?" These feelings are deeply rooted and often cannot be easily dealt with in a coaching scenario. The client, however, is not always open to psychotherapy and may even resist "going there" at all. This makes it extremely difficult to address, much less resolve, the trauma.

This chapter outlines the difficulties I have encountered in working with clients during the COVID-19 pandemic, a time of high unemployment and generalized anxiety. It explains my approach to assisting clients in reclaiming a sense of power and capability, from the first step—recognizing their stress symptoms—to the final step of securing a new job. It encompasses ways to build their mental strength and confidence even when their preferences and their state of distress limit the possibilities for direct therapeutic work.

Unemployment, Trauma, and COVID-19

As a trained psychotherapist and a coach for job-seeking professionals, I have clients coming to me for very different reasons. Some clients who come to me for job placement services are happy to explore the deeper psychological issues that figure in their professional lives. However, not all clients are willing to delve into the roots of their situation. When the client's focus is strongly centered on getting a job, and not being analyzed, it is hard as a clinician to witness and understand how avoidance of underlying issues may be increasing the client's trauma and mental anguish.

This resistance to analysis on the part of many clients speaks to the difference between psychotherapy and coaching. In psychotherapy, the clinician looks to both the individual's past and current state to uncover the issues that are causing stress in their life. In coaching, the client identifies the problem they want solved, and as the coach you look to the current state the client is in to see what must be changed. As a trained psychotherapist who has specialized in job coaching with the option of a therapeutic component for over 20 years, I have had the opportunity to see up close and personal the angst losing one's job can cause. I can usually tell within the first 20 min of meeting the client whether they will be willing to work on personal issues or whether they are solely interested in getting another job. Under normal circumstances I would simply assist the latter type of client in getting a new job, a task that would usually take 3–4 months. Now, however, I am seeing it takes 6–9 months, and for many people, this is too long to hold it together under the pressures unemployment creates. A form of decompensation begins to take hold, which presents a professional dilemma for me because I am ethically bound to try to help them maintain their mental health. This can create a very uncomfortable and difficult situation for both of us. With jobs hard to come by, there is only so much I can do to help them succeed in their search. Often all I can do is to offer comfort and support. I find myself turning into a "cheerleader," not a role I am comfortable with nor enjoy, as I try to keep their spirits up and keep them motivated. If they are clients who do not want the comfort and support, they are likely to take their frustration out on me.

In a sense, during the COVID crisis, my job-seeking clients and I are united in our frustration at an intractable situation. This, coupled with the fact that we are individually and collectively facing the perils of the COVID-19 pandemic for ourselves and our loved ones, makes the situation fraught with anxiety, helplessness, and loss of control. One of the most common complaints I hear from clients seeking new opportunities is "I hate this, I feel so out of control, so at the mercy of others. I cannot 'make' anything happen but must rely on others to get things done. At my job I got stuff done, now I have to wait for others to do it." And, sadly, there is truth to this statement. If one is successful in their job, they are often seen by others as being accomplished, "getting things done." On the other hand, when one is asked to leave a job, even a job one did not necessarily like, through no fault of one's own, one can feel violated and out of control. This was not their decision; they had no input. The loss can be equated to the loss of any type of relationship: one never likes to be dumped. Along with a painful sense of rejection, there is a feeling of helplessness that can recall the powerlessness of childhood.

With the unemployment rate in the United States as of June 2020 standing at 11.1%, an increase of more than 200% from 3.5% unemployment when the pandemic began, there are now 17.8 million Americans out of work (Bureau of Labor Statistics 2020). This huge increase causes a multitude of problems, including increased domestic violence (Schneider et al. 2016), increased crime (Raphael and Winter-Ebmer, 2001), and the personal psychological problems experienced by the out-of-work individual and their loved ones (Finnegan 2015). With unemployment numbers at June 2020 levels, stress is also magnified for the clinician/coach. My colleagues and I have more and more clients facing extended unemployment, and we feel like we can do less and less for them. Having worked in many industries, in many locations, with many organizations, my subjective sense is that the current moment is more overwhelming and desperate than anything I have encountered before. It is harder to find that "silver lining," that nugget of hope or wisdom, that will make it better.

As the clients become more fraught with angst, it spills over to the clinician. Though I consider myself a positive person, it is draining and exhausting to hear consistent negativity from so many clients, no matter how understandable that negativity may be. A lack of positive feedback chips away at the clinician's optimism. This demoralization combines with the stresses that everyone is feeling during the pandemic, particularly that of isolation. As a gregarious person, I find it difficult to spend my life on Zoom. I do not find the same human energy in a virtual setting, and it is much harder or near impossible, when seeing only a client's face, to pick up on the many nonverbal cues that supplement a person's verbal communication for a full picture of their state of mind.

Under such circumstances, both client and clinician may lose confidence in their own efficacy. My experience is that the most effective approach is to address the client's immediate dilemma—i.e., their unemployment and resulting frustration—with a keen awareness of their disorientation, helplessness, and hopelessness. Clients have a daunting task before them; by breaking it down into manageable steps, each building on the last, we are able to address both emotional and practical needs.

What Can Be Done?

My first goal when a client struggles with helplessness is to assist them in understanding what they are experiencing. This is a prerequisite to helping them regain some of their control. When an individual goes into shock (and sudden unemployment is certainly a form of shock), they may not know what is happening to them and lack the distance or perspective to put their experience in context. As a first step, I try to help them understand what they are experiencing and how it may affect them by explaining the symptoms and challenges that stress can cause, such as forgetfulness, aches, pains, sleeplessness, weight fluctuation, digestive problems, anxiety, poor judgment, chest pains, nausea, dizziness, and loss of sexual drive (https://www.apa.org/topics/stress-body), which are all potential.

Allowing the individual to understand what they are experiencing and that this is "normal" for the circumstances can be very helpful, because it can provide reassurance and a chance to learn ways of reducing stress and taking back control. In many cases, clients will notice stress symptoms without understanding that those symptoms are stress-related. For example, they may comment, "I keep forgetting things; maybe I'm losing my mind." I like to explain how humans are hard-wired for survival, and that times of stress can be likened to being under attack. As our bodies go on the defense, less primal functions, like memory and reason, are the first functions to be sacrificed, and we begin to act impulsively. Clients under extreme stress, therefore, are often not thinking clearly or rationally. Understanding that their symptoms are predictable in their situation and attributable to stress tends to come as a relief for clients.

Figure 12.1, which I developed for my own stress management workshops, outlines symptoms of stress, showing its impact on the body and mind.

Strategies for Improvement

Once the individual understands what they are experiencing and has begun managing their stress, they can move on to the next step, taking some control. This is a crucial step, as their loss of control is at the very heart of the issue. I find the best way to foster a sense of control is to assist clients in creating schedules, routines, and processes: simple measures that focus their attention on what they can control in their life, even if they cannot make a new job happen at will. By making a daily agenda listing all the activities they want to accomplish for the day, by what time, they help themselves accomplish concrete, measurable goals and set up a system to

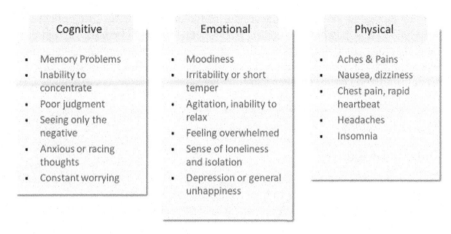

Cognitive	Emotional	Physical
• Memory Problems • Inability to concentrate • Poor judgment • Seeing only the negative • Anxious or racing thoughts • Constant worrying	• Moodiness • Irritability or short temper • Agitation, inability to relax • Feeling overwhelmed • Sense of loneliness and isolation • Depression or general unhappiness	• Aches & Pains • Nausea, dizziness • Chest pain, rapid heartbeat • Headaches • Insomnia

Fig. 12.1 Signs and symptoms of stress

acknowledge those achievements. Agendas/schedules should project plans for at least 2 weeks into the future; this time span gives the client a sense of anticipation and advance goals, but does not look so far into the future that goals seem out of reach. Planning 2 weeks ahead also gives them an opportunity to create a structure encompassing the steps they need to take, and to work within a process.

Another practice I encourage among clients is that of looking back on past accomplishments and considering how they can share these with hiring organizations. The process of reviewing their successes builds self-esteem and resilience, and deciding how to present these successes lets them take control through the process of shaping this part of their professional narrative.

Building on Successes

Once a client understands where they are and has regimented what they are doing, they then can move on to the third step, which is to build on their successes. I encourage clients to push themselves to achieve more each day. At this point in their strategy, they should be less stressed and therefore able to step back from their situation enough to systematically take stock of their past accomplishments, successes, enjoyments, and wishes. I ask them to look for similarities between past circumstances and those of the present moment in order to share with prospective employers any key examples of past successes that may be relevant now.

For example, I may ask a client to describe two things they did well in their most recent job. If they tell me they designed and implemented a new program, I ask them to break those successes down into the steps that were required. Once they have identified the steps, I ask the following: What are the steps you would need to take now to show that you can be successful in looking for a job? Often clients will worry aloud that they have no control over whether they will be hired. I point out to them that they could not guarantee their success in any project undertaken at a previous job, but they convinced bosses or colleagues to believe in or to accept their work. Similarly, I point out, they can convince potential employers to believe in and hire them.

Documentation

The fourth step is for clients to document their successes. Doing so gives them a way to see what they have achieved, and to identify patterns in where they have been successful, increasing their chances of being successful again. Literally creating a document or table to record past successes also makes it easier to identify them appropriately in an interview. This step often requires significant effort from the clinician/coach, because you may need to tease out for the client what they have achieved, and where they have been successful. When a client is depressed, it is very difficult for them to see success or achievement, and working with them to identify their selling points can sometimes be painstaking. It cannot be glossed over.

Sharing Success

Once the client is able to collect and document what they have achieved, they will often experience a feeling of pride and self-esteem. It is extremely important to capture this and bring it to the client's attention. They will need to hold on to these thoughts and feelings when they begin to present their qualifications to prospective organizations. This process of sharing successes is the fifth step of the process I undertake with clients. Networking is a vital skill in the job-seeking process. Since sharing successes is an important part of networking, it must be practiced.

I share with clients that they need to create a compelling story about their past successes. These successes need to be shared in the same way someone would tell their friends what they did on Saturday night; the story needs a beginning, a middle, and an end. I ask clients to tell me the story of what they have done in the past, and if they tell it in a boring way, I stop them. Together we polish the story, until it is both a good story and one that they are comfortable with. It is crucial that the client is comfortable with the story and confident telling it; if they are not, they certainly will not be able to sell it to somebody else.

Closing the Deal

The sixth and final step of my strategy with clients comes when they receive a job offer. "Closing the deal" involves assisting a client in negotiating, as they consider the pros and cons of what they are accepting and why. This phase should also include staying cognizant of the issues they have struggled with in the hope that they will avoid repeating them and will be happy in the position they accept. For example, many clients may struggle with "imposter syndrome": the belief that they don't deserve any position they may attain. It's important for me to have such clients step back to consider and discuss why they do deserve their professional attainments. Until they can accept their successes, they will constantly look for others' approval and external validation, never finding a sense of security and fulfillment at work. If we cannot get clients to address such issues, we as clinicians will be frustrated by the knowledge that their damaging cycles are bound to be repeated. We will carry with us the unsettling sense that nothing has been learned.

Conclusion

As clinicians, we are interested in helping clients, and there is no better feeling or outcome than to improve clients' habits and outcomes. Conversely, there is no greater frustration than to see your client unable to discern their way out of a suboptimal situation. However, maintaining our perspective and distance as clinicians is imperative in helping clients. When we cannot assist our clients and succumb to helpless feelings, we then share their trauma and loss. The COVID-19 pandemic has proved especially challenging as both client and clinician have their own concerns about the impact of the virus on their lives, in addition to job-related concerns. Managing our own emotions and helping our clients to manage theirs can become a parallel process, far preferable to the one in which we are suffering along with them, and thus incapable of providing meaningful assistance. Over the years I have worked for four of the major international consulting firms and I have seen a lot of trauma, but today's clients seem to face a particularly difficult situation, with fewer options and a faster, more demanding pace in most professional roles. Workers are expected to be available 24/7 because our technology allows that to happen. Working from home, though convenient for—even preferred by—many, can further erode the boundary between professional and private life. This makes for greater levels of stress during periods of employment, and this raises the potential for disorientation when unemployment strikes and the structure provided by work has disappeared.

As clinicians and/or coaches, we will need to be there to support our clients amid changes that challenge them and us. Our ability to be open to such new challenges will be critical to our client's success, and our own.

References

Bureau of Labor Statistics. (2020, July 2). *News release: The unemployment situation—June 2020.* https://www.bls.gov/news.release/pdf/empsit.pdf

Finnegan, A. (2015). *Unemployment: How it affects family Behavioral health.* Durham: Duke Center for Child and Family Policy.

Raphael, S., & Winter-Ebmer, R. (2001). Identifying the effect of unemployment on crime. *The Journal of Law & Economics, 44*(1), 259–283. https://doi.org/10.1086/320275.

Schneider, D., Harknett, K., & McLanahan, S. (2016). Intimate partner violence in the great recession. *Demography, 53*(2), 471–505. https://doi.org/10.1007/s13524-016-0462-1.

Tosone, C. (2012). Shared trauma. In C. Figley (Ed.), *Encyclopedia of trauma: An interdisciplinary guide.* Thousand Oaks: Sage.

Chapter 13
Considerations in Working with Veterans During COVID-19: When the Battle Is at Home

Jillian Tucker

Introduction

US veterans are uniquely poised to manage a global crisis when it arrives on their doorstep. Their reservoirs of crisis response skills honed in the military have broad applications to managing a pandemic like COVID-19. However, like many people in the world, some veterans struggle with the sudden threat of an invisible and deadly virus and the accompanying major changes to activities of daily life. For some, their time in active combat overseas did not prepare them for the experience of fighting an enemy at home that endangers everyone they love. Moreover, the particulars of the pandemic can trigger veteran-specific emotional vulnerabilities. This chapter discusses my personal and professional experiences working with US combat veterans from the Iraq and Afghanistan wars and reflects on the key resiliencies these veterans possess in adaptively facing a pandemic crisis while highlighting unique pandemic stressors triggered for some in the combat veteran population.

It should be noted that this chapter is being written in the midst of the pandemic and that the veterans discussed saw active combat in the Iraq and Afghanistan wars and lived in New York City at the time of the pandemic outbreak. This biographical information is an important context throughout the discussion. The former fact places their age range between mid-20s and late 30s and means they were involved in a war that is ongoing. Living in New York City at the outbreak might separate the experiences of these veterans from other veterans in the United States in some ways. Several of the veterans still actively serve in the National Guard or the Reserves, which were called on to respond to the crisis in New York. As one of the first big cities to have a coronavirus outbreak in March 2020, New Yorkers had limited

J. Tucker (✉)
Silver School of Social Work, New York University, New York, NY, USA
e-mail: jt1875@nyu.edu

© The Author(s), under exclusive license to Springer Nature Switzerland AG 2021
C. Tosone (ed.), *Shared Trauma, Shared Resilience During a Pandemic*,
Essential Clinical Social Work Series,
https://doi.org/10.1007/978-3-030-61442-3_13

115

information about how the virus spreads, what public health safety measures needed to be enacted and what that would logistically look like, what impact the pandemic would have on food and provisions supply chains, and how long it would go on for. At one point there was a rumor that in an effort to contain the virus from spreading out of New York, all bridges and tunnels would be closed, essentially marooning the residents on four of the five boroughs that are islands. New York City quickly became the world epicenter for virus infections, calling on many everyday New Yorkers, from nurses and emergency responders to bodega owners and transportation workers, to become frontline workers and placing further strain on resources. In the succeeding months while still fighting the coronavirus, New York City would also become one of the primary cities with anti-racism and police brutality protests that triggered mass gatherings of people and the deployment of police and other security forces. In June 2020, reports of random firework detonations occurring throughout the city caused such distress to some residents that they protested at the mayor's house in the middle of the night. Finally, in the past 19 years, New York City suffered two major disasters, one man-made with the terrorist attacks of September 11, 2001 and one natural disaster with Hurricane Sandy in October 2012. Some of the veterans in this chapter joined the military in response to September 11, and many suffered personal losses in the two disasters.

Resilience and Posttraumatic Growth

In many ways the veteran community is uniquely equipped to handle a pandemic. Their extensive training is specifically aimed at assessing and responding to crises and danger both logistically and mentally (Russell and Figley 2013; Grossman 2007). Their military work required a significant ability to gather information, plan, and anticipate short- and long-term consequences. In the first days of shutdown in New York City, many of my clients were more animated than usual, connecting with friends still in the military and the Reserves, gathering critical information that was scant at the time, and laying out possible scenarios and action plans. A common refrain was, "I've seen how things like this unfold." It was also an opportunity for me as their therapist to witness certain organizational and initiative-taking characteristics that I had not previously seen in our work. This is discussed further in the "Clinician Self-Disclosure" section.

Military training and deployment often involve long periods of time away from family and loved ones. Therefore, veterans have already navigated long-term distance from loved ones similar to what stay-at-home orders required. Additionally, certain aspects of military training and missions require personnel to be isolated or on their own. As one veteran put it to me, "I've spent a lot of time alone in a field." In early conversations during the pandemic, we itemized the techniques they used to cope with isolation and boredom on missions. While there is significant focus on posttraumatic stress injuries in veterans, many veterans also benefit from posttraumatic growth, which are character traits and adaptive perspectives that are formed or strengthened as a result of navigating traumatic experience (Tedeschi and Calhoun 2004). Examples of posttraumatic growth attributed to some military service include pride, appreciation of life and liberty, deep and loyal bonds, as well as positive feelings of accomplishment and self-efficacy (Russell and Figley 2013). Many of the veterans were pleased to realize the ample skills they already had in their tool chest, and some started sharing their coping skills with loved ones managing social isolation and traumatic stress for the first time. As pictures and stories of honorable deeds of everyday Americans were published, veterans also took solace in the courage and compassion of their neighbors. One veteran commented, "When I see people selflessly helping each other, it makes me proud to be an American, and proud of my service."

The Threat at Home

Perhaps the primary and most immediate difference the veterans I work with noticed between the pandemic and combat was summed up in the statement, "This time my family's in danger." As intense as active combat and lengthy deployments were, my clients recognized that there was comfort in knowing the danger they faced was not experienced by their loved ones. While in the pandemic they had concerns for their personal wellness and safety, worry over their loved ones triggered emotional struggle and a sense of helplessness anathema to people who take pride in their identity as protectors (Russell and Figley 2013). This was made worse by the global scale of the pandemic, which put every one of their loved ones in harm's way and thwarted contingency plans of trying to move loved ones to safety. Moreover, as the pandemic spread and stay-at-home orders took effect, some veterans struggled with the idea that "nowhere is safe or the same anymore." Many veterans appreciated that despite what they witnessed in combat, "home" was still relatively as they left it and would be there when they returned. Remembering his long stretches of deployment, a veteran said, "I would always think, 'If I make it through this, then there's home at the end of the tunnel. All the great things about life are there and waiting,' and everything was amplified because you knew it was still there. Now home isn't the same. What's waiting at the end of this pandemic fight?"

The struggle of deferring their role as the protector to medical personnel and other essential workers was more acute for the veterans whose loved ones filled these roles. Some veterans were distressed by the idea that not only were loved ones in danger, but they were also not in industries trained to come together and confront a crisis the way veterans could rely on their units and commanders. One veteran started calling her aunt daily who works in a grocery store, running a check list of precautions and becoming frustrated when her aunt did not think such safety measures were necessary, contrary to what the veteran was seeing in New York. Another veteran was beside himself with worry as his nurse practitioner wife went to work in one of the hospitals hit hardest by COVID-19 while he worked from home and cared for their son. His concern was compounded by his wife being 8 months pregnant with their second child. With tears in his eyes he kept saying, "I'm the one who is supposed to go into danger, instead it's my wife and child. I'm supposed to protect them. It's not right."

While worried for family and loved ones, especially those in essential jobs, some veterans took issue with referencing these jobs as being "on the front line" and referring to New York as "a war zone." These veterans acknowledged the difficulty and fear of the unique situation but felt the nomenclature normalized their experience of war instead of its intended purpose of highlighting how serious the situation was in some areas. Hearing and reading these combat-specific phrases served as one of many triggers during this time.

Posttraumatic Stress Triggers

In addition to a universal concern about the safety of loved ones, many situations that emerged from the pandemic served as triggers for posttraumatic stress disorder symptoms for the veterans including hypervigilance, nightmares, and feelings of isolation (Grossman 2007). The triggers were exacerbated in the beginning by limited information about how the virus spread, how it would impact supply chains, and whether the city as an epicenter would be shut down with no residents able to leave. Many felt "on guard" against an "unseen threat" due to the virus being highly transmissible, invisible, and pervasive. One veteran reported a return of combat-related nightmares in which she shoots at targets that vanish before they are hit. After a rumor about bridges and tunnels potentially being shut down, another veteran woke up in the middle of the night panicking as if he were in a night raid on deployment. He urged his girlfriend to help him pack, and they left the city first thing the next morning.

During the height of the pandemic, emergency vehicle sirens were incessant. While it might be assumed that these sirens are triggers for veterans, most veterans I have worked with over the years say that helicopters are more of a trigger than sirens. At the beginning of the pandemic, helicopters were suddenly ubiquitous, whether for emergency response or monitoring stay-at-home and physical distancing orders, and many veterans commented on how disturbing the sound was. Another common trigger for the combat veterans I work with is fireworks. At every "fireworks holiday," including Memorial Day and the Fourth of July, the veterans who are triggered by them establish a plan to be somewhere they cannot hear the blasts. In late July 2020, a rash of random firework detonations occurred throughout the city, further triggering posttraumatic stress symptoms for some veterans.

Stay-at-home orders also resulted in the sidewalks of New York being depopulated. Data estimates that 400,000 New Yorkers, approximately 5% of residents, left the city in the first 2 months of stay-at-home orders (Quealy 2020). In Jane Jacobs' (1961) seminal work *The Death and Life of Great American Cities*, she outlines how cities are made lively and safe by the sidewalks being utilized at all times of the day and night with people patronizing stores, shops, parks, offices, and schools. The resulting "eyes on the street" foster a sense of communal responsibility and identity cohesion (Jacobs 1961). Almost overnight the physical environment of New York shifted as it became vacant. Veterans started making direct comparisons to night patrols during deployment, with accompanying hypervigilance and other protective instincts kicking in. One veteran expressed surprise at how quickly it felt natural to sleep with weapons again. The hypervigilance was compounded for the veterans living with significant others who they knew were not as trained in assessing for danger. In one session with a veteran, we processed a major disagreement that resulted from him wanting to take a longer route home one night after not feeling safe on a street, with his wife flaunting his concern. He said, "She doesn't understand, she acts like I'm paranoid but this situation is different. I know how to spot danger and she wants to think the city is the same."

A Loss of Adaptive Coping Skills and a Return to Maladaptive Skills

One of the most difficult consequences of the pandemic is people's loss of the social and recreational outlets that they engaged in for exercise, entertainment, and camaraderie. Many veteran support groups have an activity component, catering to a common veteran characteristic of enjoying being active and outdoors (Russell and Figley 2013). During the pandemic, many of these outlets closed, including gyms and fitness facilities that many of the veterans went to together. In-person support groups for mental health and substance abuse concerns also had to move to the virtual sphere. The increase in isolation was ideal for more introverted veterans, while it was a detriment to extroverted veterans and veterans trying to build their social networks and socialization skills. Developing plans for activity and physically spaced socialization within the significant stay-at-home restrictions became a key component of early sessions.

Many veterans appreciate the structure that the military offered and mimic this routine in their post-military occupations and activities. A switch to working from home or job loss led to some veterans struggling with changes to routines that had been regulating. With a move to telehealth for therapy sessions, some veterans became more consistent in attending sessions and more active in their verbal processing, while others struggled with not having the routine of coming to my office and meeting in person. For some veterans, their weekly session was one of their only outings from their apartment, and they utilized this to take steps toward being less isolated. With virtually attending their session without leaving home, the isolation persists.

It is estimated that more than 20% of veterans struggle with a substance use disorder ("PTSD and substance abuse in veterans," n.d.-b). Since twelve-step and most intensive outpatient substance abuse programs are group therapy and peer support-based, the elimination of large gatherings caused some veterans to struggle with getting support, especially if they did not feel connected in the virtual meeting rooms. Limited social and recreational options and an increase in physical isolation led some veterans to revert to coping with drugs and alcohol. The longer the pandemic stretches on, the harder it becomes for some veterans. One veteran with 10 years of sobriety had his first alcohol use cravings in years after building up a significant sober social life: "It feels like when I got back from deployment and would drink and just sit alone at home. I feel like I did this to myself, I know that I didn't, but I'm just at home all day like I used to be when I drank, and so it makes me want to drink."

Survivor Guilt

While not recognized as a stand-alone diagnosis by the *Diagnostic and Statistical Manual of Mental Disorders (DSM), 5th Edition* (American Psychiatric Association 2013), survivor guilt is defined by the American Psychiatric Association ("Survivor guilt.", n.d.) as, "remorse or guilt for having survived a catastrophic event when others did not or for not suffering the ills that others had to endure." The phenomenon has been studied in veterans since the World War II (Menninger 1948) and is noted among survivors of other disasters and deadly illnesses. In my practice, I learn from my veterans to look more specifically for signs of survivor guilt, as they are easily mistaken for posttraumatic stress disorder or overlooked altogether due to the nature of the phenomenon, being that the veteran does not recognize the guilt as outsized or illogical. It was not a surprise when one veteran for whom survivor guilt is a primary focus in therapy started feeling anxiety about not being able to "fight this fight," as it was up to the medical personnel and essential workers. Moreover, the veteran struggled with his identity as a healthy young man at low risk for sickness and death, while the streets filled every few minutes with the wail of ambulance sirens. During the height of the pandemic, our sessions were punctuated on both his and my end with these acute reminders of the crisis, and he would whisper with a shake of his head, "There's another one." Existential frustration also set in when some of the client's friends and family reported they were not following stay-at-home and other safety guidelines, filling the client with simultaneous survivor guilt and helplessness at not being able to convince loved ones to take recommended precautions.

Some of the potential results of military service and posttraumatic growth include deep loyalty to a group and mission, as well as pride in taking part in history-making (Russell and Figley 2013). Almost immediately in our sessions, the veterans identified having a common bond with everyone in New York as we navigated being the global epicenter of the pandemic. This extended to the therapeutic alliance, breaking the invisible hierarchy of clinician-client into two equal residents of New York, a concept explored further in the "Clinician Self-Disclosure" section. Additionally, many of the veterans either joined the military as a response to the September 11th terrorist attacks or were living in or involved in the response to

Hurricane Sandy, creating protective roots to the city. This camaraderie with the city of New York and its residents might contribute to a sense of place attachment (Manzo and Perkins 2006). On the one hand, this ability to quickly feel allegiance with strangers allows veterans to effectively harness the power of coming together as a community. On the other hand, it can possibly trigger feelings of survivor guilt if the veteran left the city during the pandemic for safety, to be with friends and family, due to sudden economic changes or other logical reasons. Veterans with a predisposition for survivor guilt are particularly at risk.

For one veteran client who left the city only to come back a few weeks later, place attachment and its contribution to a sense of survivor guilt echoed in his statement that, "I just feel like I should be there, going through what everyone else is going through. How can I say I'm a New Yorker if I'm not there during this, even though I know I can't help much?" While he was away, his survivor guilt first revealed itself through an increase in questions about "How is the city doing?" and asking for more personal anecdotes from my day-to-day life. I had the sense that the personal questions were not about me as his therapist but about me as a fellow New Yorker. At one point his survivor guilt started to taint our therapeutic relationship as he saw me as someone going through the collective trauma with the city, while he had left: "I'm sorry to keep telling you about my stress when I'm out in the countryside and you're in the heart of it." Even his use of the word "heart" instead of an objective locator is revealing about his connection to the city and its people. His survivor guilt became problematic because he returned to the city to soothe the guilt, but his return exacerbated the issue of his isolation because many of his friends had left the city or were not close by.

Moral Injury

Another deep emotional burden some veterans return from service with is moral injury. The US Department of Veterans Affairs (VA) defines moral injury as when people "perpetrate, fail to prevent, or witness events that contradict deeply held moral beliefs and expectations" ("Moral injury," n.d.-a). This can result in long-standing feelings of guilt, shame, disgust, anger, and betrayal and can lead to self-sabotaging behaviors and a diminishing of spirituality ("Moral injury," n.d.-a). Moral injuries include individual, amoral acts. However, in my experience, the combat veterans from the Iraq and Afghanistan wars often struggle with macro-level moral injuries in terms of what the American Idea represents. Perhaps this is because these wars are ongoing and therefore the question of what their service "was ultimately for" remains unanswered. The gap is filled by the nebulous notion that they upheld the American Idea around the world. Changes in politics and policy that shift the perception of America domestically and internationally can cause ethical dissonance for veterans and threaten how they emotionally and spiritually hold their service and the sacrifice of comrades who gave their life in defense of the American Idea.

During the early months of the pandemic, many of the veterans were troubled by perceived lack of moral authority in the response to the pandemic, on macro, mezzo, and micro levels. Some veterans found fault with federal, state, city, and military leadership, coordination, and initiatives. As the United States' response to the pandemic evolved and was compared to the responses of other countries, some veterans were distressed by a perceived relinquishing of moral authority. Some veterans became more bewildered when some friends, family, and fellow Americans throughout the country pushed back on restrictions mandated and suggested to protect health. As one veteran put it, "We would go into combat wearing the American flag, knowing it might be the last thing we wore. I took pride in the work we did with our allies, with the leadership the flag conveyed. I went into battle so my countrymen wouldn't have to, and in return people can't wear a mask? Who are we now? What even is the American Idea? Is this experiment of democracy just not going to work out? What was my service for after all?" At the same time, other veterans viewed individuals' choices as exercising the American freedom they fought to defend.

Clinician Self-Disclosure in the Context of Shared Trauma

One of the most significant shifts in our therapeutic alliances involved role reversals and clinical self-disclosure. Much has been written, particularly after 9/11, about shared traumas between clients and clinicians when they both experience the same natural or man-made disaster. The research suggests that shared trauma can lead to "blurring of clinician-client roles, increased clinician self-disclosure and emphasis on the shared nature of the experience" (Tosone 2011, p. 25). I experienced all three of these to varying degrees during the pandemic.

The blurring of clinician-client roles happened during the first sentence of my first telehealth call with a veteran. I did not even have time to say a salutation before the veteran declared, "Are you okay?" The parting salutation of that call was equally urgent, "Please stay safe." Variations of these phrases still bookend most sessions with clients as the pandemic continues. The clients also started asking about my family. Usually I would maintain clinical boundaries by inquiring why it is helpful to know about the well-being of my family, but in a shared trauma it seemed clear that this was a more objective question, and it felt more than usual that it would cause a therapeutic rupture to decline to answer. I came up with a response I felt allowed me to answer their questions, assuage their fears, and join in the shared experience while also maintaining self-disclosure boundaries: "I am fortunate that all of my loved ones are healthy and safe, thank you." Unfortunately, as some friends and family became ill and passed away, it was harder not only to modify this response truthfully but also to be reminded at the beginning of the session about my escalating personal struggles. As with non-veteran clients, the sessions were laced with more mutual sharing of firsthand reports of what was happening in different parts of the city, since stay-at-home orders prevented usually mobile New Yorkers from understanding what was happening even a few blocks away. Aside from merely being self-disclosing, this was an effort by both parties to gather information that might be important for personal decision-making. As the de facto expert in the room on emotional safety, it was an interesting role reversal to be collaborating with the client on the uncertain basics of physical safety.

While I experienced this same pattern with non-veteran clients, the veteran clients were much more likely to engage with me in role reversal in a bid to preserve my safety. As aforementioned, part of the issue with New York being one of the first epicenters of the virus outbreak is that information about virus spread, supply chain impacts, and social consequences was minimal. Early sessions with veterans were filled with updates on information that they had received from friends and colleagues involved in the response, as well as predictions of what might happen and what action should be taken. At times, whether directly or indirectly, my clients suggested ways for me to stay safe, either by staying at home or leaving the city. The veteran who left the city after awakening in the middle of the night in a panic was so insistent that I leave the city that it was upsetting to him when he could see on the video telehealth system that I was still in my same living room. For the first time in my clinical career, I was navigating how to explain what sources of information I trust and personal circumstances within which I was making potentially life-and-death decisions while maintaining appropriate clinical boundaries. While my veteran clients are always respectful of my decisions, it was clear that the roles of crisis manager were reversed when the crisis was now logistical instead of emotional.

A key difference between the pandemic and other disasters is how long it is continuing. With most natural and man-made disasters, the acute danger has passed in a matter of hours, days, or weeks. By contrast, the pandemic continues as this chapter is written, nearly 5 months after the first stay-at-home orders were issued in New York. Clients continue to express concern for my well-being and end sessions with wishes for continued good health. Even though it took certain sections of the city months to return to normal after Hurricane Sandy, my clients only expressed similar worry for my well-being the first week or two because the storm had, literally, passed. As one client explained it recently, "The hurricane is still sitting over us."

Organizational Pressures

Even at the beginning of the pandemic it was clear that resulting economic strife would take its toll on donations to nonprofit organizations. Veterans' organizations are not immune to this. Some independent veteran organizations were set up to specifically fill support gaps in the VA, in particular allowing for more frequent and longer treatment sessions than the VA can support. Organizations facing funding cuts might have had to curtail treatment services in order to meet new budgetary restraints. Moreover, potential widespread mental health concerns triggered by the pandemic could lead to an increase in demand in the mental health sector. While an accompanying increase in funding and support for mental health organizations is imperative, it could further deplete financial resources traditionally provided to veterans.

Conclusion

The COVID-19 pandemic presents challenges and opportunities when working with veterans, igniting preexisting triggers while tapping into reservoirs of posttraumatic growth. In particular, the virus threatening loved ones at home can spur posttraumatic stress symptoms including hypervigilance and anxiety. Some veterans have reverted to maladaptive coping mechanisms such as isolating and substance abuse. Other less recognized emotional wounds that veterans carry are also being reinforced, including survivor guilt. Dishearteningly, as behavioral and ethical decisions are made by Americans on micro, mezzo, and macro levels, some veterans experience a doubling down on moral injury, calling into question what America stands for in the world and what is the ultimate meaning of their service and the sacrifice of peers they lost. At the same time, veterans have been heartened by communities coming together and the courage of everyday Americans, whose lives they fought to protect, fighting to save the lives of others. The pandemic provides an opportunity for veterans to showcase their significant crisis management skills to the benefit of loved ones, their neighborhoods, and country. Finally, unexpectedly navigating a long-term shared trauma has shifted but ultimately strengthened our therapeutic alliances, allowing for the facets of our humanity only emergent in a crisis to adaptively connect.

References

American Psychiatric Association. (2013). *Diagnostic and statistical manual of mental disorders* (5th ed.). Arlington: Author.

American Psychiatric Association. (n.d.). *Survivor guilt.* Retrieved July 25, 2020 from https://dictionary.apa.org/survivor-guilt

Grossman, D. (2007). *On combat: The psychology and physiology of deadly conflict in war and in peace* (2nd ed.). Belleville: PPCT Research Publications.

Jacobs, J. (1961). *The death and life of great American cities.* New York: Vintage Books.

Manzo, L. C., & Perkins, D. D. (2006). Finding common ground: The importance of place attachment to community participation and planning. *CPL Bibliography, 20*(4), 335–350.

Menninger, W. C. (1948). *Psychiatry in a troubled world.* New York: Macmillan.

Quealy, K. (2020, May 15). The richest neighborhoods emptied out most as coronavirus hit New York City. *New York Times.* https://www.nytimes.com/interactive/2020/05/15/upshot/who-left-new-york-coronavirus.html

Russell, M. C., & Figley, C. R. (2013). *Treating traumatic stress injuries in military personnel: An EMDR practitioner's guide.* New York: Routledge.

Tedeschi, R. G., & Calhoun, L. G. (2004). The posttraumatic growth: Conceptual foundations and empirical evidence. *Psychological Inquiry, 15*, 1–18.

Tosone, C. (2011). The legacy of September 11th: Shared trauma, therapeutic intimacy and professional posttraumatic growth. *Traumatology, 17*(3), 25–29.

United States Department of Veterans Affairs. (n.d.-a). *Moral injury.* Retrieved July 25, 2020 from https://www.ptsd.va.gov/professional/treat/cooccurring/moral_injury.asp

United States Department of Veterans Affairs. (n.d.-b). *PTSD and substance abuse in veterans.* Retrieved July 25, 2020 from https://www.ptsd.va.gov/understand/related/substance_abuse_vet.asp

Chapter 14
Reflections on the HIV/AIDS Crisis, COVID-19, and Resilience in Gay Men: Ghosts of Our Past, Demons of Our Present

Nicholas Santo

Introduction

In March 2020 panic radiated throughout the world as it became clear that a novel flu-like illness, COVID-19, was spreading unchecked. Cities, towns, and whole countries were encouraged to engage in quarantine protocol, wear masks, and limit any social interaction outside their households to slow the rate of infection. Many Americans did not heed the warnings of public health officials, in part because of minimal solid information on the treatment of this virus and political leaders minimizing its danger. As infection and death rates started to climb in New York City, families were unable to participate in their mourning rituals for lost loved ones. Disturbing images emerged of body bags being hoisted into refrigerated trucks summoned once the morgues had reached capacity. Empty city streets resembled a post-apocalyptic landscape.

Some aspects of this scenario felt familiar to those who had been alive long enough to remember the HIV pandemic. Approximately 40 years ago HIV emerged, a pandemic that, at the time, seemed to target gay men. The headlines declared it a cancer among gay men and medical professions coined the diagnosis Gay Related Immunodeficiency (GRID) (Cervini 2020; Shernoff 1999). People diagnosed with the virus were subject to openly homophobic and transphobic attitudes from healthcare providers (Shernoff 1999). Government officials refused to make public statements regarding its spread or to address it in a humane and ethical manner (Cervini 2020). Eventually, largely through the efforts of activists, scientists learned more about the spread of HIV/AIDS. The public came to understand that it was not simply "a gay men's disease," and treatment advanced so dramatically that it is now

N. Santo (✉)
Silver School of Social Work, New York University, New York, NY, USA
e-mail: nps320@nyu.edu

© The Author(s), under exclusive license to Springer Nature Switzerland
AG 2021
C. Tosone (ed.), *Shared Trauma, Shared Resilience During a Pandemic*,
Essential Clinical Social Work Series,
https://doi.org/10.1007/978-3-030-61442-3_14

127

possible to manage HIV with medication. However, the emotional impact of the HIV crisis on gay men who lived through it was deep and far-reaching.

How does a group of people survive a deadly virus with little to no help from those sworn to protect and serve its citizens? The gay men who lived through the HIV/AIDS crisis had to show resilience. Nonetheless, they bear the scars of that time, particularly the pain of watching their community's dread, being neglected by those in power, and being publicly shamed for their sexual identity because of its connection to a contagion. This chapter will briefly discuss the commonalities between the handling of the HIV/AIDS and the COVID-19 pandemics, then address the emotional and behavioral impact of COVID-19 on gay-identifying men through the lens of expectations and violation of expectations.

HIV/AIDS and COVID-19 Mishandled

When HIV emerged into public awareness in 1981, the virus was directly tied to gay men. The government was slow to respond to the climbing infection rates of what was first known as gay cancer, then GRID, and now HIV/AIDS (Cervini 2020). The lesbian, gay, bisexual, transgender, and queer (LGBTQ) community was already marginalized and faced adversity on multiple fronts: discrimination in the workplace that could result in termination; violence from fellow citizens and law enforcement; and automatic discharge from the armed services upon being "outed," to name a few. The perception of deviancy was projected onto LGBTQ people, creating an environment where dehumanization was generally considered acceptable. Instances of dehumanization included public officials calling for the tattooing of gay people living with AIDS as an identifier; a vote in California to quarantine and isolate AIDS patients; government's preoccupation with testing gay men only; and hospitals' disposing of the deceased in garbage bags (Cervini 2020). "Silence = Death" became an advocacy motto for the thousands affected by the virus who demanded political action for improved care. Several organizations emerged from this crisis, made up of the people affected who fought for change and sought to treat, educate, and advocate: Gay Men's Health Crisis (GMHC), People Living with AIDS (PLA), and AIDS Coalition to Unleash Power (ACT UP) (Cervini 2020). These organizations stepped in where the government failed.

As with the emergence of HIV/AIDS, the government was slow to respond to the COVID-19 pandemic. Government officials, including the President, made numerous public statements denying the severity of the virus, and many made dehumanizing statements, such as one public official suggesting that older people risk their lives by returning to work for the sake of the economy (Levin 2020). The Trump administration demonstrated xenophobic and racist attitudes in calling the virus the "China virus" (Chiu 2020) and callously deflected the demands for federal assistance from governors (Martin 2020). Each state had to fight for assistance and develop their own policies and procedures to contain the spread of the virus.

It seems clear that the United States' conspicuously severe infection and death rates from COVID-19 are directly tied to this government mishandling (Yong 2020). It has resulted in difficulties gaining access to testing (Siegler 2020); certain communities of people (particularly Black and brown communities) being disproportionately affected by the virus' impacts (i.e., health, financial, and social) (Godoy and Wood 2020); overflowing hospitals with death rates in the hundreds per day, and as mentioned previously, images of bodies in black bags being hauled onto refrigerated trucks due to insufficient space in morgues. The COVID-19 pandemic is far from over. At the time of this writing, the United States continues to have the highest infection rates. In addition to, and in part because of, government mishandling, many members of the public did not adhere to public health safety recommendations issued by the Centers for Disease Control and Prevention (CDC).

The director of the National Institute of Allergy and Infectious Diseases, Dr. Anthony Fauci, has noted similarities between HIV/AIDS and the current COVID-19 pandemic (Kim 2020). He has aptly pointed out the disproportionate rate of infection of COVID-19 in Black communities, and its similarities to HIV/AIDS infection in communities of color. The nature of both viruses is non-discriminatory, yet blame and shame has been weaponized as a means to deflect responsibility in both crises (Kim 2020). It remains to be seen to what extent private citizens and organizations must follow in the footsteps of the HIV/AIDS activists and organizers to help ourselves, since the current administration has persistently failed the American people to the tune of approximately 150,000 deaths within 8 months (Craig 2020).

Violation of Expectations and Resilience

The government's ongoing failure to meet the needs of citizens during a public health crisis can be categorized as a violation of expectations. From birth through the first year of life, we develop expectations of affective responsivity from our caregivers (Lachmann 2006). Violation of expectations occurs when caregivers do not meet our needs. The long-term effects of experiencing violations of expectations can shape the way an individual perceives and interacts with their environment, and in some cases heightening fears, pessimism, and distrust (Lachmann 2006).

In this pandemic, expectations have been violated by the lack of a coherent, empathetic, and competent response to lethal public health issues. The New York City LGBTQ community specifically experienced a violation of expectations when city officials permitted an organization with an anti-LGBTQ agenda to set up a medical camp in Central Park to treat overflow patients from hospitals. According to a New York Times article, "Franklin Graham is taking down his N.Y. hospital, but not going quietly," the organization required employees and volunteers to sign a statement of faith that affirms their belief in Jesus Christ and that marriage is between a man and a woman (Stack and Fink 2020). News of this arrangement violated the expectations that LGBTQ people had for their elected officials to show empathy and solidarity with all citizens equally during a citywide health crisis.

Silence = Death rings true through this troubling experience, while the country is also in the midst of civil unrest. Silence and inaction have incited anger and protest as people of various identities (race, gender, sexual identity) have banded together to fight injustices such as police brutality, inadequate provision of personal protective equipment (PPE), and inadequate guarantees of safety standards for planned school returns. Black Lives Matter has sharply raised its profile and grown its numbers, with support from the LGBTQ community advocating for Black Trans Lives Matter. As with the emergence of HIV/AIDS, injustices during a public health crisis have brought communities together to fight and engage in robust advocacy efforts to be treated with dignity.

The capacity of individuals and communities to come together in this way is evidence of resilience. Resilience is an adaptive behavior defined as the ability of children to function well in the face of adversity (Cummings et al. 2000), and to overcome those conditions through self-care and a recognition of self-efficacy (Bender and Ingram 2018), with a move toward a positive outcome or to reduce a negative one. Prominent LGBTQ figures who have demonstrated resiliency include Marsha P. Johnson, Sylvia Rivera, Marion Banzhaf, Alexis Danzig, Bayard Rustin, Larry Kramer, and Harvey Milk, to name a few. Each of these people displayed acts of courage in their efforts to enact positive change for those suffering, despite their own personal trials. They serve as role models and beacons of hope for the hopeless.

From the start of this pandemic I have noticed themes of guilt and shame regarding sexual identity re-emerge among my gay clients as each passing day brought grim news and sometimes tighter restrictions. The Silence = Death motto resonates today but in a slightly different way. Some have reacted to the quarantine with the thought that closeness may equal death. There is truth to this concern, given the highly contagious nature of this respiratory virus. The psychological impact the COVID-19 crisis has had on those gay men who lived through the HIV/AIDS crisis is a nightmare of expectations being violated, again.

Case Vignette

The following case vignette is provided to explore how living through the COVID-19 pandemic has triggering effects on a gay-identifying client who has also lived through the HIV/AIDS crisis. His name and identifying information have been altered in order to maintain confidentiality.

Wayne

Wayne, a gay-identifying male, first moved to New York City in his twenties. HIV/ AIDS was already ravaging the LGBTQ community. He struggled with anxiety and shame most of his life. He had a tenuous relationship with his father, who has shamed Wayne's gay identity when Wayne came out. He recalls a long history of being mocked for not being masculine enough and not participating in "boy" activities like sports throughout his childhood and adolescent development. His arrival in NYC was jarring. On the one hand, a virus was slowly killing people all around him, and on the other hand, the world continued to send rejecting messages of the people affected not being good enough (i.e., good enough for health care, equal rights, etc.). Wayne's capacity for empathy and compassion for others motivated him to dedicate time to volunteering within the LGBTQ community. Through this experience he established deep, meaningful relationships and tragic loss as friends and people he cared for were passing away.

Wayne has spent time in therapy working through feelings of inadequacy and internalized unresolved issues with his father. As the COVID lockdown wore on, social distancing orders and the frequently revised expectations of the length of time to socially distance began to weigh on Wayne. Days at home grew longer and news more dire. He recalled memories of the losses he witnessed and adverse and discriminatory events that chipped away at his self-worth. Wayne's first triggering experience was brought on by the sounds of sirens blaring throughout his neighborhood all throughout the day and night; this reminded him of times volunteering when he would sit with someone as they take their last breath and wait for ambulance transport. His anxiety was exacerbated further by imagery of refrigerated trucks at local hospitals. Wayne felt a swelling of helplessness. That feeling reignited a narrative of lack of self-worth. Treatment moved toward deeper exploration of those experiences as memories continued to resurface. At one point, he recalled some journal entries which he later found and shared in session. The entries revealed similar themes of lack of self-worth and helplessness, while also highlighting, unknowingly to Wayne, his resilience. Therapy focused on the role those experiences played in his life and highlighted his resiliency through acts of advocacy and support through troubled times.

Shared Trauma

We do not have to look far back in history to identify various events that mental health clinicians and clients have had a dual exposure to the same collective trauma, such as 9/11 (Tosone et al. 2012). The COVID-19 pandemic, as with HIV/AIDS, is a global crisis that affects clients and clinicians alike. Clinicians have been faced with the task of resolving their anxieties about safety for self and loved ones, while helping clients with similar concerns. Clinicians have also had to contend with transitions to remote practice, as well as providing a secure, remote space for effective psychotherapeutic treatment of trauma, both past and present.

The relational aspect of this traumatic event removes the autonomous choice for clinician self-disclosure. Client inquiry into my affective experience has been an interesting turn of events in treatment. Self-disclosure is always a personal choice that should be made carefully and yet during a worldwide crisis, it can be difficult to avoid. I found that after careful self-exploration, my decision to selectively self-disclose to clients has been met with a deepening of the therapeutic process. The sense of unity can also foster a sense of shared resiliency (Nuttman-Shwartz 2014); the dual exposure experience may temporarily quell the feelings of isolation. My self-disclosure included feelings of worry for the health of loved ones, adjustment to safety protocols, and at times, confusion as it pertains to receiving conflicting safety information. While this level of self-disclosure may seem to scratch the surface, it is what lies beneath that became truly challenging.

A close heterosexual cousin of mine died of HIV/AIDS-related complications in the late 1990s. I was an adolescent when I became aware of and had my first exposure to death due to HIV/AIDS. My final memory of him is vividly etched into my brain. My parents told me of his diagnosis, and spoke to me about its severity and the toll it took on his physical appearance compared to last seeing him during the holidays. After answering my many questions, we decided that I could visit his bedside, unknowingly for the last time. My cousin looked frail, pale, and had scars on his skin that I had never noticed before. Surprisingly, he maintained his strong sense of humor and warmth despite his weakness. Not much time passed after that visit when we received word of his passing. I remember feeling helpless and a deep sadness; it was a loss that I could not understand.

My adolescent mind desperately sought answers. I spent time researching HIV/AIDs in my spare time and, with approval from certain teachers, even wrote about the topic for some assignments. I started to develop a deeper sense of shame and anxiety as I learned more about how gay people were treated unfairly and inhumanely in a critical time of need. I may not have lived through the experience like my client, but I got a glimpse into the pain and despair of the time. I carry this experience with me to my sessions. This personal memory helped me to attune to my client's experience in a deep way. It also helped me to further realize my resiliency and its usefulness in treatment.

Conclusion

The similarities between the HIV/AIDS crisis and the COVID-19 pandemic are unsettling. History is repeating itself with devastating consequences and little evidence of progress. Current events have stirred up similar traumas experienced by gay men who lived through the HIV/AIDS crisis. Their anxieties about safety, nurturance, and acceptance were reignited by this global traumatic event. Marginalized groups are especially feeling the impact of the virus, and recognizing anew the great disparities woven into the fabric of this country. Those with lesbian, bisexual, transgender, and other intersecting identities are faced with their unique challenges throughout this pandemic, and clinicians working with them need to be mindful of the ghosts and demons that may remain.

References

Bender, A., & Ingram, R. (2018). Connecting attachment style to resilience: Contributions of self-care and self-efficacy. *Personality and Individual Differences, 130*, 18–20. https://doi.org/10.1016/j.paid.2018.03.038.

Cervini, E. (2020). *The deviant's war: The homosexual vs. the United States of America*. New York: Farrar, Straus and Giroux.

Chiu, A. (2020). Trump has no qualms about calling coronavirus the 'Chinese Virus.' That's a dangerous attitude, experts say. *The Washington Post*. https://www.washingtonpost.com/nation/2020/03/20/coronavirus-trump-chinese-virus/

Craig, J. (2020). Charts: How the US ranks on COVID-19 deaths per capita – and by case count. *NPR*. https://www.npr.org/sections/goatsandsoda/2020/08/05/899365887/charts-how-the-u-s-ranks-on-covid-19-deaths-per-capita-and-by-case-count

Cummings, E. M., Davies, P. T., & Campbell, S. B. (2000). *Developmental psychopathology and family process: Theory, research, and clinical implications*. New York: The Guilford Press.

Godoy, M., & Wood, D. (2020). What do coronavirus racial disparities look like state by state?, *NPR*. https://www.npr.org/sections/health-shots/2020/05/30/865413079/what-do-coronavirus-racial-disparities-look-like-state-by-state

Kim, M. (2020). Dr. Fauci praises the "courage and dignity" of the gay community next to Mike Pence, *them.*, https://www.them.us/story/fauci-mike-pence-coronavirus-aids-gay-community

Lachmann, F. M. (2006). Violations of expectations in creativity and perversion. *Psychoanalytic Inquiry, 26*(3), 362–385. https://doi.org/10.2513/s07351690pi2603_6.

Levin, B. (2020). Texas Lt. Governor: Old people should volunteer to die to save the economy, *Vanity Fair.* https://www.vanityfair.com/news/2020/03/dan-patrick-coronavirus-grandparents

Martin, J. (2020). Trump to governors on ventilators: 'Try getting it yourselves'. *New York Times*. https://www.nytimes.com/2020/03/16/us/politics/trump-coronavirus-respirators.html

Nuttman-Shwartz, O. (2014). Share resilience in a traumatic reality: A new concept for trauma workers exposed personally and professionally to collective disaster. *Trauma, Violence, and Abuse, 16*(4), 466–475. https://doi.org/10.1177/1524838014557287.

Shernoff, M. (1999). Introduction. In M. Shernoff (Ed.), *AIDS and mental health practice: Clinical and policy issues* (pp. xxiii–xxviii). Binghamton: The Haworth Press.

Siegler, K. (2020). Many who need testing for COVID-19 fail to get access. *NPR*. https://www.npr.org/2020/04/03/826044608/many-who-need-testing-for-covid-19-fail-to-get-access

Stack, L., & Fink, S. (2020). Franklin Graham is taking down his N.Y. hospital, but not going quietly. *New York Times*. https://www.nytimes.com/2020/05/10/nyregion/franklin-graham-samaritans-purse-central-park-hospital-tent-coronavirus.html

Tosone, C., Nuttman-Shwartz, O., & Stephens, T. (2012). Shared trauma: When the professional is personal. *Clinical Social Work Journal, 40*, 231–239. https://doi.org/10.1007/s10615-012-0395-0.

Yong, E. (2020). How the pandemic defeated America. *The Atlantic*. https://www.theatlantic.com/magazine/archive/2020/09/coronavirus-american-failure/614191/

Chapter 15
School Social Workers Responding to the COVID-19 Pandemic: Experiences in Traditional, Charter, and Agency-Based Community School Agency Settings

Dayna Sedillo-Hamann, Jessica Chock-Goldman, and Marina A. Badillo

Introduction

The role of the school social worker varies, depending on setting and population; however, what remains consistent is their commitment to supporting the mental health of students and advocating for their needs. During times of larger crises, such as historical events like September 11 and Hurricane Katrina, school social workers have been vital responders. As the world grapples with the COVID-19 pandemic, school-based social workers are in a unique position as schools close and transition to remote learning to prevent further spread of the deadly virus. Presently, it is unclear when schools will fully open in person across the country. The pandemic has shed light on a plethora of systemic inequities and challenges that impact the lives of young people and their families, particularly as they relate to schools and education. As a result, schools have relied on the expertise, leadership, and skills of social workers to address multiple issues such as access to technology, food insecurity, services for students with disabilities, mental health support, and crisis intervention.

School social workers work in a variety of settings that can include public, private, charter, agency-based settings, school-based health clinics, and more (Richard et al. 2019). The writers of this chapter currently work in a large public high school, a transfer charter high school, and a non-profit program based full-time in a small

D. Sedillo-Hamann (✉)
Silver School of Social Work, New York University, New York, NY, USA
e-mail: dch323@nyu.edu

J. Chock-Goldman
Stuyvesant High School, New York, NY, USA

M. A. Badillo
A Transfer Charter High School, Brooklyn, NY, USA

© The Author(s), under exclusive license to Springer Nature Switzerland AG 2021
C. Tosone (ed.), *Shared Trauma, Shared Resilience During a Pandemic*,
Essential Clinical Social Work Series,
https://doi.org/10.1007/978-3-030-61442-3_15

135

public high school, all located in New York City (NYC), the largest school district in the United States (Department of Education 2020). Working in the early epicenter of the US COVID-19 outbreak, each of the social workers had a unique experience preparing for and supporting remote learning, as well as navigating the mental health needs of students, families, and staff who were greatly affected by the pandemic and its economic impacts.

School social workers are not a mandated Department of Education (DOE) position in NYC public schools, and many schools are without one; in fact, the ratio of students to in-house social workers in Manhattan schools is 800:1 (Brewer 2017). Schools have the option to add a social worker to their budget, dependent on the priorities of an individual principal and school. Furthermore, when a school chooses to hire a social worker, their role is not uniform: some provide mandated counseling for students with Individualized Education Plans (IEPs); some provide psychosocial testing for initial IEP evaluation; and some provide social-emotional support or crisis intervention in multiple schools. The lack of uniformity and clear supervision of school social workers in the DOE has meant additional challenges for public school social workers attempting to continue their work remotely.

In addition to the nearly 1600 public schools located in NYC, there are currently over 260 charter schools (DOE 2020); however, there are no current statistics and data on how many social workers are employed in charter schools in New York State or NYC. Nevertheless, social workers are employed by most charter schools in NYC and proved to be an integral part in the response to COVID-19. Due to their deregulation from local and state authorities, charter schools are provided with more flexibility and independence to choose their curriculum, how school days can be structured, and teaching pedagogy (Kahlenberg and Potter 2014). This may also be true of the situation of the COVID-19 response in NYC within charter schools.

Another model for school social work is for outside agencies to place social workers in public schools; since the early 2000s community-based organizations (CBOs) have increasingly begun partnering with individual schools or school districts in order to provide social services and other resources to public school staff, students, and families (Johnston et al. 2017). The Community School model has become popularized and is generally well-accepted as an evidence-based approach to providing wraparound services to less-resourced communities (Oakes et al. 2017). Hundreds of partnerships between public schools and CBOs are in existence throughout the country, and they are meant to boost overall attendance and graduation rates, and improve schools in communities with higher rates of poverty (What is a Community School? 2020).

In NYC, there are currently 267 community schools that have full-time staff hired by non-profit partners (Community Schools 2020). The writer that works as a CBO social worker manages a school-based counseling program designed to help support high school students with their attendance, graduation, and overall mental health. Though they are employees of the non-profit rather than the school district, the social work team operates full time in the school and is at the forefront of communication with students and families regarding crises, resource needs, mental health services, and advocacy.

The Challenge of Preparing for and Communicating About Closing School

As the news of COVID-19 cases being documented in NYC spread, public school staff in all different schools and settings expressed their disappointment in communication and decision-making from the DOE leadership. As the largest school system in the country, DOE school staff recognized the emergent threat that COVID-19 presented to the health and safety of staff and students alike. Some teachers, students, and DOE faculty expressed feeling trapped in schools and the desire to shut down the system in order to stay at home, as other cities had already done. Many families decided in the weeks leading up to mass school closures to stop sending their child to school, instead of attempting to reach out to faculty and staff in order to explain or get their children excused. In an op-ed published prior to the closing, NYC public school teachers expressed their apprehension and fear about commuting to and teaching in buildings with up to thousands of students (Daves et al. 2020). The fear for the safety of students and of the numerous school-based staff was palpable and proved valid; as of August 2020, at least 70 DOE staff members have been reported to have passed away as a result of contracting COVID-19 (Cruz 2020).

In the week prior to the start of remote learning, DOE required staff to come to their individual school to learn the strategies to transition to remote learning. Though some recommendations were provided for guidance counselors, this was not the case for school social workers, given their varied roles and responsibilities. While many school social workers across districts banded together for mutual aid and assistance with finding resources, the lack of centralized leadership and timely communication led to many social workers feeling paralyzed or unsure of how best to support their students. Different timelines of communication across the large school system meant that social workers were not consistent in their approach and ability to provide immediate support to students and families in crisis. As of mid-April 2020—almost a month into remote learning—social workers had yet to receive guidance on providing teletherapy.

While some DOE social workers expressed feeling directionless and frustrated with the district's lack of action prior to the closing, several charter school networks in NYC, including Uncommon Schools and Public Prep, had already begun working on their remote learning plans (Public Prep Network 2020; Uncommon Schools Network 2020). The charter school-based writer—a school administrator and a licensed clinical social worker—was given the task to develop and provide a school COVID-19 closure plan along with other school administrators. Because of their charter status, the writer's school was able to announce closure earlier than the DOE and begin preparations for remote learning.

With the guidance of their Charter Management Network (CMO)—an organization that provides management services to charter schools that can be either not-for-profit or for profit—provisions were made to provide academic and family resources and structures/plans of the school closure. Each school in the charter network had the autonomy to create their own plans and structures on how they were going to conduct remote learning, provide support for students and families, and decide how they were going to support teachers and staff in their respective schools. These remote school closure plans were provided by each school to the CMO for feedback and subsequently implemented.

Similarly, the community school staff employed by the non-profit were informed by their agency that they would begin remote work days before the school system was shuttered and were thus able to plan slightly ahead for the transition. While the non-profit was attempting to make the best decision to keep their staff safe, it caused some emotional discomfort as the social work team navigated telling their students and DOE colleagues that they would not be returning to work in person. The social work team was relieved that their employer was valuing their health, but also felt that they were abandoning their school community in its time of need. This proved untrue, ultimately, as just days later the school chancellor announced the closure of all schools in the system.

It is very likely that the charter school network and non-profit were able to make decisions more quickly and adroitly to protect their staff and students as a result of their smaller size; the DOE is a huge system responsible for thousands of buildings, over a hundred thousand staff, and one million students (DOE 2020). For schools that already had systems in place for social service delivery and regular communication with families (i.e., Community Schools), the transition to remote work and support was made more smoothly.

Working Remotely with Vulnerable Students

Once the schools shifted fully to remote learning, resource and access disparities emerged quickly. Of primary importance for learning was ensuring that all students had internet access and a laptop or other remote learning device. The next challenge was designing a system of tracking student engagement and identifying ways to support all learners, including those with disabilities. Additionally, as layoffs and illnesses began to impact communities, social workers were privy to the challenges that families were facing in securing adequate food resources, accessing money for necessities, and coping with the many COVID-related deaths and hospitalizations that occurred. These challenges were even more acute for those already in vulnerable positions, including undocumented families who were unable to receive stimulus money or other benefits.

The uniqueness of charter school governing provided ample opportunities for charter schools to be innovative and creative in finding ways to support their students, families, and staff through COVID-19. It is not uncommon for charter schools to service students from underserved communities. In fact, students who are enrolled in charter schools are more likely to come from communities of color and poverty (Kahlenberg and Potter 2014). In New York City, over 80% of students who are enrolled in charter schools are economically disadvantaged (New York City Charter Center 2020). As a result, social work expertise was utilized to support families and students in crisis who were parenting, living in temporary housing, and coping with grief and loss. A system for ensuring communication based on the "primary person model" was implemented; this model consists of every student being connected to and having a relationship with at least one adult from the school (Alliance for Excellence in Education 2020). Researchers have found this model improves student engagement and attendance for students. Each student was assigned to a social worker, counselor, or student advisor who was instructed to make daily outreach communication to students and their families to ensure wellness, safety, and academic progress.

In addition, a laptop distribution program was created. All students were assessed, and those who indicated they needed a laptop either were mailed one or had picked up a laptop from a central location. Google forms were also created and emailed out to families providing opportunities for them to communicate with the school if needing assistance. Families who responded to the Google form had requested emergency supplies and food. As a result, the school responded by purchasing items for families and having them shipped directly to their homes along with providing resources to families in the community. Lastly, a grant was also written by the school administration team requesting funding from the NYC Charter Center and the grant was accepted. This additional funding was used toward purchasing mobile hotspots for students, online tutoring services (especially for students with individual education plans), and laptops.

In contrast, DOE-based social workers were left paralyzed by legal questions regarding how to begin remote counseling. Three weeks passed before clear instructions were provided as to how to communicate with parents/caregivers and students, which electronic consent forms to obtain, whether or not these forms were necessary, new service plans for students, and how to record care. Because of this lack of organization and cohesiveness in the DOE's leadership, students lost services. School social workers would provide check-ins so as to continue to care for their students without having any liability issues in the process. In a time of community crisis, school social workers as a unit were not prepared.

As agency-based social workers, the CBO staff had more flexibility in their response to the pandemic, untethered by NYC DOE mandates such as when and how to conduct remote counseling. Prior to the pandemic, a significant number of students reported mental health symptoms due to past trauma, anxiety, depression, chronic stress related to poverty, and more. Even before the schools began remote learning, the agency-based social workers began reaching out to as many students as possible, prioritizing students who were already deemed at-risk (due to mental health concerns, housing instability, or other factors), in response to growing concerns about COVID-19. During these check-ins conducted via text, telephone, video, or even using social media platforms such as Instagram, students expressed their feelings to the mental health staff.

Social work leadership and expertise were required and leaned upon during this time. Because families were struggling with economic disadvantages and resources, social work knowledge of agencies and programs were utilized. The CBO school social work team also played a large role in the resource response for students and families. Utilizing a social work-based needs assessment survey and training school staff to screen for immediate needs, the CBO was able to divert funding that was to be used for trips and events to emergency assistance for students and families. Cash grants and gift cards to purchase necessities were provided to families, as well as support with connecting to additional emergency assistance via non-profit and city agencies.

Mental Health Needs of Students, Families, and Staff

In the context of a global health crisis, the role of the school social worker became even more vital. As remote learning progressed and moved into its second and third weeks, the agency-based social work team identified several emergent themes from their sessions with students. Many of the high school students described their high stress levels, frustration with the amount of work being assigned, and their worries about the future of their high school careers; that is, whether they would be able to pass their classes, graduate on time, and more. Additionally, students felt overwhelmed with balancing home responsibilities and remote learning, while also managing anxiety about the future, their families' health, and financial stability. Alongside the daily struggles of parental job loss due to the virus, food/housing insecurity, and the other stressors that persisted before the pandemic, the pressure from teachers to continue to produce felt alienating and infuriating to some.

The charter school social work team held a virtual professional development session for the entire staff on coping skills and managing the crisis of the new virtual work experience at supporting staff's own families at home. The professional development provided a space for staff members to process their feelings, engage in social support, and learn concrete skills on how to manage their feelings, new work schedules, and competing work/life balance needs. Similarly, the CBO team held multiple community staff check-ins to connect and share regarding their shared experiences of COVID-19. The stress of having to care for others professionally while also experiencing direct effects, including fears of contagion, contracting COVID-19, and hospitalizations for one's self or loved ones, was overwhelming for many. These effects of dual exposure to a trauma-laden environment are consistent with the findings regarding shared trauma for other communal disasters, including ongoing terrorism (Baum 2010), September 11 (Bauwens and Tosone 2010; Tosone et al. 2014), Hurricane Katrina (Boulanger 2013; Tosone et al. 2014), and Hurricane Sandy (Nyapati and Mehra 2015).

In addition to supporting staff, advocacy on behalf of students' mental health continued to be a top priority for social workers in all three settings. In conversations with school administrators, the agency-based school social work team regularly emphasized the importance of students' mental health needs during the time of crisis and worked together to craft messaging to the teaching staff, encouraging them to adopt a more flexible approach to work completion and a softer tone when communicating with students. The team also provided different types of spaces in which students could share their feelings and receive support and suggestions for how to practice self-care in the midst of the pandemic. Through group meetings on Zoom, social media interactive posts, texting, and phone calls, the team used whatever opportunity they had to connect with students and assess their mental health.

School social workers quickly observed that students were in dire need of both mandated and non-mandated services. Although closing schools prioritized physical health of students during the pandemic, the emotional toll of social isolation from peers and other adults began to take shape. Children at home during remote learning experienced loneliness and disconnection, clearly linked to lack of social engagement. Home confinement may also put some young people at risk of experiencing increased intrafamily violence, in addition to increasing the risk of depression, anxiety, and PTSD (Guessoum et al. 2020). Relying solely on remote means of engaging with their students proved frustrating for social workers who understood that in-person school was often a safe haven for vulnerable youth.

Research has shown that in times of community trauma, children are susceptible to symptoms of PTSD and other mental health effects; for example, 6 months after 9/11, the NYC Board of Education conducted a study of 8266 children in grades 4 through 12 for psychiatric diagnosis (Calderoni et al. 2006). This study demonstrated that 10.5% of students overall met the criteria for PTSD, as well as risk factors for PTSD that included personal physical exposure to the attack as well as family exposure and loss (Calderoni et al. 2006). The experience of COVID-19 has already begun to cause longer term symptoms of PTSD as a result of students losing immediate family members, living in communities where many lives have been lost, and constant fear and anxiety of becoming ill. In sessions with students, social workers listened as they articulated feeling low-energy, difficulty sleeping and eating, loss of interest in normal activities, and hopelessness about the future. In a weekly COVID-19 Coping Skills group run by the writer in a DOE public school, the most shared experience expressed by students was their feelings of mourning for social interactions and connection to others.

The difference between COVID-19 and 9/11 is the additional experience of individual and community loneliness and isolation. Humans are a social species: we are born into and live our lives in social organizations that vary in size and membership, and we need to socialize with others to survive (Laursen and Hartl 2013). With all opportunities for social contact outside of family removed, this leaves youth potentially feeling an increase of anxiety and depression.

Practice Implications and Future Directions

While much can be learned from the start of the COVID-19 crisis, it is important to recognize that the effects of the pandemic will be felt by young people for a long time to come, particularly as related to their mental health (Kramer 2020).

In considering the future of K-12 education, educators, administrators, students, and families must advocate for continued services for the already most vulnerable students—those who are faced with mental health challenges or have a trauma history, those who are dealing with the effects of oppression and poverty, and those with disabilities. Schools may reopen in the short term, but there is possibility of a resurgence of the virus until an effective vaccine becomes widely available, leading to additional closures. In planning for this and any future crisis, social workers must remain strong advocates for the most vulnerable and for themselves, ensuring that they are seated at the table when planning for a crisis response.

While no one could have predicted how COVID-19 would have paralyzed our nation, schools and school systems have learned quickly the importance of preparing for crisis more generally and the important role that social workers can play in creating connections and systems that keep communities together. Unfortunately, in many public schools the lack of clarity in the role that school social workers should play in responding to the crisis demonstrated the often overlooked nature of their job. Where there is a unified force and clear protocols allowing school social workers to provide both mandated counseling and high-risk counseling immediately, students and families benefit.

Students, families, *and* school staff will need support and counseling in the aftermath of COVID-19. The amount of loss—including deaths to COVID-19, job loss, food insecurity, and social isolation—has taken a large toll on communities of color and, therefore, on the public school system in New York City and around the country. While the future is uncertain, it is important that social workers and their allies advocate that *every* school hire at least one social worker to mitigate the impact of COVID-19; in fact, some elected leaders have called for just that, noting the positive impact that school social workers can have on students' mental health (Brewer 2017).

Finally, it is worth noting how difficult it was for such a large institution like the NYC DOE to make important decisions regarding health, mental health, and safety for all of its stakeholders. In part due to their smaller size, charter schools and nonprofits were able to jump into action more quickly in some instances. The DOE and other similarly large and diverse urban school systems should consider ways to allow more autonomy and innovation so that schools can better meet the needs of their particular student and family populations. The Community School model may be the most effective way to approach K-12 education moving forward as it joins academic and social needs, and provides a school community with a plethora of resources and strategies for addressing crises.

This reflection illustrates how macro-level policies, mezzo-level innovations, and micro-level interventions influenced responses in NYC schools to COVID-19. Furthermore, this reflection demonstrates the social work leadership and expertise that is required in crisis situations in order to protect, support, and advocate for those most in need.

References

Alliance for Excellence in Education. (2020). *Getting students back on track*. Retrieved from https://all4ed.org/getting-students-back-on-track/

Baum, N. (2010). Shared traumatic reality in communal disasters: Toward a conceptualization. *Psychotherapy Theory, Research, Practice, 47*(2), 249–259.

Bauwens, J., & Tosone, C. (2010). Professional posttraumatic growth after a shared traumatic experience: Manhattan clinicians' perspectives on post 9/11 practice. *Journal of Loss and Trauma, 15*(6), 498–517.

Boulanger, G. (2013). Fearful symmetry: Shared trauma in New Orleans after Hurricane Katrina. *Psychoanalytic Dialogues, 23*(1), 21–34.

Brewer, G. (2017). Who's caring: The state of school-based mental health care in NYC schools. Gale Brewer - Manhattan Borough President. https://www.manhattanbp.nyc.gov/downloads/pdf/School%20Mental%20Health%20Report%20-%202017%20-%20Final.pdf

Calderoni, M. E., Alderman, E. M., Silver, E. J., & Bauman, L. J. (2006). The Mental Health Impact of 9/11 on Inner-City High School Students 20 Miles North of Ground Zero. *Journal of Adolescent Health, 39*(1), 57–65.

Community Schools. (2020). Retrieved July 30, 2020, from https://www.schools.nyc.gov/learning/programs/community-schools

Cruz, D. (2020, July 16). *NYC teachers union head vows schools won't open if they deem unsafe*. Gothamist. Retrieved from: https://gothamist.com/news/nyc-teachers-union-head-vows-schools-wont-reopen-if-they-deem-it-unsafe

Daves, S., Dwyer, M., & Thoms, A. (2020, March 14). We are New York teachers. Close the schools. *New York Times*. Retrieved From: https://www.nytimes.com/2020/03/14/opinion/contributors/close-new-york-schoos.html

Department of Education. (2020). DOE data at a glance. Retrieved July 30, 2020, from https://www.schools.nyc.gov/about-us/reports/doe-data-at-a-glance

Guessoum, S. B., Lachal, J., Radjack, R., Carretier, E., Minassian, S., Benoit, L., & Moro, M. R. (2020). Adolescent psychiatric disorders during the COVID-19 pandemic and lockdown. *Psychiatry Research, 291*, 113264.

Johnston, W., Gomez, C., Sontag-Padilla, L., Xenakis, L. & Anderson, B. (2017). *Developing community schools at scale: Implementation of the New York City Community Schools Initiative*. Rand Corporation. Retrieved from: https://www.rand.org/content/dam/rand/pubs/research_reports/RR2100/RR2100/RAND_RR2100.pdf

Kahlenberg, R., & Potter, H. (2014). *A smarter charter: Finding what works in charter schools and public education*. New York: Teachers College Press.

Kramer, A. (2020). *Kids and Covid-19: A mental health crisis looms*. New York: Center for New York City Affairs.

Laursen, B., & Hartl, A. C. (2013). Understanding loneliness during adolescence: Developmental changes that increase the risk of perceived social isolation. *Journal of Adolescence., 36*(6), 1261–1268.

New York City Charter Center (2020). NYC Charter School Facts. Retrieved from https://www.nyccharterschools.org/sites/default/files/resources/NYC-Charter-Facts.pdf

Nyapati, R., & Mehra, A. (2015). Hurricane Sandy and therapist disclosure. *Psychiatry; Interpersonal and Biological Processes, 78*(1), 65–74.

Oakes, J., Maier, A., & Daniel, J. (2017, June 05). *Community Schools: An evidence-based strategy for equitable school improvement*. Retrieved July 30, 2020, from https://nepc.colorado.edu/publication/equitable-community-schools

Public Prep Network [@publicprepnyc]. (2020, March 13). *Covid-19 school updated* [Instagram Post]. Retrieved from https://www.instagram.com/p/B9sCsIiJO6s/

Richard, L., Monroe, P. A., & Garand, J. C. (2019). School social work roles, caseload size, and employment settings. *School Social Work Journal, 2*, 18.

Tosone, C., McTighe, J., & Bauwens, J. (2014). Shared traumatic stress among social workers in the aftermath of Hurricane Katrina. *British Journal of Social Work, 40*(1), 226–238.

Uncommon Schools Network [@uncommonschools]. (2020, March 13). Update [Instagram Post]. Retrieved from https://www.instagram.com/p/B9rzre_nDMu/

What is a Community School? (2020). Retrieved July 30, 2020, from http://www.communityschools.org/aboutschools/what_is_a_community_school.aspx

Chapter 16
Transition to Teletherapy with Adolescents in the Wake of the COVID-19 Pandemic: The Holding Environment Approach

Cierra Osei-Buapim

Introduction

Governor Andrew Cuomo's executive order for New York State schools to close by March 18, 2020, came suddenly, with the expectation that schools would plan for alternate educational instruction during closure (Governor Andrew M. Cuomo 2020). The order, made on account of the COVID-19 pandemic, caused an array of programmatic concerns and disruptions in the way residential schools provide services to students. Clinical staff, accustomed to the structure and direct contact with students that exists within schools, were challenged to create and adapt to innovative ways of providing services as we moved our interactions with students to the telephone or online. Social workers were challenged to adjust their lives and living space to accommodate this new norm; bedrooms, living rooms, dining rooms, and kitchens became the home office for many, including myself. In addition, my personal laptop became the device that I used to complete paperwork and to participate in teletherapy sessions with some students. Personal cell phones were also utilized to maintain contact with students. We faced this challenge while navigating our own feelings of uncertainty, shock, and surprise at this unprecedented reality.

Students, meanwhile, had varying reactions to the change. Many had come to know both program and staff as the primary providers of structure in their lives, both familiar and therapeutic. In ideal instances, students had come to know staff as being flexible, understanding, and respectful of privacy and boundaries, as well as consistent, warm, empathic, and sensitive to their needs, both spoken and unspoken; such qualities are those that Zelechoski et al. (2013) identify as best qualities for staff working with youth in residential treatment settings. Other students met participation and engagement in residential schooling with reluctance or even hatred. Closures thus prompted mixed

C. Osei-Buapim (✉)
Behind the Expression Inc., Orange County, NY, USA
e-mail: coseibuapim@behindtheexpression.com

© The Author(s), under exclusive license to Springer Nature Switzerland AG 2021
C. Tosone (ed.), *Shared Trauma, Shared Resilience During a Pandemic*,
Essential Clinical Social Work Series,
https://doi.org/10.1007/978-3-030-61442-3_16

feelings among the students; some were willing and excited to go home during this time, while others experienced dread, anxiety, and fear not knowing what the next steps would entail. Whatever their initial feelings about the closure, residential students negotiated an abrupt change as they went from residing in the program full time to remaining home without a date of return. This caused a surge of anxiety in almost all of the students served, as did the "new norm" of receiving therapy by phone or online.

Cell phones, Google hangout chats and meets, and Zoom video conferencing provided the means for school social workers to continue to provide treatment to students during the COVID-19 pandemic. These modes challenged clinicians to adapt their face-to-face treatment interventions to remote implementation, which has proven to be advantageous but challenging. Studies have shown the efficacy of providing treatment interventions utilizing technology (Barak and Grohol 2011; Beeson et al. 2013; Epstein 2011). However, a drawback to this method is compromised confidentiality; the potential release of student's personal information, their identity, and particularly the vulnerability to hackers that became evident when Zoom, a platform that many school districts utilized to conduct teleservices, was hacked (Strauss 2020; Wilson 2011). In addition to technological issues, there is a risk that students will refuse to answer the social worker's call or respond to their messages or that some students may be unwilling to talk in detail due to lack of privacy at home, which has been my experience. I have also experienced a student's willingness to talk in greater detail over the phone. In such cases, the phone serves as a psychological defense mechanism against the anxiety and discomfort that can surface when talking about thoughts, feelings, and past experiences in person.

The change in clinical services from face-face to remote provided social workers with opportunities to implement essential and innovative therapeutic interventions. While treatment approaches are many and varied, creation of the holding environment should be considered paramount given its function of creating a space in which students feel safe enough to express their deepest anxieties in both face-to-face and remote treatment. The purpose of this chapter is to discuss the importance of the holding environment: its creation and its continuation during face-to-face sessions and following the change to teletherapy. Beginning with a brief overview of Winnicott's (1956) concept of the holding environment, followed by two case vignettes using the holding environment as a fundamental approach, the chapter also discusses the best practices for creating a holding environment, both in person and by phone, as well as obstacles and complications that can arise in remote treatment. For the purposes of this chapter, the technological maintenance of the holding environment during COVID-19 is limited to the use of the cell phone.

Holding Environment

As a clinical social worker in a residential treatment center, I utilize a psychodynamic approach when working with high school students, focusing on past and present experiences and the way in which they manifest in present behavior. Such an approach creates a safe space for adolescents to feel vulnerable and share their anxieties, thereby creating opportunities for a therapeutic alliance to be formed and therapy to progress. Winnicott (1956) described the holding environment as the relationship established between a mother and infant within the infant's first few years of life, which creates a sense of security and "hold" within the mother/infant relationship. Winnicott described a mother's uterus as the first holding environment, one in which "maternal preoccupation" becomes apparent (Applegate 1997). The mother in Winnicott's description is preoccupied with the care of her infant, often neglecting any other responsibilities. The attention and devotion that the mother dedicates to her infant during his/her first weeks offer a secure psychological hold, creating an environment that is safe.

This type of hold, one that provides safety and security, can be applied to the therapeutic relationship (Wright 1992). Winnicott drew parallels between the mother/infant relationship and the client/therapist relationship, emphasizing the need for parents and therapists alike to be "good enough" or attuned enough to the needs of the infant/patient to understand and accept the struggles that the infant/patient is faced with and to withstand assaults from the infant/patient without retaliation or withdrawal (Altman et al. 2002; Wright 1992; Chescheir 1985). The client's view of the therapist as "good enough" is important in creating the foundation of a holding environment. Once the holding environment is established, opportunities are presented for clients to feel safe to explore their feelings, experience growth, and communicate (Lanyado 1996). While there are many elements to the holding environment, I suggest that there are interpersonal qualities therapists maintain that allow clients to see them as "good enough." Such qualities included consistency, reliability, mirroring/vocal matching, and presence. A display of these qualities during session pave the way for safety and trust to be established, thereby creating the "holding environment." These qualities are outlined in the cases that follow and are further explored in the discussion section of this chapter. In addition, this chapter discusses ways in which administrators can implement the holding environment in school settings when shared trauma is experienced between employees and students.

The Case of Jane

Jane[1] was a 17-year-old female who became a student at a residential program due to truancy, risky behavior, and parental discord. Jane had a difficult time adjusting to the new program. On the day of her admission, she appeared stoic as she sat with her parents and two strangers: a school administrator and me, her new social worker. Jane was adamant about her refusal to participate in therapy, stating that it was pointless and a waste of time.

---

[1] All names and other personal identifiers in the cases have been changed to protect privacy and confidentiality.

After years of working together, our therapeutic relationship was well-established and founded upon the holding environment. This therapeutic relationship allowed Jane to feel safe enough to express her deepest anxieties, which were many. Whereas at first she engaged in superficial conversation responding to a verbal prompt, she eventually delved deep into her feelings of depression, anxiety, and insecurity as manifested through her body language, facial expressions, and behavior on campus.

In March of 2020, Jane and I suddenly changed from face-to-face sessions to remote therapy due to the COVID-19 pandemic. Though it felt uncomfortable at first, the phone rapidly became our primary connection. We continued with regularly scheduled appointment times, with me the one responsible for calling. Jane came to expect my phone call on the scheduled day and time, which quickly became the "new norm" for our session. While some sessions were cancelled by Jane or me for specific reasons, I sought to avoid cancelling sessions whenever possible in order to maintain the holding environment.

During our phone sessions, Jane opened up about her life experiences, recalling and sharing details of her past that she was reminded of as she sat in her room. The phone connection became personal, and Jane discussed issues relating to her family members that were prompted by being at home. She discussed deep issues and feelings related to peers and relationships. During a phone session, Jane expressed, "You are one of the top people that I feel most comfortable with because you know me. I can tell you a lot." She also noted, "As a high school worker you are way more on a personal level. I didn't tell you a lot of things [at first] because I wasn't used to having a social worker and didn't want one."

The holding environment and therapeutic relationship was established with Jane prior to the pandemic, allowing therapy to continue by phone. In contrast, my experience with Alex was difficult and largely unsuccessful, as you will read in the next brief vignette.

The Case of Alex

Alex is a 17-year-old Caucasian cisgender male who became a residential student months prior to the COVID-19 pandemic. During our face-to-face sessions, Alex was minimally engaged and often needed prompts and reminders to attend his sessions. When he did attend, he would discuss topics relating to his interests, mostly animals and video games. Alex avoided talking about his feelings and often asserted his uncertainty as to the reason for his placement in a residential program. He lacked motivation and was unwilling to engage in the program. Creating the holding environment and establishing a therapeutic relationship with Alex were my two main goals in working with him, and I attempted to do so by remaining consistent in my efforts to engage him, even when my efforts were met with refusal. Alex's lack of motivation to engage in the program led him consistently to refuse my overtures toward establishing a holding environment and therapeutic relationship, and this presented a major obstacle to my efforts.

As much as my attempts to establish a therapeutic relationship and holding environment with Alex prior to the pandemic were unsuccessful, my efforts to engage him remotely following the arrival of the pandemic was even more challenging. Whereas on campus I had the option to visit with him in the cottage when he refused to attend session, this option was not available with remote therapy. If Alex missed a session while we were still meeting face-to-face, I contacted his cottage staff, who offered a level of therapeutic support to help get through to Alex. This was not an option during remote therapy. Instead, Alex's mother, whom I contacted weekly when Alex did not answer my calls, served as the liaison between Alex and me. Though I continued to make the effort to call him, he refused to get on the phone, often stating in the background "I don't need therapy" and asserting his unwillingness to speak with me. Engaging in remote therapy was unsuccessful with Alex, as was the establishment of the therapeutic relationship and the holding environment.

Discussion

In any treatment approach, it is important to create a space for adolescents to feel safe enough to express themselves and their anxieties. While treatment approaches, diagnosis, and psychopharmacology have their place in work with adolescents, such interventions are best introduced in the context of a "holding environment"; its creation in residential school settings is essential, given that treatment tends to be long term.

The importance of the therapeutic relationship can be lost amid the demands of our jobs, heavy workloads, and back-to-back meetings with students, leaving us to focus on addressing the student's presenting behavior without giving weight to the need for the secure foundation of the "psychological hold." In the wake of COVID-19, when therapy changed from in person to remote, the results of having established or missed establishing a holding environment were seen starkly, as revealed in the cases of Jane and Alex. While time demands as professionals are inevitable, I suggest the following best practices for creating and maintaining the holding environment that will allow for a therapeutic relationship to grow: consistency, reliability, mirroring/vocal matching (Beebe 2010), and presence, all of which create the ability to hold the child's anxiety and presence.

Consistency

During the first months of our acquaintance, Jane often missed appointments. I would meet Jane in her classroom to encourage her to attend her appointment, visit her in the cottage when she refused school, and attempted to engage her in the hallway whenever an appointment was missed. Many of these efforts were met with opposition, while some with compliance. Regardless of Jane's reaction, I attempted to remain consistent in my efforts to engage her, though at times this was a challenge.

I approached my work with Alex similarly in that I remained consistent with encouraging him to attend his therapy sessions and would often meet with him in his cottage when an appointment was missed. There were days where he responded to my efforts, while other days he refused my efforts. In either case, I attempted to remain consistent. When my efforts were met with refusal or opposition, I felt discouraged and unsure of my ability to engage both Jane and Alex. The self-doubt hampered my ability to be present with both students and, at times, interfered with the creation of the holding environment; instead of holding their anxieties, I focused on my own. A level of self-awareness helped me to contend with such feelings when they arose and to remain consistent in my efforts to engage Jane and Alex. Like Winnicott's "good enough" holding figure, I recognized that being "good enough" included my imperfections. This recognition allowed me to remain consistent and "good enough," which in turn created the foundation for the holding environment for Jane both in person and by phone. However, my "good enough" was not enough to engage Alex in person or by phone. It's possible that the COVID-19 pandemic may have hindered the establishment of an in-person holding environment that could have extended to teletherapy. Regardless, the creation of the holding environment was unsuccessful with Alex, which was in part due to his lack of engagement in the therapeutic process and my lack of consistency with attempts to engage him therapeutically when my efforts were met with refusal.

Reliability

Jane's ability to rely on me started with my availability to Jane during our planned sessions. Following through on requested tasks also helped establish me as reliable in her view. With Alex, as best as I was able to, I stayed committed to my word in doing what I said I would do. For example, I would often tell Alex that I would stop by his cottage to check in on him and would follow through when he requested actions of me. Showing reliability is critical when creating the holding environment.

The change from face-to-face sessions to phone sessions presented another opportunity to demonstrate reliability with both students. When remote therapy began, I was sure to call both students at the allotted time. Jane remained consistent with answering my calls while Alex refused. In fact, in a conversation with Alex's mother, he was in the background insisting that he did not need therapy and asserted his refusal to participate. Jane came to expect my calls at the same time and on the same days. Unfortunately, although I was reliable with Alex (i.e., calling him at our scheduled time), he nonetheless refused my calls which hindered his progression and interfered with the establishment of the holding environment.

Vocal Matching

Vocal matching is a topic that has been greatly researched in the context of the mother-infant relationship; it describes a communication between mother and infant that is "a nonintrusive way of helping the infant feel sensed" (Beebe 2010, p.0.22). Just as Winnicott's work drew a parallel between mother/infant and therapist/client, my approach with Jane used a similar type of matching to what has been shown effective in mother-infant communication. I was careful to match my tone of voice with hers as a way to connect with her. I attempted to match Alex's tone as well when we met in person. There were times when he showed excitement about his interests in animals and video games and other times where he expressed his anxiety about life and past experiences; I attempted to match my tone of voice with his in order to connect with him. I offered Jane and Alex my attention during session and was mindful to ensure that my tone of voice created a space for them to feel sensed.

Both Jane and Alex reserved a large part of themselves for themselves, often avoiding talking about topics relating to romantic relationships, past experiences, and incidents that would reveal their negative sides. When I broached such topics with Jane, she usually replied, "I don't want to talk about it." I respected her boundaries; however, I often mirrored back to her the feelings she was evincing, often sadness or depression and occasionally happiness, which she rarely admitted to feeling. I found that when I respected her expressed desire to not talk about a topic, but rather focused on the underlying feeling, the session tended to be productive. My mirroring her feelings often led to her opening up about them. Her eyes often welled up, and on several occasions, she commented, "I wore waterproof mascara today," or became giggly when a feeling of discomfort arose or was acknowledged. She sometimes apologized for crying. In a calm, empathic tone, I would respond, "I see that you are crying and that's OK." This response was often followed by further tears. Mirroring Jane's feelings was the start of our therapeutic relationship and was the very intervention that caused her to further open up. Remote therapy did not provide me with the same opportunity. Jane chose not to video chat and instead chose our sessions to be held over the phone. I was unable to look her in the eyes to mirror the expressions that often contradicted her words. Vocal matching, therefore, became more important; my attunement to her tone of voice created a space for her to feel sensed, which is important for creating the holding environment.

Presence

Being present was important, both over the phone and in person. In person, prior to distance learning, my sense of presence was maintained through consistent eye contact, stillness in body language, facial expressions, and follow-up responses to things said. I was careful not to look at the clock or answer phone calls during our session. As much as I was able to, I avoided answering the door when students knocked, instead offering a gesture letting them know that I was in session. There were times that I needed to answer the phone or a knock at the door, or be mindful of the time. Ideally, I would have rescheduled my appointment with Jane or attended to whatever the interruptions were prior to session, in order to avoid a disruption in my attention. I warned Jane and Alex about any interruptions that were known in advance, and if not known, I would apologize for the interruption.

I recognized that it was my responsibility to ensure that I was able to provide Jane and Alex with my undivided attention during remote therapy. I did this by doing my best to hold the session in a location free of interruptions. As a mother of an infant, however, some distractions were inevitable during a lockdown when normal child care options were not available. When sessions were interrupted by my son's crying or "happy sounds," I apologized and acknowledged the interruption: "That's the baby talking in the background." "I know, Cierra" and "No need to apologize" were Jane's usual responses, which demonstrated an understanding of the need for me to be present both for her and for my son. I further discuss these challenges in the next section.

Challenges of Remote Therapy

The COVID-19 pandemic was unexpected; students and staff alike were not prepared or equipped to engage in remote therapy. Forced to manage professional as well as personal matters, many social workers had to attend to family needs and be present with a child or loved one while also being present with their students. Other unusual challenges included ensuring confidentiality and securing a location within our homes to hold sessions. Furthermore, dealing with the personal effects of COVID-19 and living through it as a shared experience with our students, while offering hope to many students during a time that felt hopeless, proved difficult. Engulfed by many feelings, I appreciated the opportunity to work from the comfort of my home while also being able to spend time with my loved ones. However, I found that the situation was not always conducive to my work in the same way the office environment that I've grown accustomed to was conducive. Going into work provided a level of privacy that made it much easier to give my undivided attention to my students during session. At home, distractions were inevitable, and many required my instant attention, such as responding to the cry of my son. Additionally, I had grown accustomed to going to a student's classroom, cottage, or even checking in with them in the hallway when they missed session. Remote therapy did not provide that option.

My colleagues and I shared common concerns when sessions moved to teletherapy:

> students would not participate in therapy; there would be a regression in a student's behavior; and the once personal therapeutic relationship was now more impersonal. The physical distance between my students and me was sometimes mirrored by an emotional distance. Some students maintained a stoic affect over the phone, appeared agitated when I called,

and at times kept their responses to a minimum. Although I've attempted to create a holding environment with all of my students, I acknowledge the difficulty in establishing such a holding for many students in a remote therapy situation. Reasons included the lack of a preexisting therapeutic relationship, their dislike of talking on the phone, and experiencing boundaries being crossed when I called their cell phone, the usual mode of communication during remote therapy.

Such problems were particularly evident in the case of Alex. When sessions became remote, I found it difficult to maintain my drive to engage him. My efforts to contact him by phone became infrequent, the more so as he continued to refuse. I might have explored different ways of engaging him, be it through messaging him on Google hangouts, arranging a teletherapy session and inviting his parents to participate for additional support, or even continuing to call him at the time of our arranged sessions, rather than calling his parents. Creation of the holding environment was unsuccessful with Alex, in part because I did not maintain the practices outlined in this chapter to fidelity and in part because of his unwillingness to engage in therapy.

For some of my students, these issues (the lack of a therapeutic relationship, refusal to talk on the phone, and lack of willingness to engage in therapy) proved to be major obstacles in creating the holding environment, both in person and over the phone. In these cases, my "good enough" actions were, perhaps, not good enough, which points to the question of what constitutes "good enough" and how it might be gauged. Understanding that what may be "good enough" for one student can fail to move another is important, given their unique experiences and individual makeup. Perhaps my interactions with Jane were "good enough," and I was attuned enough for the holding environment to be established, which allowed for the successful implementation of the practices identified in this chapter.

Shared Trauma and the Holding Environment

Shared trauma is a term used to describe a collective traumatic occurrence simultaneously experienced between the therapist and client, affecting their thoughts, feelings, and actions (Tosone et al. 2012). School social workers, staff, and students experienced the coronavirus pandemic as a shared traumatic experience, as it impacted the well-being of staff and students alike. The shared trauma created opportunities for school social workers to create innovative therapeutic treatment approaches for working with students, which have led to sessions that were personal and intimate in nature. It also created mixed feelings within social workers (fear, anxiety, uncertainty), which I previously described and further addressed in this section. Such feelings should be acknowledged and attended to by school administrators as a way to be in tune with staff both personally and professionally.

The unexpectedness of the COVID-19 pandemic required workers to immediately shift from their "normal" lives to the unexpected reality of working remotely. Schools required workers to fulfill their work responsibilities without missing a beat, so to speak. We were expected to continue with our work responsibilities, frankly with limited to no acknowledgment or discussion of the emotional or psychological impact the situation had on us. It would have been preferable if more attention had been given to our potential for compassion fatigue, which Tosone et al. describe as "reactions to working with trauma survivors" pg. (2012, p. 232). Figley (1995) describes the long-term effects of compassion fatigue and its negative impact on employee work performance. This lack of acknowledgment and discussion can lead to employees feeling unprepared to return to their work environment and their general dissatisfaction with organizational responses (Bauwens and Tosone 2010). While COVID-19 may not have been a direct "physical happening" for most of us, its impact continues on our work environments and may cause feelings of stress, anxiety, and depression, including long-term effects on the mental well-being of clinicians (Tosone et al. 2012). School administrators should consider implementing a strategic approach for addressing feelings elicited from their employees by shared traumatic experiences such as the present pandemic and recent protests and social upheaval relating to the Black Lives Matter (BLM) movement, police violence, and inequality afflicting Black Americans.

As they weigh this strategic approach, school administrators should consider the impact of trauma experiences on both their employees and students from a perspective of shared trauma. Creating a holding environment for staff within school settings is crucial in the wake of shared trauma experiences. Any organizational response to addressing the anxieties of school staff should be supplemented with an offer of therapy that staff may benefit from, given the long-term effects of trauma experiences. Whatever its features, an administrative response to shared trauma experiences should be implemented, and the holding environment, which can be established by outsourced therapists, should be prioritized as an effective approach for staff experiencing the same trauma as the clients served. Such an approach can create a space for staff to feel safe enough to express their anxieties relating to the traumatic event and can, perhaps, decrease compassion fatigue and increase productivity, work ethic, and efficiency within the organization and in the service of students' needs.

Conclusion

The COVID-19 pandemic presented school social workers with opportunities to connect with students in new, technologically facilitated ways, be it via Zoom or Google Hangouts or over the phone. Though the change from face-to-face sessions came suddenly and unexpectedly, school social workers adapted to this "new norm" in the provision of services. Winnicott's concept of the holding environment proved relevant and successful in the case of my student Jane, both before and during COVID-19. Instead of retaliating or withdrawing from Jane when she displayed resistance to therapy, I remained consistent in efforts to engage her, showed reliability in various ways, mirrored her tone of voice and manner, and stayed present to her feelings. These efforts served as the foundation for the sense of safety and trust on which the holding environment can be established. Unfortunately, attempts to create a holding environment were not fruitful with Alex. Though I attempted to implement the practices outlined in this chapter to fidelity, I came across challenges that hindered my implementation, including Alex's lack of engagement in the program and my own loss of motivation as a result. Nonetheless, the holding environment should be considered as a useful treatment approach working with adolescents in person and by phone. The holding environment reflects the social worker's availability to the student and the student's need for a social worker's devotion to them and their unique needs.

School social workers are presented with many opportunities to "hold" students. These opportunities must be handled carefully, but they should always be considered valuable opportunities to build the therapeutic relationship. This approach can be used to engage adolescents in person and by phone; in either case, best practices center on consistency, reliability, presence, and mirroring/vocal matching, which foster the student's sense of trust and ultimately allow for the establishment and progression of the therapeutic relationship. School administrators should also consider implementing these best practices in order to create a holding environment for employees experiencing shared traumas. Implementation of the holding environment from an organization's administrative team, through the outsourcing of therapists, creates opportunities for relational experiences between administrators and employees to be established. Such experiences can provide opportunities for staff to feel safe enough to express their anxieties surrounding the traumatic event, thereby enhancing school staff's productivity and compassion in working with students.

References

Altman, N., Briggs, R., Frankel, J., Gensler, D., & Pantone, P. (2002). *Relational child psychotherapy*. Other Press.

Applegate, J. S. (1997). The holding environment: An organizing metaphor for social work theory and practice. *Smith College Studies in Social Work, 68*(1), 7–30.

Barak, A., & Grohol, J. M. (2011). Current and future trends in internet-supported mental health interventions. *Journal of Technology in Human Services, 29*(3), 155–196. https://doi.org/10.1080/15228835.2011.616939.

Bauwens, J., & Tosone, C. (2010). Professional posttraumatic growth after a shared traumatic experience: Manhattan clinicians' perspectives on post 9/11 practice. *Journal of Loss and Trauma, 15*(6), 498–517.

Beebe, B. (2010). Mother-infant research informs mother-infant treatment. *Clinical Social Work Journal, 38*(1), 17–36. https://doi.org/10.1007/s10615-009-0256-7.

Beeson, P. M., Higginson, K., Rising, K., & Oetting, J. (2013). Writing treatment for aphasia: A texting approach. *Journal of Speech, Language and Hearing Research, 56*(3), 945–955. https://doi.org/10.1044/1092-4388(2012/11-0360.

Chescheir, M. (1985). Some implications of Winnicott's concept for clinical practice. *Clinical Social Work Journal, 13*(3), 218–233.

Cuomo, A. M. (2020, March 16). *No. 202.4: Continuing temporary suspension and modification of laws relating to the disaster emergency.* Governor.ny. https://www.governor.ny.gov/news/no-2024-continuing-temporary-suspension-andmodification-laws-relating-disaster-emergency

Epstein, R. (2011). Distance therapy comes of age. *Scientific American Mind, 22*(2), 60–63. Governor Andrew M. Cuomo (2020, June 1). Governor Andrew M. Cuomo. Retrieved from https://www.governor.ny.gov/.

Figley, C. R. (Ed.). (1995). *Compassion fatigue: Coping with secondary traumatic stress disorder in those who treat the traumatized.* New York: Brunner Mazel.

Lanyado, M. (1996). Winnicott's children: The holding environment and therapeutic communication in brief and non-intensive work. *Journal of Child Psychotherapy, 22*(3), 423–443.

Strauss, V. (2020, April, 4). School districts, including New York City's, start banning zoom because of online security issues. *The Washington Post.* https://www.washingtonpost.com/education/2020/04/04/school-districts-including-newyork-citys-start-banning-zoom-because-online-security-issues/

Tosone, C., Nuttman-Shwartz, O., & Stephens, T. (2012). Shared trauma: When the professional is personal. *Clinical Social Work Journal, 40*, 231–239.

Wilson, J. (2011). Texting patients could breach confidentiality. *Pulse, 71*(37), 12.

Winnicott, D. W. (1956). Primary maternal preoccupation. In *Through pediatrics to psycho – analysis* (pp. 300–305). New York: Basic Books.

Wright, B. M. (1992). Treatment of infants and their families. In J. R. Brandell (Ed.), *Countertransference in psychotherapy with children & adolescents* (pp. 127–139). Jason Aronson Inc.

Zelechoski, A. D., Sharma, R., Beserra, K., Miguel, J. L., DeMarco, M., & Spinazzola, J. (2013). Traumatized youth in residential treatment settings: Prevalence, clinical presentation, treatment, and policy implications. *Journal of Family Violence, 28*, 639–652.

Chapter 17
Autism in the COVID-19 Pandemic: Reflecting on Loss and Resilience

Samantha Fuld

For several years now, I have had a complicated relationship with the concept of resilience. Resilience can be defined as the ability to withstand and perhaps even grow from challenging circumstances or to have a better-than-expected outcome (Szatmari 2018; Sinclair and Wallston 2004). We all encounter struggles in life, though our positionality – the aspects of our identity that allow us privilege or are subject to marginalization – has a significant impact on the intensity and frequency of the struggles we encounter. This means that some of us are forced to be more resilient than others. The current global COVID-19 pandemic has only enhanced this dynamic.

It makes sense that as social workers, we like the idea of resilience. It is strengths-oriented. It offers a sense of hope both for us and for our clients, a belief that we have the strength to persevere. It is an essential ingredient in recovery (Hobbs and Baker 2012). Yet in my role at a university where we are charged with preparing students to be competent, anti-oppressive social work practitioners, I worry at times that we place too much emphasis on resilience. Much of our role, at least in clinical social work, is helping people maintain and strengthen resilience. We offer support and work to help our clients enhance coping skills in the face of challenging circumstances. However, I often caution students that this orientation toward individual resilience can have the unintended consequence of complacency. Challenging circumstances are virtually always the result of or enhanced by structures of oppression: racism, ableism, sexism, heterosexism, ageism, classism, etc. COVID-19 has been no exception. The pandemic itself may be a biological and environmental phenomenon, but the response in the United States reflects the American cultural emphasis on individualism. Such an orientation allowed this pandemic to grow,

S. Fuld (✉)
University of Maryland School of Social Work, Baltimore, MD, USA
e-mail: samantha.fuld@ssw.umaryland.edu

© The Author(s), under exclusive license to Springer Nature Switzerland   157
AG 2021
C. Tosone (ed.), *Shared Trauma, Shared Resilience During a Pandemic*,
Essential Clinical Social Work Series,
https://doi.org/10.1007/978-3-030-61442-3_17

disproportionality harming communities of color and those groups of people most impacted by the *isms* that are deeply embedded in the American social fabric. It is not acceptable that some people must beat the odds in order to survive. Yet, especially now, that is often our role: to help them survive and try to thrive through the challenges. Resilience offers hope, but it also comes with baggage. As a social work field, we cannot lose sight of this reality.

While we are all sharing the impacts of this pandemic, we are not all forced to be equally resilient. Our positionality dictates the risk factors and protections that foster resilience (Kapilashrami and Hankivsky 2018). My own field of practice and scholarship has been working to address the mental health needs of autistic people.[1] Resilience has been a requirement for this community, long before the pandemic. You must be resilient to live as autistic, operating in a society that does not inherently welcome neurodiversity or difference. Fiorillo and Gorwood (2020) note that people "who are already vulnerable to biological and psychosocial stressors" (p. 1) are one group most at risk for suffering adverse mental health consequences as a result of the current pandemic. For most autistic people, the shifts necessitated by COVID-19 only add to the life stressors requiring resilience. This struggle is further exacerbated if an autistic person belongs to other marginalized identity groups, experiencing the impacts of racism, classism, etc. in addition to ableism.

Autism, Mental Health, and COVID-19

COVID-19 has brought about a mental health crisis or what Mortazavi et al. (2020) describe as a "psychiatric pandemic" (p. 225) that is only likely to grow as the new post-COVID reality continues over the course of months, if not years. Autistic people were already experiencing high rates of mental health struggles prior to the COVID-19 pandemic, while having limited access to clinicians trained to identify and offer clinical services to address these struggles which are often incorrectly dismissed as an inevitable part of an autism diagnosis (Fuld 2018). Historically, social work has relied on a medical model of understanding autism spectrum disorder (ASD) rather than interrogating the social structures which require conforming to certain neurological and social ways of being and interacting with the world (Meekosha and Dowse 2007; Roulstone 2012; Fuld 2019). As a result, our clinical treatment models are primarily behavioral – focused on helping an autistic person alter their behavior to look more like society's expectation of normal. This critique is not to say that the ability to *fit in* cannot improve someone's quality of life, but what is often missed is the validation and support of one's identity. We know that validation is central to developing positive self-esteem and overall well-being for

---

[1] In this chapter, I am using identity-first language to describe autistic people. This choice in language is based on the recommendation of the Autistic Self Advocacy Network (n.d.). I want to acknowledge that this may not represent the choice that every autistic person or person with autism spectrum disorder may be most comfortable with in describing their identity.

the client and a hallmark of good practice for social workers. Discussing the impact of COVID-19, self-advocate Amy Louise Simmons (2020) speaks to this describing, "our lives are restricted by marginalisation, which is veiled by the social deficit model of autism and misinterpreted as the inevitable outcome of impaired social communication, and impaired social interaction" (p. 1011). In sharing this insight, Simmons (2020) makes the point that social distancing is not new for many autistic people. It has been an imperative because our sociopolitical structures create a context where autistic people face "overstimulation, social-exclusion, and stigma" (p. 1011). As social workers, if we are not attuned to this reality, we risk amplifying this experience and disaffirming autistic identity.

Research on implicit bias (Banaji et al. 2015) has been relatively clear: when we are tired, stressed, overwhelmed, or overworked, we tend to slip in our ability to intervene on unconscious bias. As social workers, we all are impacted by unconscious bias as a result of living in an ableist society with little recognition for and support of neurodiversity. In working with autistic people, this often plays out as an emphasis on behavioral goals and strategies that work toward *normalcy*, emphasize the goals of others (caregivers, schools, residential staff, etc.), and take an overly diagnostic, deficit-oriented approach in understanding ASD. As a result of COVID-19, autistic people, having already been struggling with mental health, might experience an exacerbation in symptoms (Centers for Disease Control and Prevention 2020) as they work to adjust to a world that is so off-balance. At the same time, social workers are sharing this trauma of a world unexpectedly altered. Many of us are facing significant losses in our own lives, while simultaneously needing to be emotionally present to support others who are struggling. This shared traumatic experience creates a perfect scenario for enacting bias in our work: we are stressed, anxious, and overwhelmed ourselves as we try to maintain well-being in an unwell social context. Meanwhile, our clients' needs are likely to be greater than ever before. Acknowledgment is meaningful in preventing this dynamic. We must be mindful and use our own experiences, our own sense of instability, to build empathy and relate to autistic people with a shared sense of humanity and understanding of the depth of trauma a pandemic like COVID-19 has caused.

We are in uncharted territory here. There is little research on supporting mental health and well-being in autistic people and none yet that could address effective ways to do this during the current pandemic. Understanding the significant impact such events are likely to have on this group of people, many of whom were already struggling, can offer some guidance for social workers to be effective advocates, supports, and allies in this pandemic.

Acknowledging Trauma and Loss

Several government agencies, nonprofit organizations, and scholars have offered guidance for supporting autistic people struggling with the impacts of COVID-19 (Centers for Disease Control and Prevention 2020; Frankova 2020; Narzisi 2020;

National Autistic Society 2020). Most of these recommendations focus on establishing structure and routine, as well as behavioral mechanisms for stress reduction such as avoiding news outlets and setting up a relaxing (or sensory-friendly) physical space. These suggestions are helpful, but I worry that in all the focus on behavior management and regaining *normality*, we miss the emotional component of the current experience. As a result of an unconscious ableist bias, I believe we have a tendency to reduce this group of people to merely a set of behaviors rather than understanding the psychological and more importantly the emotional basis of those behaviors. A 2017 report on autistic people's reactions to behavioral interventions sponsored by Autistic Self Advocacy Network (ASAN) and the Office of Developmental Primary Care at the University of California, San Francisco, speaks to this. The personal narratives contained in this report emphasize that there is a focus among therapists and professionals (including social workers) on changing appearance rather than promoting well-being, working toward identity-affirmative coping strategies, and maintaining sensitivity to the trauma many autistic people face growing up in a neurotypical-centric world.

Nyatanga (2020) emphasizes the importance of acknowledging the multiple losses associated with COVID-19 that each of us has experienced (or will experience) as a result of this virus and its impact on our lives. ASD is often characterized in part by a need for routine. Many autistic people have spent years working to find a place in their communities, find routine, and find stability. Expressing resulting sense of loss may be challenging as some autistic people have great difficulty with verbal communication, especially around social and emotional experiences. It is critical that as social workers and fellow humans we see grief for what it is and not let it get lost and labeled as merely "behavior." In that label, we risk losing the true meaning and communication behind the actions we observe and also the humanity and the shared experience.

I have previously written about the lack of evidence-supported frameworks for trauma-informed clinical care for autistic people (Fuld 2018). Acknowledging this issue and working with the knowledge we currently have, I have suggested that clinicians can utilize the Substance Abuse and Mental Health Services Administration's (SAMHSA) six principles of trauma-informed care (2014) to guide practice in this realm (Fuld 2020). The themes of this model include establishing safety; being consistent, trustworthy, honest, and transparent; finding opportunities for peer support or identity-affirmative role models; using a stance of collaboration and mutuality; shifting power dynamics to promote self-expression and choice; and staying attuned to the impact of culture, ableism, and other intersectional aspects of oppression. While these themes do not offer a clear roadmap for social workers, they do provide a therapeutic stance that will be essential in addressing the impact of COVID-19 on mental health in autistic people. Keeping these principles in mind can guide us in seeing beyond the behavior and structuring interventions that address the loss and trauma that is both acute and cumulative for the autistic community.

Resilient Coping

While resilience has been a popular field of study in the social sciences recently, there is a dearth of research on supporting resilience in autistic people (Szatmari 2018). Research associated with resilience and ASD has explored ways to support resilience among family members and caregivers, but resilience in the individual is often overlooked in favor of a behavioral focus. This oversight misses a potential strength: the term perseverate is commonly used in reference to autistic people when describing the propensity for repetition and/or a singular intense focus on routine or on a particular topic. It is often used with a negative clinical connotation by professionals, but the term perseverate is directly related to perseverance, and perseverance is something we likely all need to cope in this pandemic.

Kocalevent et al. (2017) discuss the concept of *resilient coping*. Resilient coping refers to one's skills for managing challenging situations in an adaptive way that allows for positive outcomes and potential growth (Sinclair and Wallston 2004). Sinclair and Wallston (2004) developed the Brief Resilient Coping Scale, which measures four characteristics indicative of resilient coping: ingenuity in adapting to challenging circumstances, confidence in one's ability to control their reaction to challenging circumstances, a belief that positive growth can come from challenging circumstances, and an ability to recalibrate following loss. These features, which are mostly cognitive, might provide some clinical guidance for social workers looking to support autistic clients in strengthening resilient coping skills during the COVID-19 pandemic. This framework resonates for me as having potential in our current sociopolitical context because of its emphasis on adapting not just behaviorally, but also psychologically to this new post-COVID environment and addressing the experience of loss.

Final Thoughts

There are many additional questions that arise when thinking about the impact of a COVID-19 era on autistic people that seem important to pose even if they cannot yet be answered: What does social distancing mean for people who typically struggle in social situations? Could the adoption of new forms of communication that allow physical distance create space for neurodiverse ways of relating and connecting in our communities? There are still so many unknowns. Our increased reliance on technology for work and socialization could make both communal and professional spaces more accessible and less anxiety-provoking for some autistic people. Conversely, it could also enhance the challenge of reading social cues. An autistic person may need to learn a whole new set of unspoken norms (often referred to as the hidden curriculum) for these newer forms of social interaction.

It is also important that as social workers we understand that difficulty with social communication does not mean that most autistic people do not want close social relationships and connection (den Houting 2020). Many struggle to create those connections but want them very much, which can foster a sense of isolation that is likely to be heightened by the social distance of COVID-19. Certainly, this sense of isolation and loss is shared among all of us. In working with autistic people during and after the COVID-19 pandemic, I am hopeful that we as social workers will tap into this sense of shared trauma, shared loss, and shared resilience. The acknowledgment and empathy that come from this shared experience have real potential to address the ableism that has existed in social work's adherence to a medicalized understanding of ASD.

References

Autistic Self Advocacy Network. (n.d.). *Identity first language.* https://autisticadvocacy.org/about-asan/identity-first-language/

Banaji, M. R., Bhaskar, R., & Brownstein, M. (2015). When bias is implicit, how might we think about repairing harm? *Current Opinion in Psychology, 6,* 183–188. https://doi.org/10.1016/j.copsyc.2015.08.017.

Centers for Disease Control and Prevention. (2020, May 27). *Coronavirus disease 2019 (COVID-19): People with developmental and behavioral disorders.* https://www.cdc.gov/coronavirus/2019-ncov/need-extra-precautions/people-with-developmental-behavioral-disabilities.html

den Houting, J. (2020). Stepping out of isolation: Autistic people and COVID-19. *Autism in Adulthood, 2*(2), 103–105. https://doi.org/10.1089/aut.2020.29012.jdh.

Fiorillo, A., & Gorwood, P. (2020). The consequences of the COVID-19 pandemic on mental health and implications for clinical practice. *European Psychiatry, 63*(1), 1–2. https://doi.org/10.1192/j.eurpsy.2020.35.

Frankova, H. (2020). The impact of COVID-19 on people with autism, learning disabilities and mental health conditions. *Nursing and Residential Care, 22*(6), 1–3. https://doi.org/10.12968/nrec.2020.22.6.10.

Fuld, S. (2018). Autism spectrum disorder: The impact of stressful and traumatic life events and implications for clinical practice. *Clinical Social Work Journal, 46*(3), 210–219. https://doi.org/10.1007/s1061.

Fuld, S. (2019). De-marginalizing intellectual and developmental disabilities in graduate social work education. *Journal of Social Work Education.* Advance online publication. https://doi.org/10.1080/10437797.2019.1656584.

Fuld, S. (2020). ASD, trauma, and coordinated care. In M. B. McClain, J. D. Shahidullah, & K. R. Mezher (Eds.), *Interprofessional care coordination for pediatric autism spectrum disorder: Translating research into practice* (pp. 325–339). Springer. https://doi.org/10.1007/978-3-030-46295-6_21.

Hobbs, M., & Baker, M. (2012). Hope for recovery–how clinicians may facilitate this in their work. *Journal of Mental Health, 21*(2), 144–153. https://doi.org/10.3109/09638237.2011.648345.

Kapilashrami, A., & Hankivsky, O. (2018). Intersectionality and why it matters to global health. *The Lancet, 391*(10140), 2589–2591. https://doi.org/10.1016/S0140-6736(18)31431-4.

Kocalevent, R. D., Zenger, M., Hinz, A., Klapp, B., & Brähler, E. (2017). Resilient coping in the general population: Standardization of the brief resilient coping scale (BRCS). *Health and Quality of Life Outcomes, 15*(1), 251–259. https://doi.org/10.1186/s12955-017-0822-6.

Meekosha, H., & Dowse, L. (2007). Integrating critical disability studies into social work education and practice: An Australian perspective. *Practice, 19*(3), 169–183. https://doi.org/10.1080/09503150701574267.

Mortazavi, S. S., Assari, S., Alimohamadi, A., Rafiee, M., & Shati, M. (2020). Fear, loss, social isolation, and incomplete grief due to COVID-19: A recipe for a psychiatric pandemic. *Basic and Clinical Neuroscience, 11*(2), 225–232. https://doi.org/10.32598/bcn.11.covid19.2549.1.

Narzisi, A. (2020). Handle the autism spectrum condition during coronavirus (COVID-19) stay at home period: Ten tips for helping parents and caregivers of young children. *Brain Sciences, 10*(4), 207–210. https://doi.org/10.3390/brainsci10040207.

National Autistic Society. (2020). *Tips for autistic people and families.* https://www.autism.org.uk/services/helplines/coronavirus/resources/tips.aspx

Nyatanga, B. (2020). Impact of COVID-19 on loss and grief: A personal lens. *British Journal of Community Nursing, 25*(6), 306–307. https://doi.org/10.12968/bjcn.2020.25.6.306.

Office of Developmental Primary Care & Autistic Self Advocacy Network. (2017). *First-hand perspectives on behavioral interventions for autistic people and people with other developmental disabilities.* https://autisticadvocacy.org/wp-content/uploads/2017/05/Behavioral-Interventions-Report-Final.pdf

Roulstone, A. (2012). 'Stuck in the middle with you': Towards enabling social work with disabled people. *Social Work Education, 31*(2), 142–154. https://doi.org/10.1080/02615479.2012.644942.

Simmons, A. L. (2020). COVID-19 social distancing: A snippet view of the autistic social world. *Disability & Society, 35*(6), 1007–1011. https://doi.org/10.1080/09687599.2020.1774866.

Sinclair, V. G., & Wallston, K. A. (2004). The development and psychometric evaluation of the brief resilient coping scale. *Assessment, 11*(1), 94–101. https://doi.org/10.1177/1073191103258144.

Substance Abuse and Mental Health Services Administration. (2014). *SAMHSA's concept of trauma and guidance for a trauma-informed approach.* Rockville, MD: Substance Abuse and Mental Health Services Administration.

Szatmari, P. (2018). Risk and resilience in autism spectrum disorder: A missed translational opportunity? *Developmental Medicine & Child Neurology, 60*(3), 225–229. https://doi.org/10.1111/dmcn.13588.

Part III
Practice Perspectives, Innovations, and Impact on Social Work Practice

Chapter 18
The Impact of the COVID-19 Pandemic on the Relational World of the Patient-Clinician Dyad: Obstacles and Opportunities

Constance Catrone

The COVID-19 pandemic has created a traumatogenic environment across our country and the globe. This unfolding and unpredictable public health crisis has reverberated throughout our society and communities, upending institutions and challenging social and cultural norms. Early on, van der Kolk (2020) shared his view that the pandemic's traumatic impact upon the American public is exacerbated by leadership's failure to provide predictability and trust, thus contributing to one's feeling of vulnerability and helplessness. In exploring the impact of this collective trauma, it is necessary to consider the sociocultural and political environment in which this devastating health crisis is unfolding.

This chapter assumes a relational lens to explore how this pandemic and the ensuing upheaval in our major institutions and daily lives affect the practice of clinical social work. Several clinical concepts facilitate this examination: therapeutic frame, holding environment, embodiment, self-object functions, self-regulation, and intersubjectivity. The purpose is to explore how the traumatogenic context of COVID-19 challenges the structure and process of the treatment relationship and how this challenge benefits or undermines the treatment experience of client and clinician.

This chapter reflects several practice issues that have emerged and challenged me during this period of collective trauma. These include the following: How does the shared trauma experience of my patients and me affect the therapeutic relationship? What does it mean and how does it affect our work that our bodies are not in the same room due to meeting via telehealth? Is the holding environment *holding and*

C. Catrone (✉)
Silver School of Social Work, New York University, New York, NY, USA

Southern Connecticut State University, New Haven, CT, USA
e-mail: catronec1@southernct.edu

© The Author(s), under exclusive license to Springer Nature Switzerland AG 2021
C. Tosone (ed.), *Shared Trauma, Shared Resilience During a Pandemic*, Essential Clinical Social Work Series,
https://doi.org/10.1007/978-3-030-61442-3_18

containing as well over a screen as it does in the office? I will explore each of these issues through case material, personal reflection, and discussion.

The trauma literature provides a framework to navigate these uncertain times and this new territory. These include compassion fatigue (Figley 2002), shared trauma (Tosone et al. 2012), collective trauma (Hirschberger 2018), secondary traumatic stress (Stamm 1995), vicarious trauma (Saakvitne 2002), and shared traumatic reality (Baum 2010). The current pandemic shares many characteristics described by Tosone et al. (2012) and Baum (2010). Most notably, we share with our patients the threat of illness and death. Further, with public health recommendations and executive orders prescribing stay-at-home orders and self-quarantining, we share the loss of social connection, anxiety about the future, and significant upheaval in the rhythm and routine of our daily lives. When conducting psychotherapy with our patients, we are likely to experience subjective states and countertransference feelings that are affectively charged and dysregulating.

The current collective trauma has characteristics that distinguish it from other experiences, disasters, and catastrophes. First, while the pandemic has reached into all our communities, its impact is mediated by sociocultural factors such as race, age. and socioeconomic status (Centers for Disease Control and Prevention [CDC] 2020). The disproportionate risk to Black and Brown individuals has exposed major health, social, and economic inequities. These revelations have become part of our shared traumatic reality. Second, this pandemic is not an event as much as it is an unfolding, unpredictable threat to our safety and security. The impact of living with a continuous threat such as the coronavirus seems more akin to chronic trauma or the threat of terrorism. Third, there is no end in sight.

My Personal Trauma Narrative

My experience of this health crisis has been mediated by my age, a risk factor, and my status, a protective factor. I feel quite grateful to be healthy and economically secure. This pandemic has underscored the power and privilege of my whiteness. Concurrently, anxiety regarding my risk status and that of those dear to me is chronic. The continual warnings regarding the risk of COVID-19 for those over 60 years of age confronted me with my mortality and physical vulnerability for the first time. This age-related self-consciousness was and is exacerbated by the now increased reliance on technology that has entered my professional and personal life. The generational divide between the young and old is quite apparent in this age of Zoom meetings, Doxy sessions, and FaceTime calls. Conducting any type of relationship over a screen is alien to me personally, let alone as a professional caregiver.

Given these stressors, I found myself questioning life choices and doubting my commitment to continued work. I asked myself, "What am I doing with my remaining years? Am I too old for this?" Despite decades of experience, I feel like a novice. These feelings of vulnerability, questions regarding my worth professionally, and anxiety about a forestalled future have become the backdrop of my personal and professional self. The last several months have been a personal exercise in managing grief and social isolation. The loss of connection and intimacy with others has been challenging. I especially miss being with my patients face to face. Little did I realize how much our shared embodiment gratified me! Yet, these subjective experiences are now part of what I bring to the treatment relationship.

The Therapeutic Frame

Cherry and Gold (1989) elaborate the importance of the therapeutic frame for the clinician. I have found the disruption to my usual way of working a challenge. I have learned, to my surprise, how reliant I am on the structural aspect of conducting my practice. Activities such as driving to the office and having that 20 min of travel time to prepare psychologically and to transition from my personal self to my professional self and vice versa are very grounding. I continue to maintain my routine of time, space, and separateness from my personal life, though I am now in my office alone with my screen. Apparently, these rituals serve as an important component of my holding environment by supporting my self-regulation and sense of agency. In addition, I miss the simple rituals of waiting for, greeting, and meeting patients in the waiting room. These have been exchanged for the sending of Zoom and Doxy invitations and a click of the mouse upon beginning and ending the hour.

The conceptualization of the therapeutic frame, the relational context in which psychotherapy occurs, has undergone considerable analysis, reconsideration, and adaptation since its original formulation by Freud (Cherry and Gold 1989). Widely embraced by therapists representing a variety of clinical approaches, the concept of frame includes both structural and relational components. Structural components include timing, payment, setting, and mutually agreed upon expectations regarding the parameters of the relationship. Relational components include confidentiality, ethics, and self-disclosure as components of one's therapeutic stance. The structural and relational components of the therapeutic frame provide safety, predictability, and continuity for both patient and clinician. Well-established elements of the frame include neutrality, abstinence, and anonymity (Cherry and Gold 1989). In the last several decades, therapist interpretation of these therapeutic attitudes has shifted and evolved to include a variety of practices and reinterpretations to allow for increased self-disclosure and flexibility.

Given the shelter at home order, psychotherapists and their patients were required to co-create a structure that enabled the work of the therapeutic dyad. For most therapists who had been conducting an office-based practice, this required an administrative redesign. We shifted from meeting with clients face-to-face to a telehealth meeting format within a few days. The anxiety, confusion, and insecurity of this shift was well illustrated by the hundreds of e-mail messages, webinars, and informational alerts filling our in-boxes from colleagues, professional organizations, and third-party payers. As professional helpers, we were driven and preoccupied by our commitment to our patients. On a personal level, I and others found it grounding and reassuring to continue our work – one shred of the normalcy of pre-pandemic life. Even so, the necessary administrative adaptations were accompanied by feelings of insecurity and uncertainty. Would patients continue? Would insurance companies pay equitably? Can I do this?

As van der Kolk (2020) observed, in this accommodation to the pandemic, we lost agency and control over our professional lives, while simultaneously managing a threat to our health and those of our loved ones. Once the structural dimension of the therapeutic frame was established and agreed upon, our attention shifted to mastering a new medium through which the holding environment could be sustained. Flexibility and humor have been essential. I have reevaluated the therapeutic frame with many patients, attempting to accommodate their developmental, relational, and social needs. I have met with clients who are in their cars parked at a Wi-Fi hot spot, with adolescents whispering because they're afraid their parents will hear them, and with an adult woman who let me know that there were rainbows (pixels) over my head as I shared (what I thought was) a very wise interpretation.

Impact Upon the Holding Environment

Several scholars (Baum 2010; Tosone et al. 2012) have identified shared trauma as contributing a unique dimension to the relational world of the therapist-client relationship. During the pandemic, I have experienced shared trauma as an added real and psychological dimension to the holding environment of the therapeutic relationship. The concept of holding environment (Winnicott 1986) is derived from the archetype of the early maternal-child relationship and the provision of good-enough parenting. Throughout my career, I have found this concept to be a guiding principle in my work with children, adults, and families. In considering the relevance of this concept as a guide for practice during the pandemic, I was and am heartened that the Winnicott's thinking about this relational dimension of development and healing emerged from their work during a collective trauma, World War II (Applegate 1997). Though their writings do not explicitly explore the impact of the war upon them, they were managing a dual exposure to trauma.

Winnicott's (1986) early conception of a holding environment portends the need for change and adaptation. Winnicott describes how the infant's needs are met and adapted to by the mother: The care "is not mechanical… It is reliable in a way that implies the mother's empathy" (p. 245). Ogden (2004) stresses the changing functions of holding as a means of accommodating and facilitating the individual's emerging sense of self. These principles have guided me through this pandemic.

Tosone (2011), in describing her clinical experience post-9/11, refers to a "leveling experience" (p. 26) within the therapeutic relationship. The experience of a shared trauma exposes one's vulnerability and fears both to oneself and one's patients. Saakvitne (2002) noted that the frame of psychotherapeutic works shifts when the therapist's vulnerability is revealed to the patient. Anonymity is not possible with this change. Boundaries are loosened, and therapist neutrality seems withholding and inauthentic.

From the Office to the Screen: Furthering the Mind-Body Split

The opportunity to meet with patients over a video platform or audio call has allowed the therapeutic work to continue uninterrupted. The chance to maintain the connections with our patients, and for our patients to be able to access treatment during this crisis, has been an extraordinary benefit to both therapist and patient. Many clinicians have recently extolled the benefits of working on a screen: improved access, convenience, a lens into patients' personal lives, and inclusion of other family members, including pets.

Challenges are imposed upon the intersubjective sphere of the treatment when the relationship is mediated through a computer screen. In a recent interview, Sherry Turkle (Chakrabarti and Martin 2020) notes that connection through screen is "efficient;" yet, relationships are "messy." Todd Essig, in a YouTube video presented by the American Psychoanalytic Association (2020), cautions that "telepresence" is distinctly different from "actual presence." The following section explores one major aspect of this difference: the absence of shared embodiment.

Shared Embodiment as a Component of the Intersubjective Sphere of Treatment

Schore (2012), a developmental researcher, enjoins clinicians to "get the body in the room." Drayson (2009) identified embodiment as an essential component of clinical practice. Clinicians have embraced the observation that the mind is embedded in a body that communicates nonverbally and nonconsciously. Body language is no longer a communication only from patient to therapist; rather, the bodies of the patient and the therapist communicate reciprocally through gesture, subtle shifts in gaze, and head nods. With the discovery of mirror neurons, Lehrer (2018) has shed light on the neurobiological basis of embodied communication. Bodies communicate with each other, and this unconscious synchrony contributes to feelings of well-being (Galbusera et al. 2019). As clinicians, we are trained to take it all in, the posturing, the facial tensions, and the subtle shifts. We respond with our own unconscious movements that communicate understanding, empathy, and interest. The Boston Change Project (Boston Change Process Study Group 2018) describes this dimension of our intersubjective connection with our patients as living "in the bodily experiences of others as we interact with them or even merely observe them" (p. 301).

America is a body-conscious society. The pandemic has affected our experience of our own and others' bodies. Pre-pandemic, our bodies were easily categorized: healthy or ill, able or disabled, old or young, attractive or unattractive, and white or non-white. The pandemic has leveled this playing field (Tosone et al. 2012). We are all physically at risk, albeit some more than others. Others' bodies are now perceived as threatening, so we must socially distance. Do not get too close and no touching. A cough and throat clearing have assumed new meaning. Where once these involuntary acts invited others to lean in with concern, now they move away.

In this context, our inability to invite our patients' bodies into our offices and to sit with each other's bodies represents a loss and a challenge to the intersubjective sphere. While we are capable of "holding" the patients' minds, we are not able to hold their bodies. An 8-year-old patient brought this challenge to my attention during a telehealth session. As we were meeting on a video chat, the screen began to move around her room. When I asked what was happening, she explained that she decided to do some pushups while we talked. I joined her, doing pushups while we talked.

Children's relationship to their bodies is quite different than adults'. This child's body, quite directly, was a means of self-regulation and mastery. Eventually, during the pandemic, we transitioned to outdoor walks while wearing face masks. As she climbed on a stone wall, she explained that by engaging in these somewhat challenging activities, her mind was occupied and she did not have to think about her worries.

An Actual and a Virtual Holding Environment

In late February I began assessing D,[1] a 17-year-old Caucasian male who presented with depressive symptoms, ruminating thoughts, low self-worth, and depressed mood. After two in-person sessions, we shifted to telehealth sessions, a very comfortable medium for him given his proficiency with computers and technology and interest in becoming a software designer. In late March I received a referral for J, a 20-year-old Latinx-Caucasian male who experienced low self-worth, poor sleep, low energy, and depressed mood. This young man chose to wait until we could meet in person. Our first in-person meeting was delayed until mid-May, when phase II of coronavirus shelter-in-place orders allowed for offices to open with precautions.

Working with these two young men who present with similarities developmentally, share symptoms, and struggle with the social losses of the coronavirus has provided an opportunity to consider how the differing delivery systems of psychotherapy mediate both the therapeutic relationship with each and the therapy experience for both of us.

---

[1] All clients' names and other personal identifiers in this chapter have been altered to protect privacy and confidentiality.

Both young men are bright and introspective. D relies on intellectualization to manage his feelings and has difficulty letting me in to his inner world. Instead, he independently processes his difficulties and shares the metabolized analysis with me. I can intrude on this and join him in this processing, but he ultimately feels quite dysregulated and withdraws from our work. As the younger of two successful boys, his early development seemed to lack appropriate mirroring and idealizing from his parents. He presents as isolated and psychologically cutoff from them and their "holding."

J, a very sociable and sensitive young man who writes poetry and is pursuing an art degree, has failed to meet his expectations for social acceptance, belonging, and leadership. He sees himself positively but is disappointed that he was not as success-ful socially and romantically at college as he "should" have been. He is the older of two children in a family where he is clearly the apple of his mother's eye.

In retrospect it seems quite understandable to me that J needed to be in the office. He is a very physical young man. He is very connected to his body as an expression of his identity. He is aware that he is attractive and views himself as a good athlete. He needed to be seen and heard in his entirety. Our actual presence provides an enlivened holding environment that supports his sense of self and where his need to be mirrored positively facilitates his self-reflection and growth. I believe that he rightly knew that a virtual environment would not hold him adequately.

D's relationship to his body is quite different. He sees himself as fat, unattractive, and unathletic. This negative self-perception fuels his poor self-esteem, self-consciousness, and social isolation. Without an embodied component to our work, I have only been able to know how he thinks about what he *had* been feeling. And, I have no ability to respond to the physical dimension of his self. I cannot even see his body. There is an absence of intimacy in this virtual relationship that I feel would have benefitted from having both our bodies in the room. As I have come to know D as a bright, very appealing young man, I believe that the holding environment pro-vided cannot hold all his needs, longings, and wishes. This deficiency undermines the safety of the relationship, and he is left feeling overwhelmed and affectively dysregulated by our sessions.

These two young men are managing painful affect, complicated family, and social relationships and trying to construct a healthy sense of self. J seems clear that his self is represented through his body and mind and both need to be experienced in his therapy. D's experience of his body is full of pain and loathing, and the treat-ment frame has mirrored his overvaluing of his intellect over his body and a seem-ing devaluing or lack of integration of his physical self in his attempt to construct a healthy sense of self.

Boundary Alterations with an Ongoing Psychotherapy Patient

Baum (2010) describes the impact of a shared trauma upon patient-therapist dyads when a collective trauma occurs within the context of an ongoing therapeutic relationship. Boundaries may be blurred (Tosone 2011; Tosone and Bialkin 2003). Patients may experience and express concern for the therapist's well-being (Gelso 2002). The following case material represents one of the most intimate therapeutic encounters that I have experienced with a patient. My increased vulnerability due to health concerns as well as the sociopolitical context enhanced our connection, causing me to think about her outside of session and to anticipate her reaction to unfolding events.

T is a middle-aged, African American woman, a retired police detective. She is married to a man, raising two sons, and very involved in her grandson's life. She began treatment approximately 1 year prior to the pandemic for help with her depression and suicidal thoughts. T is a highly intelligent, compassionate individual who joined the police force to provide service to her community. While she loved the role of helping others and solving problems, she holds much resentment toward the force, where she witnessed corruption, and was the victim of sexist and racist treatment and biased policies. Her inability to trust her fellow officers and the system is best evidenced in her decision to work alone, without a partner. In this way, she shielded herself from other officers' unacceptable behavior and their expectation that she would support them unquestioningly.

Her retirement after 23 years on the force was the result of injuries incurred on the job that left her with chronic medical problems, as well as a significant history of trauma. Because of these physical problems, her body is a frequent topic of our attention. Pain, the inability to get out of bed some mornings, the loss of physicality and strength, and the side effects from medications represent significant losses to her. Her discomfort is quite visible to me in the sessions.

She had experienced several quite frightening events as a police detective. She described unflinchingly running "toward the danger," explaining, "That's what we're trained to do." She described dangerous patrol assignments in housing projects where there was only one entry and exit, thus increasing one's vulnerability when a problem arose. She described a particularly painful and sad experience that occurred early in her career. This event has emerged as a "model scene" (Lichtenberg 2001) because she and I would return to this event as an exemplar of her real and subjective experience representative of her helplessness, isolation, and oppression.

She was called to assist another officer who had apprehended a suspect. When she arrived, the officer in charge and two other officers had subdued the suspect. The suspect, a young African American male, was face down with hands handcuffed behind his back. The officer in charge had his knee on the suspect's neck, and the suspect was yelling that he "couldn't breathe." T registered the officer's disregard for this young man and intervened, telling the officer, "You can take your knee off his back. He's cooperating." The officer responded with expletives and accused her of interfering. This scene led to a series of complaints by T of the arresting officer and by the arresting officer about T's interference. Ultimately, neither were reprimanded, and there was no finding of wrongdoing for either of them. In her telling of this story, she directly expressed limited affect. It was an event – one of many. However, her body revealed her despair and anger.

T entered treatment wondering, "What should I do with my life?" Yet, her caretaking of her family and devotion to their safety consumed her. Her well-practiced need to dissociate and deny her needs compromised her ability to care for herself emotionally and physically. Her need to caretake extended to her neighbors and community.

She shared many early and current experiences with racism, though she did not label them as such. However, her awareness of and concern for her son's and grandson's safety were an ongoing theme. She worked hard to equip them with the language and skills to manage their worlds. An avid consumer of news, she often arrived at session in a fury about something that the president proposed. I struggled not to join her in her anger, while validating her fear and anger.

At one point she shared that she feared that there would be another "civil war." In early March, at our last in-person session, she stood up and approached me. We hugged. Despite public health advice, I could not deprive us of this ritual. Our in-person sessions had promoted an intimacy, mutual respect, and positive regard that would form the frame for our telepresence sessions. We brought a holding environment into the telehealth world that absorbed the impact of the collective trauma that we were about to share.

The pandemic's exposure of the disproportionate impact upon Black and Brown individuals provided a context to explore her concerns for her own and her family members' health. After a few weeks of lockdown, her husband had to return to work, where safety measures were in place, but loosely. She worried about his health and perceived that he was "not well." We discussed the reality of his health and ability to access health care. I moved the conversation a bit deeper. Did she trust the medical provider and the healthcare establishment? We were able to acknowledge the extreme vulnerability and risk that her husband, as a Black man, carried and the burdens she experienced trying to keep everyone safe and healthy.

An opportunity to share and hold her experience of racism emerged following the shooting of Ahmaud Arbery. Having heard about this on the news, I was prepared to hear T's experience of this event. She was despondent as she described having watched the video and seeing him "gunned" down like an "animal." Her despair and frustration with the authorities were palpable. I was able to link her grief to her identification with Ahmaud's mother and her experience of being the mother and grandmother of Black boys. She wept openly. My heart broke.

Several weeks after this session, news of George Floyd's murder hit the news. I learned of this several days prior to a scheduled session with T. I felt immediately attuned to her experience of this shooting. After all, Floyd's death was painfully reminiscent of the situation that had occurred in her police work over 20 years earlier. My instinct was to reach out to her and call and to engage in a conversation. But I held back, thought about it, and sent a text expressing my shared grief and acknowledging the impact of this upon her. She let me know that she and her family were "hanging in."

In the following session, she stated that she had found the complaints that had been written about that long-ago incident. Could she read them to me? Of course, I listened as she read the officer in charge's complaint about her. He was describing a woman who did not in any way resemble the woman I had come to know. She then read her complaint, submitted when she was only 27 years old. During her reading, I felt an intimacy that I had rarely shared with patients.

My work with T illustrates how our sharing of a traumatic reality reduced the asymmetry of the relationship and enhanced the intimacy between us. As Tosone (2012) pointed out, our responses were not identical. These shifts in the therapeutic frame facilitated the discussion of heretofore unspoken issues: race, privilege, injustice, and death. The layers of our shared trauma facilitated our work as individuals and as an intersubjective couple in making meaning of our experience.

The vicarious traumatization (Saakvitne 2002) that I have experienced in this work has served my personal and professional growth. This transformative experience is captured in the recently coined concept of shared resilience (Nuttman-Shwartz 2015).

`   Several weeks ago, I walked a path alone and saw a police officer on her bicycle. This sight comforted me and created a feeling of safety. I thought of T's experiences. I was aware that my experience of safety is not shared across the community. This awareness is another aspect of my privilege and another benefit of our sharing the trauma together.

Conclusion

Just as the coronavirus has presented a "novel" challenge to the field of infectious disease, the pandemic and associated upheaval also have provided a "novel" challenge to the practice of clinical social work. This chapter shared my observations regarding how the collective traumas of our external world intrudes upon the clinical encounter and shapes the *potential space* as described by Winnicott (1971) of the therapist-patient dyad. Relying on familiar theoretical concepts and my experience, I have attempted to make meaning of my professional experiences. It seems ironic that in a time of such social isolation, distress, threat, and loss, opportunities for growth and intimacy emerge.

References

American Psychoanalytic Association. (2020, March 31). *Emergency conversion to tele-treatment: Making it work* [video file]. Retrieved from https://www.youtube.com/watch?v=hZW1LBrtveo&feature=youtu.be

Applegate, J. (1997). The holding environment: An ongoing metaphor for social work theory and practice. *Smith College Studies in Social Work, 68*, 84–97.

Baum, N. (2010). Shared traumatic reality in communal disasters: Toward a conceptualization. *Psychotherapy: Theory, Research, Practice, Training, 47*, 249–259. https://doi.org/10.1037/a0019784.

Boston Change Process Study Group. (2018). Moving through and being moved by: Embodiment in development and in the therapeutic relationship. *Contemporary Psychoanalysis, 54*, 299–321. https://doi.org/10.1080/00107530.2018.1456841.

Centers for Disease Control and Prevention. (2020). *Covid-19 in racial and ethnic minority groups* [Your Health]. Retrieved from https://www.cdc.gov/coronavirus/2019-ncov/need-extra-precautions/racial-ethnic-minorities.html

Chakrabarti, M. (Presenter), & Martin, W. (Producer), & Turkle, S. (Interviewee). (2020, April 1). *Staying connected virtually: What we lose online* [Audio podcast]. Retrieved from https://www.wbur.org/onpoint/2020/04/01/connected-physical-distancing-coronavirus

Cherry, E. F., & Gold, S. N. (1989). The therapeutic frame revisited: A contemporary perspective. *Psychotherapy: Theory, Research, Practice, Training, 26*, 162–168. https://doi.org/10.1037/h0085415.

Drayson, Z. (2009). Embodied cognitive science and its implications for psychopathology. *Philosophy, Psychiatry, & Psychology, 16*, 329–340. https://doi.org/10.1353/ppp.0.0261.

Figley, C. R. (2002). Compassion fatigue: Psychotherapist's chronic lack of selfcare. *Journal of Clinical Psychology, 58*, 1433–1441. https://doi.org/10.1002/jclp.10090.

Galbusera, L., Finn, M. T. M., Tschacher, W., & Kyselo, M. (2019). Interpersonal synchrony feels good but impedes self-regulation of affect. *Scientific Reports, 9*(14691). https://doi.org/10.1038/s41598-019-50960-0.

Gelso, C. J. (2002). Real relationship: The "something more" of psychotherapy. *Journal of Contemporary Psychotherapy, 32*, 35–40. https://doi.org/10.1023/A:1015531228504.

Hirschberger, G. (2018). Collective trauma and the social construction of meaning. *Frontiers in Psychology, 9*. https://doi.org/10.3389/fpsyg.2018.01441.

Lehrer, J. (2018). The mirror neuron revolution: Explaining what makes humans social. *Scientific American.* Retrieved from http://www.scientificamerican.com/article/the-mirror-neuron-revolut/

Lichtenberg, J. D. (2001). Motivational systems and model scenes with special references to bodily experience. *Psychoanalytic Inquiry, 21*, 430–447. https://doi.org/10.1080/07351692109348945.

Nuttman-Shwartz, O. (2015). Shared resilience in a traumatic reality: A new concept for trauma workers exposed personally and professionally to collective disaster. *Trauma, Violence, & Abuse, 16*, 466–475. https://doi.org/10.1177/1524838014557287.

Ogden, T. H. (2004). On holding and containing, being, and dreaming. *The International Journal of Psychoanalysis, 83*, 1349–1364. https://doi.org/10.1516/T41H-DGUX-9JY4-GQC7.

Saakvitne, K. W. (2002). Shared trauma: The therapist's increased vulnerability. *Psychoanalytic Dialogues, 12*, 443–449. https://doi.org/10.1080/10481881209348678.

Schore, A. N. (2012). *The science of the art of psychotherapy.* New York: W. W. Norton.

Stamm, B. H. (1995). *The professional quality of life scale: Compassion satisfaction, burnout, & compassion fatigue/secondary trauma scales.* Pocatello: Sidran Press.

Tosone, C. (2011). The legacy of September 11: Shared trauma, therapeutic intimacy, and professional posttraumatic growth. *Traumatology, 17*, 25–29. https://doi.org/10.1177/1534765611421963.

Tosone, C., & Bialkin, L. (2003). Mass violence and secondary trauma: Issues for the children. In L. A. Straussner & N. K. Phillips (Eds.), *Understanding mass violence: A social work perspective* (pp. 157–167). New York: Pearson, Allyn, & Bacon.

Tosone, C., Nuttman-Shwartz, O., & Stephens, T. (2012). Shared trauma: When the professional is personal. *Clinical Social Work Journal, 40,* 231–239. https://doi.org/10.1007/s10615-012-0395-0.

van der Kolk, B. (2020, April). *When Covid 19 leaves clients feeling helpless* [video file]. Retrieved from http://www.nicabm.com

Winnicott, D. W. (1971). *Playing and reality*. Oxford: Penguin.

Winnicott, D. W. (1986). The theory of the parent-infant relationship. In P. Buckley (Ed.), *Essential papers in psychoanalysis: Essential papers on object relations* (pp. 233–253). New York: New York University Press.

Chapter 19
Wholeheartedness in the Treatment of Shared Trauma: Special Considerations During the COVID-19 Pandemic

Jill Zalayet

Introduction

I left my office on Thursday evening, March 12, 2020. Before crossing the threshold of my doorway, I stopped and took a long pause. Normally, I am rushing to leave at the end of my work day, trying to catch my train home, which only leaves twice each hour. On this evening, though, I felt the need to take in the contents of my office, the chair that I sit on, the couch that my patients sit or lay down on, the art on my walls, and the papers on my desk. I stood there for several minutes before turning off the light and closing the door. While it was not clear at that time how long I would be away from my professional home – the safe and cherished space where I see my patients – I had a visceral sense that it would be some time before I returned.

In the weeks leading up to this evening, news about the virus had been circulating. I supervise psychotherapy students in China over Zoom and had been aware of COVID-19 for several months and the impact that it was having there. People in my neighborhood had begun stocking up on cleaning supplies and dry foods, anticipating shortages. A highly charged debate about closing school buildings was brewing as stay-at-home orders were being issued in New York City. Many people were beginning to anticipate separation and loss, but it was not until that evening when I left my office that the magnitude of the loss began to set in and become real, the loss of the shared physical space with my patients.

Like many of my colleagues, I was tasked with rapidly transitioning to a telehealth platform from home, attempting to provide a holding environment (Winnicott 1960) for my patients in a climate wrought with tremendous uncertainty. As a clinician, in any environment, self-awareness, reflection, and insight into one's areas of vulnerability are necessary, as a means of informing and mitigating

J. Zalayet (✉)
Silver School of Social Work, New York University, New York, NY, USA

© The Author(s), under exclusive license to Springer Nature Switzerland AG 2021
C. Tosone (ed.), *Shared Trauma, Shared Resilience During a Pandemic*, Essential Clinical Social Work Series, https://doi.org/10.1007/978-3-030-61442-3_19

countertransference responses. However, in the context of this shared and unprecedented environment, my ability to discern and decipher my own blind spots and fears has been even more essential in order to provide the holding function that my patients desperately need. How do I manage the relational "disconnect" of not being with my patients physically, maintaining attunement, while also managing countertransference reactions that are inherent to navigating a shared trauma? In an effort to provide for my patients as well as for myself, I have found myself leaning into the work of Karen Horney, a formidable psychoanalyst and Neo-Freudian, whose theory and ideas have provided the holding and maternal function that *I* have so deeply needed during this uncertain time in our country and in our world. I am grateful for this space to share some of my thoughts and reflections related to Horney's concepts of wholeheartedness and basic anxiety, as they relate to the vicissitudes of shared trauma (Saakvitne 2002; Altman and Davies 2002; Tosone et al. 2003).

Karen Horney's relational theory and constructs have served as a guidepost throughout my psychoanalytic training and practice. Horney (1937) privileged the individual's cultural environment in psychotherapy and believed that we cannot wholly understand another person's plight and help relieve suffering unless we understand and attend to the full range of an individual's environmental and cultural variables. This perspective was pioneering for her time as she dared to challenge drive theory, which largely disregarded environmental factors. Further, we are not blank slates as Freud contended, and we now understand how pivotal the relationship between the therapist and patient is in the effectiveness of the treatment. (Altman 1994). My focus and attention to Horney's work in my doctoral studies have been an attempt to revitalize a groundbreaking theory within the social work community as I believe her theory and constructs to be as applicable today as they were over 100 years ago. Understanding the significance of historical trauma as well as the impact that environmental, social, and cultural factors have on an individual's development is vital to understanding the whole person. Early trauma impacts an individual's defensive structure. Recognizing the dynamic underpinnings connected to *early* trauma is essential to being able to respond to *current* trauma in a way that allows for greater insight, providing the opportunity for growth in the face of heightened anxiety and insecurity. The unfortunate and devastating impact of COVID-19 has served to further augment the relevance of Horney's concepts of basic anxiety and wholeheartedness.

Wholeheartedness and Basic Anxiety

Defining wholeheartedness has proven to be a somewhat difficult and elusive project that I have grappled with. As it turns out, so have many before me. Ultimately, what I have come to understand is that wholeheartedness is experiential; you can only fully understand it by having the experience of being with a wholehearted other. There are many clinical concepts that share some similar aspects with wholeheartedness such as attunement (Stern 1985; Beebe and Lachman 2002), the working alliance (Greenson 1965), genuineness/congruence (Rogers 1957), and empathic immersion (Kohut 1984). What I have sought to discern over the last several years in my doctoral studies is, what is unique and distinctive to wholeheartedness? What personal attributes of the therapist are important for the patient to feel safe and understood? Patients are better able to access their own constructive forces via their relationship with a therapist who has worked through their own inner conflicts and is able to draw upon all aspects of themselves and their emotions as a result. Cantor's (1959) paper, "The Quality of the Analyst's Attention," based on various lectures Horney gave on technique before she died, states:

> The whole-hearted aspect of the analyst's attention involves observing with all one's capacities and faculties. Here we are listening, seeing, and feeling with our intuition, undivided interest, reason, curiosity, and specialized knowledge. This knowledge involves awareness of our own selves, generalized professional knowledge and experience, and all that we are aware of in the particular patient. We are focusing ourselves as fully as we can on all the patient's communications, verbal and non-verbal. It is the faculty of not being distracted, either by our own deeper problems or by situations which have upset us acutely. (p. 28).

How is one able to achieve this therapeutic state of wholeheartedness? As stated, we cannot always be wholehearted as we have our own blockages and countertransference. Wholeheartedness is a therapeutic ideal. Safran (2002) describes the attitude of openness and receptivity on the part of the therapist as being an idealized state and discusses the importance of the therapists' ongoing and intuitive assessment of his/her own impact and countertransference in the therapeutic relationship. He explains that as humans we inevitably have desires, goals, and expectations and that "The task is not to rid ourselves of them, but to strive to the best of our ability to become aware of the impact they are having on the way we relate to the present moment in an ongoing fashion" (p. 237). What is essential is the therapists' unwavering attention and commitment to understanding his/her own personal variables and inner conflicts as well as being continually mindful of times when we are unable to be wholehearted so that we may redirect ourselves. It is the therapist's continual striving to be a "whole" presence when working with deeply traumatized people that embodies wholeheartedness.

Wholeheartedness is embedded in Horney's concept of basic anxiety. She describes basic anxiety as the child's experience of feeling alone and helpless in a potentially hostile world (Horney 1945). The infant is innocent, brought into the world with the potential for a full development. Horney (1950) describes the real self as the nucleus of one's potential, explaining that it is the "alive, unique, personal center of ourselves" (p. 155). When trauma occurs, that potential and those early aspects get disregarded, and the demands of the environment become the focus. Horney describes how the person's development under these circumstances becomes driven by the need to avoid or lessen basic anxiety so as not to feel alone and helpless in a hostile world. When the early environment is particularly inconsistent and/ or abusive and neglectful, defensive solutions often become compulsive. Horney (1945) explains that the child will often split off from aspects of their real self, what she terms alienation, in an attempt to find safety. However, this sense of safety is precarious because it is not based upon shoring up the array of internal resources and agency but rather it is based upon a shaky defensive system. This splitting off lends itself to the significance of wholeheartedness, as the child's development is impacted and fractured. Gaining more access to the real self is one of the goals of treatment; alienation from the real self is viewed by Horney as a "psychic death" (p. 185). Psychotherapy becomes focused on healing these splits in the individual. The word heal means to make whole ("Heal," 2020).

There are three defensive and unconscious solutions that Horney (1937) put forth. These solutions are utilized to circumvent and bind their experience of vulnerability and helplessness. They are moving toward (compliance), moving against (aggression), and a moving away (detached) solution. A compliant child is generally self-effacing and works hard to please and appease their caretaker(s); this child is most afraid of being alone. The moving against child feels that she/he needs to fight in order to be seen and heard and get what she/he needs. The moving away child is a more resigned child. Having attempted to move toward and move against, she/he learns that neither solution will allow them to get their needs met and so she/he detaches; hostility from friction with others increases this child's basic anxiety. People cope with feeling unsafe, unloved, and undervalued by compulsively moving toward, against, and away from others. When the early environment is consistently unresponsive, the child feels particularly vulnerable, and he or she may adopt one mode of relating (one specific solution), more compulsively, and is usually to the exclusion of the other two solutions. In other words, the defenses that one uses to circumvent anxiety can become so rigid and compulsive that they interfere with the whole development of the individual. One of the goals of treatment is to help the individual utilize a less rigid, less compulsive solution, moving more fluidly among all three solutions as the current circumstances require.

Horney's Concepts and COVID-19

Horney's concepts and ideas are particularly vital and relevant now during the COVID-19 pandemic, as we are all experiencing the uncertainty and vulnerability of living in an unsafe world. The basic anxiety of feeling alone in a hostile world is being re-experienced by both patient and therapist – a shared trauma. How do we navigate this shared experience, helping our patients cope while managing our own reactions and responses? Horney (1945) shares with us that "Nobody divided within himself can be wholly sincere" (p. 163). In order to be able to provide for our patients, we need to be deeply reflective and introspective with regard to our own personal variables, well examined, in order to understand the ways in which we, too, are porous to responding to the current trauma and our own defensive structure and triggers.

The uncertainty in our current environment has thrust many patients back to the familiar experience of helplessness and vulnerability. Older defensive solutions are being utilized, often compulsively, in the face of tremendous insecurity. Many of my patients have questioned their reactions and anxieties related to the environmental unrest, feeling that they are regressing and not handling their personal variables in a more constructive way. Some have shared feeling that the progress they have made and the flexibility they feel they have developed with regard to negotiating and managing their anxiety are at risk. Normalizing these feelings and reactions is critical. Basic anxiety helps us to understand the vulnerability that so many of our patients are re-experiencing. The current culture of social distancing lends itself to isolation, which for many patients is only serving to perpetuate and affirm their early experience of feeling alone and vulnerable in a hostile world. Deeply entrenched defensive solutions developed early on to mitigate helplessness have resurfaced in the face of this unprecedented environment, leaving many patients feeling particularly vulnerable and unsafe.

Helping patients understand that they do not have to be alone with their thoughts and fears is essential. Often as clinicians, we seek to cure or fix our patients' pain and distress. We cannot fix the unimaginable pain and suffering that are taking place in the world and in our patients' lives as a byproduct of the public health crisis and social/political climate we are navigating. In fact, affirming our patients' subjective realities is essential. Their fears and anxieties are not all based in neurotic underpinnings – rather, they are based in the reality of the world in which we are living. What we can do is serve as a witness. As a wholehearted other, we can provide a safe and constructive space where the reality of the current environment and patients' lived experiences are processed, while slowly deciphering derivatives and defenses from earlier traumas that may now be impacting current coping. As stated, wholeheartedness is a process of healing splits, the parts of oneself that were split off from early on, in the service of binding basic anxiety. It is a commitment to helping patients reconnect with their "whole" self and more of their capacity as a means of helping them to experience a deeper sense of their own agency. The therapist serves as a container and holds the patient in mind, an experience which is often unique for a person who was not acknowledged by their earliest caretaker(s) (Horney 1946). Through this process we can help transmute feelings of helplessness into a lived experience in which there exists greater possibility, hope, and meaning.

Toward the end of her life, Horney became interested in the principles of Zen Buddhism and the writings of Daisetz T. Suzuki (DeMartino 1991), further developing her concept of wholeheartedness and the idea of being able to operate with all of one's faculties while remaining "oblivious to oneself" (Vida and Molad 2004, p. 338). Vida and Molad (2004) share that wholeheartedness is a concept that is very difficult to grasp because it is connected to having the "highest presence and the highest absence" (Horney 1987, p. 34 in Vida and Molad 2004). The idea of absence in this context is not suggestive of the therapist's avoidance; rather, it is the Zen state of being completely present via a "self-less self" (DeMartino 1991, p. 277). It is only through deep, ongoing introspection and examination of our own inner lives that we can attempt to achieve such wholehearted moments. If as clinicians we are split and divided ourselves, we cannot serve as containers for the full range of our patients' feelings and projections.

Final Thoughts

I have been back to my office once, since leaving in March, to gather a few things that I have needed. Standing once again in my space, alone, mask and surgical gloves on, it felt as if time had stood still. Everything was exactly where I left it, and yet everything had changed. Patients have asked me when and even "if" I will return to my office. I want nothing more than to be with my patients again, to return to the physical space that we seemingly lost overnight. Many of my patients have asked questions about my health, my overall well-being, as well as my plans regarding my practice and my office. At a previous time, I would have likely explored these questions for deeper meanings. Now, however, I feel the need to respond to these types of inquiries more directly. We have *all* been destabilized by the state of the world and the many real-life issues that we are attempting to negotiate. My patients need to know that I am able to be with them completely. Providing a safe space to authentically address their concerns and provide a mirror in which their fears are affirmed and not pathologized is my commitment to them. Safety in the therapeutic relationship is about attending to the well-being of the whole person, in every way that is needed, and that is what I will continue to strive to provide. For the time being, we all have to live with uncertainty. While we cannot forecast or know exactly what the future will look like, we can retain hope for better days ahead. For many of my patients, I am holding this hope for them, and I feel privileged to be able to provide this function.

References

Altman, N. (1994). A perspective on child psychoanalysis 1994: The recognition of relational theory and technique in child treatment. *Psychoanalytic Psychology, 11*(3), 383–395.

Altman, N., & Davies, J. M. (2002). Out of the blue: Reflections on shared trauma. *Psychoanalytic Dialogues, 12*(3), 359–360.

Beebe, B., & Lachman. (2002). *Infancy research and adult treatment.* Hillsdale: The Analytic Press.

Cantor, M. B. (1959). The quality of the analyst's attention. *The American Journal of Psychoanalysis, 19*(1), 28–32.

DeMartino, R. J. (1991). Karen Horney, Daisetz T. Suzuki, and Zen Buddhism. *The American Journal of Psychoanalysis, 51*, 267–283.

Greenson, R. R. (1965). The working alliance and the transference neurosis. *The Psychoanalytic Quarterly, 34*, 155–181.

Heal. (2020). In *Merriam-Webster.com* dictionary. Retrieved July 19, 2020, from https://www.merriam-webster.com/dictionary/heal

Horney, K. (1937). *The neurotic personality of our time.* New York: W.W. Norton & Company.

Horney, K. (1945). *Our inner conflicts.* New York: W.W. Norton.

Horney, K. (1946). What does the analyst do? In K. Horney (Ed.), *Are you considering psychoanalysis?* New York: W.W. Norton.

Horney, K. (1950). *Neurosis and human growth.* New York: W.W. Norton.

Horney, K. (1987). *Final lectures.* New York: W.W. Norton.

Kohut, H. (1984). Chapter 6: The curative effect of analysis: The self psychological reassessment of the therapeutic. In A. Goldberg (Ed.), *How does analysis cure?* (pp. 300–307). Chicago: University of Chicago Press.

Rogers, C. R. (1957). The necessary and sufficient conditions of therapeutic personality change. *Journal of Counseling Psychology, 21*, 95–103.

Saakvitne, K. W. (2002). Shared trauma: The therapist's increased vulnerability. *Psychoanalytic Dialogues, 12*(3), 443–449.

Safran, J. D. (2002). Reply to commentaries. *Psychoanalytic Dialogues, 12*(2), 235–258.

Stern, D. (1985). *The interpersonal world of the infant.* New York: Basic Books.

Tosone, C., et al. (2003). Shared trauma: Group reflections on the September 11th disaster. *Psychoanalytic Social Work, 10*(1), 57–77.

Vida, J. E., & Molad, G. J. (2004). The Ferenzian dialogue: Psychoanalysis as a way of life. *Free Associations, 11*(3), 338–352.

Winnicott, D. W. (1960). The theory of the parent-infant relationship. *International Journal of Psycho-Analysis, 41*, 585–595.

Chapter 20
Reflections on the Impact of Remote Counseling: Friendship in a New Therapeutic Space

Meredith Hemphill Ruden

Introduction

During a global crisis where unexpected death looms and occurs, I find it apropos to consider existentialist Irvin Yalom's viewpoint on therapy's gifts. Yalom (2003) considered the fear of death as ever-present and commanding in every patient's distress and the "deathbed scene" as a potential moment of openness and honesty as that fear is realized and released at last.

As I have counseled individuals throughout the coronavirus pandemic, I do not believe that it is coincidental that my thoughts have turned to my past work in hospitals with people who are critically or chronically ill. I find myself drawing upon hospital social work terminology in conceptualizing my private practice clients' problems – terms and phrases like "uncertainty" and "struggle to wait" – as new COVID-19-related issues overlay old ones and bring new clients to my "door." We (both therapists and clients) are being presented with daily life-threatening/death-bed scenes. We are at that bedside as we watch the news and hear stories of serious illness through our extended networks. And, of course, if we contract COVID-19, we are in that bed and manage its symptoms without knowing if we will survive or return to good health.

M. H. Ruden (✉)
City Center Psychotherapy, New York, NY, USA
e-mail: Drruden@citycenterpsychotherapy.com

© The Author(s), under exclusive license to Springer Nature Switzerland
AG 2021
C. Tosone (ed.), *Shared Trauma, Shared Resilience During a Pandemic*,
Essential Clinical Social Work Series,
https://doi.org/10.1007/978-3-030-61442-3_20

Case Vignette

Counseling Through Illness

My counseling of Richard[1] through his illness with COVID-19 demonstrates how a serious illness positioned me as a bedside witness.

> *I had worked with Richard on depression, underemployment, and procrastination for 1 year prior to quarantine with weekly in-person sessions. In early spring 2020, he had contracted COVID-19. I counseled him as he sat in his bed, being unable to move from it for several weeks, and as I sat in my home office, I felt trepidation prior to our remote sessions ("was he feeling better?"). I was nervous about how little seemed predictable about the illness's course, according to the news. People who were low risk for serious complications were getting them; people who seemed to be minimally symptomatic one day were critically ill the next. In awareness of this, I checked on Richard's health, inquired about his strategies for care, and offered suggestions for additional support, in each session. He was under-standably anxious, saying that he was unsure of how to interpret current symptoms and what to expect. As well as thinking of ways to minimize "unknowns," we discussed coping with uncertainty. These coping strategies were directed toward him but served as useful reminders for myself, as I coped with limited data on his health and welfare. To lessen my own worry, I occasionally texted Richard between sessions during this time to see how he felt physically.*

Prior to COVID-19, I was less curious about a client's health and details of his day-to-day routine, preferring those lines of inquiry that appeared more directly linked to his presenting problem and therapeutic goals. This purview was not developed out of an uncaring, prescriptive, and hierarchical approach. On the contrary, it was derived out of a profound respect for my client's agency and capacity and willingness to have them guide me. Like Tosone (2006) prior to the traumatic impact of 9/11, I prided myself on my warmth and caring but these feelings as existing within the confines of the therapeutic space. During Richard's illness, I noticed that my caring extended beyond the parameters of therapy.

What changed in therapy and the therapeutic relationship, and what caused this change?
Had the therapeutic relationship simply become *less formal*?
If yes, then, this would explain why I thought less about how what I asked and was told related to Richard's therapeutic challenges and why I thought about his welfare in a more personal way. It made sense to me that my interactions with Richard during his illness should resemble my past counseling work in hospitals. Like my relationship with those patients, my relationship with Richard was starting to resemble an amalgam of many types of relationships, including personal ones. And, similar to my approach to my hospital work and its heightened sense of

---

[1]The client's name and other personal identifiers have been changed to protect privacy and confidentiality.

intimacy with patients, I saw the shift in therapeutic dynamics as a positive one, full of therapeutic potential. It

did not qualify as an overstepping of client boundaries, of the sort that concerns Reamer (2002) in *Eye on Ethics*. Rather, this shift struck me as an ethically and therapeutically good fit for the client and situation (i.e., illness at home) in which it occurred. But, did *less formal* adequately capture what *more* I gained through this relational change?

Was I "lending ego"?

Psychoanalytic tradition theorizes that the client can borrow cognitive abilities and emotional capacities from the therapist's own mind (Misch, 2000). Although possible to do so, I think my earlier, pre-pandemic work with Richard in assisting him to plan ahead and problem-solve to combat procrastination better fits this concept. I think that my work during his illness involved less of his borrowing of a faculty missed or undeveloped than of my supporting him as a friend might. Like a friend, my motivation for supporting him was simple: to support him so that he did not have to manage his illness and its accompanying stress alone. I will say more on this later in this chapter.

Had the relationship shifted toward a more sensitized and compassionate form, as a result of a shared trauma?

During the time that Richard was ill, our therapeutic exchanges were typical of that seen in a shared trauma reality. In such a reality, a therapist can develop an altered perspective, wherein the line between professional concern and personal caring is seen as superfluous (Tosone 2006). And, indeed, my caring for Richard took on a different hue. This is illustrated by the fact that I felt compelled to text him, so that I could be assured that he was improving. Drawing on research in vicarious post-traumatic growth and vicarious resilience, Nuttman-Shwartz (2014) describes how shared trauma leads to numerous positive outcomes (i.e., greater self-confidence, sensitivity, compassion, and hope) that impact the therapist's outlook and therapeutic work. Combined, these outcomes suggest that the therapist attempts to understand a client's problem more and increases her part in the effort to overcome it. This delineation aptly describes my purview and intense effort to help and support Richard during his illness when his "problem" was, first and foremost, his poor health.

Counseling Following Illness

As Richard recovered from his illness and was able to leave his bed during our sessions, he sat in his living room which faced an outdoor patio. He invited me to look at what he saw.

Richard – "I've been working on my garden. Do you want to see it?"

Me – "Yes, I'd love to. I've heard so much about it…Wow, you've put a lot of work into it. You really like gardening, don't you?"
Richard – "I do. I think it really might be my thing. It makes me happy."

I felt interested in what he had to share. My interest did not feel necessary or the result of an altered perspective brought on by existential questioning (what matters most?), as can occur when the impact of trauma continues to be felt. It was the result of being invited into more parts of my client's life, and it was the result of my decision to explore that new terrain without any preconceived notions of therapeutic value. A voluntary aspect of relationship formation is a precondition for friendship. Moyer and Hajjat (2017) describe friendship as a "negotiated attachment" (p. ix) that is separate from group affiliation or categorization; it is a chosen relationship entered into voluntarily when one gravitates toward some aspect of another's personhood. It is an "affective bond" (Moyer and Hajjat 2017; p. x) that one may or may not have with, say, a sister – or, say, a client. And, indeed, in the warmth that I felt as Richard shared his garden project with me, I noticed affection, affection for a person who had taken a risk to share with me an interest and part of himself that he had not, until now. Our relationship shifted toward professionally based friendship. Without extending the bounds of professionalism, I expressed more interest in all aspects of Richard's life. I did not guide my assessment and inquiry by what seemed relevant to therapy; and, Richard shared more openly, apparently also ridding himself of such strictures.

Richard's case, and others like it, suggests to me why Yalom (2003) considers friendship in the "a necessary condition in the process of therapy" (p. 181). If fear of death is the source of our psychological distress and causes a sense of loneliness as Yalom supposes, it makes sense that confrontation with our own mortality should need companionship to tolerate and survive psychologically. COVID-19 is confronting us with our own mortality. We can no longer be certain that death is in the distant future (in fact, we never could). And, as the pandemic confronts us with a threat to our well-being, we are aware that we are alone. It makes sense that in such moments, moments of profound loneliness, we benefit most from a metaphorical hand to hold. Such a "hand" does not deny the aloneness we feel but challenges our sense of its totality (recognized in such self-statements like "I am completely alone") and, thus, helps better tolerate it. Again, I argue that holding a metaphorical or literal hand outreached in such a situation is ethical.

But, while Yalom's link between friendship and mortality coheres with part of the story of Richard's therapy during this pandemic, it does not wholly explain how therapeutic intimacy developed. Richard recovered quickly from the virus without any long-term change in his emotional well-being, outlook, and self-concept, or me to mine. When the *bedside* was left, it became a nontraumatic memory. We continued therapy remotely as virus rates surged, and our therapeutic intimacy, that personal, contextual, and "evolving" (Tosone 2006, p. 89) phenomenon that is commonly considered part of effective therapy, grew. It did not grow out of a processing of a life-threatening experience, and it was formed as a result of a shared reality in that it was remote because pandemic precautions meant that we could not meet in-person.

How could professionally based friendship and therapeutic develop remotely? It seems unlikely given the lack of curated therapeutic space and the physical distance between client and therapist in remote counseling, which arguably disrupts the intimacy of a shared therapeutic space. Research and literature abound with concern about the limiting qualities of remote counseling. In Morin's (2019) article "Does Online Therapy Work?," the author expresses common worry that the absence of face-to-face therapeutic exchange limits therapist's observations and, thus, their ability to make informed interpretations and interventions. Research on the impact of the therapy office environment on client perception also suggests that, without it, we, therapists, are at a disadvantage. Pressly and Heesacker (2001) cite studies that link art, furniture selection and positioning, and other environmental cues in therapists' offices with a client's feelings of comfort, degree of self-disclosure, and view of their therapist's competence. It is also striking that, in a group of seven clinical social workers whom I interviewed recently for a qualitative study underway, all expressed loss connected with transitioning to remote counseling and all described efforts to maintain the quality of their therapeutic work. They worry that the quality of their therapeutic work will suffer when it is remote.

Today, I no longer have access to that designated space in which I use the positioning of my chair, certain décor, and the way I sit and hold myself within it to communicate my therapeutic approach and expertise; and, my clients no longer benefit from going to a designated space that often supports the therapeutic relationship in orienting her/him/them toward therapy.

Yet, despite this space's absence, I have experienced more intimacy with Richard and other clients. In the removal of the specialness of a curated therapy space, there is room for the ordinariness of my clients' lives. I see and hear things that may not have been mentioned, deemed unworthy for, or irrelevant to therapy. I also shared more of me as a person, as Richard and others saw my un-curated, personal space. This had a two-part therapeutic benefit: (1) it revealed interests and motivation unknown beforehand. Richard's real interest in his garden work was not emphasized in therapy previously, and it was uncharacteristic. By meeting him in his home, we found a possible path toward a brighter future for him; and (2) it worked toward greater equality between me and my clients. The dynamic wherein my clients self-reveal necessarily and I self-disclose in a controlled, minimal manner has changed. Now, they learned and could assess things about me, just as I them. This calls upon me to have greater humility in my work. To use the consensus drawn from Rowden, Harris, and Wickel's (2014) study on humility in relational therapy, I define it as "an attitude of openness," "recognition.... (and) comfort with one's limitation(s) or problems," and "recognition of one's own contribution to relational problems" (p. 385). My lack of awareness of Richard's garden prior to the pandemic illustrates a problematic, blinkered approach. I looked for motivation to get a job; I looked for interests that had strong potential to develop into employment opportunities. I did not ask more broadly: "tell me about your interests." The new, co-created therapeutic space primes me through environment to more deeply understand that my catalyst for change lies in greater openness – openness to know them and them (within the reasonable limits of the computer screenshot) me.

Remote Counseling's Potential

There is hesitancy to accept remote video counseling as a viable long-term alternative to in-person therapeutic sessions within the community of social workers and therapists. Yet, in this chapter, I chose to focus on its therapeutic possibilities, partially for pragmatic reasons. We must consider the possibility that video counseling may be the only viable alternative to in-person counseling for some time and work with it in order to best support our clients. I also focus on these possibilities because I am seeing them realized with some of my clients and believe more is possible. While the therapeutic relationship is not all that therapy rests on, it is a significant mechanism for change. In that regard, I think that remote counseling has something to offer: the potential for a greater sense of friendship between therapist and client.

References

Misch, D. A. (2000). Basic strategies of dynamic supportive therapy. *The Journal of Psychotherapy Practice and Research, 9*(4), 173–189.

Morin, A. (2019, , July 17). *Does online therapy work? Here's what science says. Inc.* Retrieved from https://www.inc.com/amy-morin/does-online-therapy-work-heres-what-science-says.html

Moyer, A., & Hajjat, M. (2017). *The psychology of friendship*. Oxford: Oxford University Press.

Nuttman-Shwartz, O. (2014, November). Shared resilience in a traumatic reality: A new concept for trauma workers exposed personally and professionally to collective disaster. *Trauma, Violence and Abuse.*

Pressly, P. K., & Heesacker, M. (2001). The physical environment and counseling: A review of theory and research. *Journal of Counseling & Development, 79*(2), 148–160.

Reamer, F. (2002). Eye on ethics. *Social work today.* Retrieved from https://www.socialworktoday.com/news/eoe_030402.shtml

Rowden, T. J., Harris, S. M., & Wickel, K. (2014). Understanding humility and its role in relational therapy. *Contemporary Family Therapy, 36*, 380–391.

Tosone, C. (2006). Therapeutic intimacy: A post-9/11 perspective. *Smith College Studies in Social Work, 76*(4), 89.

Yalom, I. (2003). *The gift of therapy: An open letter to a new generation of therapists and their patients*. New York: Harper Perennial.

Chapter 21
The Natural World: The Role of Ecosocial Work During the COVID-19 Pandemic

Michelle Willoughby

Introduction

There have been birds chirping outside my apartment window for the past several months. During my 8-year residency in my Manhattan apartment, they have not presented in such volume or in such numbers, signaling an environmental change. Throughout my 10-year professional career as a hospital social worker, coupled with personal observation, I have experienced and witnessed the value of connecting to the natural world. The COVID-19 pandemic decreased the frequency of outdoor experiences for many people across the globe. Patients in the hospital already face this disconnect and are largely relegated to interaction with plants, flowers, or technology. There is a human desire to connect with nature that is now receiving more recognition since so many people are now facing limitations or restrictions to their outdoor activities. The COVID-19 pandemic is the catalyst for social and natural isolation from the world around us.

In the 1980s and 1990s, social workers looked at shifting the understanding of the environment to go beyond the social aspects to include the natural perspective. Carel Germain (1981) was the first to discuss an ecological approach to social work practice acknowledging the role of the physical environment and the natural world. Since the 2000s, social work literature has grown around social work and the natural environment with varying terminology. Ramsay and Boddy (2017) conducted a concept analysis of environmental concerns and social work. They identified a list of terms throughout social work literature including green social work, environmental social work, ecological social work, and sustainable social work. For the purpose of this chapter, the term ecosocial work will be used. "An ecosocial approach might

M. Willoughby (✉)
Silver School of Social Work, New York University, New York, NY, USA
e-mail: mw1983@nyu.edu

C. Tosone (ed.), *Shared Trauma, Shared Resilience During a Pandemic*,
Essential Clinical Social Work Series,
https://doi.org/10.1007/978-3-030-61442-3_21

be defined as an anti-oppressive model of social work practice that sees the natural world as a central variable in human development and well-being and promotes environmental sustainability as a core professional consideration" (Norton 2012, p. 304). Social workers should question the impact of technology and its ability to solve problems (Crews and Besthorn 2016). An ecological approach also critically analyzes many industrialized societies' viewpoint that the environment is a separate entity and viewed as property (Zapf 2010).

The history of social work practice has largely excluded the natural and physical environment, instead focusing mostly on social elements. Social work should expand the understanding of person-in-environment to include the natural environment (Miller et al. 2012; Zapf 2010; Heinsch 2012). Zapf (2010) created a new paradigm for the twenty-first century, "people as place," replacing the person-in-environment model. "People as place" emphasizes community, the inclusion of the natural world, and illustrates the interconnectedness of humans and nature. The purpose of this paradigm is "living well in place" (Zapf 2010, p. 40). A radical shift is needed to address the natural world in social work practice.

Miller et al. (2012) drew a distinction between environmental justice, which analyzes the impact of the natural world on humans, and ecological justice, which takes it a step further with the viewpoint of humans as part of a larger universe. Environmental justice brings attention to the disproportionate impact environmental issues have on people of color, poor, and other marginalized communities. Maas et al. (2006) found that people who live near green natural environments report higher levels of overall health than those who live near less-green environments. Marginalized communities often do not have the access to green natural environments in comparison to affluent communities (Mitchell et al. 2011).

Ecosocial Work

Crews and Besthorn (2016) identified facets of ecosocial work to include recognizing that the environment is inclusive of the natural world, the value of intuition and spiritual experiences, and acknowledging the interconnectedness of humankind and the natural universe. Ramsay and Boddy (2017) discussed four characteristics of ecosocial work including capitalizing on present social work competencies, being open to different viewpoints including indigenous values, the ability to critique dominant culture, and the ability to work across disciplines. Community, diversity, and the interdependence of nature are indigenous values that can be incorporated into social work practice (Gray et al. 2007). The ecosocial work literature contains terms that may be new to some social workers such as biophilia (Besthorn and Saleebey 2003; Fromm 1964) and deep ecology (Besthorn 2012; Mosher 2010).

Biophilia

The psychoanalyst Erich Fromm (1964) first used the term *biophilia* stating, "its essence is love of life in contrast to love of death" (p. 45). Fromm was a humanist and his description of biophilia included natural and social aspects. The American biologist E.O. Wilson (1984) later described biophilia as "the innate tendency to focus on life and lifelike processes" (p. 1). Wilson's book, *Biophilia: The Human Bond with Other Species*, depicts his immersion in the natural world, modernizing the term biophilia to focus on the natural world. Besthorn and Saleebey (2003) discussed the interconnection between humans and the natural world, addressing biophilia in social work practice. Biophilia acknowledges that humans and other living and nonliving things are all interconnected in a web of relationships, are inherently valuable, and should be respected. There are opportunities to incorporate animals and nature into social work practice to improve overall well-being.

Deep Ecology

The term *deep ecology* was coined by the Norwegian philosopher Arne Naess in the 1970s to explain mutual dependency and interconnectedness in an ecosystem. Deep ecology posits that humans are entrenched in a network of relationships. Naess rejected the belief that humans have a higher hierarchical place in nature (Naess 1973). Besthorn (2012) used the term deep ecology to challenge social work's anthropocentric view, placing humans at the center of social work practice. Besthorn (2012) discussed *deep justice*, shifting the focus from anthropocentricity to the interconnectedness of ecological and social elements in social work practice. Traditional ideas of social justice emphasize importance of the individual and social experience, sending a message that other nonhuman aspects of the natural environment have lesser value.

Ecosocial Work in Practice

There are numerous ways to incorporate the natural environment into direct practice. Space to discuss the client's relationship with nature including plants and animals could be included in an initial assessment (Norton 2012). Environmental concerns impacting client well-being should also be explored (Borrell et al. 2010). There has been growing interest in human-animal relationships including pet ownership and animal-assisted interventions (Chalmers et al. 2020). According to the International Association of Human-Animal Interaction Organizations, "an animal assisted intervention is a goal oriented and structured intervention that intentionally includes or incorporates animals in health, education and human services (e.g., social work) for the purpose of therapeutic gains in humans" (Jegatheesan 2018, p. 5). Dogs are most often used in animal-assisted interventions (Chalmers et al. 2020), but horses are also growing in popularity (Acri et al. 2016). Risley-Curtiss (2010) found that, in a national study of 1649 social workers, only one-third of respondents indicated that they asked about animals in their assessment and less than one-quarter of respondents reported they used animal-assisted interventions.

Engaging in therapy outdoors may be beneficial for mental health professionals and their clients to make connections in the natural world (Cooley et al. 2020). Berman et al. (2008) found in their study that participants taking a 50- to 55-min walk in a green space improved cognitive performance. The Japanese tradition of forest bathing (shinrin-yoku) is the practice of being fully "present" in a forest through the use of the senses. Results of a study on forest bathing in Japan showed that adults who participated in forest bathing exhibited lower blood pressure and lower cortisol levels (Park et al. 2010). Viewing pictures of nature and living near green spaces have shown benefits for overall health. Research has shown that viewing pictures of nature improves cognitive functioning (Berman et al. 2008). Van den Berg et al. (2003) found that participants who watched a video depicting nature demonstrated better mood and concentration as compared to a group who viewed a video of an urban environment. Social work practitioners could include pictures of nature, plants, water fountains, and windows with nature views in social work settings (Besthorn and Saleebey 2003).

Community organizations such as healthcare facilities, schools, and prisons must recognize the role of biophilia and provide outdoor spaces (Norton 2012). These organizations can also explore biophilic design or animal-assisted interventions to help residents to connect to nature while indoors. Dijkstra et al. (2008) found in their study that participants viewing a hospital room with indoor plants reported reduced stress compared to a hospital room with no plants. Heinsch (2012) recommended that hospital settings consider the importance of nature since patients often are not able to connect with nature. Community gardening, the promotion of farmers' markets, recycling programs, and buying local products are other ways social workers can become involved in community-level work (Norton 2012).

Advocacy and influencing the creation of new green policies are integral to making positive change for the natural world. Social workers are encouraged to work across disciplines and with various types of organizations in advocacy and policy efforts on local, state, national, and international levels (Norton 2012). Social workers can also advocate within social work governing bodies such as National Association of Social Workers (NASW), International Federation of Social Workers (IFSW), and Council on Social Work Education (CSWE) in order to shift social work policy and education to recognize a person-in-environment framework including the natural world. Biophilia, deep ecology, and environmental justice must be addressed in social work polices for best practice.

Experiences in the outdoors can contribute to personal and professional growth. Lichtblau (2010) found in a self-study that outdoor experiences impacted the writer's thinking, emotions, and physical body and offered a holistic approach to well-being. This study implies that social workers should immerse themselves in the natural world and reflect upon it for professional development. Crews and Besthorn (2016) advocate for experiencing moments of silence in the natural world to promote personal and professional development. Listening to nature allows social work practitioners to better understand their clients. Embracing silence in nature may also lead to a better understanding of areas for personal growth for social work practitioners.

Crews and Besthorn (2016) identified two exercises that can be used to connect to the natural world. The exercises do not involve much instruction or planning. The first exercise is to take a walk outside, alone, and without technology, using the senses, being present and reflective. The second exercise can be used in an agency setting. The social work practitioner can invite a client to look out the window or at a picture of nature or a plant and focus on that for 1–2 min. Crews and Besthorn (2016) recommend the use of silence in direct practice with clients, the values of being present, and using the senses. Being attuned to silence in nature may allow social work practitioners to express more empathy and care in their practice.

Alternate Nature Connections

There are opportunities outside of social work to connect to the environment through other mediums such as art, music, theater, film, food, wine, and biophilic design (Zapf 2010). There are many examples of artwork throughout history, such as the paintings in the Lascaux Cave in France, that have drawn inspiration from the natural world. The natural world served as an inspiration for artists such as Frida Kahlo, Vincent van Gogh, and Georgia O'Keefe. Most recently, the portrait of President Barack Obama by Kehinde Wiley in the National Portrait Gallery in Washington, DC, depicts Obama surrounded by foliage with flowers signifying meaningful places in his personal life: jasmine for his birthplace in Hawaii, chrysanthemum as the official flower of Chicago, and African blue lilies honoring his Kenyan heritage (Cotter 2018). Creating or viewing art inspired by the natural world can be a pleasurable and therapeutic experience. Art can also raise awareness for environmental change. Visits to sculpture gardens and botanical gardens are active ways to connect to artistry in the natural world.

Film screenings, theater performances, and concerts have been held in outdoor spaces and offer an opportunity to experience the arts outdoors. Composers have often been inspired by the outdoors. The twentieth-century French composer Olivier Messiaen famously incorporated birdsong into his compositions. The Liceu Opera Barcelona reopened in June, 2020, after the COVID-19 pandemic with a string quartet performing to an audience of plants. The artistic director was motivated to bring attention to nature. After the performance, the plants were donated to local healthcare professionals (Treisman 2020).

There is also opportunity for innovative biophilic designs in a variety of environments such as homes, healthcare settings, and prisons. Urban planners who take inspiration from the natural world may help to allow more interconnectedness in our ecosystem within urban habitats. Community gardening has gained popularity in urban spaces and can be a positive way to strengthen community ties while connecting to the natural world (Besthorn and Saleebey 2003). Shopping at farmers' markets creates a feeling of being nourished by the earth. The connection to the earth is also pronounced in viniculture with an emphasis on terroir and the desire to taste the grapes representative of a healthy ecosystem (Asimov 2020).

COVID-19

A negative effect of the COVID-19 pandemic for many Americans, especially in urban settings, has been increased isolation from natural environments, leading to questions as to the level of impact isolation has on their overall health. Fewer cars on the road have positively impacted noise pollution, allowing birdsong to be heard (Bui and Badger 2020). Though many park spaces remained open, some people felt safer staying in their homes, limiting their exposure to green spaces. So many conversations professionally and personally seem to revolve around technology fatigue, social isolation, and separation from nature.

The pandemic altered normal routines and limited time spent in natural surroundings. The pandemic has also reminded us of the importance of connection to other humans and the natural world. It is a signal that deep ecology and biophilia have their place in social work practice. Now that restrictions are lifting in much of the United States, more people are feeling comfortable going outdoors. Current societal values often do not provide for the opportunity to experience nature without distraction, to be present in the moment (Lichtblau 2010). The fallout of the pandemic highlights the importance of the natural world and environmental issues in the social work field including theory, education, and practice.

During the COVID-19 pandemic, being able to step outside for fresh air has become more important than ever. During 13-hour hospital shifts, even amid the chaos, I made every effort to leave the physical building for a walk on my break. There was something restricting about the simple act of just breathing in enclosed hospital spaces. My office was on a COVID unit, and even with my mask, there was something special about being able to breathe in outdoor air. This is one of the privileges I had that my patients did not. I got to go home at the end of my shift. I felt appreciative that I had a green space within walking distance from my apartment where I could feel more disconnected from urban life and my work at the hospital.

Isolation has been especially trying for hospitalized patients confronted with a strict no-visitation policy and a quarantine restriction to their rooms. Under normal circumstances, patients subjected to prolonged hospitalization face a disconnect from nature when they are unable to leave the hospital. In multi-bed hospital rooms, the bed with the window view is always prime real estate. Patients look longingly out the windows in the hospital hallways, especially standing near a window when it is sunny. People like to stand near windows in the hallway to talk and bask in the glow of that moment of light.

With the pandemic, my work at the hospital changed. Patients with COVID-19 were restricted to their rooms and barred from social encounters and open spaces. Face-to-face encounters were not possible, but even over the phone, patients were able to express their motivations for leaving the hospital. Beyond reunification with family, patients also discussed basic wishes, such as returning home to their pets, enjoying the beach, sailing, fishing, gardening, or just sitting on a porch. Patients were very willing to trade the confinement and isolation of a hospital bed for strict precautionary measures at home.

I received more frantic calls from families. The time spent on these calls seemed to double as the need to provide emotional support was greater than usual. Oft-changing New York City protocols for nursing homes, assisted living facilities, shelters, and hospital transportation proved challenging. Priorities shifted to providing guidance to families navigating the difficult landscape of funeral and burial services. With this shared trauma, patients and families shared their fears, and I remember thinking that I was afraid, too. COVID-19 forced me to confront many of the same questions my patients and their families were facing. What if I get COVID-19? What if I bring it home to my spouse? News spread of hospital staff dying. I am in here, too. In my social work role, I am the person families and patients come to for answers. The pandemic forced me to get comfortable with not having answers.

I remember providing support to a woman whose partner had COVID-19 and died in the hospital overnight. She was sobbing and said repeatedly, "Just don't tell me that you are putting him in one of those refrigerator trucks." There had been a lot of negative publicity in the news about decomposing bodies found in a U-Haul rental outside a funeral home in Brooklyn, New York (Feuer et al. 2020), and reports about the overflow of bodies being held in mobile morgues (Feuer and Salcedo 2020). I realized that the patient who died was around the same age as my husband and was just hospitalized the day before. The woman was not able to be with her partner at his end of life. What if my spouse got sick and I couldn't be with him at his end of life? Would I be thinking about the mobile morgues upon news of his death? How could I talk about the reality of the mobile morgues in that moment? Having 10 years of experience in hospital social work, I have handled many tense and highly emotional situations. This was different. My heart was racing. I had to collect myself before returning her initial call. I provided emotional support and concrete resources during the five phone conversations we had throughout the day. She did have questions about burial services, which I answered to the best of my ability, knowing that funeral homes were facing their own challenges.

Additional negative aspects of the pandemic were increased anxiety and fear about patients going to nursing homes and the process of burial arrangements. Many family members who normally visited patients at nursing homes would relay their concerns that they didn't trust the nursing homes and didn't want the patients to return to residency. Even though the hospital had a strict no-visitation policy, many families had more trust in the hospital than the nursing homes. Eventually, due to the sudden rise in deaths, the funeral homes became overwhelmed. Some family members were worried that their loved ones would end up in a mobile morgue or, even worse, missing.

I felt a tremendous amount of pressure from patients who didn't have COVID-19 to be discharged from the hospital as soon as possible. Several patients would adamantly express their desire to leave prematurely, concerned about the likelihood of contracting the virus while in the hospital. Many patients were anxious about the number of staff coming in and out of their rooms. Hearing their anxiety and concerns about being in a hospital with so many COVID-positive patients, they were echoing feelings I also had. They just wanted to feel safe. I wanted to feel safe, too.

Throughout the COVID-19 pandemic and my isolation from nature, I have reflected on my own history with the outdoors. It seems to be a tale of two cities. My memories as a kid growing up in suburban Chicago in the 1990s were not rife with an affinity to nature. I did not like going to the beach and getting sandy. Motion sickness hampered my enjoyment of fishing on a boat with my granddad and made long car rides miserable. During these rides, my dad refused to turn on the AC, and my mom kept the windows shut because the breeze from the open windows gave her a stiff neck. The sticky vinyl seats and my younger siblings draped all over me created a hot box. To this day, I need to feel air on my face during car rides. Every summer the family vacation involved camping in a cramped 1964 FAN travel trailer with a family of nine. Just thinking about it makes my temperature rise.

After moving to Manhattan in 2008, there was a greater need to transcend the dense, compact urban sprawl. Planning and taking vacations domestic and abroad to connect to the outdoors became a vital part of my inner balance. It now gives me the feeling of being plugged in to the world around me. Time spent outdoors has proved invaluable in my adult life with its healing and restorative components. Throughout this experience of shared trauma, I noticed that elements of my professional and personal life had shifted. Shared trauma can create a shift in clinical practice with a greater emphasis on self-care (Tosone et al. 2012). My self-care shifted from Broadway shows and gym workouts to time spent in nature. Sitting alone in the Central Park with my floral face mask has served as a way for me to decompress and center myself after working at the hospital. I sit on a blanket, listen to the birds, and watch the swaying trees and pollinating bees in silence. Without a backyard, porch, or even balcony, I resorted to larger green spaces near my home, not feeling comfortable with the risks associated with taking public transportation. Living in a small New York City apartment facing COVID-19 restrictions heightened my interest in ecosocial work.

Conclusion

The pandemic has brought attention to the role of biophilia and deep ecology in our lives. More thoughtful approaches to combat isolation in hospitals are needed, such as access to outdoor spaces and community gardens. There are possibilities in creating more supportive spaces not only for those hospitalized but also for all people facing isolation. More innovation is needed in biophilic design of work environments and the client experience to increase interpersonal and environmental connections. Biophilic design, the use of plants in practice, nature views, walking therapy, animal companionship, and animal-assisted interventions should be explored. Social workers should consider advocating for environmental justice on local, national, and international levels. The social work principle of advocating for social justice must also include environmental justice through individual and collective action (Miller et al. 2012). Social workers are called to be global environmental citizens moving beyond the importance of the individual, nation, or a particular generation to collective engagement (Zapf 2010).

My personal and professional growth flowered this early summer during a short stay in the Catskills after spending months working as a hospital social worker in New York City during the COVID-19 pandemic. Pleasure reading, which is normally a top priority, took a backseat to staring at trees and squirrels, feeling the breeze, and listening to birds. My excursions in the Central Park have turned from an amenity into a necessity. Learning about biophilia and deep ecology has transformed the way I encounter outdoor space. I feel that my recent experiences in the natural world have led to my personal and professional growth. With the COVID-19 pandemic restrictions still in place in parts of the United States, it is more important than ever for social workers to incorporate biophilia and deep ecology into our personal and professional lives. The COVID-19 pandemic has prompted a new paradigm shift of what social work will become.

References

Acri, M., Hoagwood, K., Morrissey, M., & Zhang, S. (2016). Equine-assisted activities and therapies: Enhancing the social worker's armamentarium. *Social Work Education, 35*(5), 603–612.

Asimov, E. (2020, July 20). From good wine, a direct path to the wonders of nature. *The New York Times.* Retrieved from https://www.nytimes.com/2020/07/20/dining/drinks/wine-vineyard-viticulture-farming.html

Berman, M. G., Jonides, J., & Kaplan, S. (2008). The cognitive benefits of interacting with nature. *Psychological Science, 19*, 1207–1212.

Besthorn, F. H. (2012). Deep ecology's contributions to social work: A ten-year retrospective. *International Journal of Social Welfare, 21*(3), 248–259.

Besthorn, F. H., & Saleebey, D. (2003). Nature, genetics, and the biophilia connection: Exploring linkages with social work values and practice. *Advances in Social Work, 4*(1), 1–18.

Borrell, J., Lane, S., & Fraser, S. (2010). Integrating environmental issues into social work practice: Lessons learnt from domestic energy auditing. *Australian Social Work, 63*(3), 315–328.

Bui, Q., & Badger, E. (2020, May 22). The coronavirus quieted city noise. Listen to what's left. *The New York Times*. Retrieved from https://www.nytimes.com/interactive/2020/05/22/upshot/coronavirus-quiet-city-noise.html

Chalmers, D., Dell, C., Rohr, B., Dixon, J., Dowling, T., & Hanrahan, C. (2020). Recognizing animals as an important part of helping: A survey exploring knowledge and practice among Canadian social workers. *Critical Social Work, 21*(1), 1–29.

Cooley, S. J., Jones, C. R., Kurtz, A., & Robertson, N. (2020). 'Into the wild': A metasynthesis of talking therapy in natural outdoor spaces. *Clinical Psychological Review, 77*(1–14), 101841.

Cotter, H. (2018, February 12). Obama portraits blend paint and politics, and fact and fiction. *The New York Times*. Retrieved from https://www.nytimes.com/2018/02/12/arts/design/obama-portrait.html

Crews, D., & Besthorn, F. H. (2016). Ecosocial work and transformed consciousness: Reflections on eco-mindfulness engagement with the silence of the natural world. *Journal of Religion & Spirituality in Social Work: Social Thought, 35*(1–2), 91–107.

Dijkstra, K., Pieterse, M. E., & Pruyn, A. (2008). Stress-reducing effects of indoor plants in the built healthcare environment: The mediating role of perceived attractiveness. *Preventive Medicine, 47*, 279–283.

Feuer, A., & Salcedo, A. (2020, April 2). New York City deploys 45 mobile morgues as virus strains funeral homes. *The New York Times*. Retrieved from https://www.nytimes.com/2020/04/02/nyregion/coronavirus-new-york-bodies.html

Feuer, A., Southall, A., & Gold, M. (2020, April 29). Dozens of decomposing bodies found in trucks in Brooklyn funeral home. *The New York Times*. Retrieved from https://www.nytimes.com/2020/04/29/nyregion/bodies-brooklyn-funeral-home-coronavirus.html

Fromm, E. (1964). *The heart of man: Its genius for good and evil*. New York: Harper & Row.

Germain, C. (1981). The ecological approach to people-environmental transactions. *Social Casework, 62*(6), 323–331.

Gray, M., Coates, J., & Hetherington, T. (2007). Hearing indigenous voices in mainstream social work. *Families in Society, 88*(1), 55–66.

Heinsch, M. (2012). Getting down to earth: Finding a place for nature in social work practice. *International Journal of Social Welfare, 21*(3), 309–318.

Jegatheesan, B. (2018). *IAHAIO white paper*. Retrieved from https://iahaio.org/wp/wp-content/uploads/2020/07/iahaio_wp_updated-2020-aai-adjust-1.pdf

Lichtblau, D. (2010). Learning from the fields: Reflection on experience in the outdoors as professional development. *Critical Social Work, 11*(3), 9–28.

Maas, J., Verheij, R. A., Groenewegen, P. P., de Vries, S., & Spreeuwenberg, P. (2006). Green space, urbanity, and health: How strong is the relation? *Journal of Epidemiology and Community Health, 60*, 587–592.

Miller, S. E., Hayward, R. A., & Shaw, T. V. (2012). Environmental shifts for social work: A principles approach. *International Journal of Social Welfare, 21*, 270–277.

Mitchell, R., Astell-Burt, T., & Richardson, E. A. (2011). A comparison of green space indicators for epidemiological research. *Journal of Epidemiology and Community Health, 65*, 853–858.

Mosher, C. (2010). A wholistic paradigm for sustainability: Are social workers experts or partners? *Critical Social Work, 11*(3), 102–121.

Naess, A. (1973). The shallow and the deep, long-range ecology movement: A summary. *Inquiry, 16*(2), 95–100.

Norton, C. L. (2012). Social work and the environment: An ecosocial approach. *International Journal of Social Welfare, 21*, 299–308.

Park, B. J., Tsunetsugu, Y., Kasetani, T., Kagawa, T., & Miyazaki, Y. (2010). The physiological effects of Shirin-yoku (taking in the forest atmosphere or forest bathing): Evidence from field experiments in 24 forests across Japan. *Environmental Health and Preventive Medicine, 15*(1), 18–26.

Ramsay, S., & Boddy, J. (2017). Environmental social work: A concept analysis. *British Journal of Social Work, 47*, 68–86.

Risley-Curtiss, C. (2010). Social worker practitioners and the human-companion animal bond: A national study. *Social Work, 55*, 38–46.

Tosone, C., Nuttman-Shwartz, O., & Stephens, T. (2012). Shared trauma: When the professional gets personal. *Clinical Social Work Journal, 40*, 231–239.

Treisman, R. (2020, June 22). Barcelona opera reopens with an audience of plants. *NPR*. Retrieved from   https://www.npr.org/sections/coronavirus-live-updates/2020/06/22/881943143/barcelona-opera-reopens-with-an-audience-of-plants

Van den Berg, A. E., Koole, S. L., & Van der Wulp, N. Y. (2003). Environmental preference and restoration: (how) are they related? *Journal of Environmental Psychology, 23*, 135–146.

Wilson, E. O. (1984). *Biophilia: The human bond with other species*. Cambridge, MA: Harvard University Press.

Zapf, M. (2010). Social work and the environment: Understanding people and place. *Critical Social Work, 11*(3), 30–46.

Chapter 22
Building the Capacity of Neighborhoods and the Resilience of Neighbors to Respond to COVID-19: The Neighbor to Neighbor Volunteer Corps

Stacey Gordon, Ernest Gonzales, and Jillian Hinton

Background and Historical Perspective

By the end of March 2020, there were 44,771 cases of COVID-19 and 1096 COVID-19-related deaths in New York City (NYC Health 2020). Most businesses were closed with the exception of essential goods and services. By mid-March, social distancing (hereinafter referred to as physical distancing) was adopted state-wide, leaving many residents who needed help with activities of daily living and instrumental activities of daily living wondering how they were going to survive. And for individuals who lived alone, the fear of becoming exposed to and infected with COVID-19 with implications of daily survival was palpable. Federal programs were slow to respond to local needs of individuals. Federal and state agencies provided information on the pandemic with broad implications for physical distancing, but tangible assistance was absent.

Residents of university Faculty Housing, the majority of whom were faculty members, partners, and family members, wanted to help their neighbors however they could. Previously, the president and provost of the university, along with their leadership team, had identified urban issues, inequality, and supporting families of all ages as crosscutting themes important to the university in practice and in the development of scholarship and implementation of real-world resolutions. These priority areas guided the provost to establish a Work Life office in 2017. The Work Life office is committed to improving the well-being of its faculty members and administrators and serves as a bridge between university-wide policy and the unique needs of the university faculty and staff. An experienced social worker, hired as the executive director of Work Life, created a comprehensive program of support for

S. Gordon (✉) · E. Gonzales · J. Hinton
Silver School of Social Work, New York University, New York, NY, USA
e-mail: stacey.gordon@nyu.edu

© The Author(s), under exclusive license to Springer Nature Switzerland AG 2021
C. Tosone (ed.), *Shared Trauma, Shared Resilience During a Pandemic*, Essential Clinical Social Work Series,
https://doi.org/10.1007/978-3-030-61442-3_22

faculty and administrators throughout their work span in parenting, childcare, and early childhood to grade 12 education; in issues of aging, caregiving, and retirement; and in self-care, mental wellness, telework, and financial wellness. Work Life positioned itself at the center of multiple interdepartmental conversations about how to address faculty and administrator concerns at the university. Programming and consultations at Work Life were well underway when the pandemic hit, and because of Work Life's involvement in the university community, the office was able to pivot, engage, and respond with administrators from the Faculty Housing office to incorporate a civic engagement arm. The goal of this new initiative, Neighbor to Neighbor (N2N), was to help local residents with basic needs through telephone check-in assessments. With the absence of a national intervention combined with a strong desire among local residents to help, interacting with the university's institutional capacity, N2N was launched.

COVID-19 has a disproportionate impact not just among older adults when compared to their younger counterparts but also among individuals with underlying health issues, who are often racial and ethnic minorities and individuals with lower levels of socioeconomic status (Morrow-Howell and Gonzales 2020). We wanted to recognize, recruit, and train residents (Volunteers) who wanted to give back to society in this great time of pain. All of our Volunteers and clients (Neighbors) were living in Faculty Housing. Some had aged in place over the decades prior to the university's housing acquisition, while others were affiliated with the university. Volunteers were mostly female (60%), either faculty or partnered with a faculty member, highly educated with the majority having a PhD or MA degrees. Volunteers were 20% Black, 30% Latinx, and 50% White and represented at least 15 countries. They were, on average, 45 years of age. Nearly 8 out of 10 of the Neighbors identify as female. Approximately 20% of Neighbors served had been living in Faculty Housing since the late 1970s, prior to the time that the university took ownership of the buildings. Many Neighbors had underlying health conditions prior to COVID-19, and some employed home health aides who could not commute to work in the early days of the pandemic.

Conceptual Framework

The institutional framework of productive aging (Morrow-Howell et al. 2001; Gonzales et al. accepted) was an important heuristic tool that guided the development of our civic engagement program. We prioritized the values of health equity, choice, opportunity, and inclusion, given the great heterogeneity found within our neighborhood, as well as the various needs and preferences of the neighborhood residents. This model exemplifies aspects of the ecological framework with macro-, mezzo-, and micro-factors that interact with each other to develop a corps of Volunteers with subsequent outcomes. At the same time, the model can be used to help identify at-risk populations who might need assistance with basic and mental health needs by Volunteers.

The Program

The goals of N2N were to create connection and support between adults of all ages and abilities in Faculty Housing in an effort to build community social ties between residents. Residents were recruited to the program through a hand-delivered recruitment form sent to everyone living in Faculty Housing. The form provided space for residents to indicate whether they wanted to work as a Volunteer or receive a check-in call from a Volunteer. There was also space on the form to indicate whether residents were particularly concerned about another resident in Faculty Housing. Volunteers entered the program with varying levels of civic experience, and all were required to attend a virtual training session and several optional Volunteer check-ins conducted by the program leads. Program leads provided scripts to guide Volunteers through their telephone conversations with their Neighbor, with tips for conversation and space for the Volunteer to indicate the needs and preferences of the Neighbor, as they arose during the interaction. In the initial stage of contact, the Volunteer was requested to submit anonymous results of conversations to the program leads. Information collected helped the program leads assess whether the program was appropriately targeting the needs of the population. The language used in the script was designed to encourage mutual support between Volunteer-Neighbor pairs, promote autonomy and integrity, and draw careful attention to ageist assumptions and language. Neighbors were encouraged to discuss their coping strategies with Volunteers and to elicit coping strategies and tips from Neighbors, especially those tips and strategies they had employed in difficult situations in the past. Encouraging mutual support was also intended to reduce ageism and ableism, and ageist and ableist attitudes, and to promote a sense of solidarity between the Volunteers and Neighbors. Volunteers were encouraged to discuss with their Neighbor about how often to make contact. Many in the initial phase of the program were making weekly check-in telephone calls.

Health Care

In the initial phase of the project, we found that many residents in Faculty Housing did not have access to their regular healthcare providers. There were several incidents where Neighbors and Volunteers needed an emergency checkup and a prescription for an antibiotic or other medication, and it was widely regarded as unsafe to go to the local emergency room. In response, we created a collaboration with a visiting medical provider who carefully conducted home visits, informed by CDC guidelines, to Faculty Housing residents. This provider used personal protective equipment and followed proper protocol when entering and exiting the residence of each program participant.

Food Resources

When the shelter-in-place order in NYC first occurred, several employees in the Work Life office and residents in Faculty Housing purchased large amounts of dry goods and toiletries to keep on hand as pantry items in case residents needed supplies and were unable to leave their homes or purchase supplies online. As the weeks progressed, it became clear that some grocery stores in the area were remaining open and continued to be well-stocked. The program leads decided to keep the dry goods for Neighbors or Volunteers who expressed food insecurity, and program leads worked with building staff, such as door attendants and superintendents, to deliver bags of food and toiletries. We created a collaboration with the director of the university's philanthropic campaign who connected us with a local senior center that regularly provides meals to older adults in the community. During the COVID-19 pandemic, they began offering "grab-and-go" meals to their community members and extended their grab-and-go food service to our program participants. We offered these meals to anyone in the program. Each week the meals were delivered to a spot set up by Faculty Housing, and participants picked up meals themselves, or their Volunteers picked them up and delivered them to their Neighbor.

Mental Wellness

Mental wellness was an area of great concern for the program leads. A scale to gauge the mental wellness of Faculty Housing residents was included in the Volunteer script. Volunteers were instructed to ask Neighbors to indicate where they stood on a scale ranging from "content as usual" to "quite concerned about myself and my mood and need a mental health referral."

Volunteers were instructed to be in contact with the program leads immediately if the Neighbor indicated that they were beginning to feel concerned about themselves or were quite concerned about themselves. Volunteers were also instructed to offer a professional mental health assessment to Neighbors. The in-depth assessments were conducted by the university's School of Social Work doctoral students and faculty members who volunteered to assess Neighbors and, if necessary, refer them to a network of clinical practitioners in the community.

Technology Assistance

With the imposed isolation during the pandemic, we recognized that people unfamiliar with technology might not have their usual means of support when technology problems arose. We also wanted to provide support for those who wished to connect with others through virtual means. To help as many people as possible find access to various ways of technological connection, we created a collaboration with Cyber-Seniors, an organization providing meaningful intergenerational contact through mentorships between younger and older generations who teach each other technology and life skills, a reciprocal and beneficial exchange. Neighbors were given the website and telephone number of Cyber-Seniors and were instructed to connect with their Volunteer to help them research courses available. Given the lack of normal activities over the summer months, Work Life put out a call to recruit teenage community members to become mentors for the Cyber-Seniors program during the summer months.

Outcome and Critique of the Program

At the beginning of the program, there were 100 Volunteers and 125 Faculty Housing residents who signed up to be part of the program. By the time we had completed the first training and Volunteers made their initial first check-in telephone calls, a major unforeseen issue arose. Many individuals living in New York City during the early phase of the pandemic, including those living in Faculty Housing, left the city to go to second homes or the homes of family members who lived outside of New York City (Bellafante 2020). Many of those who left had signed up to receive a telephone check-in from a Volunteer and were not answering their home telephone numbers. After trying several times to make contact with their Neighbor and receiving no response, several Volunteers grew wary of the program altogether and dropped out. Some Volunteers requested another Neighbor to check in on, and others expressed frustration that they were unable to "do" anything to help and were resentful because they had been promised a job to do and could not do it. Volunteers also expressed frustration with the program, saying that they wished there was more to do to help their Neighbors, and offered a critique of the Neighbors, saying that they were "too independent," potentially implying a wish that the Neighbors were less competent so the Volunteers could feel more useful and valuable. This is an area for further inquiry and relates to the research on ageism in general and specifically to ageism in the family (Gordon 2020). Often family members express frustration at the independent decision-making of their older loved ones, when they are offering help or asserting control in managing their affairs. Expressing low expectations of the capabilities of older adults is a form of affective ageism which can, in certain circumstances, lead to age discrimination.

Although we provided instruction in conducting the mental wellness part of the script, two Volunteers decided to withdraw from the program because they felt uncomfortable inquiring about mental health. After a discussion, it was revealed that in one case there was also a language barrier, and the Volunteer did not feel that he could fully understand the language expressed around mental health concerns. The other Volunteer revealed that she was battling with her own mental health and felt overwhelmed by her own needs at the time and could not find the energy to help her Neighbor.

Emerging Evidence on Shared Trauma and Shared Resilience

The literature on trauma informs us of both the potential for negative consequences and of the potential for positive consequences and growth of individuals exposed to traumatic experiences (Nuttman-Shwartz 2014). Participation in N2N during the COVID-19 pandemic provided an opportunity for both Volunteers and Neighbors to give and receive support from one another, during a time when both parties were experiencing trauma stemming from COVID-19. The concept of shared trauma (Tosone et al. 2012) usually relates to the therapist-client dyad but is applicable to our Volunteer-Neighbor pairs in this instance of shared pandemic-related trauma. Clinicians also report positive consequences of working with trauma victims, such as increased resilience and emotional expressiveness, independence, and self-confidence (Nuttman-Shwartz 2014; Arnold et al. 2005). Volunteers in N2N reported satisfaction in their ability to provide services and see their Neighbors thrive with the support they gave. Volunteers expressed satisfaction at the opportunity to give back to their community and to feel productive during a time when the surrounding community seemed to be spiraling out of control. Below are some themes from Volunteers about their experiences:

> One of my relatives died from COVID-19 in a hospital not far from where I live. There was a sort of helplessness because I couldn't see the person or memorialize their life. I felt it was incredibly depressing for all of us, and the act of volunteerism and just thinking about other people kind of prevented me from going down into a hole, I think. There's nothing like helping other people to encourage you to forget your own woes. So yeah, it was good for that. Did it help me deal with the first wave of the pandemic? I guess there's this sort of psychological place where when you're forced to console other people and tell them everything's going to be ok, then you kind of believe it yourself, so in that way it was helpful, I suppose. But it was also good and it was mutually beneficial, in that they turned out to be my upstairs neighbors whom I'd wanted to get to know better anyway. They're such nice people. I'm grateful for that match.
> [Female, age 49, married]
>
> I think it was just good, in general, to help us remain connected to the community and to remind ourselves to support each other, and it also gave me the opportunity to meet people within my own building that I had never really met before...I think it has given me a stronger sense of community within my own building and within the community at large.
> [Female, age 56, married]

Neighbors also experienced growth and satisfaction in their participation in the N2N project. The experience of mutual help through empathic bonding (Nuttman-Shwartz 2014) is illustrated in the quotes below. The Volunteer-Neighbor pairs felt empathy toward one another and formed tight bonds with one another and expressed interest in keeping in touch with one another:

> I felt so glad to be connected with someone who was near me during this time. It took a while to get to know him, but now I am happy that we have a good relationship. We speak every week, and I'm looking forward to getting to know him better when we can socialize together outside.
> [Female, age 72, lives alone]

My Volunteer brought me groceries and food and I am so grateful to her. I really feel like she cares about me, and I didn't even know her before the pandemic. We talked a lot over the phone, and discussed books and plays, and I felt comfort because I knew that she was there, especially during the time that we could not leave our apartments.
[Male, age 76, lives alone]
    I had a medical issue and my Volunteer made sure that I was seen by a doctor, and she got my prescription and food for me when I was ill. This helped me feel less alone.
[Female, age 81, lives alone]

Productive Aging: The Civic Dimension

The N2N program was based on the premise that residents were able to choose whether to become a Volunteer or a Neighbor, and while the majority of the Volunteers were young to middle-aged adults, many were over the age of 65 years and either still working at the university or retired from their faculty position. Older Volunteers contributed their own knowledge of community resources and experiences as community members, and this added richness and depth to the training and follow-up Volunteer community discussions. The desire to give back may have satisfied important psychosocial developmental goals, such as generativity and integrity (Slater 2003; Erikson 1974). Recognizing the positive impact of volunteering on older adults (Gonzales et al. 2015, 2019) and the positive impact of the N2N program on the community as a whole, the program leads intend to continue and expand the N2N program in the future to include additional communities within the university.

References

Arnold, D., Calhoun, L. G., Tedeschi, R., & Cann, A. (2005). Vicarious posttraumatic growth in psychotherapy. *Journal of Humanistic Psychology, 45*, 239–263.
Bellafante, G. (2020, March 14). *The rich have a coronavirus cure: Escape from New York.* Retrieved August 03, 2020, from https://www.nytimes.com/2020/03/14/nyregion/Coronavirus-nyc-rich-wealthy-residents.html.
Erikson, E. H. (1974). *Dimensions of a new identity.* New York: Norton.
Gonzales, E., Matz-Costa, C., & Morrow-Howell, N. (2015, April). Increasing opportunities for the productive engagement of older adults: A response to population aging. *The Gerontologist, 55*(2), 252–261.
Gonzales, E., Suntai, Z., & Abrams, J. (2019). Volunteering and Health outcomes among older adults. In D. Gu & M. Dupre (Eds.), *Encyclopedia of gerontology and population aging.* Cham: Springer.
Gonzales, E., Morrow-Howell, N., Angel, J., Fredman, L., Marchiondo, L. A., Harootyan, R., Choi, J., Choudhury, N., Carolan, K., Lee, K., Tan, E., Yu, P., Shea, E., & Matz, C.. (accepted). Integrating AASW&SW's grand challenges of productive aging and health equity to guide efforts to improve the health of an aging population. In M. Teasley, M. Spencer & M. Bartholomew (Eds). *Racism and the grand challenges for the social work profession.* New York: Oxford University Press.

Gonzales, E., Gordon, S., Whetung, C., Connaught, G., Collazo, J., & Hinton, J.. (under review). *Acknowledging structural discrimination in the context of a pandemic: Advancing an anti-racist, anti-sexist, and anti-ageist movement.*

Gordon, S. (2020). Ageism and age discrimination in the family: Applying an intergenerational critical consciousness approach. *Clinical Social Work Journal., 48,* 169.

Morrow-Howell, N., & Gonzales, E. (2020). Recovering from COVID-19: Recommitting to a productive aging perspective. *Public Policy & Aging Report, XX*(X), 1–5.

Morrow-Howell, N., Hinterlong, J., & Sherraden, M. (Eds.). (2001). *Productive aging: Concepts and controversies.* Baltimore: John Hopkins University Press.

Nuttman-Shwartz, O. (2014). Shared resilience in a traumatic reality: A new concept for trauma workers exposed personally and professionally to collective disaster. *Trauma, Violence, and Abuse,* 1–10.

NYC Health. (2020, March 31). *Coronavirus disease 2019 (COVID-19) daily data summary.* NYC Health | City of New York. https://www1.nyc.gov/assets/doh/downloads/pdf/imm/covid-19-daily-data-summary-03312020-2.pdf

Slater, C. L. (2003). Generativity versus stagnation: An elaboration of Erikson's adult stage of human development. *Journal of Adult Development, 10*(1), 53–65.

Tosone, C., Nuttman-Shwartz, O., & Stephens, T. (2012). Shared trauma: When the professional is personal. *Clinical Social Work Journal, 40*(2), 231–239.

Jill Hinton is pursuing a BA in Psychology at CUNY-Brooklyn College in New York City and is completing an internship through the Center of Health and Aging Research, Policy, and Practice at NYU Silver School of Social Work. She is especially interested in geriatric mental health.

Chapter 23
The Importance of Pets During a Global Pandemic: See Spot Play

Katherine Compitus

Shared trauma can be defined as a traumatic event or experience that is experienced simultaneously by the clinician and the client. This parallel process may help strengthen the rapport between the client and clinician since the client already knows that the clinician is experiencing similar stressors (Tosone 2020). For example, during the current pandemic, both clients and clinicians may fear for their own health and the health of a loved one and may feel worsening mental health symptoms such as derealization and loneliness due to isolation. Professors at social work schools must deal with another layer, since they must help the students process their own feelings of trauma and guide the students in their care for clients while simultaneously navigating their own feelings of loss and confusion.

For educators and clinicians who work at animal-assisted therapy (AAT), there is another party involved in the shared trauma experience – the therapy animal. Although the animals may not understand what is happening in the world, they certainly feel the effects. The therapeutic benefits of the human-animal bond have taken center stage during this global pandemic, and people who may not know the science behind the human-animal bond still realize that interacting with animals can help people feel better. The relationship between humans and animals is being looked at in new and interesting ways. Pets are being adopted from shelters in record numbers never seen before, and many people are considering whether factory farming practices are the root cause of the current pandemic (Rothan and Byrareddy 2020). Clinicians, such as myself, who primarily utilize animal-assisted therapy as a treatment model, have had to make significant adaptations to the treatment protocol since public visits have been limited due to government restrictions. This chapter will discuss my own experience as a clinician who contracted COVID-19, the shared trauma experienced by myself and my clients, and necessary adaptations to

K. Compitus (✉)
New York University, New York, NY, USA

© The Author(s), under exclusive license to Springer Nature Switzerland AG 2021
C. Tosone (ed.), *Shared Trauma, Shared Resilience During a Pandemic*, Essential Clinical Social Work Series, https://doi.org/10.1007/978-3-030-61442-3_23

the animal-assisted therapy model in order to ensure the continued health and well-being of clients, their pets, and the clinician (myself).

The human-animal bond has shown to be a powerful relational tool, effective in treating a number of mental and physical ailments, from anxiety to diabetes. Interacting with animals provides people with a sense of joy, perhaps because they appear to love us unconditionally and without judgment (Compitus 2019). The benefits are not only psychological and social but also biological. Studies show that when we spend time with pets, oxytocin (the love hormone) is raised and cortisol (the stress hormone) is lowered in the body (Beetz et al. 2012). For example, recent research shows that we can increase the quality of life in older adults who have been diagnosed with dementia by increasing the amount of time they spend interacting with animals (Baek et al. 2020). When older adults with dementia spend time with pets, including their own, it may alleviate depression, boredom, and anxiety and even help to improve cognitive functioning (Baek et al. 2020). They may remember the name of their pet or a visiting pet (even when they are no longer able to remember the names of their own family members); they may smile more, laugh, and report a greater sense of happiness.

The therapeutic benefits of interacting with animals are not limited to the patients but also extend to caregivers and may be a welcome break in the day from the burnout that often plagues them. But what happens when the caregiver is the one who is unwell? When I contracted COVID-19 in March 2020, I had all the typical symptoms: pressure in the chest, a sore throat, body aches, chills, and horrible fatigue. My doctor believes that I had a relatively mild case, since my fever never went above 101 degrees Fahrenheit. Although it was called a mild case, it felt crippling to me. The fatigue was the worst aspect for me – when I walked across my living room, I felt as if I had just run a marathon. These symptoms lasted for 4 weeks and severely limited my activities of daily living.

At the time that I contracted COVID-19, I was teaching classes at three major universities. I also live on my micro-farm sanctuary which provides AAT for trauma survivors. I currently have 37 animals at the sanctuary, and we include a variety of species in our AAT, from cows to dogs. I was suddenly unable to care for the animals at the sanctuary, since I was too sick to muck out a barn or to carry bags of grain. In fact, I was so weak that I was unable to feed our indoor dogs and cats. It was near impossible to have friends and family, or volunteers, to come help care for the animals, since they would be at risk of contracting COVID-19 if they came to our property. Luckily, my husband has an extremely strong immune system and, with my direction, was able to care for the animals during my illness. It caused me to wonder how we would have managed to care for our pets if we both had become sick at the same time or how people who lived alone, and had to shelter alone, cared for their pets if they became ill. I started thinking about how COVID-19 not only affected people but also how the human-animal bond had altered the way people interacted with pets. As a clinician, I also had to quickly learn how to adapt the AAT to a virtual format, since people were no longer able to attend therapy in person.

My university classes all moved to an online format, and my students were extremely understanding and helpful while I recovered from COVID-19.

Nuttman-Shwartz (2015) wrote that "empathic mutual aid relationships" (p. 4) are one of the most important aspects of resilience in shared traumatic situations. Although my students were also experiencing the multiple fears involved in experiencing a world pandemic (health fears, financial fears, academic fears), they were incredibly supportive of my recovery. It was the shared experience and empathic bonding between myself and my students that helped us all create a holding environment (Winnicott 1960) (albeit virtual) that allowed us to become more connected with each other and to share strategies to help navigate the shared trauma that we were experiencing with our clients. Since none of us had ever lived through a world pandemic, the students in my human-animal bond class were instrumental in brainstorming ways to adapt AAT to a virtual environment. Research into shared trauma shows that "in situations of adversity, resilience is observed when individuals engage in behaviors that help them navigate their way to the resources they need to flourish" (Nuttman-Shwartz 2015, p. 4). It was the collaborative nature of the class that I believe helped both myself and my students feel an increased sense of self-efficacy at a time when many of us felt so out of control. I was later able to share some of our ideas with other animal-assisted therapists, thus helping the scope of our project reach other clients and pets outside of our own.

O'Haire et al. (2019) state that "in the wake of crisis (e.g. natural disasters, acts of community violence and terror), communities are shaken. Normalcy seems a distant memory; and panic, loss, and numbness pervade. In these times, many people take great comfort in the presence of a friendly animal, such as a therapy or companion animal" (p. 16). My students and I hypothesized that the presence of an animal during a world crisis was naturally comforting to many people. Many states implemented shelter-in-place orders, and restaurants and other public venues were shut down. People became afraid to visit friends and family for fear of spreading or contracting the virus. Older adults, especially those in assisted living facilities, were not allowed visits from family members since they were considered highest at risk. My students and I postulated that during the pandemic animals were being adopted from shelters for a variety of reasons.

Primarily, the animal would provide a companion for people who were socially isolated, especially for those who were sheltering alone. Social isolation is a grand challenge in social work because the effects of loneliness can result in internalizing disorders such as dysthymia and major depression and may even lead to death (Grand Challenges for Social Work 2015). Of course, isolation is not the same as loneliness, and perhaps by socially isolating with a companion animal, many people were able to avoid feeling lonely, while still being mindful of the government regulations.

Another reason that we believe that people were adopting animals was the effect of oxytocin (briefly mentioned above). Oxytocin is a hormone that causes people to feel safe, secure, and happy. Studies show that oxytocin is released when people fall in love, when a mother holds her child, or when a person pets an animal (Beetz et al. 2012). Kruger and Serpell (2010) suggest that AAT is an effective treatment modality because it creates a relationship and offers affection in a nonthreatening manner. Certainly during in-person AAT, the therapy animal is often seen as more trustworthy than a person and, therefore, may facilitate the development of trust between the therapist and client. During the pandemic, other people were seen as physically untrustworthy, since it is impossible to tell who carries the virus, and yet it is considered unlikely that animals can contract or spread the coronavirus. Perhaps people were naturally turning to animals as a source of companionship and affection, for a sense of physical and emotional safety, and as a trustworthy companion. Other reasons for increasing human-animal interactions in a traumatogenic environment include providing people with "a source of non judgmental support, stress-reducing companionship, positive outlets for joy and laughter, a safe haven for physical touch and emotional vulnerability" (O'Haire et al. 2019, p.16). My students and I began to share more stories about our own pets, as the news of the spreading virus worsened. Speaking about a purring cat or a silly dog seemed to give us back a sense of normalcy during a time when we were all experiencing a sense of disequilibrium and derealization.

Pets are common companions to people of all ages from young children to older adults, and a strong bond may form between people and their pets (Peretti 1990). The pet becomes a companion, a buddy, and someone to talk to and to care for and may even provide a purpose to continue living after friends and family have passed away (Cohen 2002; Irvine 2013). People began to die from COVID-19 in record numbers, and for those who have friends that have passed away, the pets may become surrogate friends, while pets may function as surrogate family members for those who are unable to hug their own kin (Veevers 2016). My students and I hypothesized that pets not only model mindful and joyous living (Compitus 2019) but that they also were less at risk of dying from the illness and, therefore, were a more dependable attachment figure at a time when even young healthy people were dying.

Since none of us had ever experienced such a global crisis before, my students and I thought of ways to adapt AAT to fit the current health restrictions. There are multiple types of animal-assisted interventions, and we tried to come up with ideas to fit a variety of circumstances. For example, a common scenario in animal-assisted education is when a child is nervous about reading out loud, but the nonjudgmental presence of a therapy animal may help increase their sense of confidence. Since we could no longer bring therapy animals into schools or hospitals, my students suggested animal-assisted teletherapy for students who were now being schooled at home. Many clinicians had already moved their practice to teletherapy, so moving AAT to a virtual model was a natural suggestion. Of course, the tactile stimulation and soothing effects of petting an animal would no longer be available, but the child would still be able to read and interact with the therapy animal. Another suggestion for virtual animal-assisted education was to have children write letters to the therapy animals. This would only work for clients who had already established a relationship with the therapy animal, but it was a great way to engage children through animal-assisted learning.

Interestingly, many large corporations also began integrating animals in a therapeutic capacity in their staff meetings. Naturally, people's children and pets would appear in the background of a virtual meeting. But corporations began to solicit the appearance of therapy animals, such as llamas, horses, and dogs, to weekly virtual meetings. Perhaps the appearance of the therapy animal lightened the mood, provided a sense of cohesion among the staff (a shared common experience), or simply was a welcome distraction from the serious health and economic crisis that was happening. O'Haire et al. (2019) suggest that "in the face of trauma, people can feel ostracized, stigmatized, and alone … the trusted presence of an animal may help foster social engagement … as well as their meaningful reconnection with society" (p. 24). People may not have known or understood why they were naturally moving toward animal-assisted interactions, but these new trends certainly illustrate that our reliance on animals for emotional support should not be overlooked.

Conclusion

During times of uncertainty, animal companions can provide us with a stable attachment object, an increased capacity for self-efficacy and self-regulation, and a method of safely engaging with the social environment (from a safe distance). For those with dogs, they still had to leave the house to provide relief walks for the dog, and this got people moving, exercising, and out of the imposed isolation of their house. For people with other types of pets, sharing pictures and stories of their pets' antics on media outlets like Instagram and Facebook was another way to remain connected to the outside world. As we prepare to slowly reopen our sanctuary to clients (while observing strict health regulations), I am cautious but optimistic that we will be able to continue to help people regain a sense of equilibrium. A cow or a pig, a dog or a cat, they all live in the moment, even while being cautiously aware of their surroundings. There is a lot that we can learn from our relationships with animals, and although the current health crisis is certainly tragic, at least people have naturally found an adapting coping strategy that has fur and four feet. Although we share in this traumatic experience, we are also sharing our strategies for resilience. Animal companionship is a type of self-care that, perhaps, we all could use right now.

References

Baek, S. M., Lee, Y., & Sohng, K. Y. (2020). The psychological and behavioural effects of an animal-assisted therapy programme in Korean older adults with dementia. *Psychogeriatrics*.

Beetz, A., Uvnäs-Moberg, K., Julius, H., & Kotrschal, K. (2012). Psychosocial and psychophysiological effects of human-animal interactions: The possible role of oxytocin. *Frontiers in Psychology, 3*, 234.

Cohen, S. (2002). Can pets function as family members? *Western Journal of Nursing Research, 24*(6), 621–638.

Compitus, K. (2019). Traumatic pet loss and the integration of attachment-based animal assisted therapy. *Journal of Psychotherapy Integration, 29*(2), 119–131.

Grand Challenges for Social Work. (2015). http://grandchallengesforsocialwork.org/wp-content/uploads/2015/12/180604-GC-social-isolation.pdf, retrieved April 25, 2019.

Irvine, L. (2013). Animals as lifechangers and lifesavers: Pets in the redemption narratives of homeless people. *Journal of Contemporary Ethnography, 42*(1), 3–30.

Kruger, K. A., & Serpell, J. A. (2010). Animal-assisted interventions in mental health: Definitions and theoretical foundations. In *Handbook on animal-assisted therapy* (pp. 33–48). New York: Academic Press.

Nuttman-Shwartz, O. (2015). Shared resilience in a traumatic reality: A new concept for trauma workers exposed personally and professionally to collective disaster. *Trauma, Violence, & Abuse, 16*(4), 466–475.

O'Haire, M. E., Philip Tedeschi, M. S. S. W., Jenkins, M. A., Braden, S. R., & Rodriguez, K. E. (2019). The impact of human-animal interaction in trauma recovery. In *New directions in the human-animal bond* (Vol. 15). West Lafayette: Purdue University Press.

Peretti, P. O. (1990). Elderly-animal friendship bonds. *Social Behavior and Personality: An International Journal, 18*(1), 151–156.

Rothan, H. A., & Byrareddy, S. N. (2020). The epidemiology and pathogenesis of coronavirus disease (COVID-19) outbreak. *Journal of Autoimmunity, 109*, 102433.

Tosone, C. (2020). Shared trauma and social work practice during communal disasters. In J. Duffy, J. Campbell, & C. Tosone (Eds.), *International perspectives on social work and political conflict* (pp. 50–64). New York: Routledge.

Veevers, J. E. (2016). The social meanings of pets: Alternative roles for companion animals. In *Pets and the family* (pp. 11–30). New York: Routledge.

Winnicott, D. W. (1960). The theory of the parent-infant relationship. *International Journal of Psycho-Analysis, 41*, 585–595.

Chapter 24
Dialectical Behavior Therapy and the COVID-19 Pandemic: Building a Life Worth Living in the Face of an Unrelenting Crisis

Madelaine Ellberger

Introduction

"What on earth is going on and how are we going to make this work?". These were the words that repeatedly came to my mind beginning in March 2020 as news of the novel coronavirus, formally known as COVID-19, spread across the media as quickly as the virus itself spread throughout the globe. I, along with the rest of the world, watched as nation after nation swiftly entered into crisis mode and culminated in a screeching halt. In all areas of life, people swiftly did what they could to adapt their professional and personal lives to the new socially and physically distanced reality. This phenomenon, which is still persisting, shifting, and changing, is known among the psychiatric community as shared trauma (Tosone 2012). Shared trauma is defined as the multidimensional response that mental health clinicians experience as a result of primary or secondary exposure to the same collective trauma as their patients (Tosone 2012). While one can argue that the appearance of COVID-19 has left the entire world enmeshed together in an experience of collective trauma, this experience is particularly unique for mental health providers. As mental health clinicians, we immerse ourselves in the pain, joy, triumphs, and failures of other people's lives. However, with good training and supervision, we learn to separate ourselves from our patients' experience. It is rare that we find ourselves immersed in simultaneous trauma with our patients, and yet that is exactly what has occurred in the wake of the global pandemic. I, like my other clinician constitutes, observed with dread as we quickly were forced to accept that we must learn to practice and treat our patients through an Internet-linked webcam.

M. Ellberger (✉)
Silver School of Social Work, New York University, New York, NY, USA

The Center for Cognitive and Dialectical Behavior Therapy, Lake Success, NY, USA
e-mail: mellberger@ccdbt.com

© The Author(s), under exclusive license to Springer Nature Switzerland AG 2021
C. Tosone (ed.), *Shared Trauma, Shared Resilience During a Pandemic*,
Essential Clinical Social Work Series,
https://doi.org/10.1007/978-3-030-61442-3_24

As a clinician practicing dialectical behavior therapy (DBT), I have spent many days and years staring directly at death and joining my patients on a journey toward navigating how and what it means to build a life worth living. DBT, written by Dr. Marsha Linehan (1993), is an evidence-based treatment aimed directly at treating borderline personality disorder, chronic suicidality, self-injury, and extreme emotion dysregulation. The treatment provides a blueprint of skills for clinicians to help patients learn a new way of living, once described to me by a middle-aged patient as a new lease on life. From the start of the COVID-19 pandemic, I have leaned on DBT as a guide for myself both clinically and personally, just as I have helped my patients do so.

The COVID-19 pandemic has ravaged the bodies, finances, minds, and souls of every individual in more ways than one. The entire human population is feeling the impact of the increase in these stressors, with the psychological impact being potentially as great as the physical. Prior to the onset of this global pandemic, suicide was already considered a major public health problem (World Health Organization 2018). According to the National Institute of Mental Health (2018), suicide is the 10th leading cause of death overall in the United States. It is important to note that the current pandemic did not cancel out all other health crises but rather is occurring alongside them. In reflecting on the experience of providing DBT in the age of COVID-19, I am reminded of a radical acceptance, a core strategy taught in the distress tolerance module in DBT skills training (1993). Rejecting reality does not change it, and in order to change reality, you must first accept it. This chapter will offer a reflection on the experience of providing dialectical behavior therapy during the ongoing COVID-19 pandemic. In doing so, the chapter will provide an overview of DBT in order to highlight the impact of the pandemic on the provider, the patient, and implementation of the treatment itself. Obstacles and adaptations to treatment will be presented through the lens of the four components of DBT. Throughout the chapter, clinical case examples will be provided in italics to bring the discussion to life. Names, gender, and all other identifying information have been altered in order to maintain confidentiality.

Dialectical Behavior Therapy: An Overview

Dialectical behavior therapy (DBT) was first created by Marsha Linehan (1993) as a cognitive behavioral treatment to reduce suicidal behaviors as a result of emotion dysregulation in individuals diagnosed with borderline personality disorder (BPD). The combination of interpersonal difficulties, the complexity of presentation with other comorbid issues, and high-risk behaviors often exhibited by individuals with BPD has led many mental health clinicians to label individuals diagnosed with BPD as untreatable patients (Fava and Ellberger 2020). A large body of evidence exists to substantiate DBT as a successful treatment for individuals who meet criteria for BPD. Randomized controlled trials with adults diagnosed with BPD indicate that compared to psychotherapy by clinicians not trained in DBT (referred to as "treatment as usual"), standard DBT significantly reduces suicidality, self-harm, hospital admissions, emergency room visits, anger outbursts, and hopelessness (Feigenbaum et al. 2012; Linehan et al. 1991, 1993; Verheul et al. 2003). This finding has been validated with adult populations being treated in outpatient clinics, on inpatient units, and in forensic institutions. According to the Cochrane Collaboration Review, DBT is the only treatment adequately supported by data to be deemed an effective, empirically supported treatment modality for BPD (Stoffers-Winterling et al. 2012). DBT has also been identified as a primary or supplementary treatment modality for individuals with substance disorders (Lee et al. 2015; Pennay et al. 2011), eating disorders (Harned et al. 2008), and posttraumatic stress disorder (Harned et al. 2014).

Linehan has provided a solution to this problem in the psychiatric community in the form of DBT, an empirically validated, comprehensive, and effective mode of treatment for BPD. DBT is comprised of four main facets: individual therapy, group skills training, phone coaching, and consultation team (Linehan 1993). At its most basic core, DBT is a treatment of emotions. Through a dialectical synthesis balancing acceptance and change strategies, patients learn how to both accept and manage their big emotions in order to gain more competence and sense of control over their life. As a DBT practitioner of several years, I will describe each of these facets using my own clinical experience to create a more robust picture of the way in which DBT works.

Individual Therapy

In considering the breakdown of the different components of DBT, I think about individual DBT as the place in which the patient and the therapist take a fine-tooth comb to the patient's experiences. The goal of individual therapy is to increase awareness of ineffective behavioral response patterns and create goals targeting changes in these areas in order to establish a more secure and rewarding life. In individual therapy, time is spent helping patients apply and generalize skills learned in group to specific areas of their life. At the same time, a part of the session time is also spent observing and processing the transactions between the therapist and the patient as a way to address patterns of behavior in vivo. These two components are crucial to the success of treatment, as in DBT we believe that without the mindfulness of what is pulling at us in the moment, we cannot begin to do something differently. Through the use of various interventions such as diary cards, behavior chain analysis, validation, and irreverence, the patient learns and practices slowing down their cognitive process enough to begin to understand the function of his or her behavior.

DBT clinicians are required to maintain the basic assumptions of the treatment, which call for a nonjudgmental and radically genuine way in communicating with the patient (Linehan 1993). There is a broad base of literature that maintains that one of the greatest predictors of therapeutic success, regardless of disorder or treatment modality, is the relationship between the provider and patient (Choi-Kain et al. 2017; Flückiger et al. 2012; Woolcott Jr 1985). Patients engaging in DBT have often endured prior relationships in treatment and in their lives in which they may have experienced rejection as a result of their pathology. The only way in which to help such patients believe that change is possible is through a trusting and caring therapeutic relationship.

Skills Training Group

Primary to the model, DBT also includes a group skills training component. When explaining the treatment to a new patient, I like to call skills group the "bread and butter" of DBT. Skills training group is where patients learn replacement behaviors in order to reduce and extinguish engaging in dangerous or impulsive behaviors in the context of emotion dysregulation. From a behavioral perspective, the concept of replacement behaviors is important. It allows people to practice a new way of being, rather than just expecting people to be different or feel different without instruction. In fact, learning and practicing skills builds a sense of mastery over the self and the internal experience and is considered by Linehan and those of us who practice DBT to be a significant component in recovery from borderline personality symptoms (Linehan 1993).

Within the adult DBT model, there are four modules of skills, each of which correspond to the problem behaviors that bring folks into DBT (Linehan 1993). These modules are mindfulness, distress tolerance, emotion regulation, and interpersonal effectiveness. In my own experience, I would argue that the entire treatment model is couched in mindfulness. That is to say that one can't opt in their awareness to "do something different" if they aren't aware of what exactly is pulling at them and what else they could do to get what they need. That is what mindfulness provides, in my opinion – choices. Distress tolerance is the crisis management module. In this module, patients learn how to delay urges and decrease impulsivity by mindfully turning their awareness onto other stimuli (Linehan 1993). This module is particularly important in building behavioral control over suicidal and self-injurious urges, as well as other target behaviors (Linehan 1993). The rationale for this module is simple and founded in basic learning principles: the less one reinforces a thought or behavior, the less likely it is to remain present and will eventually become extinct. Emotion regulation skills are what I like to call "life worth living skills." These skills help patients become more effective problem-solvers of their emotions, learn to create and break down reasonable goals, and behaviorally activate (Linehan 1993). They literally help someone begin to live a life that looks like that which he or she may describe as desirable. Lastly, interpersonal effectiveness skills help people bring more balance into their relationships in order to maintain positive relationships and create effective boundaries. This set of skills is particularly helpful in helping patients tolerate and reduce ineffective behavior in the context of fears of abandonment or rejection (Linehan 1993).

Phone Coaching

By definition, phone coaching is the opportunity for DBT patients to engage in brief, out-of-session communication with their individual therapist in times of extreme emotion dysregulation and crisis. The main goal of phone coaching is skills generalization (Linehan 1993). Particularly at the beginning of treatment, it is helpful for patients to reach out to their therapist in a time of crisis in order to utilize a skill in their environment in the moment, rather than engage in an ineffective behavior out of habitual patterns of responding. However, based on my clinical experience, I might argue that an equally valuable secondary effect of phone coaching is building and reinforcing the relationship between the patient and therapist. I have found that simply the knowledge that I am available to patients outside of session, in my "real life," helps the patient feel held even in the context of behavioral treatment. Out-of-session contact can also be used to make repairs between the patient and therapist or to share good news. We bring ourselves, our personalities, and our emotions into treatment in order to reinforce to patients that this relationship, even if it is therapeutic, is real.

Consultation Team

The final component of DBT is the weekly consultation team meeting. The purpose of the consultation team is to ensure that each clinician is providing the best care possible with each patient. Each week, my DBT team meets for 3 h to discuss aspects of cases each clinician might be struggling with or have questions about. The team provides the clinician with valuable feedback from multiple perspectives on how to best help the patient. The consultation team upholds the primary tenant of the dialectical thinking, in that there is no one correct way of seeing a situation and solving a problem and no one absolute truth. The consultation team serves as "therapy for the therapist," providing validation and support in problem-solving to help the clinicians deal with their own therapy-interfering behaviors, emotions, thoughts, or burnout. DBT is not a treatment that should be done in isolation, as that stands in complete opposite of the notion of dialectical thinking. DBT clinicians deal primarily and consistently with very complex issues such as suicidality, self-harm, and trauma. Just as the therapist is on a journey with the patient, so, too, is the consultation team on a journey with the therapist.

Providing DBT During COVID-19

I am a senior staff clinician at a private DBT outpatient therapy center in the New York metro area. We are considered one of the longest standing and largest DBT teams in the county, with the founders of my practice trained by Linehan herself. In early March, as the severity of the spread of COVID-19 increased in the United States, our team decided to begin working remotely via a HIPAA-compliant video platform. Suddenly, my team members and I went from seeing each other and working collaboratively for 10–12 h a day, to working in solitude, often haphazardly, in whatever room with a door we could find in our respective homes. Our patients went from the ritual of driving to our office twice weekly for individual session and skills group to having to face themselves alone over a video camera in order to receive treatment. True to the treatment itself, therapists and patients alike had to engage in a shared and collaborative experience of acceptance and change in order to maintain the continuity and quality of care that has saved and continues to save so many lives. It remains a testament to the strength and resilience of my patients, the solidarity and steadfastness of my team, and the brilliance and timelessness of this treatment modality that we have, and continue, to achieve the aforementioned goal of helping people build a life worth living in the face of what Linehan (1993) might call an unrelenting crisis. The remainder of this chapter will highlight the ways in which the pandemic climate has impacted clinicians and patients throughout the four facets of the treatment.

Individual Therapy and COVID-19

I never signed up to sit in front of a computer screen for what feels like endless hours. The art of psychotherapy is punctuated by the connection formed between two human beings, therapist and patient, in the service of a shared goal, healing. One of the greatest professional adjustments I have had to face during the pandemic is the experience of providing treatment, particularly individual therapy, over video conferencing. There is a notable, though difficult to operationalize, difference in the experience of connecting to a patient in person versus via teletherapy. Since the beginning of the transition, I find myself physically and emotionally exhausted after sessions because of the sheer amount of effort that is required to obtain what feels like the closest thing to an in-person session.

The identification and repair of therapy-interfering behaviors, and integral component of relationship-building and movement in DBT, has expanded to include online behaviors that get in the way of effectively engaging in session. It is important to state that in DBT we focus on therapy-interfering behaviors engaged in by both the patient and the clinician. This is a nod to the core assumption that therapists are not infallible and we make mistakes. This allows us to utilize our own ineffective behaviors to model and normalize to patients the process of problem-solving and effective interpersonal communication when issues arise. Teletherapy provides many opportunities for therapy-interfering behaviors on "both sides of the couch," as I like to say. Issues such as texting or using the phone during session, browsing the Internet/social media, and just general difficulty maintaining attention for 45 min on video are some of the most common behaviors that both myself and my patients have engaged in. Across the board my patients have reported having difficulty feeling connected to treatment at different times, regardless of whether they started treatment during the pandemic and have only experienced teletherapy or have been seeing me for many years and have established strong rapport. Many patients with borderline personality disorder struggle with fear of abandonment and feelings of emptiness (American Psychiatric Association 2013). The sometimes disjointed and sometimes distracted experience of individual therapy over Zoom has created circumstances in which patients' fears of abandonment or feelings of emptiness are sometimes activated and become part of the problem-solving of therapy-interfering behaviors.

Avery is a young adult patient and DBT graduate whom I have been treating on and off for 3 years, beginning when she was in high school. While at college Avery would seek treatment from a local provider as she attended school out of state and come back to see me over the various break periods. At the start of the pandemic, Avery's campus closed down, and she was forced to return home for the remainder of the semester. Upon returning home, Avery began seeing me again for weekly individual sessions. Initially, sessions focused on the goal of adjusting to living back at home with family, maintaining social engagement in a socially distanced climate, and creating a structure so that depressive symptoms would not worsen. Avery would come to session every week on time; however, after about 6 weeks or so, Avery seemed to have adjusted well to being home and began to have less and less to say in session. This has been a previously identified therapy-interfering behavior in the past with Avery, the function of which was identified as a fear of ending treatment and sadness around losing the relationship. As I became aware of this iteration of the behavior, I planned on addressing it directly in session with the goal of helping Avery to create a plan for temporary termination in the service of her learning how to assess her needs, effectively say goodbye, and tolerate feelings of sadness and emptiness.

During our Zoom session, I followed my plan and discussed what I saw going on in session and discussed problem-solving in what I thought was both a validating and yet firm manner. After session, I received an angry message from Avery outlining the ways in which I had failed as a provider, most notably highlighting observations of teletherapy-specific therapy-interfering behavior such as the sound of the mouse clicking or my eyes seemingly moving across the screen. While this was predominantly an emotional reaction to feeling abandoned by my suggestion that she may be ready to take a break from treatment, I had to acknowledge that dialectally speaking, there was some validity to her feedback, albeit the severity of the identified behavior may not have been accurate. In the moments of long silence or shrugs on Zoom, I had often found myself pulled to glancing down at my phone or briefly scrolling through an email. Both their truth and my truth were occurring side by side at the same time, and I knew that I had to address my own therapy-interfering behavior in session with the patient. I knew that modeling tolerating my own shame and guilt for my behavior would provide a corrective experience for the patient about being able to say goodbye effectively, without having to devalue me as an individual or the relationship. In our next session, we openly and genuinely discussed her email and my reaction to it. I was able to validate what was valid about Avery's side, apologized for my ineffective behavior, and processed the emotions and thoughts fueling her email. Avery, in turn, was able to effectively express her sadness, feelings of shame as a result of a perceived abandonment, and anxiety about losing the relationship. Collaboratively, we problem-solved a way in which to both preserve the relationship and yet still take a pause from treatment. As a result, we created a plan that involved several DBT skills used for coping and a scheduled number of sessions we would maintain before taking a break from treatment. In addition, we directly outlined how to assess the need to return to treatment and how to utilize session time effectively.

Skills Training Group and COVID-19

There are striking differences between in-person group pre-pandemic and video conference group necessary during the pandemic. Aside from the face value importance of the role that skills group plays in the overall structure of the treatment, there are several secondary benefits that patients receive from engaging in skills group. Group can be considered a multilevel group, with participants at varying points of the first year of their treatment. Based on my observations from spending years leading DBT skills groups, this multilevel experience provides so many benefits for patients. It allows veteran members to display mastery over skills and model positive outcomes of engaging in the treatment through sharing their experiences over time in treatment. For newer members, participating in group with longer-standing patients provides concrete, real-life examples that this treatment does work and things actually can get better. Skills group in its design is inherently validating for the DBT patient, as it brings together a group of people all struggling with different and yet similar problems, with the goal of learning how to manage big emotions in a world where they have often felt othered. During in-person groups, members enter one by one, have the opportunity to say hello to each other and catch up in a friendly way before starting, and often continue to share in a casual manner during the 10-minute break that occurs during every group. While many DBT patients have struggled tremendously with interpersonal relationships and loneliness, the group provides the opportunity to experience a sense of belongingness in an effective manner.

The experience of Zoom group creates a barrier to the experience of community that is created during in-person groups. Patients can't really have side conversations with one another when everyone can hear every part of a conversation, and only one person's audio can be heard at the same time. Although there is still a break, it now involves each member muting themselves and turning off their video so they can take some time off the screen in order to account for the sheer fatigue that occurs from attending a 90-minute video session. Similar therapy-interfering behaviors that occur during individual therapy occur during group as well. In-person group leaders would address therapy-interfering behavior by speaking privately with the patient either before or after group. Over video, it has become much harder to effectively manage therapy-interfering behaviors in group and address them in an effective and non-shaming way. In addition, I find that there are more technological issues such as a participant's Zoom freezing in the middle of their example or someone being unable to access the link. These technological difficulties are particularly disruptive, especially because I have very little control over preventing them and solving them.

Due to the needs of our center, I began running a new skills group time slot in late November of 2019, prior to the COVID-19 outbreak. Generally speaking, running a new group tends to be more challenging because you are literally starting from scratch, with all members starting from zero in terms of skills group experience. With the onset of the pandemic only a couple of months after the start of group, just as the group was barely beginning to get its groove, we transitioned to teletherapy, and the group went virtual. Within the first few weeks, my group members dwindled from six to four, as several patients couldn't tolerate the experience of teletherapy. With an already somewhat lower energy group, the loss of two voices left me feeling like I had to work harder to make up for the challenges faced in virtual group. My usual teaching and engagement strategies did not seem to land in the same manner in teletherapy, and I noticed people engaging in other activities or even getting up and leaving the screen during non-break times, a distraction that did not occur in all of my years of leading in-person skills groups. I would do my best to find innovative ways to engage participants; however, the management of therapy-interfering behaviors felt like they were getting in the way. I tried many different behavior management strategies, such as irreverence, whole group contingencies, and reinforcing online group rules several times, none of which have seemed to maintain change.

I have noticed my own increasing frustration in and out of group session. I have started engaging the help of members' individual therapists to address effectiveness in group with their patients in order to remove some of the burden from me, and overall my team has been very helpful in validating my frustration. More recently, the dynamic of the group has shifted in a somewhat positive and more effective direction with the addition of a new member who has been in treatment for longer than my other group members. I have begun enlisting this patient in providing homework examples and have seen this person provide feedback to other group members in a friendly and appropriate manner. While group has probably been one of the most continuously challenging aspects of providing DBT during the pandemic, I am hopeful that the natural flow of treatment will take its course, with new members being added over time. This might provide my current group members the opportunity to take on a veteran role and engage more, as I have seen happen so many times during in-person groups.

Phone Coaching and COVID-19

I have always had fairly broad limits with my phone coaching rules. However, I decided that in the wake of the pandemic, I would adjust my limits to reflect the ongoing crisis nature of the pandemic environment. While for many years I had made myself available for coaching calls between the hours of 7 AM and 1 AM every day, I decided to, for the first time ever, expand these limits to provide coaching 24 h, 7 days a week. I offered these new hours not only to my patients but also extended that to different doctors working the warzone of the hospitals to share with their colleagues in need of intervention. In my years practicing DBT, my friends and family have become accustomed to my "give me one second, I'm getting a patient call," as a dart away from the bar, dinner table, movie theater seat, or out of bed. The experience of working from home and particularly being quarantined for several months during the peak of infection in New York initially left me feeling like I had no break from or escape in my work. I would go from seeing patients for 12 h in my tiny little makeshift home office to transitioning onto the couch only to get a coaching call or text asking for help. I had nowhere to dart away to.

In addition, the extreme hospital overload in the initial months of the pandemic created a very uniquely complex dilemma surrounding patients at imminent risk for suicide. While the function of phone coaching is to help patients effectively manage a crisis in the moment through skill use, there are times in which the patient is not willing or able to maintain safety and needs to be hospitalized. Additionally, there have been times I have received calls from patients after making an attempt in which they needed to seek immediate medical treatment. These occurrences, though somewhat infrequent, are not uncommon among DBT clinicians, and I, myself, have had my fair share of them. However, COVID-19 threw a wrench in my otherwise well-oiled machine that was the process of hospitalizing a patient. Especially in the first few months of the pandemic outbreak, I have had to ask myself at each and every suicidal crisis call questions like "Is this person's risk truly great enough to chance exposing them to COVID?", "Are psychiatric units even operating? Would this bed be better used to treat a dying COVID patient?", and "What will happen if the hospital is at capacity and the patient gets turned away?". Ultimately, if someone's life is imminently in danger, I have and always will send them to the hospital, as I don't take gambles with people's lives. That being said, COVID-19 has forced me to re-evaluate my own risk assessment process and has created situations in which I must handle crises much more intensively than I would were hospitalization not to become another causality of the pandemic.

Lorena is an adult DBT patient who has not yet completed her first 6 months of treatment. Lorena has a significant developmental trauma history and meets criteria for borderline personality disorder. She has been chronically and acutely suicidal for several years in the wake of a number of significant interpersonal losses among family members and friends. Lorena thinks constantly about dying, has written suicide letters many times over the years, keeps several box cutters in different places throughout their house in order to have them available at any time, and engages in cutting as self-injury in order to practice and prepare herself for the act of suicide by cutting and bleeding out. In addition, at the beginning Lorena shared with me a few specific potential suicide dates she had planned in the upcoming months. One of these dates has come and gone since the start of the pandemic. As the date approached, Lorena and I spent a lot of time working on commitment to safety and willingness to staying alive on that day. Lorena, although willing and very talkative in session, was and remains to this day very clear about her ambivalence to live, making any safety plan very flimsy at best. Additionally, Lorena had stated since the beginning of treatment that she did not see the value in phone coaching or using skills to regulate emotions, and had not really engaged in out-of-session communication with me at any time.

Several times in the weeks prior to the date I had made my contingencies about hospitalization very clear, stating and truly meaning that as long as she was willing to collaborate with me and commit to safety even if only for hours at a time, I would not hospitalize her. I was clear that on that day if she could not commit to safety, I would need to call 911. She was worried about contracting COVID and was willing with great difficulty to agree. I knew how attached Lorena was to her plan and how difficult it was for her to consider alternatives particularly in a state of high emotions. Cases were rapidly on the rise on Lorena's planned date, and many hospitals were at capacity already.

While I normally wouldn't think twice about hospitalizing a patient of this status or even arranging a planned admission, I wanted to make sure I truly exhausted any and all measures in order to keep this patient out of the hospital during this time. I decided to reach out to her spouse 1 week prior to the date in order to create a backup contingency plan for maintaining safety. I had known that Lorena's spouse was already aware of this as well as the other dates and in the past had previously struggled to act in a clinically effective manner in past suicidal crises simply because he didn't know how. I created a plan with the spouse to remove all box cutters and other sharps from the house and lock them up early in the morning on the specified date. I informed Lorena's spouse to keep an eye on her every few hours that day and to update me on their status beginning the night before through the following morning when I was scheduled to see them. I also instructed the spouse to hide the car keys and to call 911 and then me with any escalation of behavior or threats. During the day of the plan, there were several escalations, none of which included the patient utilizing phone coaching directly. However, as a result of my pre-planning with Lorena's spouse, I was in constant communication with the spouse and was able to provide them with "in the moment" coaching on how to manage Lorena's threats and help maintain her safety.

Consultation Team and COVID-19

Among all of the professional and practice adjustments I have had to make in the wake of the pandemic, the change in the consultation team experience has been the most significant. The consultation team is the heart and soul of every DBT practice, and there is nothing more special than my team. In between the heaviness that sometimes comes with treating our patients, the ability to socialize, debrief, or distract with my team members in the office has given me the support and comradery to be the expert DBT therapist I have learned to be. The milieu in my office is second to none, and it is sorely missed. Although my team and I all have one another's cell phone numbers and are available to each other at any moment in time, the special experience of the DBT team milieu is lost in the abyss of the Internet. My colleagues and I are no longer able to walk into each other's offices to get brief "hallway consultation" for a difficult situation. We no longer eat lunch together every week during our 3-hour consultation team meeting. The loss of interaction is, in my opinion, tangible.

The value of consultation team model is an often overlooked facet of the treatment; however, in the wake of the drastic restrictions placed on all of us during COVID-19, its place and purpose in the treatment have become impossible to replace. Simply put, DBT clinicians were not meant to practice alone. The consultation team is present not only to maintain the highest standard of care for patients, but, most notably, it also exists so that we can reduce the inevitable experience of burnout that comes with pouring your heart and soul into treating a group of patients whom are judged by the psychiatric community as "the most difficult patients to treat." Team meeting via video conference has significantly diluted the ability to mitigate burnout, sometimes actually adding to the burden that spending hours of Zoom places on all of our well-being.

Prior to COVID-19 I almost never looked at my phone during team time. The team was sacred, and therefore my phone would stay on "do not disturb," only ringing on the instance that I received a call from a patient. COVID-19 has changed that for me. Another moment is where the shared trauma phenomenon has influenced my behavior, in an almost sneaky, seemingly undetectable way. Sitting in a room in my apartment for hours and hours has been taxing on my body and mind. I have found myself feeling emotionally and physically exhausted bearing the weight of this new world, my own emotions surrounding the pandemic, the impact it has had on my family and friends, and the uncertainty of it all. Pair that with the normal stress in DBT that comes with treating patients who often struggle with any combination of impulsivity, suicidal and self-injurious behavior, poor interpersonal relatedness, and extreme emotional reactions. It has been more difficult to catch my breath at times while juggling all of the professional and personal moving parts. To add to the potential for burnout, a sizeable portion of my former patients asked to return to treatment, and in both lucky and shocking ways, the center has been incredibly busy. My caseload has grown tremendously, and while I'm not treating more people than I effectively can, I am very mindful of the impact that the number of patients I'm currently taking care of has on me. Dialectically speaking, I feel both very lucky to be able to continue to treat people, save lives, and maintain my job and my salary. At the same time, treatment over Zoom has been complex and difficult. The fallout of COVID-19 has changed my team meeting experience, and for basically the first time ever, I find myself drifting away to social media or text messages when I usually listen mindfully, share gratefully, and support collaboratively. This is a shared experience among our team, and in true DBT fashion, we have spoken explicitly about this shift in the service of validating one another, problem-solving what we can, and collectively accepting what we must do about the reality of our current needs as clinicians and human beings. We lean on the treatment, which dictates that we lean on each other, as a way to move from shared trauma to shared resilience (Nuttman-Shwartz 2014).

As a final vignette, I will share a story about my team from our second week of quarantine. About 10 minutes before our team meeting was scheduled to begin, I received a call from a colleague and close friend of mine, frantically reporting that a very significant person in their life had died fairly suddenly from what was believed to be complications from COVID-19. On a personal level, I felt devastated for my friend and teammate. On a professional level, I knew I had to mobilize and help this person solve the immediate work-related issues that arose as a result of the crisis. I told my friend to inform the partners of our practice via text message of what occurred and swiftly drafted a text for this person to send to our bosses. In addition, I got a list of patients that would need coverage in the coming days while my friend grieved this loss from a distance. I provided that list to my bosses so they could figure out whom would cover each patient, because that's just what we do for each other. My bosses somberly shared the news with us before our mindfulness practice, and I know my colleague was flooded with concerned messages, cards, and fruit platters from our team both collectively and individually. We as a team reached out to my colleague's patients to inform them of coverage, managed any additional risk that came our way, and mindfully experienced the array of emotions that came with this experience. This is the value of the DBT team, and while things have drastically changed and continue to do so, the spirit of the DBT consultation must be maintained as a constant.

Conclusion

DBT asks both providers and patients to be willing to find a synthesis between acceptance and change. In DBT we are often looking at our patients' lives, our treatment, and ourselves and asking the question "what do we need to change and what do we need to accept in order to move forward?". The COVID-19 pandemic has called on the entire world to practice this dialectic in order to keep moving in the face of the uncertainty of the pandemic. This is true from on a global level all the way down to an individual treatment level. As DBT clinicians, the charge of adapting DBT to both maintain adherence to the model and adjust to the obstacles in the pandemic environment has, as I like to say, provided therapists with many opportunities to practice using skills. One of Marsha Linehan's most famous dialectical assumptions states that each and every person is doing the best they can at any given moment and at the same time can try harder and do better (Linehan 1993). We as DBT therapists have been and will continue to do the best we can in any given moment to meet the needs of our patients and the treatment during this global pandemic. And, at the same time, we must continue to pause, reflect, problem-solve, and adapt as the world continues to shift and change with COVID-19.

References

American Psychiatric Association. (2013). *Diagnostic and statistical manual of mental disorders* (5th ed.). Arlington: Author.

Choi-Kain, L. W., Finch, E. F., Masland, S. R., Jenkins, J. A., & Unruh, B. T. (2017). What works in the treatment of borderline personality disorder. *Current Behavioral Neuroscience Reports, 4*, 21.

Fava, J., & Ellberger, M. (2020). Treatment of borderline personality disorder using Dialectical Behavior Therapy. In C. M. Leprowsky (Ed.), *Borderline personality disorder* (pp. 163–204). Hauppauge: Nova Science Publishers.

Feigenbaum, J. D., Fonagy, P., Pilling, S., Jones, A. H., Wildgoose, A., & Bebbington, P. (2012). A real-world study of the effectiveness of DBT in the UK National Health Service. *The British Journal of Clinical Psychology, 51*(2), 121–141.

Flückiger, C., Del Re, A. C., Wampold, B. E., Symonds, D., & Horvath, A. O. (2012). How central is the alliance in psychotherapy? A multilevel longitudinal meta-analysis. *Journal of Counseling Psychology, 59*(1), 10–17.

Harned, M. S., Chapman, A. L., Dexter-Mazza, E. T., Murray, A., Comtois, K. A., & Linehan, M. (2008). Treating co-occurring Axis I disorders in recurrently suicidal women with borderline personality disorder: A 2-year randomized trial of Dialectical Behavior Therapy versus community treatment by experts. *Journal of Consulting and Clinical Psychology, 76*(6), 1068–1075.

Harned, M. S., Korslund, K. E., & Linehan, M. (2014). A pilot randomized controlled trial of Dialectical Behavior Therapy with and without the Dialectical Behavior Therapy prolonged exposure protocol for suicidal and self-injuring women with borderline personality disorder and PTSD. *Behaviour Research and Therapy, 55*, 7–17.

Lee, N. K., Cameron, J., & Jenner, L. (2015). Review of treatment for substance use and borderline personality disorder. *Drug and Alcohol Review, 34*, 663–672.

Linehan, M. (1993). *Cognitive behavioral treatment of borderline personality disorder*. New York: Guilford Press.

Linehan, M. M., Armstrong, H. E., Suarez, A., Allmon, D., & Heard, H. L. (1991). Cognitive behavioral treatment of chronically parasuicidal borderline patients. *Archives of General Psychiatry, 48*(12), 1060–1064.

Linehan, M. M., Heard, H. L., & Armstrong, H. E. (1993). Naturalistic follow-up of a behavioral treatment for chronically parasuicidal borderline patients. *Archives of General Psychiatry, 50*(12), 971–974.

National Institute of Mental Health. (2018). *Suicide*. Retrieved from https://www.nimh.nih.gov/health/statistics/suicide.shtml#part_154968

Nuttman-Shwartz, O. (2014). Shared resilience in a traumatic reality: A new concept for trauma workers exposed personally and professionally to collective disaster. *Trauma Violence, & Abuse, 16*, 1–10.

Pennay, A., Cameron, J., Reichert, T., Strickland, H., Lee, N. K., Hall, K., & Lubman, D. I. (2011). A systematic review of interventions for co-occurring substance use disorder and borderline personality disorder. *Journal of Substance Abuse Treatment, 41*(4), 363–373.

Stoffers-Winterling, J. M., Völlm, B. A., Rücker, G., Timmer, A., Huband, N., & Lieb, K. (2012). Psychological therapies for people with borderline personality disorder. *The Cochrane Database of Systematic Reviews, 8*, CD005652.

Tosone, C. (2012). In C. R. Figley (Ed.), *Encyclopedia of trauma: An interdisciplinary guide.* Thousand. Oaks: Sage Publications.

Verheul, R., Van Den Bosch, L. M. C., Koeter, M. W. J., De Ridder, M. A. J., Stinjen, T., & Van Den Brink, W. (2003). Dialectical Behavior Therapy for women with borderline personality disorder. *British Journal of Psychiatry, 182*, 135–140.

Woolcott, P., Jr. (1985). Prognostic indicators in the psychotherapy of borderline patients. *American Journal of Psychotherapy, 39*, 17–29.

World Health Organization. (2018). *Suicide.* Retrieved from https://www.who.int/newsroom/fact-sheets/detail/suicide

Chapter 25
Reflections on Providing Virtual Eye Movement Desensitization and Reprocessing Therapy in the Wake of COVID-19: Survival Through Adaptation

Gillian O'Shea Brown

The spread of the COVID-19 virus has led to severe public health challenges, including detrimental physical and mental health outcomes nationwide. In this time of collective trauma, the effects of COVID-19 will undoubtedly give rise to unequal degrees of hardship, primarily impacting those who are most vulnerable to structural and systemic inequality. This phenomenon has presented many challenges for therapists, particularly those who utilize eye movement desensitization and reprocessing (EMDR) when treating populations who often present with an underlying diagnosis of complex posttraumatic stress disorder (C-PTSD). The negative effects of layered relational trauma, particularly through childhood abuse and neglect, have long been recognized as contributing factors towards the development of C-PTSD (Courtois 1988; van der Kolk 2015), a diagnostic entity included in the *International Classifications of Diseases*, 11th revision (*ICD-11*). According to the *ICD-11*, C-PTSD is associated with a broad spectrum of psychopathological symptoms and is conceptualized as including the core elements of PTSD such as re-experiencing the trauma, deliberate avoidance of internal and external traumatic reminders, and a sense of current threat expressed as hypervigilance and hyperarousal. The *ICD-11* has also recently identified additional C-PTSD symptoms, including emotional regulation difficulties, persistent negative views of the self, and interpersonal problems characterized by difficulties forming and maintaining relationships with others (WHO 2018). Until recently, C-PTSD was never officially codified in any diagnostic nomenclature. Endorsement of the *ICD-11* definition of C-PTSD will come into effect on January 1, 2022.

G. O'Shea Brown (✉)
Silver School of Social Work, New York University, New York, NY, USA
e-mail: gob226@nyu.edu

© The Author(s), under exclusive license to Springer Nature Switzerland AG 2021
C. Tosone (ed.), *Shared Trauma, Shared Resilience During a Pandemic*, Essential Clinical Social Work Series, https://doi.org/10.1007/978-3-030-61442-3_25

The chapter will first discuss the development of C-PTSD, with special consideration for how the COVID-19 pandemic may heighten the risk of retraumatization and exacerbate symptoms. This chapter will also provide an overview of EMDR as a psychotherapy modality for treating C-PTSD, specifically focusing on the application of *resource development and installation* (EMDR-RDI) for stabilization. EMDR-RDI refers to a set of EMDR protocols that focus exclusively on strengthening connections to positive affective states and resourceful memories (Korn and Leeds 2002; Leeds 1995; Leeds and Shapiro 2000). Additionally, this chapter will review the existing relevant literature and provide an analytical take on the ethical and clinical implications of providing virtual EMDR (V-EMDR) therapy. A composite case will illustrate how EMDR-RDI is provided via teletherapy. Finally, reflections of the practice benefits and challenges of providing V-EMDR will be discussed, including limitations and recommendations guiding future practice.

C-PTSD in the Time of COVID

C-PTSD transcends the category of posttraumatic stress disorder (Herman 1992), including both the core elements of PTSD, such as re-experiencing, avoidance, and hypervigilance, as well as symptoms of poor affect regulation, negative self-concept, and difficulties with establishing and maintaining healthy interpersonal relationships (WHO 2018). The long-term psychological impact, of both the spread of the COVID-19 virus and the restrictive policies adopted to counteract it, remains uncertain. However recent research has indicated heightened risk of trauma-related symptoms, which has the capacity to exacerbate C-PTSD symptoms for several reasons (Forte et al. 2020; Shigemura et al. 2020; Zandifar and Badrfam 2020). Social distancing, confinement, and quarantine were adopted to contain diffusion. This has altered the fabric of society, creating changes to consciousness and awakening a climate of trepidation. For many individuals who struggled to adapt to survive, strong relational bonds, community ties, education institutes, and places of religious practice were abruptly taken away. This abrupt loss of social norms has the potential to activate hypervigilance in many trauma survivors, while also creating a large-scale sense of uncertainty that is characteristic of a global pandemic (Forte et al. 2020). Additionally, for many trauma survivors, therapy represents a stable, predictable, reliable, and trustworthy foundation that instantiates a sense of trust and connection. Just like the parent-child dyad, the clinical relationship promotes the formation of a secure attachment in which the therapist demonstrates sensitivity to the individual's emerging intentionality (Fonagy et al. 2007). This relationship requires the therapist to possess the ability to demonstrate attunement and mirroring, an interpersonal phenomenon in which the attachment figure adjusts the timing and content of their behavioral movements to mirror another's behavioral and emotional cues, fostering empathy and rapport (Chartrand and Bargh 1999). Secure attachment experiences require mentalizing (i.e., the ability to understand the child's subjectivity) and, in turn, lead to the formation of epistemic trust (i.e., the individual's willingness to experience the environment and consider new information as trustworthy) (Corriveau et al. 2009). An individual who has endured numerous experiences of rejection by the attachment figure has a memory network that can be easily triggered (Ainsworth 1982; Bowlby 1989). Consequentially, clients presenting with C-PTSD will likely have complex relationships with themselves and their attachment figures, which should be addressed compassionately when quarantine restrictions prevent in-person therapy sessions, as these experiences could be perceived by the client as abandonment, rejection, or even punishment.

In the wake of COVID-19, clients were abruptly directed to self-quarantine, and the usual considerations for treatment planning and termination planning were unavailable. Changes to treatment which ordinarily would be carefully co-created and discussed over weeks or months were hastily made as this large-scale crisis began unfolding precipitously. Teletherapy is one potential alternative to in-person session; however, teletherapy is a privilege reserved only for those who can afford a phone, stable Internet connection, and/or a laptop, as well as a place of solitude where they can confidentially and safely process their emotions. When clients are unable to partake in teletherapy, preferring the safety and familiarity of their weekly in-person session, treatment shifts towards termination. Ordinarily at termination, a client's symptoms have declined, and treatment can address the loss of the therapeutic relationship, culminating in the metaprocessing of emotions related to termination of the treatment. However, in the wake of this pandemic and the essential move toward quarantine, some clients were placed in a situation where they had to unexpectedly terminate the therapeutic relationship. For those who transitioned to teletherapy, the ramifications of COVID-19 became evident through expressions of reported survivor's guilt, helplessness, emotional reactivity, hypervigilance, and in some cases, avoidance and numbing (Forte et al. 2020; Shigemura et al. 2020; Zandifar and Badrfam 2020).

The EMDR Resource Development and Installation Protocol

EMDR is a modality which addresses both the brain and body. Since its inception, EMDR has been understood by both therapists and clients as a powerful vehicle for processing traumatic experiences but only when the client has achieved stabilization (Shapiro 1995). The efficacy of EMDR therapy in the treatment of PTSD has been well established in over 30 positive randomized controlled studies during the past three decades (Ahmad et al. 2007; Marcus et al. 1997, 2004; Shapiro 2014; Wilson et al. 1997). Such research findings led to the World Health Organization (2013) stating that trauma-focused cognitive behavioral therapy (TF-CBT) and EMDR are the only psychotherapy modalities recommended in the treatment of children, adolescents, and adults who meet the diagnostic criteria for PTSD. It is important to note that most of the above study participants differ from survivors of complex trauma with chronic abuse and neglect histories in terms of symptom presentation and capacity for tolerating trauma-focused work (Korn 2009). EMDR is a trauma resolution approach that involves a standard set of procedures and clinical protocols including specific types of bilateral sensory stimulation.

The EMDR approach incorporates the adaptive information processing (AIP) model, which posits that memories of distressing experiences are dysfunctionally stored in the brain in an unmetabolized state in the memory networks that contain perceptions, negative beliefs, affect, and body sensations that arose during the experience of trauma (Shapiro 2007). The unmetabolized memories, much like a "skipping disc," will replay the most distressing part of the memory, which can cause intrusive thoughts, shame-based cognition, and psychological reactivity that can be activated by sensitivity cues. EMDR classically involves eight phases, which include (1) history taking, (2) preparation and stabilization, (3) assessment, (4–7) desensitization, reprocessing, closure, and finally (8) reevaluation (Shapiro 1995). Specific focused strategies and bilateral stimulation (administered through eye movements, tapping, or tones) help the client access dysfunctionally stored memories and related affect which, in turn, desensitizes the emotions and physical sensations and enables them to access more adaptive material stored in the brain. Ultimately this promotes the formation of new, positive associations with the original event, such as "the risk of harm has passed and I am now safe."

Research has found that the treatment of complex trauma should be phase-oriented, multimodal, and skill-focused, with a core emphasis on symptom relief and functional improvement (Briere and Scott 2006; Courtois et al. 2009; van Der Kolk et al. 2005). In the treatment of complex trauma, the EMDR model is adapted to be phase-oriented, highlighting the importance of the role of resource development strategies that address the needs of patients with compromised affect tolerance and self-regulation (Korn 2009). This allows the client to operate out of deep self-awareness rather than conditioning. The preparatory steps of EMDR involve history taking and providing clients with a sense of safety so that they can begin to identify memories and communicate more openly, facilitating effective trauma reprocessing. This involves the therapist consciously observing and gathering information on the client's background, while assessing their suitability for EMDR. The second phase of the EMDR protocol centers on preparation by providing clients with tools that will prepare them for EMDR, including enhancing their ability to independently tolerate positive affect regulation. During this preparatory phase of treatment, there is a strong emphasis on building affect tolerance and psychoeducation; this is known as resource development and installation (RDI).

Leeds (1995) introduced RDI along with the proposed principles for the use of bilateral stimulation along with positive images and memories. RDI was incorporated into the EMDR protocol early on and has been utilized to strengthen affective, cognitive, and behavioral coping skills (Korn and Leeds 2002; Shapiro 1995). EMDR-RDI refers to a set of EMDR protocols that focus exclusively on strengthening connections to positive affective states and resourceful memories (Korn and Leeds 2002; Leeds 1995; Leeds and Shapiro 2000). EMDR-RDI is used to help clients access existing resources and develop new and effective coping skills such as mindfulness, self-soothing, distancing, grounding, and emotional regulation (Leeds and Shapiro 2000). EMDR-RDI focuses on stabilizing and preparing the clients for the next phases of treatment, when attention will turn to the processing of traumatic memories. A central feature of complex trauma is a loss of the ability to physiologically modulate stress responses in addition to a diminished capacity to utilize bodily signals (van der Kolk et al. 1996). EMDR-RDI can be very effective in increasing affect tolerance when it is used to enhance mindfulness, the ability to notice a feeling or bodily sensation and accompanying emotions (Korn 2009). Survivors of complex trauma often present with increased dissociative symptoms; therefore, establishing safety in the body is paramount to the healing process (Forgash and Copeley 2008). The efficacy of EMDR can be challenged by symptoms of dissociation and complex trauma; therefore, RDI is highly beneficial to the efficacy of treatment (Fisher 2002; Korn and Leeds 2002). When administering EMDR-RDI, Korn and Leeds (2002) recommend shorter sets of bilateral stimulation – six to twelve bidirectional movements are used – to ensure that the client is installing a positive resource and not accessing painful material as with standard processing.

EMDR-RDI offers a range of valuable resourcing interventions and exercises that can relinquish maladaptive defenses, as new coping skills, self-capacities, and resources are developed and strengthened (Korn 2009). The basic EMDR-RDI protocol (Korn and Leeds 2002) involved a range of resources that the client could choose from which included mastery of experiences, relational resource, and symbolic resources. EMDR-RDI has been further developed and adapted to include many other positive resources and grounding protocols by other EMDR clinicians including Janina Fisher PhD Fisher (2001) and Laurel Parnell PhD Parnell (1999). Korn and Leeds (2002) proposed the "Relational Resource," which involved resourcing the client with a "supportive figure," a trustworthy, reliable person who could serve as their imagined guide before they engaged in processing of painful material. This approach fosters a sense of safety, stabilization, and empowerment in trauma survivors. During the upheaval caused by COVID-19, utilizing EMDR-RDI might assist individuals in establishing a sense of safety in their body, even when faced with uncertainty, loss of resources, and isolation.

Virtual EMDR

Continued advancement in the technology domain has enhanced the development and utilization of mobile health applications, especially those using EMDR techniques to facilitate the therapeutic process. EMDR has always been tightly tied to technology, as various technological devices were created to assist with bilateral saccadic eye movements and other forms of sensory dual attention mechanisms (Shapiro 2018). With EMDR mHealth applications, the EMDR therapist can attach headphones to a mobile phone device and then use the application to administer bilateral tones to the client. In alternative versions, the therapist will play the application on a computer, providing the client with both visual and auditory bilateral stimulation (Lee and Cuijpers 2013). However, research measuring the efficacy and safety of these applications is limited, particularly for clients who may present with complex posttraumatic conditions and associated comorbidities (Marotta-Walters et al. 2018).

As individuals adapt to survive during the COVID-19 global pandemic, the potential dangers associated with this kind of technology cannot be disregarded. At the present time, there are no federal or state agencies overseeing the confidentiality of data collected by mHealth applications, which are available in the mobile application stores. The Federal Communications Commission (FCC), Food and Drug Administration (FDA), and the Office of Civil Rights can only regulate mHealth applications when the applications interact or exchange personally identifiable data with Health Insurance Portability and Accountability Act (HIPAA)-covered entities (Marotta-Walters et al. 2018). Marotta-Walters and colleagues (Marotta-Walters et al. 2018) caution that the easy accessibility to unregulated mHealth applications for the treatment of severe mental health issues such as C-PTSD pose a number of serious risks, including a lack of HIPAA-compliant data privacy and security. These applications also have the potential to cause harm to clients if used improperly, including triggering dissociation and emotional dysregulation. In terms of EMDR mHealth applications, generally a brief description of the mechanism of bilateral stimulation using a sensory-based stimulus is provided; however, many do not provide the theoretical basis for EMDR (Marotta-Walters et al. 2018). Unfortunately, the widespread distribution of these applications also allows for individuals to access disturbing memories via self-administered bilateral stimulation without the guidance of a trained EMDR therapist.

Despite its structured protocol, EMDR therapy remains a highly relational process. EMDR therapists are formally trained to assist clients through experiencing intense reactions during processing, such as dissociation, looping (getting stuck in painful material), emotional dysregulation, and unexpected somatic responses. Shapiro (2018) has cautioned that there is a significant risk of retraumatization in the context of self-directed EMDR, postulating that memories may merely be dissociated rather than reprocessed. Furthermore, most of the mHealth applications are developed without the involvement of healthcare providers and with no assurance of security and privacy of private health information (Boulos et al. 2014; O'Neill and Brady 2012). Consequentially, in a review on mHealth applications designed to facilitate Virtual Eye Movement Desensitization and Reprocessing (V-EMDR), Marotta-Walters and colleagues (Marotta-Walters et al. 2018) recommended that applications should only be used by trained EMDR therapists as a tool to facilitate V-EMDR treatment, as long as the therapist provides an "appropriate and regulated environment"| to facilitate EMDR treatment. However, the terms of "appropriate and regulated" are not clearly outlined or discussed in this review, leaving it largely open to the interpretation of the EMDR-trained therapist.

In January 2020, the EMDR International Association's Report of the Virtual Training and Therapy Task Group was released with the intention of providing clearer direction concerning best V-EMDR practices. In this report, references to virtual delivery of EMDR therapy pertain exclusively to EMDR therapy that is administered by an EMDR-trained therapist online via HIPAA-compliant telecommunications that have a business associate agreement (BAA). References to

V-EMDR in the report do not concern companies, websites, or services that offer EMDR self-therapy without live guidance from an EMDR-trained therapist. Mirroring the concerns expressed by Marotta-Walters and colleagues (Marotta-Walters et al. 2018), self-administration of EMDR therapy is strictly forbidden in the policies outlined in this report. Additionally, this task group highlighted the necessity for EMDR-trained therapists to complete a tele-mental health certification in order to maintain a safe standard of online practice, prior to providing V-EMDR. The task group further recommended that EMDR therapists stay abreast of the rapidly changing technologies and guidelines in order to adequately maintain safety and security within their practice. Along with these technology guidelines, this task group recommended that EMDR clinicians providing virtual treatment must demonstrate online attunement, ethical integrity, and fidelity to the EMDR therapy model. While EMDR-trained therapists are guided to be attentive to the client's safety and comfort level during reprocessing, V-EMDR may heighten the risk for misattunement because of limited eye contact, limited visual cues (noticing motor activity), and the forfeiture of the in-person connection. Furthermore, when conducting V-EMDR, there is no possibility of providing clients with a confidential therapeutic environment. Despite these potential limitations, the utilization of V-EMDR places emphasis on attunement and stabilization. The focus on connection can prove to be anchoring particularly during the social isolation caused by the COVID-19 pandemic.

Case Study

The following case study is a composite case which contains elements and techniques derived from a number of EMDR sessions. Savannah[1] is a 36-year-old married Hispanic female, employed full time in the media industry. Savannah has a diagnosis of complex posttraumatic stress disorder and presented to treatment with symptoms of a trauma-related mood disorder and anxiety due to history of relational trauma including child sexual abuse, physical abuse, and emotional abuse. She has engaged in EMDR-oriented therapy for over 6 months. Over the course of her treatment thus far, history taking has revealed pervasive negative cognition, including thoughts of weakness and inadequacy. Savannah reported repeated disturbing memories, somatized symptoms related to trauma, pervasive guilt, low mood, and hypervigilance arising from childhood complex trauma. Due to the onset of COVID-19, Savannah was unexpectedly placed in quarantine, putting an abrupt end to her in-person sessions. The following paragraphs contain a reflection of Savannah's first virtual EMDR session from the perspective of the therapist.

During this session, I was mindful to ensure that Savannah was in a quiet and confidential space in her home. I positioned myself so that I appeared in the center

---

[1] A pseudonym has been used to preserve confidentiality.

of her screen, showing my face and upper torso in a well-lit room to resemble how I would appear if I was sitting adjacent to her in the therapy suite. Some décor from my therapy office was intentionally placed in the background to create a sense of familiarity, warmth, and comfort. I noticed and remarked that we could see each other's facial expressions more closely, and she remarked that because my earphones were attached to my computer, she felt that this space was safe, intimate, and confidential. In the beginning of this session, Savannah was facilitated through processing her emotions regarding this period of adjustment. She reported feeling anxious and reported other familiar somatized symptoms of trauma, such as pervasive nausea and gastrointestinal upset. She was provided with psychoeducation and information regarding the use of technology-assisted bilateral stimulation via the mHealth applications. Savannah was guided through downloading the application and instructed to listen to auditory bilateral stimulation through her earphones attached to her cellphone, while simultaneously engaging in telepsychotherapy on her laptop. Once comfort and ease were established concerning the tempo, volume, and sound quality of the audio, she was guided through the grounding protocol. The following excerpts illustrate the process of Savannah being guided through the installation of a "relational resource" (Korn and Leeds 2002) as adapted from Fisher's modified EMDR-RDI protocol (Fisher 2001).

Therapist: Sit back in the chair, connect with your body, and begin to breathe deep in to the stomach. You are seated with your feet on the ground (pause). Please think about a place that feels calm (pause). When you have the image of what represents your calm place, I want you to let me know by nodding.

Client: (Nods).

Therapist: Tell me what you see.

Client: I am at a house that David[2] and I sometimes visit upstate. I am sitting on the back deck. I have just practiced yoga. I can hear bees buzzing in the distance. It's a warm day. I feel Zen.

Therapist: As you think of that experience, notice what you see, hear, and feel. Notice what emotions you are experiencing and how you feel in your body (6–8 sets of bilateral stimulation).

Client: The air is cool. I feel calm. It is peaceful up here. I am present. I feel relaxed in my body. I feel like I can breathe easily up here. My body feels calm.

Therapist: Focus on your calm place and its sights, sounds, smells, and sensations (pause). Tell me more about your experience (6–8 sets of bilateral stimulation).

Client: I can see the sky; the greenery looks so beautiful and I hear the leaves move in the wind. The air is cool and fresh; I am enjoying the view. My shoulders are loose and I am breathing deeply and easily.

Therapist: Bring up the current image (pause). Concentrate on where you feel the pleasant sensations in your body, and allow yourself to enjoy them. Concentrate on those sensations. (6–8 sets of bilateral stimulation).

---

[2] A pseudonym has been used to preserve confidentiality.

Client: (Shoulders drop, jaw is unclenched, client has a slight grin).

Therapist: What are you noticing now (6–8 sets of bilateral stimulation)?

Client: Cool and fresh air and the gentle movement of the leaves. There is no chaos up here, only harmony. My body is rested. I have deep breaths. It is peaceful up here.

Therapist: Focus on that. What do you notice now (6–8 sets of bilateral stimulation)?

Client: I feel calm in my body. I feel it in my chest.

Therapist: Is there a word or phrase that represents your calm place (6–8 sets of bilateral stimulation)?

Client: I am at peace.

Therapist: Think of the words "I am at peace," and notice the positive feelings and sensations you are having when you think of those words (substantial pause). Concentrate on those sensations and the words "I am at peace," and be curious about the sensation. What are you noticing now (6–8 sets of bilateral stimulation)?

Client: I am strong and I am at peace.

Therapist: Now say the words "I am at peace" and notice how you feel (6–8 sets of bilateral stimulation).

Client: I feel strong.

Therapist: Allow those words to metabolize in your body. (Pause). Ok wonderful, come back again to the room. Gently come back to your body and open your eyes.

Client: I am back (laughs) – I needed that!

Therapist: You did wonderfully. We need to find a way to support you in processing painful material. What inner strength or resource would help you feel less overwhelmed?

Client: I feel like I am always alone when I am most hurt. It scares me when people lose control and become unpredictable and crazy. Everyone is so crazy right now!

Therapist: Is there a reliable, nurturing figure that could serve as a supportive guide to you?

Client: My sixth grade teacher Mrs. Elgin[3] would always remember my birthday, and sometimes she would see that I was alone and find a way to make me feel important. She was so kind; the way she looked at me – there was a warmth in her eyes I had never seen before – it felt like home. Even though home at that time was a house of horrors, when she smiled at me, I felt safe, important, and even special.

Therapist: That is a wonderful choice for a warm nurturing figure. I could hear the warmth in your voice as you recalled her warm nurturing presence. Close your eyes and imagine what it would feel like to have her presence as a resource (6–8 sets of bilateral stimulation).

---

[3] A pseudonym has been used to preserve confidentiality.

Client: I would feel guided and protected. When I would enter her classroom, I always felt calm and heard. She has a smile on her face that reaches her eyes and I feel a smile on my face. She makes me feel safe.

Therapist: Yes, and if you felt safer, what would follow from that (6–8 sets of bilateral stimulation)?

Client: I feel strong and powerful.

Therapist: Once again, imagine yourself with Mrs. Elgin; imagine her warm presence and gentle smile. In every cell of your body, you feel safer and even protected. (Pause). Notice the feeling in your body that goes with having a warm nurturing figure available to you (6–8 sets of bilateral stimulation).

Client: (Smiling – eyes closed – head held high). My throat is open; stomach feels neutral. This is the first time my stomach has felt neutral all week. I feel very Zen right now.

Therapist: Yes, with your Mrs. Elgin available to you, you feel calmer and more peaceful – go with that (6–8 sets of bilateral stimulation).

Client: (Smiling). (Hands are placed on heart center).

Therapist: What would Mrs. Elgin say to that sensation (6–8 sets of bilateral stimulation)?

Client: You are here and you are safe.

Therapist: You are here and you are safe. Slowly, slowly come back into this room, noticing toes in shoes, tongue in your mouth, eyes fluttering, and when you're ready I want you to switch off the bilateral stimulation. How are you feeling Savannah (6–8 sets of bilateral stimulation)?

Client: I feel safe and I am powerful.

Reflections on Proving Virtual EMDR

The EMDRIA task group for virtual EMDR advised that it is prudent for EMDR clinicians providing any treatment virtually to demonstrate online attunement, ethical integrity, and fidelity of the EMDR therapy model. Heeding the cautions of the timely EMDRIA report and being mindful of the need for continuity of care in the wake of COVID-19, I found it critical to balance the duty of care and the dignity of risk to meet Savannah's needs for grounding and stabilization during this time of collective trauma. I initially felt ill-equipped to adapt treatment to V-EMDR without the appropriate training; however, because of COVID-19, I was forced to lean into this discomfort and venture into an unfamiliar territory. Balancing both parts of my clinical discernment, I chose to proceed with caution and listen for any signs that the new adaptation was causing Savannah heightened anxiety or distress. I was conscientious to practice online attunement, and made sure to monitor her breathing, facial expressions, eye contact, and tone of voice. I practiced self-guided grounding techniques prior to the session, being mindful of my physiological responses to collective trauma. Shared trauma as described by Tosone et al. (2012) refers to the affective, behavioral, cognitive, spiritual, and multimodal responses that clinicians experience as a result of dual exposure to the same collective trauma as their clients. Despite our shared experience of the uncertainty related to the pandemic, I wanted to ensure that my own affective state and cognitive processing was regulated and not mirroring her uncertainty and activation. I was also mindful of the risk of blurring professional and personal boundaries, along with the increased risk of self-disclosure. In terms of attunement, I was conscious that my tone of voice and breathing were stabilized, so that I could fully focus on tracking somatic and non-verbal cues exhibited by Savannah. In my own countertransference, I later realized that I aspired to serve as her anchor in an unsettled world.

Despite its structured protocol, EMDR therapy remains a highly relational process. The foundational steps of EMDR processing involve providing the client with psychoeducation around dissociation, trauma, and affect regulation techniques. Savannah and I had had the benefit of completing these steps in person during our months of in-person EMDR therapy. Savannah became so comfortable during this time in the therapy room that she began to paraphrase me when exploring her newly acquired psychoeducation and complex mind-body relationship. Savannah was an eager and willing client, always demonstrating magnificent curiosity by asking for journal prompts and additional readings on theories that resonated with her during sessions. Even given these successful in-person sessions, I found V-EMDR particularly challenging for several reasons. For example, using this modality I could not see Savannah's bilateral extremities, as I generally could during our in-person EMDR sessions. This is important as I had initially observed that Savannah's left ankle would sometimes become agitated when she was processing painful material from her formative years, which served as a subtle somatic cue. As visual cues are limited when using V-EMDR, I could only observe her face and upper bilateral motor activity during these sessions, depriving me of her usual motor activity and affect regulation cues. Using this technology, I felt limited to the auditory bilateral stimulation, as eye movements directed via hand gestures presented were less effective when administered through teletherapy, according to Savannah's feedback. This may be concerning for hearing-impaired trauma survivors seeking V-EMDR. Furthermore, Savannah's previous EMDR processing had occurred exclusively with bilateral stimulation via a pulsar, though she appeared to adapt well to auditory bilateral stimulation. During our teletherapy session, Savannah lamented that she missed coming to my office; however, she reported that V-EMDR had provided her with the familiar sense of lightness she needed from stabilization resourcing. EMDR therapists must have the clinical awareness to know when to provide therapeutic assistance for grounding and restabilizing (Watson-Wong 2013). I wanted to provide Savannah with stabilization; however, I was reluctant to venture into potentially destabilizing territory as I felt limited in the quality of a safety plan I could put in place if needed, given the overwhelmed state of the healthcare systems during the early stages of the pandemic. In order to be prudent to the safety guidelines, I provided additional time for session closure and followed up with Savannah in terms of her wellness in between sessions. I also provided Savannah with follow-up instructions promoting her mind-body attunement and suggested resourcing homework to be completed in between sessions. While these are all classic components of EMDR therapy, I felt compelled to be even more consistent in the application and was more conservative when it came to V-EMDR rather than in-person EMDR.

It is critical for therapists to build strong attunement and communication skills to ensure optimal connection with the client during V-EMDR. This process is ripe with opportunities for misattunement, given unavoidable technical glitches and/or unclear processing. This is especially true for clients suffering from C-PTSD, as technological malfunctions, for instance, a frozen screen, can appear eerily similar to the "Still Face Experiment." The "Still Face Experiment" was conducted by placing an infant face to face with their nonresponsive expressionless mother following 3 min of free interaction (Tronick et al. 1978; Tronick and Gold 2020). After repeated attempts to engage their mother, the infant typically withdraws and orients their face and body away from the mother with a withdrawn, hopeless facial expression. This "still face" response, caused by connectivity issues, may inadvertently replicate this experience in emotionally vulnerable clients, which may impact the client-therapist dyad, causing undue stress and potential retraumatization. To counteract the risk of misattunement, Watson-Wong (2013) has advised that prior to beginning reprocessing, clinicians should build an alliance with a client's adult ego state to enable helpful communication and evaluate missed or confusing cues and clues during processing. Therapists should apply their transferable clinical and attunement skills, to help clients stay engaged and connected during telepsychotherapy.

Conclusion

The spread of COVID-19 has caused many public health challenges, particularly in the domain of therapeutic treatment. During this time V-EMDR has emerged as a necessary adaptation to effective clinical practice. Despite the continued treatment afforded by this technology, much is still unknown regarding the refinement and safeguarding of V-EMDR use. There is an urgent need for V-EMDR-specific training and education, the development of technological guidelines, and specific telemental health certification to ensure client confidentially, safety, and optimal treatment outcomes. These steps should be integrated into the basic EMDR training to ensure continuity of care can be assured without compromising quality in the event of a future pandemic. Chronic traumatization can lead to internalized shame and negative cognitions; however, by compassionately witnessing clients and providing V-EMDR during the unfolding collective trauma, we can begin to unburden clients and develop their inner resources, thereby paving the way for deeper trauma healing.

References

Ahmad, A., Larsson, B., & Sundelin-Wahlsten, V. (2007). EMDR treatment for children with PTSD: Results of a randomized controlled trial. *Nordic Journal of Psychiatry, 61*, 349–354.

Ainsworth, M. D. S. (1982). Attachment: Retrospect and prospect. In C. M. Parkes & J. Stevenson-Hinde (Eds.), *The place of attachment in human behavior* (pp. 3–29). New York: Tavistock.

Boulos, M. N., Brewer, A. C., Karimkhani, C., Buller, D. B., & Dellavalle, R. P. (2014). Mobile medical and health apps: State of the art, concerns, regulatory control and certification. *Online Journal of Public Health Informatics, 5*(3), 229–229. https://doi.org/10.5210/ojphi.v5i3.4814.

Bowlby, J. (1989). The role of attachment in personality development and psychopathology. In S. I. Greenspan & G. H. Pollack (Eds.), *The course of life* (Infancy) (Vol. 1, pp. 119–136). Madison: International Universities Press.

Briere, J., & Scott, C. (2006). *Principles of trauma therapy: A guide to symptoms, evaluation, and treatment.* London: Sage Publications.

Chartrand, T. L., & Bargh, J. (1999). The chameleon effect: The perception-behavior link and social interaction. *Journal of Personality and Social Psychology, 76*, 893–910.

Corriveau, K. H., Harris, P. L., Meins, E., Fernyhough, C., Arnott, B., Elliott, L., & de Rosnay, M. (2009). Young children's trust in their mother's claims: Longitudinal links with attachment security in infancy. *Child Development, 80*, 750–761.

Courtois, C. A. (1988). *Healing the incest wound: Adult survivors in therapy.* New York: Norton.

Courtois, C. A., Ford, J. D., & Cloitre, M. (2009). Best practices in psychotherapy for adults. In C. A. Courtois & J. D. Ford (Eds.), *Treating complex traumatic stress disorders; An evidence-based guide* (pp. 82–103). New York: Guilford Press.

Fisher, J. (2001). *Modified EMDR resource development & installation protocol.* Boston: Presentation at the Trauma Center.

Fisher, J. (2002) *Adapting EMDR techniques in the treatment of dysregulated or dissociative patients.* In Paper presented at the International Society for the Study of Dissociation Annual Meeting San Antonio, Texas November 12, 2000.

Fonagy, P., Gergely, G., & Target, M. (2007). The parent-infant dyad and the construction of the subjective self. *Journal of Child Psychology and Psychiatry, 48*, 288–328. https://doi.org/10.1111/j.1469-7610.2007.01727.x.

Forgash, C., & Copeley, M. (2008). *Healing the heart of trauma and dissociation with EMDR and ego state therapy.* New York: Springer.

Forte, G., Favieri, F., Tambelli, R., & Casagrande, M. (2020). COVID-19 pandemic in the Italian population: Validation of a post-traumatic stress disorder questionnaire and prevalence of PTSD symptomatology. *International Journal of Environmental Research and Public Health, 17*(11), 4151. https://doi.org/10.3390/ijerph17114151.

Herman, J. L. (1992). Complex PTSD: A syndrome in survivors of prolonged and repeated trauma. *Journal of Traumatic Stress, 5*(3), 377–391. https://doi.org/10.1002/jts.2490050305.

Korn, D. (2009). EMDR and the treatment of complex trauma: A review. *Journal of EMDR Practice and Research, 3*(4), 264. https://doi.org/10.1891/1933-3196.3.4.264.

Korn, D. L., & Leeds, A. M. (2002). Preliminary evidence of efficacy for EMDR resource development and installation in the stabilization phase of treatment of complex posttraumatic stress disorder. *Journal of Clinical Psychology, 58*(12), 1465–1487. https://doi.org/10.1002/jclp.10099.

Lee, C. W., & Cuijpers, P. (2013). A meta-analysis of the contribution of eye movements in processing emotional memories. *Journal of Behavior Therapy and Experimental Psychiatry, 44*(2), 231 239. https://doi.org/10.1016/j.jbtep.2012.11.001.

Leeds, A. M. (1995). *EMDR case formulation symposium.* In Paper presented at the annual meeting of the International EMDR Association, Santa Monica.

Leeds, A. M., & Shapiro, F. (2000). EMDR ad resource installation: Principals and procedures for enhancing current functioning and resolving traumatic experiences. In J. Carlson & L. Sperry (Eds.), *Brief therapy strategies with individuals and couples* (pp. 469–534). Phoenix: Zeig, Tucker, Theisen, Inc.

Marcus, S. V., Marquis, P., & Sakai, C. (1997). Controlled study of treatment of PTSD using EMDR in an HMO setting. *Psychotherapy, 34*(3), 307–315. https://doi.org/10.1037/h0087791.

Marcus, S., Marquis, P., & Sakai, C. (2004). Three- and 6-month follow-up of EMDR treatment of PTSD in an HMO setting. *International Journal of Stress Management, 11*(3), 195–208. https://doi.org/10.1037/1072-5245.11.3.195.

Marotta-Walters, S. A., Jain, K., DiNardo, J., Kaur, P., & Kaligounder, S. (2018). A review of mobile applications for facilitating EMDR treatment of complex trauma and its comorbidities. *Journal of EMDR Practice and Research, 12*(1), 2. https://doi.org/10.1891/1933-3196.12.1.2.

O'Neill, S., & Brady, R. R. (2012). Colorectal smartphone apps: Opportunities and risks. *Colorectal Disease, 14*(9), e530–e534. https://doi.org/10.1111/j.1463-1318.2012.03088.x.

Parnell, L. (1999). *EMDR in the treatment of adults abused as children*. New York: Norton.

Shapiro, F. (1995). *Eye movement desensitization and reprocessing, basic principles, protocols and procedures*. New York: Guilford Press.

Shapiro, F. (2007). EMDR, adaptive information processing, and case conceptualization. *Journal of EMDR Practice and Research, 1*(2), 68–87. https://doi.org/10.1891/1933-3196.1.2.68.

Shapiro, F. (2014). The role of eye movement desensitization and reprocessing (EMDR) therapy in medicine: Addressing the psychological and physical symptoms stemming from adverse life experience. *The Permanente Journal, 18*, 71–77. https://doi.org/10.7812/TPP/13-098.

Shapiro, F. (2018). *Eye movement desensitization and reprocessing (EMDR) therapy: Basic principles protocols, and procedures* (3rd ed., pp. 243–244). New York: The Guilford Press.

Shigemura J., Ursano R. J., Morganstein J. C., Kurosawa M., & Benedek D. M. (2020, February). Public responses to the novel 2019 coronavirus (2019 – nCoV): Mental health consequences and target populations. *Psychiatry and Clinical Neurosciences*. [Epub ahead of print].

Tosone, C., Nuttman-Schwartz, O., & Stephens, T. (2012). Shared trauma: When the professional is personal. *Clinical Social Work Journal, 40*, 231–239. https://doi.org/10.1007/s10615-012-0395-0.

Tronick, E., & Gold, C. (2020). *The power of discord: Why ups and downs of relationships are the secret to building intimacy, resilience, and trust*. New York: Hachette Book Club.

Tronick, E., Als, H., Adamson, L., Wise, S., & Brazelton, T. B. (1978). Infants response to entrapment between contradictory messages in face-to-face interaction. *Journal of the American Academy of Child and Adolescent Psychiatry, 17*, 1–13.

van der Kolk, B. A. (2015). *The body keeps the score brain, mind and body in the healing of trauma*. New York: Viking Press.

van der Kolk, B. A., McFarlane, A., & Weisaeth, L. (1996). *Traumatic stress*. New York: Guilford.

van Der Kolk, B., Roth, S., Pelcovitz, D., Sunday, S., & Spinazzola, J. J. (2005). Disorders of extreme stress: The empirical foundation of a complex adaptation to trauma. *Journal of Trauma Stress, 18*(5), 389–399.

Watson-Wong, J. (2013, September). Poster titled, EMDR Internet Therapy presented at the 18th EMDR International Association Conference, Austin, TX.

Wilson, S. A., Becker, L. A., & Tinker, R. H. (1997). Fifteen-month follow-up of eye movement desensitization and reprocessing (EMDR) treatment for posttraumatic stress disorder and psychological trauma. *Journal of Consulting and Clinical Psychology, 65*(6), 1047–1056.

World Health Organization [WHO]. (2013). *Guidelines for the managements of conditions specifically related to stress*. Geneva: WHO.

World Health Organization [WHO]. (2018). *The ICD-11 for mortality and morbidity statistics*. Retrieved from https://icd-who-int.proxy.library.nyu.edu/browse11/l-m/en

Zandifar, A., & Badrfam, R. (2020). Iranian mental health during the COVID-19 epidemic. *Asian Journal of Psychiatry, 51*, 101990.

Chapter 26
Shared Traumatic Stress and the Impact of COVID-19 on Public Child Welfare Workers

Deirdre S. Williams

Introduction

Child welfare authorities like New York City's Administration for Children's Services (ACS) were created to provide oversight wherever there are allegations of abuse and neglect of children (Yamatani et al. 2018). Reports are made, screened, and investigated 24/7 (Tavormina and Clossey 2015). Yet the public child welfare (PCW) system is wrought with challenges at the best of times. In the United States, too many families and children are systematically involved in the PCW system, which leads to exposure to the juvenile and criminal courts (Abramovitz 2005). Approximately 442,995 children in 2017 were reported to be placed in out-of-home placements in the PCW system due to allegations of neglect and/or maltreatment. Most of these hundreds of thousands of American children live in an "urban 'war zone'…the nightmare of neighborhood and family violence" (Webb 2016, p. 183). Witnessing or being party to violence, particularly at an early age, leads to adverse effects for children (Abramovitz 2005). Poor outcomes (i.e., lack of safety, permanency, and well-being of at-risk children) can impact the children's future capability and cause severe and long-standing physical, emotional, and behavioral risks that continue into adulthood, resulting in long-term challenges with employment, stability, and health (Lieberman et al. 2015).

The current pandemic has brought to the fore the fact that many children are not safe in their homes. The sudden closure of schools left vulnerable children with no outlet from difficult or dangerous home situations and removed them from the view of teachers and other mandated reporters of suspected child abuse. Amid concerns about the capacity of existing child protection policies to rise to this unprecedented

D. S. Williams (✉)
Silver School of Social Work, New York University, New York, NY, USA
e-mail: dswilliams@nyu.edu

© The Author(s), under exclusive license to Springer Nature Switzerland
AG 2021
C. Tosone (ed.), *Shared Trauma, Shared Resilience During a Pandemic*,
Essential Clinical Social Work Series,
https://doi.org/10.1007/978-3-030-61442-3_26

249

situation, child advocates have called for more direct and proactive oversight (Jolie 2020; Tavormina and Clossey 2015). At the heart of those conversations are the PCW workers, who risk their own safety to fulfill their roles providing adequate protection for children. During large-scale crises (e.g., terrorism, natural disasters, and pandemics), the risk of being unsafe, needing protection, and experiencing trauma is heightened for both children and workers (Tosone et al. 2011).

"The individuals working at human services nonprofits arguably have been the unsung heroes [in]…response to the coronavirus pandemic" (Amandolare et al. 2020, para. 1). Unfortunately, events like 9/11, Hurricane Sandy, and now COVID-19 require "more of the already-stretched child welfare workforce" as "Child welfare…systems have experienced significant disruptions, putting tremendous strain on children, youth and families, as well as the caseworkers…who support the healthy development and wellbeing of the next generation" (Fickler 2020, p. 32). There is a gap in the literature on the effects of large-scale crises on specific human services workforces, including PCW workers. However, given the clear difficulty such crises entail in the sector, leadership needs to be proactive on international, national, local, and interagency levels as the world faces further outbreaks of COVID-19 (Roule 2020). One area that needs further exploration is shared traumatic stress (SdTS), or the dual exposure to trauma PCW workers experience as they encounter secondary trauma from the populations they serve alongside their own reactions from posttraumatic stress (Tosone et al. 2015). Addressing this challenge is important if agencies hope to retain workers and keep them safe. This chapter, therefore, focuses on valuing PCW staff as a highly important resource in the system, in part by directly addressing the effects of SdTS in times of large-scale crisis.

Case Study

Collin[1] is a 14-year-old African American male living in Brownsville, Brooklyn, New York. He is represented in a child protective case with his 8-year-old brother and has been involved in juvenile court cases. He has an extensive history of inconsistent and inappropriate relationships with adult figures. Because of his constant displacement, moving between various family members and various levels of child welfare placements, he was vulnerable to gang involvement and began to report such involvement, which was encouraged by his mother as a source of social support. Collin was arrested and has an open delinquency case filed against him for sexual offense against an 11-year-old girl who lives across the hall from his mother. He was at risk of remand or remaining in custody of the Department of Youth and

---

[1] All names and other personal identifiers of the case have been changed to protect privacy and confidentiality.

Family Justice at a detention center. His behavior prior to his arrest increased his chances for remand, as he had a high absent without leave (AWOL) history.

Collin gained a sense of stability when he was placed and transitioned well in the care of his uncle following his last arrest. He had the opportunity to start over at a new school for a fresh start, which he verbalized that he wanted. Administrators at his new school were understanding of his circumstances and willing to work with him, albeit knowing little of his background. They reported to his caseworker that they found him to be very honest, helpful, and motivational to his peers. He admitted that he really enjoyed school and was willing to have a fresh start. Collin played sports at school (football, basketball, and track and field) and with the school social worker's assistance, became involved in clubs and activities. The school administrators directly assisted him in applying to "good" high schools. His uncle told the courts that Collin had become a kind of coach for the other students in school, telling them not to join gangs and not to "do bad."

Unfortunately, with the arrival of COVID, he was no longer able to seek stability and mentorship at school. He experienced many disruptions at his uncle's home due to his history and resulting lack of trust. His acting out behaviors led to his uncle becoming increasingly frustrated. Collin was placed in a non-kinship home and was forced to change schools. He returned on AWOL to his mother's home in an effort to protect his younger brother. He re-entered the gang and re-engaged in several illegal activities that resulted in further arrests.

Impact of COVID-19 on PCW Workers

Hearing traumatic stories like Collin's is common for PCW workers. Children who experience trauma are more likely to have heightened challenges with academic achievement, aggression, inappropriate and unsafe sexual practices, substance misuse, and court involvement. For Collin, a way of coping was through school. For other youth, school may also offer a place of respite, especially for those in whose homes and lives outside school violence, exploitation, and other challenges are commonplace occurrences. As schools offer a form of protection under specific mandates, their closure during the COVID-19 pandemic has left an obvious gap in our public means of safeguarding children. Many have identified a need to change child protection policies in response, so they entail more direct and proactive oversight (Jolie 2020).

An alarming number of American children and adolescents are, like Collin, affected by traumatic events in their families and communities, and their trauma in turn affects the workers who manage their cases. The child's exposure to these types of events can lead to severe emotional and behavioral distress for the child and the worker (Seti 2007; Smith Hatcher et al. 2011). Child welfare is a particularly daunting profession to work in: The work is highly stressful and demanding because every decision a worker makes could potentially affect their clients' lives (Daley 1979). Job demands include overtime work, work-home interference, work conflicts, job insecurity, time demands at work, recipient contact demands (home visits), and heavy workload (Amandolare et al. 2020; Corin and Björk 2016; Scanlan and Still 2019; Sharma et al. 2020). An unreasonable burden of work demands is typical, impeding service delivery and the quality of service for families (Frost et al. 2017; Gibson et al. 2018; Yamatani et al. 2018). In some cases, PCW workers may experience pain and conflict from carrying out agency policies that they perceive as counter to a child's needs (Casey Foundation 2017; Edwards and Wildeman 2018; Hanna 2018; Rosinsky and Connely 2016; Yamatani et al. 2018). High caseloads and inadequate use of resources for children in need of permanency can potentially increase harm. The actress Tiffany Haddish, talking to David Letterman in *My Next Guest* (Letterman 2019), describes how when she was in foster care, she was given garbage bags to move her possessions instead of a suitcase. Haddish eloquently describes how she interpreted this as a child to mean that she, as a person, was no more than trash (Letterman 2019). These experiences can affect a young person's self-perception that shapes a young person's image of themselves that can last a lifetime (Abramovitz 2005). Workers will witness more such experiences among the children they serve in a large-scale crisis, like a pandemic, as agencies face additional challenges and work demands increase (Roule 2020; Tavormina and Clossey 2015).

Direct care workers are expected to manage clinical challenges and make life-altering decisions that arise in cases contact like they did with Collin. They also have little to no appropriate clinical training, even though a major function of their job is to provide protection, care, professional advocacy, consistency, and appropriate placement options (Gorman 2018). Ultimately, during a crisis like the pandemic, workers are tasked with completing their already cumbersome job demands with the added factors of obligations to their own families (including children who may be home from school and family members who are high risk medically) and environmental safety concerns for the sake of accountability (Amandolare et al. 2020; Corin and Björk 2016; Scanlan and Still 2019; Sharma et al. 2020).

Disproportionate Risk

Workers typically go out in precarious situations, where they could be harmed in the communities they serve (Corin and Björk 2016; Geisler et al. 2019). The community Collin resides in is typical of a predominantly Black and Hispanic, low-income environment, where services are most needed but often not well received. In pre-pandemic times, PCW workers expressed concerns about their own safety and elevated caseloads involving families struggling with drug and alcohol addictions and children with special needs (Daley 1979). Studies have shown that about 70% of direct care case workers have been affected by violence while in the field or have been threatened while on the job (Daley 1979).

During COVID-19, there are concerns that the social service agencies will not be able to sustain operations and survive as worker safety intensified. When agencies are under stress, not only are the lives of children like Collin affected, but risks also become more significant for those considered *essential* (Leary 2020). PCW workers and their loved ones are at risk every day during COVID, since workers must go into different homes despite social distancing advisories. The profession is predominantly working-class women who are more likely to have children and require childcare, which also increases their exposure and risk of infection (Sharma et al. 2020). In addition to the gender disparity, a disproportionate number of Black and Latinx Americans make up the essential workforce (The Lancet 2020). This is particularly concerning in New York City which, as one of the early COVID-19 epicenters, included 60% of the deaths in this demographic as of May 2020 (The Lancet 2020).

Shared Traumatic Stress

Crisis affects workers' emotional sense of self, where feelings of powerlessness, anxiety, and shared trauma are present (Tavormina and Clossey 2015). The risk of workers developing shared traumatic stress (SdTS), or shared trauma, increases as interactions with children and families who have experienced trauma increase. Shared trauma is understood to be the experience of trauma by direct care providers, where they become directly traumatized as they create a professional helping relationship with traumatized clients like Collin (McTighe and Tosone 2015; Seti 2007). This affects workers professionally and personally.

Typically, a traumatic event is when a person experiences, witnesses, or is confronted with the actual threat of death, serious injury, or damage to the physical integrity of self or others (i.e., violence, natural disasters, living in a war zone, life-threatening accidents, physical/sexual abuse, and rape) (American Psychiatric Association [APA] 2013). Diagnosing posttraumatic stress disorder (PTSD) is dependent upon a specified series of events associated with a set of symptoms. These trauma-related symptoms can include dissociation, flashbacks, nightmares, numbness, aggression, irritability, anxiety, and difficulty with problem-solving (American Psychiatric Association 2013; Van Riel 2016). PTSD can manifest from collective traumatic experiences as well as individual ones. For workers, the parallel process of experiencing collective trauma as individuals in a society and then being re-exposed to the trauma in their helping capacity, working with clients, is referred to as shared traumatic stress (Tosone et al. 2015). Workers who experience SdTS can become hyper-focused on work and withdrawn or avoidant, experience emotional and physical stress, reduce personal and family time, and make life changes (Tavormina and Clossey 2015). These are all factors that lead to job dissatisfaction, job stress, or job disengagement and are predictive factors affecting employment stability in the PCW system. When a person is disengaged from their work, they are more likely to fail to be effective at their jobs (Edwards and Wildeman 2018; Hanna 2018; Letterman 2019; Rosinsky and Connely 2016).

Additional Stressors on the Sector During the Pandemic

Despite all of the stressors, PCW workers choose to remain in the profession due to an innate, intrinsically motivated, altruistic desire to help people (Geisler et al. 2019). However, their dedication to their clients is not usually enough to sustain them when pressures mount. The average PCW worker leaves the job after an average of 1.8 years, making the turnover rate between 20 and 40% (Casey Family Programs 2017; Frost et al. 2017; Li and Huang 2017; Rao Herman et al. 2018). During COVID-19, that rate is expected to rise. Fiscal constraints only exacerbate the stressed system. Typically, turnover of workers is expensive, morally and financially. Agencies cannot afford increased turnover rates as their mere survival is at risk during COVID-19 (Abel et al. 2020; Amandolare et al. 2020).

PCW agencies have been burdened with added unexpected operational costs, which have catapulted as increased need for safety affects service delivery during COVID-19 (Abel et al. 2020; Amandolare et al. 2020). Agencies were required to purchase items such as personal protective equipment (PPE) and increase services, such as IT support (remote work) and temporary workers to cover for those getting sick (Amandolare et al. 2020). The CARES Act, a federally funded policy, allowed agencies to gain more support from several grant opportunities under the Administration for Children and Families until September 30, 2021, to pay for these additional expenses. This emergency funding was sourced through community services block grants ($1 billion) for various social services and emergency aid, operating supplemental summer programs through noncompetitive grant supplements ($500 million), and family violence prevention and services grants ($45 million; Abel et al. 2020). As agencies prepare to support workers through incentivized/bonus pay, risk workers' medical safety, and mitigate risks through PPE, the city's financial state remains fragile (Amandolare et al. 2020).

The system cannot afford to see turnover rates increase. The financial cost of turnover averages about $54,000 (severance packages, overtime of retained staff, worker separation, and hiring and training of new staff) for every PCW worker who leaves the workforce (Casey Family Programs 2017). As fiscal problems affect overall service delivery, outcomes for vulnerable children and families are likely to suffer with higher turnover (Edwards and Wildeman 2018; Hanna 2018; Scanlan and Still 2019).

The already limited resources to help children like Collin and their families are much scarcer during the pandemic, as PCW agencies are concerned with their very survival (Amandolare et al. 2020; Roule 2020). Children need consistent, healthy relationships with adults who model proper behaviors (Abramovitz 2005; Madden and Aguiniga 2017). With funding tight, there is an urgent need for strategies to improve health and safety for vulnerable populations and at-risk PCW workers without incurring additional costs.

Opportunities to Shift Practices and Support Workers

By supporting the worker, we will effectively support youth like Collin. As the world prepares for a prolonged impact from COVID-19, leadership on international, national, and interagency levels needs to be proactive (Roule 2020). Institutionally supportive practices and policies would directly shift organizational culture across the PCW system and mitigate risk of shared traumatic responses for staff (Corin and Björk 2016; Deglau et al. 2018; Spielfogel et al. 2016). The literature conveys that PCW workers are best supported through organizational strategies (Corin and Björk 2016; Lietz 2018; Rao Herman et al. 2018). Implementing organizational strategies and interventions (i.e., increasing transparency) is vital in retaining highly skilled PCW workers (Rao Herman et al. 2018). PCW workers and their supervisors expressed that there are constraints in applying the appropriate skills needed to their cases due to a lack of management support (Corin and Björk 2016; Deglau et al. 2018; Lietz 2018). Without institutional practices and policy put in place to prioritize workers' needs during this crisis, they will be at increased risk for contracting COVID-19, needing to treat secondary traumatic responses, and leaving the profession altogether.

Supervisors and upper management need to create an environment that actively helps workers to gain perspective, think objectively and critically, and implement a plan of action in which management will support them (Deglau et al. 2018; Lietz 2018). Building and practicing a mandatory staff wellness policy for the workforce could also impact job satisfaction for the better. Evidence supports that increased opportunities for self-care, networking, and staff recognition enhance organizational culture and encourage the worker to remain in the job (Gorman 2018; Scanlan and Still 2019; Spielfogel et al. 2016). Such changes would shift the work culture in PCW organizations from deficit-focused to supportive, directly increasing job satisfaction.

Conclusion

Protecting children like Collin is important, but our practices in managing and supporting our PCW workers do not reflect this value. Children's best interests can only be served through supporting the workers more effectively and mitigating the risks of SdTS. If we built a foundation that adequately supports the workers, we could improve service delivery outcomes overall. Initiatives to support PCW workers need to be implemented on all levels, from practice to policies, and across child welfare agencies locally, nationally, and internationally (Frost et al. 2017).

References

Abel, J., Barnett, J. D., Callas, G., Cohn, A., Kolkin, M. B., Nussdorf, M., Pikofsky, S., Sinder, S. A., Wheeless, S.D., Zalenga, L.M., Jensen, K., & Oppenheimer, J. (2020). President Trump signs CARES Act into law. *Steptoe's Analysis*. https://www.steptoe.com/en/news-publications/president-trump-signs-cares-act-into-law.html. Accessed 22 Aug 2020, DOI: https://doi.org/10.1177/2632352420934491.

Abramovitz, M. (2005). The largely untold story of child welfare reform and the human services. *Social Work, 50*(2), 175–186. https://doi.org/10.1093/sw/50.2.175.

Amandolare, S., Bowles, J., Gallagher, L., & Garrett, E. (2020). *Essential yet vulnerable: NYC's human services nonprofits face financial crisis during pandemic*. Report. Center for an Urban Future. https://nycfuture.org/research/essential-yet-vulnerable. Accessed 21 Aug 2020.

American Psychiatric Association. (2013). *Diagnostic and statistical manual of mental disorders* (5th ed.). Arlington: American Psychiatric Association.

Casey Family Program. (2017). *How does turnover affect outcomes and what can be done to address retention?* [Information packet]. New York. Retrieved from https://caseyfamilypro-wpengine.netdna-ssl.com/media/HO_Turnover-Costs_and_Retention_Strategies-1.pdf

Corin, L., & Björk, L. (2016). Job demands and job resources in human service managerial work an external assessment through work content analysis. *Nordic Journal of Working Life Studies, 6*(4), 3–28. https://doi.org/10.19154/njwls.v6i4.5610.

Daley, M. R. (1979). Preventing worker burnout in child welfare. *Child Welfare, 58*(7), 443–450.

Deglau, E., Akincigil, A., Ray, A., & Bauwens, J. (2018). What's in an MSW? Graduate education for public child welfare workers, intention, engagement, and work environment. *Journal of Public Child Welfare, 12*(3), 238–263. https://doi.org/10.1080/15548732.2018.1457586.

Edwards, F., & Wildeman, C. (2018). Characteristics of the frontline child welfare workforce. *Children and Youth Services Review, 89*, 13–26. https://doi.org/10.1016/j.childyouth.2018.04.013.

Fickler, W. (2020). *Vulnerable populations face heightened risk*. Washington, DC: National Conference of State Legislatures.

Frost, L., Höjer, S., Campanini, A., Sicora, A., & Kullburg, K. (2017). Why do they stay? A study of resilient child protection workers in three European countries. *European Journal of Social Work, 21*(4), 485–497.

Geisler, M., Berthelsen, H., & Muhonen, T. (2019). Retaining social workers: The role of quality of work and psychosocial safety climate for work engagement, job satisfaction, and organizational commitment, human service organizations. *Management, Leadership & Governance, 43*, 1.

Gibson, K., Samuels, G., & Pryce, J. (2018). Authors of accountability: Paperwork and social work in contemporary child welfare practice. *Child and Youth Services Review, 85*, 43–52. https://doi.org/10.1016/j.childyouth.2017.12.010.

Gorman, S. (2018). Child welfare and protection professionals: How do they experience the work? An interpretative phenomenological analysis. *Irish Journal of Applied Social Studies, 10*(1), 29–44.

Jolie, A. (2020). Children seem to be less vulnerable to the coronavirus. Here's how the pandemic may still put them at risk. *TIME*. https://time.com/5818006/coronavirus-children-angelina-jolie/. Accessed 21 Aug 2020.

Leary, J. P. (2020). The slippery definition of an "essential" worker. *The New Republic*. https://newrepublic.com/article/157544/slippery-definition-essential-worker-coronavirus-pandemic. Accessed 21 Aug 2020, DOI: https://doi.org/10.2196/17835.

Letterman, D. (2019). *Netflix Special, My Next Guest* [Series]. Netflix.

Li, Y., & Huang, H. (2017). Validating the job satisfaction survey in voluntary child welfare. *Elsevier, 83*, 1–8.

Lieberman, L. D., Lausell-Bryant, L., & Boyce, K. (2015). Family preservation and healthy outcomes for pregnant and parenting teens in foster care: The Inwood House Theory of change. *Journal of Family Social Work, 18*, 21–39. https://doi.org/10.1080/10522158.2015.974014.

Lietz, C. A. (2018). Infusing clinical supervision throughout the child welfare practice: Advancing effective implementation of family-centered practice through supervisory practice. *Clinical Social Work, 46*, 331–340. https://doi.org/10.1007/s10615-018-0672-7.

McTighe, J. P., & Tosone, C. (2015). Narrative and meaning-making among Manhattan social workers in the wake of September 11, 2001. *Social Work in Mental Health, 00*, 1–19.

New York City Independent Budget Office. (2018). *Under pressure: How the city's child welfare system responded to recent high-profile tragedies.* [Brochure]. New York: NY: Hanna, K.

Rao Herman, S., Biehl, M., & Chahla, R. (2018). Views on workplace culture and climate: Through the lens of retention and Title IV-E participation. *Journal of Public Child Welfare, 12*(3), 380–397. https://doi.org/10.1080/15548732.2018.1431172.

Rosinsky, K., & Connely, D. (2016). *Child welfare financing SFY 2014: A survey of federal, state, and local expenditures* (pp. 1–31). Washington, DC: The Annie E. Casey Foundation.

Roule, N. (2020, April 6). *The Cipher Brief, DOI:* https://doi.org/10.1155/2020/4817239.

Scanlan, J. N., & Still, M. (2019). Relationships between burnout, turnover intention, job satisfaction, job demands, and job resources for mental health personnel in an Australian mental health service. *Health Services Researcher, 19*(62), 1–11.

Seti, C. L. (2007). Causes and treatment of burnout in residential child care workers: A review of the research. *Residential Treatment for Children & Youth, 24*(3), 197–229.

Sharma, V., Scott, J., Kelly, J., & VanRooyen, M. J. (2020). Prioritizing vulnerable populations and women on the frontlines: COVID-19 in humanitarian contexts. *International Journal for Equity in Health, 19*(66), 1–3.

Smith Hatcher, S., Bride, B., Oh, H., Moultri King, D., & Franklin Catrett, J. (2011). An assessment of secondary traumatic stress in juvenile justice education workers. *Journal of Correctional Healthcare, 17*(3), 208–217. https://doi.org/10.1177/1078345811401509.

Spielfogel, J. E., Leathers, S. J., & Christian, E. (2016). Agency culture and climate in child welfare: Do perceptions vary by exposure to the child welfare system? *Human Service Organizations: Management, Leadership, and Governance, 40*(4), 382–396.

Tavormina, M., & Clossey, L. (2015). Exploring crisis and its effects on workers in children protective services work. *Child and Family Social Work, 2–17*(22), 122–136.

The Lancet. (2020). *The plight of essential workers during the COVID-19 pandemic* (Vol. 395). https://www.thelancet.com/journals/lancet/article/PIIS0140-6736(20)31200-9/fulltext. Accessed 22 Aug 2020, DOI: https://doi.org/10.34172/ijhpm.2020.180.

Tosone, C., McTighe, J. P., Bauwens, J., & Naturale, A. (2011). Shared traumatic stress and the long-term impact of 9/11 on Manhattan clinicians. *Journal of Traumatic Stress, 24*(5), 546–552. https://doi.org/10.1002/jts.20686.

Tosone, C., McTighe, J. P., & Bauwens, J. (2015). Shared traumatic stress among social workers in the aftermath of hurricane Katrina. *British Journal of Social Work, 45*, 1313–1329. https://doi.org/10.1093/bjsw/bct194.

Upbring. (2017). *Achieving permanency for children in care: Barriers and future directions.* [Brochure]. Austin, TX: Madden, E.E., Aguiniga, D.M.

Van Riel, R. (2016). What is social constructionism in psychiatry? From social causes to psychiatric classifications. *Frontiers in Psychiatry, 7*, Article 57. (Open access journal), DOI: https://doi.org/10.7717/peerj.2799.

Webb, T. (2016). Children exposed to violence: A developmental trauma informed response for the criminal justice system. *Journal of Child & Adolescent Trauma, 9*(3), 183–189. https://doi.org/10.1007/s40653-015-0069-5.

Yamatani, H., Engel, R., & Spjeldnes, S. (2018). Child welfare caseload: What's, just right? *Social Work, 54*(40), 361–368.

Chapter 27
How COVID-19 Exposed an Inadequate Approach to Burnout: Moving Beyond Self-Care

Julian Cohen-Serrins

The COVID-19 pandemic has profoundly impacted the healthcare sector where a range of professionals experience an overwhelming number of acutely ill patients (Shah et al. 2020). Social work in particular represents a profession where COVID-19 has magnified the initiates and impacts of occupational stress. Social workers operate on the macro-level navigating complex systems, advocating for underserved or underrepresented clients while also providing direct clinical interventions. These occupational realities intersect with the profession's social justice values ensuring that they will be at the vanguard of any pandemic. Moreover, social workers occupy a unique position: serving those infected with COVID-19, as well as the frontline and essential workers combating the pandemic (Vlessides 2020; Wrenn and Rice 1994). In fact, the COVID-19 pandemic exemplifies the concept of a shared trauma, a traumatic event that simultaneously affects clients' as well as the professional's person life (Tosone et al. 2012). A shared trauma such as COVID-19 event may hinder a professional's ability to adequately provide care while their clients become increasingly in need of their care. Furthermore, the number of services that social workers are expected to perform both compassionately and safely during COVID-19 necessitates an acceleration of remedial approaches centered on stress and burnout reduction. Achieving this goal requires a recognition that occupationally induced stress and burnout among social workers are not confined to COVID-19. Rather, the pandemic has exposed and magnified a pervasive preexisting issue across the healthcare sector.

J. Cohen-Serrins (✉)
Silver School of Social Work, New York University, New York, NY, USA
e-mail: jcs891@nyu.edu

© The Author(s), under exclusive license to Springer Nature Switzerland AG 2021
C. Tosone (ed.), *Shared Trauma, Shared Resilience During a Pandemic*,
Essential Clinical Social Work Series,
https://doi.org/10.1007/978-3-030-61442-3_27

259

Critically Understanding the Issue: Causes and Effects of Occupational Stress

Prevalence and Effects

Occupational stress among healthcare workers had already reached endemic levels before the COVID-19 pandemic (Bridgeman et al. 2018; Dyrbye et al. 2017), and its consequences, specifically burnout, are profound economically and humanistically. Numerous studies of burnout confirm its significance as a pressing and detrimental issue for the healthcare sector (Dzau et al. 2018; West et al. 2016). While the prevalence of burnout in the aggregate healthcare sector has not been fully determined, research suggests that it may be as high as 70% (Van Mol et al. 2015) and the rate of burnout specifically among social workers has been estimated to be 60% (Martin and Schinke 1998). Additionally, the degenerative psychosocial effects of burnout are multifold, including decreased empathy (Wagaman et al. 2015), increased clinical mistakes (Cimiotti et al. 2012; Shanafelt et al. 2010), work absenteeism (Gil-Monte 2008), job turnover (Jackson and Schuler 1983), depression (Shirom 2005), and depersonalization (Jaracz et al. 2005). Burnout can be disastrous for the individual employee, client well-being, organizational sustainability, and public trust in healthcare institutions.

Why Social Work Is at Particular Risk

Citing reliable figures for the prevalence of burnout in the healthcare sector is challenging due to industry norms that galvanize healthcare workers to individually reconcile burnout, thereby stigmatizing those admitting to it and seeking support. Social workers in particular face these challenges along with negative perceptions relating to the value of their work (LeCroy and Stinson 2004). When compared with physicians and nurses, the status and social capital of the social work profession is notably less (Murphy and McDonald 2004). Too frequently social work is reduced to its historical roots in charity, suggesting that the services provided by social workers are akin to unpaid caregiving labor. This cultural devaluation places social workers at an increased risk of being overlooked during a traumatic event such as COVID-19 despite the numerous essential services that they provide (LeCroy and Stinson 2004; Peterson 2012). These services include discharge planning, service administration, psychotherapy, and establishing effective interventions across each ecological system (Moore et al. 2017). Generally, in the United States, these ecological systems are highly complex and often under resourced, but under current pandemic conditions, they are in disarray.

Moreover, social workers themselves are confronting a shared stress along with their clients. They, too, must confront and address the dramatic disruptions in their personal daily routines caused by the pandemic along with the pervasive fear of infecting themselves or a loved one. Therefore, social workers during the COVID-19 pandemic are even more likely to lack the resources necessary to bolster their own physical and psychological safety when providing clients with critical interventions.

The Status Quo: The Case for Self-Care

What Is Self-Care?

The preeminent framework for assuaging all forms of occupational stress, including burnout, is self-care. While there is no operationalized definition of self-care, it can be understood as deliberate personal or professional action to reduce stress (Lee and Miller 2013; Miller et al. 2017). Self-care has become a popular framework for individually initiated strategies or rituals to reduce stress and has incorporated evidence-based practices such as mindfulness techniques (Rudaz et al. 2017). These techniques include meditation, taking breaks during the workday to decompress and reduce exposure to occupational stressors, or taking time off from work entirely (Lee and Miller 2013). For a comprehensive guide on self-care for clinicians during the COVID-19 pandemic, see the chapter "The COVID-19 Self-Care Survival Guide: A Framework for Clinicians to Categorize and Utilize Self-Care Strategies and Practices" in this volume. Despite its popularity, self-care is not a standardized organizational intervention. Workers must subjectively identify their need for self-care and which actions would alleviate their stress. Thus, self-care can only exist as a concept that organizations can encourage among workers. Unlike other stress reduction interventions that operate at a broader organizational level, such as trainings or new management practices, self-care is limited to popular de-stressing procedures chosen by individual workers.

Why Self-Care Became the Predominate Approach

The Benefits of Self-Care

Self-care does provide some noteworthy benefits for improving employee wellness, especially for social workers who have advanced training related to building resiliency and self-sufficiency. This chapter is not meant to contend that there are no benefits to self-care,[1] rather that it fails as a primary method for burnout reduction.

---

[1] For a review of approaches and benefits of self-care, applied specifically for clinicians practicing during the COVID-19 pandemic, see the chapter "The COVID-19 Self-Care Survival Guide: A Framework for Clinicians to Categorize and Utilize Self-Care Strategies and Practices."

One reason why self-care has become so prevalent and palatable for social workers relates to therapeutic practices utilized with clients. Self-care involves tackling issues with individualized strategies to achieve self-sufficient goals. Social workers are taught that when individuals are able to cope with often uncontrollable proximal and distal stressors, they build resilience (Polizzi et al. 2020). Since these assumptions are valued when applied to clients, it is reasonable to assume that similar practices will promote resilience among practitioners.

Further, self-care is an aspect of social work education (Bressi and Vaden 2017). Nationally, there has been a promotion to incorporate self-care into social work education from CSWE and NASW (Bressi and Vaden 2017), and social work practice courses typically integrate it into their curriculum. Consequently, it is common to find self-care awareness campaigns and practice guides in both educational and professional settings (Bressi and Vaden 2017). Self-care is currently the predominate method for occupational stress prevention and burnout reduction in the social work profession despite the existence of other effective methods (Restauri and Sheridan 2020).

The Critique of Self-Care

Self-Care and Neoliberalism

An alternative explanation for self-care's popularity is its connection to neoliberal values. First, the rudimentary elements of self-care practices must be identified and enacted autonomously. It is the responsibility of the worker to identify *approachable* stressful elements of their work. Next, the worker must individually identify a self-care action to remedy their stress. This may paradoxically contribute to burnout among social workers if they invest substantial effort and belief that their self-care practices will eliminate occupationally induced stress. Unlike sociopolitical examples of auto-emancipation, individual workers cannot inoculate themselves with self-care practices to become resistant to occupational stress because the causal structures and dynamics of that stress are unaffected. Even the most thoughtful and practiced self-care strategies cannot neutralize organizationally rooted stressors. This gap between the outcomes and expectations of self-care may explain part of the increasing pervasiveness of burnout.

The theoretical foundations of self-care are based in neoliberal values, such as those espoused by the Chicago School of Economics, which views individuals as solely responsible for their socioeconomic status (Harvey 2007). Self-care's demand that workers identify the sources and solutions of their stress is akin to neoliberal economic concepts such as "rational self-interest." Self-care assumes that each individual worker has an equal capability to effectually improve their workplace conditions. Such claims discount the socioeconomic, sociopolitical, and organizational forces that exist in the workplace. In fact, the foundational principles of self-care support several tenants of American capitalism: a hyper-individualist view of work, ignoring systemic and structural oppression, and a rejection of collective values and actions to improve occupational conditions. Therefore, self-care can be characterized as a laissez faire approach to occupational stress reduction and worker well-being.

The political economy of self-care reveals why it is the most cost-effective method that an organization can endorse because it forces the worker to take on both the identification and cure for their stress. The organization is not required to invest any resources. By embracing self-care, organizations can frame their inaction as a seemingly pragmatic and individualized stress reduction effort. The organization can claim that they are supportive of workers engaging in self-care practices, falsely asserting themselves as partnering with workers in stress reduction and thereby absolving its role in producing the conditions for burnout. In doing so, self-care supports the profit motive more than it serves as a stress reduction strategy to meaningfully address occupational stress and burnout.

How COVID-19 Revealed the Failure of Self-Care

During the COVID-19 pandemic, constant pleas have been made for additional medical personnel, financial support, and equipment. While the number of people being hospitalized and dying from COVID-19 remains staggering, workers across the healthcare sector are deeply distressed by the lack of resources being provided to support their ability to function professionally. Within public hospitals these issues were more prevalent causing a greater risk of exposure and anxiety among healthcare workers (Van Dorn et al. 2020). Clearly, occupational stress during the pandemic continues to be a result of organizational resource deficiencies.

Therefore, the COVID-19 pandemic accentuates the flaws of self-care as the prevalent approach to occupational stress management. Even if a social worker maintained a strong self-care routine, such as taking time off from work when needed, practicing relaxation techniques, and taking full lunch breaks, the pandemic, as an exemplar of a shared trauma, has permeated the social spaces where those practices occur and replaced them with danger and uncertainty. For social workers who are frequently exposed to COVID-19, one of the most stressful situations relates to infecting loved ones, co-workers, or themselves. This type of concurrent professional and personal stress, synonymous with shared traumatic events, can have severe psychosocial and professional implications for the social worker and their clients (Tosone et al. 2011). Thus, a core element of any successful self-care strategy, access to a safe environment removed from the workplace, is compromised. Although social workers frequently have high caseloads and hectic work environments, the COVID-19 pandemic is so socially transformative infiltrating both their professional and personal lives, that many self-care practices are inoperable. Rather, the COVID-19 pandemic has emphasized the importance of organizations investing in structural resources and methods to support their workforce.

How to Progress: Future Directions to Support Our Workers

Shifting the Focus to Organizational Approaches

Organizations are large enough to have distinct cultural norms and are more agile than macrosystems. Therefore, organizations should be the primary arena for designing and implementing strategies to reduce burnout and its precipitators. Organizations are both key drivers of occupational stress and burnout and yet are pragmatic environments for creating robust change. There is a precedent for investing such support in organizational action, especially in relation to workforce issues that increase turnover and absenteeism (Morse et al. 2012). If an organization adopts more egalitarian and inclusive decision-making policies or improves management practices to recognize the meaning and value of their employees' work, structural resistance to precipitators of stress and burnout can be established for all employees. Organizational interventions can provide both preventative actions that build resilience to occupational stressors and the development of burnout, as well as methods to reduce stress in work environments where burnout is already endemic (Awa et al. 2010).

Refining Our Interventions

The current array of interventions to prevent and mitigate occupational stress and burnout lacks both specificity and scope. While there is a growing array of interventions, they tend to be implemented on an individualized basis (Awa et al. 2010; Morse et al. 2012), such as self-care, and are mostly tested on a single occupation (Awa et al. 2010). Yet, in nearly every healthcare organization, there is a variety of professions taking part in a client's care. For example, in emergency rooms treating those with COVID-19, doctors, nurses, social workers, nurse aides, and administrative support staff are constantly collaborating to treat incoming patients. Similarly, in a mental health clinic, treating healthcare workers traumatized from the chaos of the pandemic, a clinical social worker may work with a psychiatrist, peer specialist, and administrative specialist. With the exception of individually administered private practices, healthcare professionals work together.

Therefore, interventions should be tested in a way that we can observe which methods work well for each individual profession within a particular healthcare setting. This means fitting interventions to specific occupational environments such as emergency rooms. Since the intensity and distinctiveness of an occupation are derived largely from the work environment, it is beneficial to observe which interventions are most effective for staff working in a common setting. If future research examines interventions among all of the professionals in a given environment, then we can determine which practices are potentially effective across several professions, while identifying potential patterns of successful intervention types for specific occupational settings. If mindfulness practices tend to benefit emergency room nurses, but not emergency room social workers or physicians, then instituting a broad mindfulness intervention for the entire emergency room staff would not be effective. However, if we only focus on nurses, we may falsely conclude that mindfulness interventions will mitigate burnout among emergency room staff.

Additionally, existing intervention types are still too broad to accurately address the source of burnout within an organization. Currently, interventions not individually implemented, are considered organizational interventions (Restauri and Sheridan 2020). This is an erroneous assumption. Those categorized as "organizational" interventions may be implemented within distinct areas of an organization, in a specific department, or even in subgroups within departments. For example, a training on burnout awareness in hospital settings may be administered specifically to a social work department or just to the social work supervisors of that department. The effectiveness of such a training would depend on identifying the source of the burnout and applying an intervention to that source. If the supervisors are largely contributing to the burnout of the social work staff, providing a training for them would be most effective. If the training were provided too broadly, then it may be a waste of time and resources, which could increase stress and diminish confidence in the intervention's effectiveness. If it were too specifically applied, it could fail to address the entirety of causal factors.

Thus, it is beneficial to develop interventions and organizational procedures attuned to the situations causing burnout. Different interventions are needed if a unit of social workers were experiencing burnout due to abusive supervision practices as opposed to a shared traumatic event such as the COVID-19 pandemic. After the September 11th attacks, there was a palpable need among mental health clinicians for increased clinical supervision, peer supervision, and outlets for workers to express and process their emotions and experiences after such a unique and traumatic event (Bauwens and Tosone 2010; Tosone et al. 2012). Future studies should utilize implementation research to characterize an intervention's area of effect within an organization and to improve their specificity.

Engaging Stakeholders

The Role of the Academy

Universities where social workers are being trained for an increasingly diverse array of occupations must instill education and advocacy about organizationally rooted burnout reduction measures. Just as social workers are not taught to use uniformed treatments for their clients, they should not be taught that self-care is their only resource for stress and burnout reduction. Rather, it should be one of the several resources to ensure their ability to resist stressors integral to the social work profession, such as an Employee Assistance Program, a supportive organizational culture, and access to trainings that build recognition of and resilience to occupational stress and burnout (Lee et al. 2019; Rollins et al. 2016; Vifladt et al. 2016). Educational institutions have an obligation to ensure that students are aware of existing resources and how they can be utilized and taught to advocate for additional resources if needed.

Professional Advocacy

Once social workers enter the field, there are governing bodies that could propagate burnout awareness and burnout reduction interventions and enforce their standardization. Where unions exist, such as in major hospitals or large nonprofits, they can promote organizational resources to address burnout as a part of collective bargaining agreements. Because unions can exist across several organizations, their partnership in reducing burnout has the ability to impact industry norms, even influencing nonunionized organizations to introduce similar resources in order to remain competitive. For many health professionals, including social workers, licensing boards could provide a venue for increased awareness of burnout reduction interventions. Since these boards are responsible for continuing education requirements, they could mandate education related to burnout awareness and reduction. These boards also extend beyond individual organizations and can affect a profession's educational standards.

Conclusion

The COVID-19 pandemic has brought extraordinary strain to the healthcare system and represents a global example of shared trauma. Social workers face many of the stressors that other healthcare professionals experience along with some distinctive sources such as social work's systemic focus and social justice values. Further, the COVID-19 pandemic has underscored the structural insufficiencies of the current healthcare system including self-care, the preeminent method to reduce occupational stress, and its foundation in neoliberal values. Yet, the pandemic also provides insight into how we can develop and promote more progressive and structural methods to improve the well-being of social workers and the entire healthcare workforce. Perhaps a silver lining of this generational disaster will be the impetus to address burnout with the comprehensive, nuanced, and effective interventions that healthcare workers deserve.

References

Awa, W. L., Plaumann, M., & Walter, U. (2010). Burnout prevention: A review of intervention programs. *Patient Education and Counseling, 78*(2), 184–190.

Bauwens, J., & Tosone, C. (2010). Professional posttraumatic growth after a shared traumatic experience: Manhattan clinicians' perspectives on post-9/11 practice. *Journal of Loss and Trauma, 15*(6), 498–517.

Bressi, S. K., & Vaden, E. R. (2017). Reconsidering self care. *Clinical Social Work Journal, 45*(1), 33–38.

Bridgeman, P. J., Bridgeman, M. B., & Barone, J. (2018). Burnout syndrome among healthcare professionals. *The Bulletin of the American Society of Hospital Pharmacists, 75*(3), 147–152.

Cimiotti, J. P., Aiken, L. H., Sloane, D. M., & Wu, E. S. (2012). Nurse staffing, burnout, and health care–associated infection. *American Journal of Infection Control, 40*(6), 486–490.

Dyrbye, L. N., Shanafelt, T. D., Sinsky, C. A., Cipriano, P. F., Bhatt, J., Ommaya, A., & Meyers, D. (2017). *Burnout among health care professionals: A call to explore and address this underrecognized threat to safe, high-quality care* (NAM perspectives. Discussion paper). Washington, DC: National Academy of Medicine.

Dzau, V. J., Kirch, D. G., & Nasca, T. J. (2018). To care is human—Collectively confronting the clinician burnout crisis. *New England Journal of Medicine, 378*(4), 312–314.

Gil-Monte, P. R. (2008). Magnitude of relationship between burnout and absenteeism: A preliminary study. *Psychological Reports, 102*(2), 465–468.

Harvey, D. (2007). *A brief history of neoliberalism.* Oxford: Oxford University Press.

Jackson, S. E., & Schuler, R. S. (1983). Preventing employee burnout. *Personnel, 60*(2), 58–68.

Jaracz, K., Gorna, K., & Konieczna, J. (2005). Burnout, stress and styles of coping among hospital nurses. *Roczniki Akademii Medycznej w Białymstoku, 50*(Suppl 1), 216–219.

LeCroy, C. W., & Stinson, E. L. (2004). The public's perception of social work: Is it what we think it is? *Social Work, 49*(2), 164–174.

Lee, J. J., & Miller, S. E. (2013). A self-care framework for social workers: Building a strong foundation for practice. *Families in Society, 94*(2), 96–103.

Lee, E., Daugherty, J., Eskierka, K., & Hamelin, K. (2019). Compassion fatigue and burnout, one institution's interventions. *Journal of Perianesthesia Nursing, 34*(4), 767–773.

Martin, U., & Schinke, S. P. (1998). Organizational and individual factors influencing job satisfaction and burnout of mental health workers. *Social Work in Health Care, 28*(2), 51–62.

Miller, J. J., Lianekhammy, J., Pope, N., Lee, J., & Grise-Owens, E. (2017). Self-care among healthcare social workers: An exploratory study. *Social Work in Health Care, 56*(10), 865–883.

Moore, M., Cristofalo, M., Dotolo, D., Torres, N., Lahdya, A., Ho, L., & Fouts, S. (2017). When high pressure, system constraints, and a social justice mission collide: A socio-structural analysis of emergency department social work services. *Social Science & Medicine, 178*, 104–114.

Morse, G., Salyers, M. P., Rollins, A. L., Monroe-DeVita, M., & Pfahler, C. (2012). Burnout in mental health services: A review of the problem and its remediation. *Administration and Policy in Mental Health and Mental Health Services Research, 39*(5), 341–352.

Murphy, A., & McDonald, J. (2004). Power, status and marginalization: Rural social workers and evidence-based practice in multidisciplinary teams. *Australian Social Work, 57*(2), 127–136.

Peterson, K. J. (2012). Shared decision making in health care settings: A role for social work. *Social Work in Health Care, 51*(10), 894–908.

Polizzi, C., Lynn, S. J., & Perry, A. (2020). Stress and coping in the time of COVID-19: Pathways to resilience and recovery. *Clinical Neuropsychiatry, 17*(2), 59–62.

Restauri, N., & Sheridan, A. D. (2020). Burnout and PTSD in the COVID-19 pandemic: Intersection, impact and interventions. *Journal of the American College of Radiology, 17*(7), 921–926.

Rollins, A. L., Kukla, M., Morse, G., Davis, L., Leiter, M., Monroe-DeVita, M., & Collins, L. (2016). Comparative effectiveness of a burnout reduction intervention for behavioral health providers. *Psychiatric Services, 67*(8), 920–923.

Rudaz, M., Twohig, M. P., Ong, C. W., & Levin, M. E. (2017). Mindfulness and acceptance-based trainings for fostering self-care and reducing stress in mental health professionals: A systematic review. *Journal of Contextual Behavioral Science, 6*(4), 380–390.

Shah, K., Chaudhari, G., Kamrai, D., Lail, A., & Patel, R. S. (2020). How essential is to focus on physician's health and burnout in coronavirus (COVID-19) pandemic? *Cureu, 12*(4), e7538.

Shanafelt, T. D., Balch, C. M., Bechamps, G., Russell, T., Dyrbye, L., Satele, D., & Freischlag, J. (2010). Burnout and medical errors among American surgeons. *Annals of Surgery, 251*(6), 995–1000.

Shirom, A. (2005). Reflections on the study of burnout. *Work & Stress, 19*(3), 263–270.

Tosone, C., McTighe, J. P., Bauwens, J., & Naturale, A. (2011). Shared traumatic stress and the long-term impact of 9/11 on Manhattan clinicians. *Journal of Traumatic Stress, 24*(5), 546–552.

Tosone, C., Nuttman-Shwartz, O., & Stephens, T. (2012). Shared trauma: When the professional is personal. *Clinical Social Work Journal, 40*(2), 231–239.

Van Dorn, A., Cooney, R. E., & Sabin, M. L. (2020). COVID-19 exacerbating inequalities in the US. *The Lancet, 395*(10232), 1243–1244.

Van Mol, M. M., Kompanje, E. J., Benoit, D. D., Bakker, J., & Nijkamp, M. D. (2015). The prevalence of compassion fatigue and burnout among healthcare professionals in intensive care units: A systematic review. *PLoS One, 10*(8), e0136955.

Vifladt, A., Simonsen, B. O., Lydersen, S., & Farup, P. G. (2016). The association between patient safety culture and burnout and sense of coherence: A cross-sectional study in restructured and not restructured intensive care units. *Intensive and Critical Care Nursing, 36*, 26–34.

Vlessides, M. (2020, April 06). *COVID-19: Mental health pros come to the aid of frontline comrades.* Retrieved May 21, 2020, from https://www.the-hospitalist.org/hospitalist/article/220157/coronavirus-updates/covid-19-mental-health-pros-come-aid-frontline

Wagaman, M. A., Geiger, J. M., Shockley, C., & Segal, E. A. (2015). The role of empathy in burnout, compassion satisfaction, and secondary traumatic stress among social workers. *Social Work, 60*(3), 201–209.

West, C. P., Dyrbye, L. N., Erwin, P. J., & Shanafelt, T. D. (2016). Interventions to prevent and reduce physician burnout: A systematic review and meta-analysis. *The Lancet, 388*(10057), 2272–2281.

Wrenn, K., & Rice, N. (1994). Social-work services in an emergency department: An integral part of the healthcare safety net. *Academic Emergency Medicine, 1*(3), 247–253.

Part IV
Convergence with Racism Pandemic

Chapter 28
The Pandemic Within the Pandemic of 2020: A Spiritual Perspective

Terry S. Audate

Introduction

The colliding impact of the novel coronavirus pandemic (COVID-19) and the recent highlighting of police brutality through nationwide protests has changed the fabric of the United States, forcing the country to grapple with the two crises' traumatic effects. In the wake of these two seismic events, individuals are looking to make sense out of the changes in the world around them. They are more likely to ask themselves big questions about their place in the world or the meaning of life. Both the virus and the protests, including the violence connected to protests, have disproportionately affected communities of color.

Frantz Fanon, a twentieth-century psychiatrist from the island of Martinique and author of *The Wretched of the Earth*, articulated and struggled with the question of whether violence is "warranted in overturning colonial oppression" (Fanon 1963). His work drew on his personal experience, and his writings influenced anticolonialism movements across the globe. Fanon argued that colonialism destroyed the soul. In 2020, the convergence of COVID-19 and a large-scale reckoning with police brutality and racism have led people to question their faith, values, and spiritual journey in new ways, and Fanon's examination of oppression and its damage to the soul seems freshly relevant. With society-wide events engendering unprecedented responses from individuals, groups, and organizations worldwide, across diverse socioeconomic backgrounds, mental health professionals everywhere are engaged with clients trying to answer existential questions.

Historically, people of color have faced unrelenting racial disparities in employment, education, law enforcement, policing, and health. However, COVID-19 and

T. S. Audate (✉)
Silver School of Social Work, New York University, New York, NY, USA
e-mail: ta329@nyu.edu

© The Author(s), under exclusive license to Springer Nature Switzerland
AG 2021
C. Tosone (ed.), *Shared Trauma, Shared Resilience During a Pandemic*,
Essential Clinical Social Work Series,
https://doi.org/10.1007/978-3-030-61442-3_28

the worldwide demonstrations for justice, which have brought so many disparities to light, have affected everyone in one way or another. In my clinical practice, I have found that, while the impact of events may differ by race and socioeconomic status, my clients across the board have experienced disruption and difficulties that have the potential to cause distress. Many people, including the clinicians in my practice, have reported feeling confused and displaced and questioning the world they live in. Where does one go for therapeutic assistance when even the most skilled clinicians are personally impacted by current events?

The answer to Fanon's question of whether violence is the remedy to the violence inflicted on people of color is, from a spiritual perspective, an emphatic no. The life of John Lewis, the former civil rights leader since the times of Dr. Martin Luther King, Jr., which Americans have reflected on during this period as his death coincided with Black Lives Matter protests, spoke loudly to nonviolent change as a better alternative. Change through nonviolence is rooted in spiritual consciousness. In this chapter, I summarize two key points from a paper currently under review in which I offer an introduction on how to balance one's mind and spirit in the face of current events and to contemplate these events in such a way as to derive meaning and purpose from them.

COVID-19 Pandemic

The outbreak of COVID-19 and the constant threat of a rising infection curve have disrupted any sense of normalcy. With nearly 229,000 confirmed cases and over 23,000 deaths in New York City to date (CDC 2020), this virus has shocked the city. Mental health professionals were not immune to its impact. Those who lost loved ones faced an especially heavy burden, and all faced normal human worry about their health and the health of family and friends.

The global emotional impact of COVID-19 has yet to be determined. However, in my clinical practice, I have witnessed the prevalence of anxiety, stress, insomnia, anger, and the effects of social distancing as a result of COVID-19. These implications include feelings of loneliness, isolation, lack of motivation, and increased cognitive distortions. My clinical practice has also seen an increase in diagnoses of mild to moderate depressive symptoms, increased rates in substance and alcohol abuse, increased incidence of paranoia, and an increase in marital/relationship discord. Lastly my practice has unfortunately experienced the deaths of two clients.

This disease has been traumatic for individuals, causing them pain and chaos in their lives, inducing a sense of hopelessness and powerlessness for many (Calhoun and Tedeschi 1999). These symptoms have been reported by an influx of clients seeking help to manage their emotions and regain a sense of control. Clients have reported years of wealth building being lost and chaos in their lives on different fronts due to the COVID-19 pandemic. According to Decker (1993), events that upset our plans and sense of order can serve as lessons and are a call to reconsider our priorities and what we think the purpose of life is. In the case of the COVID-19 crisis, the disruption points to our oneness at the deepest levels and the reality that we are all in this struggle to survive and thrive. However, before we could even come to terms with the COVID-19 crisis, public outcry over police brutality led us to confront the ongoing pandemic of racism in policing.

Police Brutality

At the apex of confirmed COVID-19 cases in New York, the Centers for Disease Control and Prevention (CDC) recommended that the general public wear home-made face coverings to mitigate the spread of the disease. However, people from Black and brown communities expressed concern that if members of their communities wore homemade masks, such as bandanas, it could compound racial discriminatory behavior from law enforcement, putting additional lives in danger (Alfonso 2020). This was because colored bandanas are often associated with gang affiliation; therefore, such attire for Black and brown men made them more susceptible to racial profiling.

This concern foreshadowed the death of George Floyd, an unarmed man of color who died at the hands of police in Minneapolis, Minnesota, on Memorial Day. One officer was charged with second-degree murder and three others with aiding and abetting murder in the days that followed, as demonstrations took place in towns and cities across the country and even across the world. The intersection of the COVID-19 pandemic with widespread awakening to the "pandemic" of police brutality and sustained racism is complex. In the United States, people of color have been particularly vulnerable to COVID-19 because of economic disparities, disparities in access to health care and health outcomes, and related factors (CDC 2020; Brooks and Roy 2020; Gupta 2020). This unequal burden likely intensified the anger over racial profiling and police brutality that contributed to mass protests around the world. That anger arose from the unjust killings of Tanisha Anderson, 37, who was diagnosed with a bipolar disorder; Michael Brown, 18, who was walking home with a friend; Tamir Rice, 12, who was playing with a toy gun in the park; Eric Garner, 43, who was allegedly selling loose cigarettes; Freddie Gray, 25, who was killed in a police van while his hands and feet were shackled without a seatbelt; Alton Sterling, 37, who was apprehended for selling CDs and DVDs and later killed; Stephon Clark, 22, who was shot in his grandmother's backyard; Breonna Taylor, 26, who was killed while she was asleep; and countless others by police officers who are rarely charged and almost never convicted. According to a study conducted by Edwards, Lee, and Esposito (2019), excessive force rendered by police is a leading cause of death among men of color, and Black, Latinx, American Indian, and Alaska Native men and women are all at higher lifetime risk of the same than are white men and women.

Police brutality and racial profiling has been an issue for decades, but the public execution of George Floyd marked an apparent turning point, fueling the most pervasive protests—in terms of countries and protestors involved—in history (Buchanan et al. 2020). Government officials from all over the country pledged action; in one prominent move, the City Council of Minneapolis voted to dismantle its police department and replace it with a department of community safety and violence prevention. In addition, discussions have re-emerged related to the subpar resources in communities of color, such as medical access and insurance, employment, education, and overall access to essential resources. As Fanon (1963) declared, communities of color were forced into second-class citizenship under colonialism and have been denied these resources as a result.

Shared Trauma

Serving a community of color during these times, when a highlighting of racial injustice is coupled with the pandemic, places a heavy toll on clinicians who come from these same communities. Clients seen in my practice have reported feelings of rage, anger, fear, sadness, and hopelessness. Many ask "What is the world coming to?" and "What is the meaning of all this?". How do we, as clinicians, bring peace to those we serve in these communities and help them answer these existential questions?

The clinicians in my practice are on the front line during the current crises and have been dually exposed to trauma by living through the crises themselves while striving to help clients make sense of what is happening. Amid the prevalence of COVID-19 in New York City and the constant displays of blatant disrespect for people of color seen from law enforcement officers, in the media, in everyday life, and at the highest levels of the US government, as well as the subpar conditions so many people of color face on a day-to-day basis, clinicians have disclosed their own intrapsychic concerns as they relate to these two phenomena. Collectively, clinicians have experienced degrees of trauma in the current situation, while also increasing their susceptibility to vicarious and secondary trauma (Tosone et al. 2012; Saakvitne 2002) and giving them an important stake, along with their clients, in seeking answers to meaning-making questions (McTighe and Tosone 2015).

A Spirituality Perspective

Human spirituality can be seen as esoteric, delicate, and obscure. It is intertwined with the experience of culture, traditions, and ways of life. If the human spirit's purpose is to learn lessons and to conceptualize them as consciousness (Calhoun and Tedeschi 1999), then there is much to glean from our experiences.

These tumultuous times have given us plenty of opportunities to reflect on the fragility of life and its purpose. Having been taught to accumulate wealth and to seek external recognition for our efforts with little thought for the highest and greatest good that we can serve, individually and collectively, we may be challenged when times of trauma push us to search for deeper meaning. Things like external recognition are temporary and of less importance viewed through the spiritual lens. They fall short of bringing inner lasting peace, the goal of spiritual practice.

Spirituality suggests that traumatic events are pathways for individuals to learn lessons or make corrections in their lives. Using a spirituality-based approach to work with clients has been beneficial in my practice. In the previously mentioned paper, I outline spiritual tenets across cultures and disciplines which converge on ideas central to the process of facilitating an approach rooted in spirituality to foster posttraumatic growth. I outline steps that can assist clients in answering existential questions. The first involves connecting to feelings on a deeper level, and the other pertains to expanded consciousness.

These two steps involve a spiritually oriented therapist helping to establish a safe environment for a client. Once that space is created, the therapist is able to usher the client into the abyss of their emotions and feelings to forge a relationship with their essence, the spiritual part of them (Johanson 2012; Hegel 2016). In other words, the therapist's aim is to help the client to get in touch with and identify their true feelings about the crises. The therapist then guides the client to recognize their rationalizing thoughts and beliefs and how these are in place to justify them not dealing with their feelings. The clinician can then explore with clients, what lessons they can glean from their current trauma to advance their consciousness.

Identifying with our emotions, thoughts, and feelings is the gateway to discovering the answers to the existential questions (Frankl 1959). The acknowledgment of one's feeling is the first step to creating that bridge between mind and spirit necessary for attaining a higher consciousness. In this way, the therapist engages the client in a meaningful discussion to enrich their insights about their experiences. This involves the use of universal principles such as the second law of thermodynamics, which proposes that all things tend towards equilibrium and for every action, there is an equal and opposite reaction.

These concepts can be used not only to help clients but also to help clinicians begin to connect to higher meaning. The aim of this spiritual approach to this crisis is to guide individuals toward reconsidering their humanity and the place where we are one. It asks us to see others as part of a common struggle that we all face to make our lives individually, and our world collectively, better. It can be argued that we are spiritual beings in a physical body having physical experience (Frissell 2001). A spiritual approach to revisiting that experience could be impactful in moments of crisis, since the spiritual level is where our commonality lies, and recognizing our oneness also makes us aware that our struggles are common to all and therefore a part of the process of conscious evolution.

Discussion

Built into the experience of this pandemic is a spiritual lesson, as reluctant as we may be to receive it. For weeks, much of the world stopped, outside of activities considered essential. The quiet that followed gave us an opportunity to reflect on the condition of the planet and the damage humans have imposed on it. Our busy life-styles and drive to attain wealth and status have caused many of us to miss the kind of purpose that gives us spiritual sustenance in life. It has forced too many to live their lives in concert with the expectations of their societies. We have become too busy with external responsibilities and goals to give adequate time to our internal issues. We have learned to suppress these internal conflicts, using work and external commitments as a means of avoiding internal issues, that is, avoidance of self.

Human commonality lies in spirituality, whereas divergence is realized through our cultures, religions, beliefs, and values. Human feelings and emotions connect individuals directly to the human spirit (Audate 2020). The worldwide response to COVID-19 and the death of a man of color—part of a long, wide pattern of injustice—has prompted strong emotions, causing large swaths of humanity to reflect on our common ground. This can be seen as a spiritual perspective. We could view this moment as the spirit realm, the realm of origination seeking to manifest a different world (Dyer 2001).

In my clinical practice, I have had many individuals seek therapy to address their emotional turmoil at this time. As a clinician, I have a chance to help them look inward and face unresolved conflicts that external engagements have caused them to avoid, just as I have the chance to do in my own life. It is an opportunity that we should grab with both hands.

Based on my experience of working with clients, this pandemic forces us to reconsider what is most critical in life and what our priorities should be. As we work on ourselves individually, and bring resolution to our personal difficulties, we will ultimately grow our awareness and thus become emotionally better humans. Our contributions to our families, friend groups, and communities will improve. We each have a responsibility to create a better world for ourselves and for those that come after us, and this time of reflection is ideal to stop the slide in our personal lives, our families, our communities, and our world (Dyer 2001). Continued worldwide demonstrations about racial inequities in our societies call on us to reconsider our past relationships with, and attitudes towards, each other. Coming on the heels of a worldwide pandemic, this movement highlights the need for personal and collective change in our planet. A spiritually based therapeutic approach draws attention to how we are all the same at the deepest level and that we all desire things and struggle with the same issues that challenge our very humanity. It, therefore, provides a unique hope for our personal contribution to the conscious evolution of humanity.

Conclusion

The dual crises of COVID-19 and a widespread reckoning with racial inequity have given humans worldwide a chance to pause and reconsider our way of life and our individual and collective responsibilities to one another. History shows our failures, but crises are typically pregnant with new opportunities. This current crisis provides us with the best opportunity that we have been given in a long time to redress the ills in our societies and to make the world better. George Floyd's death has galvanized the world to respond to these ills in ways never seen before. Spiritually speaking, we may speak of a divine energy at work, beyond human thought, and this perspective suggests a tidal shift that will bring about lasting change for a more equitable world. Clinicians are among the change agents in our communities who can usher in the transformations we wish to see.

The stress that we individually struggle with in these daunting times can be viewed as a challenge to each of us, individually. It is there to remind us that each of us has a role to play in producing a better world. That role starts with a change within us. Our clinicians have a double duty: helping others to address their personal responsibilities to the greater good and addressing their own contribution to the process. A spiritual and metaphysical approach could be of great assistance, providing a sense of connection, shared experience, and mutual duty in this time of need.

References

Adewale, V., Ritchie, D., & Skeels, S. E. (2016). African American and African perspectives on mental health: A pilot study of the pre and post colonial and slavery influences and their implications on mental health. *Journal of Communication in Healthcare, 9*(2), 78–89.

Alfonso, F. (2020, April 7). Re: Coronavirus: Why some people of color say they won't wear homemade face masks. [CNN.COM Wire Service]. Retrieved from https://www.mercurynews.com/2020/04/07/coronavirus-why-some-people-of-color-say-they-wont-wear-homemade-face-masks/

Audate, T. S. (2020). *A spiritual-based approach to the understanding and advancement of post-traumatic growth*. Manuscript submitted for publication.

Bassett, M. T. (2019). No justice, no health: The black panther Party's fight for health in Boston and beyond. *Journal of African American Studies, 23*(4), 352–363.

Bleakley, P. (2019). A thin-slice of institutionalised police brutality: A tradition of excessive force in the Chicago Police Department. *Criminal Law Forum, 30*, 425–449.

Brooks, J. & Roy, T. (2020). Racial disparities and COVID-19. Retrieved from https://ncdp.columbia.edu/ncdp-perspectives/racial-disparities-and-covid-19/

Buchanan, L., Bui, Q., & Patel, J.K., (2020, July 3). Re: Black lives matter may be the largest movement in U.S. history. [New York Times]. Retrieved from https://www.newyorktimes.com/interactive/2020/07/03/us/george-floyd-protests-crowd-size.html

Calhoun, L. G., & Tedeschi, R. G. (1999). *Facilitating posttraumatic growth: A clinician's guide*. Mahwah: Lawrence Erlbaum Associates, Publishers.

Caparros-Gonzalez, R., & Alderdice, F. (2020). The COVID-19 pandemic and perinatal mental health. *Journal of Reproductive and Infant Psychology, 38*(3), 223–225.

Centers for Disease Control & Prevention. (2020. July 24). Re: Health equity considerations and racial and ethnic minority groups. Retrieved from https://www.cdc.gov

Cheng, P., Guohua, X., Pang, P., Wu, B., Jiang, W., Yong-Tong, L., & Xiaoting, B. (2020). COVID-19 epidemic peer support and crisis intervention via social media. *Community Mental Health Journal, 56*(5), 786–792.

Decker, L. R. (1993). The role of trauma in spiritual development. *Journal of Humanistic Psychology, 33*(4), 33–46. Sage Publications, Inc.

Dyer, W. W. (2001). *There's a spiritual solution to every problem.* New York: Harper Collins Publishers.

Edwards, F., Lee, H., & Esposito, M. (2019). Risk of being killed by police use of force in the United States by age, race-ethnicity, and sex. *PNAS, 116*(34), 16793–16798.

Fanon, F. (2004). *The wretched of the Earth* (trans: Philcox, R.). New York: Grove Press (1963).

Frank, V. E. (2014). *The will to meaning.* New York: Penguin Group.

Frankl, V. E. (2006). *Man's search for meaning* (trans: Lasch, I.). Boston, MA: Beacon Press. (1959).

Frissell, B. (2001). *You are a spiritual being having a human experience.* Berkeley: Frog, Ltd.

Graham, A., Haner, M., Sloan, M. M., Cullen, F. T., Kulig, T. C., & Cheryl, L. J. (2020). Race and worrying about police brutality: The hidden injuries of minority status in America. *Victims & Offenders, 15*(5), 549–573.

Gupta, S. (2020, April 10). Re: Coronavirus: Why African American may be especially vulnerable Covid 19 heath race. [Science News]. Retrieved from https://www.sciencenews.org/article/coronavirus-why-african-americans-vulnerable-covid-19-health-race

Hegel, G.W.F. (2016). *The Phenomenology of Mind* (trans: Baillie, J.B.). Middletown: Pantianos Classics. (1807).

Imran, I. H., Tiwana, F., & Tahir, S. M. (2020). Impact of the COVID-19 pandemic on adult mental health. *Pakistan Journal of Medical Sciences, 36*. (COVID19-S4).

Johanson, G. (2012). Mindfulness, emotions, and the organization of experience. *Hakomi Forum, 25*, 49–70.

Jung, C.G. (1993). Modern man is search of a soul. (trans: Dell, W.S. & Baynes, C.F.). New York: Harcourt, Inc.

Jung, C. G. (2006). *The uncovered self.* New York: First New American Library.

Lipscomb, A. E. (2020). You have the right to exclaim your pain: Honoring Black familial voices impacted by police induced trauma in the United States. *Journal of Ethnic and Cultural Studies, 7*(1), 131–142.

McManus, H. D., Cullen, F. T., Jonson, C. L., Burton, A. L., & Burton, E. S., Jr. (2019). Will black lives matter to the police? African Americans' concerns about Trump's presidency. *Victims & Offenders, 14*(8), 1040–1062.

McNamara, A. (2020, March 20). Re: New York liquor stores deemed "essential" under Cuomo's statewide order. [CBS News]. Retrieved from https://www.cbsnews.com/news/coronavirus-new-york-liquor-stores-deemed-essential-under-cuomos-statewide-order/

McTighe, J., & Tosone, C. (2015). In the long shadow of 9/11: Narratives of Manhattan clinicians' efforts to make meaning of a shared trauma. *Social Work in Mental Health, 13*(4), 299–317.

Parlotz, R.D. The Institute for the Study of Spirituality and Trauma, downloaded April 22, 2020 From http://www.geocities.com/frbobparlotz/isstparlotz.html

Peeples, L. (2020). What the data say about police brutality and racial bias - and which reforms might work. *Nature, 583*(7814), 22–24.

Saakvitne, K. W. (2002). Shared Trauma: The Therapist's Increased Vulnerability. *Psychoanalytic Dialogues, 12*(3), 443.

Sanchez, R. & Meilhan, P. (2020, June 26). Re: Minneapolis City Council advances plan to dismantle embattled police force. [CNN.COM]. Retrieved form https://www.cnn.com/2020/06/26/us/minneapolis-city-council-police-department/index.html

Snouwaert, J. (2020, March 20). Re: Liquor stores in New York are considered 'essential' business by the state and will remain open during the coronavirus shut-

downs. [Business Insider]. Retrieved from https://www.businessinsider.com/
coronavirus-new-york-liquor-stores-deemed-essential-can-stay-open-2020-3

Tosone, C., Nuttman-Shwartz, O., & Stephens, T. (2012). Shared trauma: When the professional is
personal. *Clinical Social Work Journal, 40*(2), 231–239.

Vis, J., & Boynton, H. M. (2008). Spirituality and transcendent meaning making: Possibilities
for enhancing posttraumatic growth. *Journal of Religion & Spirituality in Social Work: Social
Thought, 27*(1–2), 69–86.

Chapter 29
Black Lives, Mass Incarceration, and the Perpetuity of Trauma in the Era of COVID-19: The Road to Abolition Social Work

Kirk Jae James

Introduction

Six months in the year 2020 has demonstrated to me the importance of living in the *now*. Yet as social workers, who are needed more than ever in the era of COVID-19, we can no longer afford to solely triage oppression and trauma. No matter how dystopian this moment may feel, we must move beyond the surface and explore the root of the social ills we seek to combat. Sankofa is a word and practice in West Africa (Temple 2010), which implies that to understand the present, we need to examine its history. Rather than begin this reflection prematurely amid a global pandemic—which has significantly exacerbated the trauma and oppression of historically marginalized people—I believe it prudent to provide some brief historical context towards our understanding of trauma and its relationship to the Black experience in the United States. And finally, I will articulate why in this now—amid the COVID-19 pandemic and the Black Lives Matter (BLM) movement—social work must reckon with its history and actualize its values by embracing abolition.

Trauma: A History Rooted in War

Trauma has been a buzzword for many years. I believe understanding it is of paramount importance to liberating a world engulfed for centuries in the trauma of white supremacy. Yet there is often minimal conversation on its history or the conceptual framework which guides our understanding and practice as social workers—

K. J. James (✉)
Silver School of Social Work, New York University, New York, NY, USA
e-mail: kaj3@nyu.edu

© The Author(s), under exclusive license to Springer Nature Switzerland AG 2021
C. Tosone (ed.), *Shared Trauma, Shared Resilience During a Pandemic*, Essential Clinical Social Work Series, https://doi.org/10.1007/978-3-030-61442-3_29

281

especially as it pertains to Black people impacted by carceral systems (James and Smyth 2014).

The genesis of the word "trauma" comes from the Greek word "traumat"—which means to wound. Trauma is "often used interchangeably with post-traumatic stress disorder [PTSD]"—which seeks to understand the present-day impact of a *past* traumatic event (DeVeaux 2013, p. 261). The current clinical and conceptual framework for the understanding of trauma is rooted in war—as soldiers came home from World War I, it became clear that they were suffering. A British medical journal, *The Lancet*, would ultimately coin the term "shell shock" in February 1915 to explain the phenomenon initially thought to be a physical illness emanating from exposure to the loud discharge of weapons. Through much research, debate, and advocacy by veterans, "shell shock" would become trauma and ultimately evolve to PTSD—which was then added to the Diagnostic and Statistical Manual of Mental Disorders (DSM-III) in 1980 by the American Psychiatric Association (APA) (Crocq and Crocq 2000). In simple terms, trauma is any experience that overwhelms your ability to cope and respond as your best self. Clinical recognition and subsequent treatment of PTSD required an "etiological catalyst"—a trauma of sorts—often wide-ranging yet nevertheless rooted in extreme conditions (Goodwin 1987).

A 1990s research study on adverse childhood experiences (ACEs) further demonstrated the impact of trauma on children. They found that exposure to as little as one adverse experience (or traumatic event) could present lifelong consequences into adulthood. The outcomes included poor mental and physical health, substance use, higher risk for sexual diseases, lower socioeconomic opportunities, and ultimately, incarceration (Stensrud et al. 2019).

In my work with people impacted by carceral systems, I like to say that "trauma is drama" as it impairs numerous cognitive processes like the corpus callosum, a bridge that connects the left and right brain and is a conduit for critical thought and reality perception. Biological research on trauma demonstrates an impact on respiratory functioning, digestive functioning, immune functioning, and just about every automatic process necessary for health (Van der Kolk 1996). Understanding trauma and its genesis has been instrumental in my practice as a social worker. However, I have often felt that something was missing in trauma research and practice—which is again, mostly rooted in PTSD—implying a post or halt to the traumatic event. I am not sure if the magnitude of the question felt daunting to the APA or if its relevance would disturb white supremacy's dissonance, but I have always wondered

"How do we quantify the impact of trauma (war) that has never been 'post'?".

The Quest for White Supremacy and Its War on Black Lives

The Black Lives Matter (BLM) movement is again challenging the historical dissonance and apathy towards the oppression of Black people (and other oppressed minorities) in the United States. However, the dissonance is not limited to "racists" or pronounced "white supremacists." The student-led uprisings within social work education are similarly challenging the profession to recognize the lack of diversity and historical content afforded to students in preparation for their work with marginalized populations (James and Smyth 2014). The goal for this section is not solely to bridge the educational gap but to allow us a window to truly consider from a heart space, the trauma of oppression.

For the sake of this reflection, "Black Lives" is operationalized rather broadly. A brief historical account of the trauma African people have experienced in the quest for white supremacy—colonization, slavery, racism, and capitalism—and continuing through the journey for liberation and equity in the year 2020, is highlighted by BLM.

The root of much Black trauma is "white supremacy"—which took root in West Africa around 1471, when Portuguese sailors invaded the continent lusting after its gold. Shortly after, Europeans would go on to determine Black bodies were also of monetary value. Chattel slavery would rob millions of men, women, and children from their homes, families, languages, and history. For months they had to eat, sleep, and defecate in spaces not built for human beings. Many died in these conditions, but the ones who survived went through *the door of no return* on a transatlantic journey—where millions would perish—many choosing to jump with children into shark-infested waters to escape their predicament. It got no better for the ones who survived and made it ashore to various diasporic "captured land," including what would become the United States in 1619.

These stolen people would have to adjust to strange lands, new languages, religion, and food. They would again have to adjust to being separated and sold to plantations where brutally cold winters and hot summers awaited, with backbreaking labor enforced by whippings and other forms of public torture, where Black women had to teach their daughters how to survive rape and white men's sexual fetishization of Black bodies (Wideman 1998).

Black people would have to endure centuries of untold brutality before the passage of the 13th Amendment in 1865 feigned to acknowledge their humanity. The amendment hailed as the legislation to end chattel slavery in the United States declared slavery illegal, except for people convicted of crimes (James 2016). So as Black people awaited the promises of reconstruction, the southern states—many of which depended on the exploitation of Black bodies (via slavery) to sustain their economies—moved immediately to *exploit* the language of the amendment.

They established the "Black codes"—a series of laws that laid the groundwork for false theories and practices to substantiate Black criminality post-chattel slavery. The "codes" made it a crime to be unemployed, walk on the same side of the street as white people, look white people in the eye, and testify against white people in court (James 2016). Former slaves, lacking the ability to defend themselves against these laws rooted in anti-Blackness, were often convicted and sentenced to years in prison for minor offenses, only to be sent back to plantations—a practice termed "convict leasing system" by historians (Mancini 1996). Imputing crime to color within the American psyche could now be corroborated by the large percentages of incarcerated former slaves. Numerous media outlets then began to assert that Black people were inherently criminal. *Race Traits and Tendencies of the American Negro,* a popular publication of the time, would proclaim that "crime, pauperism, and sexual immorality" were inherent tendencies of Black people (Hoffman 1896, p. 217). This false narrative set the stage for the Jim Crow era and another century of racialized oppression and trauma.

The Civil Rights Act of 1965 (similar to the 13th Amendment) brought with it a new hope, but what followed were new Black codes in the form of "The war on drugs," mandatory minimums, truth in sentencing, three-strikes law, the 1994 crime bill, stop and frisk, etc.—all policies and practices with profound racial implications disproportionately affecting Black people (Alexander 2020). Also, true to the formula established in 1865, there was an intentional neoconservative agenda to negate social determinants of behavior—and to thus marginalize, if not extinguish, the role of poverty and varied systematic layers of oppression as causal factors of behaviors considered "criminal," while simultaneously utilizing various methods of propaganda to promote Black criminality and anti-Blackness within the American consciousness.

While the police and carceral systems are central tools in maintaining white supremacy, they are not the only structures of harm inducing trauma. Many scholars have pointed out that capitalism—with its roots in slavery—continues to be a tool of Black labor exploitation and racialized violence, leaving millions of Black people to live their lives in perpetual financial insecurity (Melamed 2011; Pulido 2017). Education—often hailed as a necessary tool to access capitalistic structures—is often denied and/or inaccessible to many Black people. Those who can enter such structures have attested to the violence they must endure to survive and succeed (Black and Garvis 2018). Even social work has a tremendous bias towards admitting formerly incarcerated people (Magen and Emerman 2000). Health care and housing—the building blocks of fundamental human rights—are still largely inaccessible to many Black people, especially those entrapped within the carceral apparatus. How does social work begin to quantify and work with that magnitude of trauma, further exacerbated by the quest for white supremacy, on Black lives? And how has the COVID-19 pandemic further impacted people who are already compromised in this way?

Mass Incarceration

George Jackson, one of the greatest advocates for the rights of incarcerated individuals, would profoundly articulate in his classic *Soledad Brother* that:

> Black men born in the US and fortunate enough to live past the age of 18 are conditioned to accept the inevitability of prison. For most of us, it simply looms as the next phase in a sequence of humiliations. Being born a slave in a captive society and never experiencing any objective basis for expectation had the effect of preparing me for the progressively traumatic misfortunes that lead so many black men to the prison gate. I was prepared for prison. It required only minor psychic adjustments. (Jackson 1994, p. 4)

Much of my current research and interventions center on "mass incarceration"—a euphemism academics used to downplay the vestiges of colonialization, slavery, and racialized oppression inherent in the United States. The term further incorrectly implies that there is an equal probability of incarceration for all people living in America—which is statistically incorrect. The truth is that more Black men are incarcerated today than were enslaved in 1850. Black men, women, and children are significantly overrepresented in every facet of the prison industrial complex erected by the United States. A country that purports to be a democracy, but with only 5% of the world's population, has managed to incarcerate 25% of the total global prison population. Almost 11 million people are jailed to await trial each year; over 2 million people are sentenced and warehoused in state and federal prisons throughout the nation. More children are incarcerated in the United States than any other country in the world. Women are the fastest-growing prison population, and millions more are trapped in their communities under the auspices of parole and probation (Alexander 2020).

The majority of people held in jails and prisons are Black—direct descendants of mothers, fathers, and children stolen from Africa beginning in the fifteenth century (Wacquant, 2002). An almost 500-year continuous history of war. Quite possibly, an "etiological catalyst" unlike any witnessed in the history of this world. Yet their trauma—one certainly exacerbated by the pandemic—is rarely a topic of conversation. I have to admit that the first time I was asked to consider the trauma of racialized oppression, I was dumbfounded. My dissertation advisor asked me to consider the traumatic impact of carceral systems and centuries of oppression on Black and brown people. Yet I was having a hard time conceptualizing the question, especially considering I had just illustrated in over 200 pages what I believed to be the impact of racialized oppression with well-sourced quantitative data. But he persisted "your work shows how people are impacted systematically, but how does the trauma of that oppression impact the people?".

It is a question that social work as a profession has spent little time contemplating—and it is a question made even more relevant during this pandemic that has disproportionately impacted Blacks, not only in deaths but economically, socially, and in ways that, frankly, have yet to be understood, which terrifies me! The resilience of Black people in the face of constant oppression speaks for itself. But COVID-19, coupled with blatant racism and gaslighting by the US government amid gross police and state-sanctioned violence, presents *another* layer of traumatic stress for extremely vulnerable people who have never had a *post* trauma. How do we quantify the impact? By now, you should know that the question is rhetorical as we have no tools at our disposal to access the trauma of 500 years of oppression—but even without a tool of measure, we know that there will be an impact. And let us not forget "trauma is drama."

COVID-19: The Personal Is the Professional

Trauma awareness needs to be a parallel process that starts internally with us as social workers—which can often feel selfish and challenging to people who have dedicated their lives in service to others. However, much like the announcement before takeoff that cautions us to put on our oxygen mask first in the case of an emergency, we must recognize that an understanding of our own trauma is paramount to our ability to show up as our best selves in work to dismantle oppression amid a pandemic. Furthermore, the truth, all of it, has to be centered in that process.

There is catharsis that awaits us all in *truth-telling*. But since March of 2020, and the Zoom invasion into my personal life, "How are you doing?" has become my most dreaded question. The often-used expression has taken on a new depth during the coronavirus pandemic. Yet, depending on the person or situation, I know the answer is often a watered-down palatable version of my truth. But in honoring Baldwin and this moment, here is the truth of how I am doing: I am a Black man living in the United States and a world rooted in anti-Blackness, where the trauma of white supremacy is an omnipresent facet of my existence, an existence that is always in question. The uncertainty the world feels, as a result of this pandemic, is the uncertainty myself and that most oppressed people have to live under each day. And much like that of my enslaved ancestors, it began at birth. Yet, for brevity, I will share only my experiences during the first 6 months of 2020.

January arrives with two of my closest friends and my 20-year-old brother, incarcerated. My brother, incarcerated for *weed possession*, has to spend 6 months in jail before his release in May. At the same time, my friends remain trapped in human cages, separated from their families and children amid a global pandemic. In February, my 27-year-old brother—a graduate of Columbia University and Duke University School of Medicine—had a mental health breakdown during which he is hospitalized for 2 weeks. Kobe Bryant died on the same weekend of his hospitalization—and as I cried for Kobe and my brother, there was no way I could have imagined the world getting any worse, but it did.

March brings the apocalyptic reality of COVID-19 and the academic transition online—a traumatic period for all—yet very little acknowledgment or support for faculty, staff, and students, especially those of color, whom, historically marginalized and traumatized, will be more vulnerable to the myriad impacts of this pandemic. March further brings the challenges of finding balance in my own life while supporting my family and children in their own emotional, educational, and professional transitions.

April begins the first wave of calls and emails reporting the death and illness of friends and relatives associated with COVID-19. The loss of my uncle to COVID-19 heralds in May, followed by another mental health breakdown for my brother—this time involving a 30-hour police and family stakeout outside his Washington, D.C. apartment—requiring my mom and dad to fly in from Georgia during the height of a pandemic. In June, on my mother's birthday, she is hospitalized for stress-related symptoms. My grandmother would follow my mom to the hospital a week later—and while the doctor could not determine what was causing her chest pains, I can tell you without a doubt that it was trauma!

And that snippet is by no means exhaustive, as I have not even mentioned the very public killings of Black people in this period: George Floyd in Minneapolis, Minnesota; Breonna Taylor in Louisville, Kentucky; Ahmaud Arbery in Glynn County, Georgia; Tony McDade in Tallahassee, Florida; Dion Johnson in Phoenix, Arizona; and countless others killed and victimized daily—a steady stream of murder, used as trauma porn on continuous media loops showing knees on necks and final cries of "I can't breathe."

It's all beyond exhausting, and there is no letup. Email alerts from students and colleagues—at all hours—each *urgent* and demanding of an immediate response continually bombard and threaten the illusion of privacy. Or maybe it's the late-night calls from Black men and women, all suffering and seeking to check in. And as much as I try to hold space for everybody, I am aware of my trauma and vulnerabilities in the present moment—especially their ability to adversely impact my health.

Self-care has often felt like an empty cliché in social work circles. However, for me and many others, its practice has become integral to survival amid a pandemic and racialized violence. Yoga, running, biking, cooking, and finding *joy* within my moments have all become tools of resilience building. But as a Black man, even one who is formerly incarcerated, I am aware of my privilege. In sharing my struggles during the pandemic, I hope to create the space for truth, healing, and resilience-building among my colleagues—and social work as a profession—which will be needed now more than ever. But to truly show up, we must recognize our own trauma on individual and organization levels—while co-creating appropriate spaces for healing.

The Road to Abolition Social Work

COVID-19 has amplified the historical harm of marginalized people to such a degree that we cannot afford to not actualize our core values at this moment. These values are intrinsically aligned with abolition—a historical call to end slavery (or jails and prisons) and transform this nation so that *everyone* has the right to self-actualize.

I believe in the possibility of an abolitionist and liberatory social work. But for social work to become the vanguard of justice it professes, it must be willing to recognize the dissonance between its values and actions. It must uproot the ideas of white supremacy, settler colonialism, anti-Blackness, racialized capitalism, and cis-heteropatriarchy that permeate its education and practice. It must reckon with its intellectualization of oppression at the expense of meaningful action. And it must also reckon with its relationship with carceral systems.

In a recent article titled "Resisting Carcerality, Embracing Abolition: Implications for Feminist Social Work Practice," the authors Richie and Martensen (2020) outline three tenants for abolition praxis. The first one requires a critique of the factors that have facilitated "mass incarceration." The authors contend that "crime is more of a social construction than an absolute phenomenon" (p. 13) and highlight eras in which "crime" rates went down as financial allocation to policing increased. Second, the authors argue that increasing funds unwarranted for policing is "associated with a simultaneous divestment of resources from programs and services that would otherwise strengthen communities with their most significant needs" (p. 13). And finally, the authors argue that we must speak to the "misnomer" of "mass incarceration" as it is a system with a clear intent to target and subjugate Black people and other vulnerable populations. At all levels, social work must be a loud voice of truth—challenging the antiquated criminal narratives and stereotypes attributed to oppressed people.

As the push to defund police coincides with a global pandemic, "inner-city violence", and nationwide protest—amid a renewed fascist-led media propaganda campaign to distort the truth while pathologizing Black people and other minorities to maintain the status quo (Giroux 2018; Stanley 2020)—social work must resist. It must loudly challenge long-held myopic narratives related to "crime," causation, and public safety. Social work must tell the truth—it must teach and give voice to the perpetuity of oppression and trauma inflicted by the quest for white supremacy. It must demand the reinvesting and redistribution of resources that support restorative and transformative practices in response to harm and community building. Social work must also be transparent and accountable to what an actualization of its core values looks like—especially as it attempts to discern actions aligned with power and domination (reformist reforms) vs. liberation. While abolition social work is an evolving concept with much room for dialogue, growth, and imagination, the questions below are a framework adapted from abolitionist activist Cameron Rasmussen and Dean Spade (Rasmussen and James 2020) and expanded by the author to gauge our collective actions as social workers toward liberation:

- Does the work shift power, give voice, mobilize, and include the leadership of impacted people?
- Does it dismantle dichotomies of good vs. bad, violent vs. nonviolent, and/or deserving vs. undeserving?
- Does it work against the expansion and legitimization of carceral systems? Or the narratives that fuel them?
- Does it provide financial relief for impacted people without compromising their agency?
- Is the work trauma-informed and rooted in a historical analysis of oppression?
- Is the work committed to an evolving process of decolonization and inquiry towards its ways of knowing, being, and acting?
- And maybe most importantly, is the work self-actualizing—meaning, are we moving towards the co-creation of a society that puts us out of business?

Conclusion

COVID-19 has disproportionately impacted Black people—am I surprised? No! Black Lives from the micro to the macro have been intrinsically linked with oppression and trauma—one that has never been *post*, and only exacerbated by a pandemic and the senseless murders of innumerable Black men and women. And while the antidote for trauma is often resilience, I would caution against social work championing resilience for the sake of solely surviving and acquiescence to oppression—and ask that we see resilience as a key to resistance and the transformation of our society. I ask that as a profession we commit to creating liberatory spaces where we can better understand the traumatic impact of COVID-19 on impacted communities—so that we may work with them in partnership to heal, build resilience, and move our society from an ethos rooted in power and domination, to one of love.

I remain an optimist, no matter how long the journey to the promised land is. But I would not be living in truth if I didn't share that I am deeply concerned to what degree social work, and our society, can commit to decolonization—meaning, are we really ready to extrapolate our ways of knowing, being, and acting, from the omnipresence of white supremacy?

We are living in a moment that demands societal change if the United States is to be considered a democracy—yet in prior moments, such as the period following the 13th Amendment and the Civil Rights Movement, what followed were false narratives and institutions amounting to "reformed" legacies of chattel slavery. We cannot allow history to repeat itself. We must evolve by standing in truth: Black Lives Matter! There can be no justice, no peace, and certainly no democracy until every human being has the right to self-actualize—and be free from the oppression and trauma of white supremacy.

References

Alexander, M. (2020). *The new Jim Crow: Mass incarceration in the age of colorblindness*. New York: The New Press.

Black, A. L., & Garvis, S. (2018). Trauma in the academy. In *Lived experiences of women in academia* (pp. 130–139). London: Routledge.

Crocq, M. A., & Crocq, L. (2000). From shell shock and war neurosis to posttraumatic stress disorder: a history of psychotraumatology. *Dialogues in Clinical Neuroscience, 2*(1), 47.

DeVeaux, M. I. (2013). The trauma of the incarceration experience. *Harvard Civil Rights-Civil Liberties Law Review, 48*, 257.

Giroux, H. A. (2018). *American nightmare: Facing the challenge of fascism*. San Francisco: City Lights Books.

Goodwin, J. (1987). The etiology of combat-related PTSD. In *Post-traumatic stress disorders: a handbook for clinicians*. Cincinnati: DC DAV.

Hoffman, F. L. (1896). *Race traits and tendencies of the American Negro. American Economic Association, 11*(1-3), 1–329.

Jackson, G. (1994). *Soledad brother: The prison letters of George Jackson*. Chicago: Chicago Review Press.

James, K. (2016). The Criminal Justice System: A History of Mass Incarceration With Implications for Social Work. In T Maschi & G. S. Leibowitz (Eds.), *Forensic Social Work: Psychological and Legal Issues in Diverse Practice Settings* (2 ed., pp. 237–248). Springer.

James, K., & Smyth, J. (2014). Deconstructing mass incarceration in the United States through a human rights lens: Implications for social work education and practice. In *Advancing human rights in social work education*. Alexandria: CSWE Press.

Magen, R. H., & Emerman, J. (2000). Should convicted felons be denied admission to a social work education program? *Journal of Social Work Education, 36*(3), 401–405.

Mancini, M. J. (1996). *One dies, get another: Convict leasing in the American South, 1866–1928*. Columbia: Univ of South Carolina Press.

Melamed, J. (2011). *Represent and destroy: Rationalizing violence in the new racial capitalism*. Minneapolis: U of Minnesota Press.

Pulido, L. (2017). Geographies of race and ethnicity II: Environmental racism, racial capitalism and state-sanctioned violence. *Progress in Human Geography, 41*(4), 524–533.

Rasmussen, C., & James, K. (2020, July 17). Trading cops for social workers isn't the solution to police violence. Truthout. https://truthout.org/articles/trading-cops-for-social-workers-isnt-the-solution-to-police-violence/

Richie, B. E., & Martensen, K. M. (2020). Resisting carcerality, embracing abolition: Implications for feminist social work practice. *Affilia, 35*(1), 12–16.

Stanley, J. (2020). *How fascism works: The politics of us and them*. New York: Random House Trade Paperbacks.

Stensrud, R. H., Gilbride, D. D., & Bruinekool, R. M. (2019). The childhood to prison pipeline: Early childhood trauma as reported by a prison population. *Rehabilitation Counseling Bulletin, 62*(4), 195–208.

Temple, C. N. (2010). The emergence of Sankofa practice in the United States: A modern history. *Journal of Black Studies, 41*(1), 127–150.

Van der Kolk, B. A. (1996). *The body keeps score: Approaches to the psychobiology of posttraumatic stress disorder*. New York: Guilford Press.

Wacquant, L. (2002). Slavery to mass incarceration. *New Left Review, 13*, 41.

Wideman, D. J. (1998). The door of no return? A journey through the legacy of the African slave forts an excerpt. *Callaloo, 21*(1), 1–11.

Chapter 30
COVID-19 and the Injustice System: Reshaping Clinical Practice for Children and Families Impacted by Hyper-Incarceration

Anna Morgan-Mullane

Introduction

The emotional effects of parental incarceration can be exhibited by children through trauma-related stress symptoms such as depression, anxiety, challenges in forming relationships, concentration problems, sleep difficulties, emotional withdrawal, substance misuse, and significant feelings of shame and stigmatization. These impacts can often last well into adolescence and young adulthood (Manning 2011; Murray et al. 2012; Miller and Barnes 2015; Phillips et al. 2006). To underscore the extensive nature of this issue in the United States (US), nearly 2 million children have at least one incarcerated parent, according to the Bureau of Justice Statistics, a number that is likely underreported as it does not take into account the custodial states of individuals who are a child's guardian or who perform other significant caretaking functions (Manning 2011; Miller et al. 2013; Murray and Farrington 2008).

Despite the large number of children and families affected by incarceration, limited research has been conducted to explore the effects of parental incarceration on children, as well as what policy interventions exist to mediate the toll exacted upon these children and families (Manning 2011). Existing research implies that parental incarceration is associated with numerous traumatic effects (Manning 2011; Murray et al. 2012; Miller and Barnes 2015; Phillips et al. 2006). However, no research attempts to interpret the traumatic and psychological implications of hyper-incarceration based on what is known about systemic racism and traumatic experience, nor does any research describe best practices for the treatment of this specific population. While current treatment methods such as relational-cultural and

A. Morgan-Mullane (✉)
Children of Promise, NYC, Brooklyn, NY, USA

Silver School of Social Work, New York University, New York, NY, USA
e-mail: amm1414@nyu.edu

© The Author(s), under exclusive license to Springer Nature Switzerland AG 2021
C. Tosone (ed.), *Shared Trauma, Shared Resilience During a Pandemic*,
Essential Clinical Social Work Series,
https://doi.org/10.1007/978-3-030-61442-3_30

attachment-focused interventions have offered new methodologies for treating children and families experiencing trauma associated with systemic racism, an extensive literature search found no evidence in peer-reviewed journals that this treatment orientation has been applied to children of incarcerated parents.

Nationwide, the known infection rate for COVID-19 in jails and prisons is about 2.5 times higher than that in the general population (Equal Justice Initiative 2020). Therefore, children of incarcerated parents remain a growing population who presently experience both the traumatic impacts of COVID-19 within their own communities, as well as the fear and anxiety associated with health concerns for their incarcerated loved ones. Poehlmann (2005), at the time, noted that there was no known empirical investigation into how parental incarceration impacts the quality of a child's attachment relationships. At the present time, there is no known published research indicating how fear associated with increased health concerns for loved ones in correctional facilities imposes a problematic pattern of attachment for children and their future relationships.

This chapter argues in favor of mental health providers utilizing relational-cultural theory and attachment theory in the expansion of the treatment of children affected by parental incarceration during the coronavirus pandemic. At present, these practices are deployed within a limited set of circumstances, even though mental health providers largely recognize their potential for broader use. The current rise in infections of COVID-19 in both jails and prisons traumatically affects children of incarcerated parents. Mental health providers can benefit from incorporating relational-cultural and attachment theory in their work with this population, as well as understanding the impact of dual exposure to trauma brought about by the COVID-19 pandemic and clinical implications of shared trauma.

Background

As mentioned earlier, the Bureau of Justice Statistics reports that nearly 2 million children have at least one incarcerated parent, a number that is likely underreported (Manning 2011; Miller et al. 2013; Farrington and Murray 2008). For the majority of caretakers, parental incarceration reinforces the racialized systemic oppression brought forth by hyper-incarceration, with its associated external stressors such as financial insecurity, elevated emotional stress, strained interpersonal relationships, and increased difficulties associated with the supervision of children (Turanovic et al. 2012).

Most children of incarcerated parents are under the age of 18 (Mumola 2000) and experience numerous sources of material and emotional insecurity. For example, children of incarcerated parents are more likely to receive public assistance, to experience interrupted phone or utility service due to nonpayment, and to experience residential insecurity through missed mortgage and rental payments causing families to move into shelters (Geller et al. 2009). These examples are symptoms of the greater socioeconomic systemic oppression that exists for children even before a parent is incarcerated, and these conditions tend to worsen after incarceration (Miller and Barnes 2015; Phillips et al. 2006).

These material and emotional consequences have been exacerbated during the COVID-19 pandemic. Families are no longer able to send care packages to loved ones due to concerns about contamination and disease prevention. Without access to care packages from relatives, the only opportunities for discretionary spending are through the custodial commissary, which is a lifeline for hygiene products like toothpaste, facial tissue, soap, and laundry detergent. Because caregivers and family no longer purchase their own supplies for their incarcerated loved ones, they are now restricted to providing actual currency, which increases the financial strain on family members to provide twice the amount of money they were contributing prior to the coronavirus pandemic.

With COVID-19's resultant intensification in physical, psychological, and environmental stress, children of incarcerated parents report increased rates of traumatic stress. Mental health practitioners working in healing spaces for children and families impacted by parental incarceration must provide expansive awareness of the significant impact of medical neglect, health disparities, and collateral consequences of COVID-19 for children with incarcerated loved ones. Unpacking the micro, mezzo, and macro systems of oppression specific to this population will reinforce safety in the lives of the impacted children through the therapeutic relationship. Applying practices such as relational-cultural and attachment theory will help enable the child to narrate their own experiences of how COVID-19 has impacted them and provide a forum to discuss commonplace losses, like limitations of visitation privileges, familial stress, and increased fear and worry for the well-being of their incarcerated loved ones. In implementing these practices, it behooves clinicians to be aware of how the increased children's needs during the COVID-19 pandemic impact them. That is, in addition to helping children negotiate these difficult times, clinicians also need to address the impact of COVID-19 on their own personal and professional lives.

Evidence Supporting Disruptions in Attachment for Children of Incarcerated Parents

Children develop representations of relationships that are less optimal when attachment figures are unavailable due to discontinuity in care or the occurrence of some prolonged separation (Toth et al. 2002). Consistent with attachment theory (Kobak 1999), the majority of children initially reacted to separation with sadness, crying, and calling for or looking for their mothers. Other common reactions include confusion, worry, anger, acting out, fear, developmental regression, sleep problems, and indifference. Although many of these responses are similar to reactions exhibited by older children following the loss of a parent to incarceration, such as loneliness, fear, anger, and aggression, young children's sleep patterns and maintenance of developmental milestones appeared highly vulnerable to disruption. Lack of mother-child contact during imprisonment may result in children viewing the mother as unavailable when needed, which may have implications for children's representations of attachment relationships. Now that parents are unable to see their children in person due to new restrictions in jails and prisons after the increased reports of infection rates for COVID-19, children report feeling even more detached from their parental figure and fear that this means they will "never see them again" (Zahir, age 8, personal interview).[1]

Prevalence of COVID-19 in Jails and Prisons

As noted previously, the infection rate for COVID-19 in US jails and prisons is 2.5 times higher than in the general population (Marshall Project 2020). This is especially concerning when considering the demographic of those at risk who are over the age of 50. In the US prison system, there are over 150,000 people over the age of 55 (Marshall Project 2020). Adults who are incarcerated report a higher prevalence of infectious diseases and chronic conditions compared to noninstitutionalized populations (Marshal Project 2020). Therefore, when COVID-19 became widespread in several state prisons, it impacted incarcerated Black people at higher rates than Black people outside of the prison system, and the consequences of infection in custodial settings was more lethal.

Across the United States, by April 2020, 48% of incarcerated people who had died of COVID-19 were Black, compared with 40% of people who died outside of correctional facilities (Marshall Project 2020). The heightened risk of infection imposed upon members of Black communities, including those who are incarcerated, should be a warning cry for mental healthcare workers of the looming mental health crisis associated with parental incarceration: as infection rates in jails and prisons increase, so, too, does the emotional and psychological burden on children and family members of those incarcerated.

Psychosocial and Medical Implications of COVID-19 for Parents and Children

The Prison Policy Initiative (2020) reports that while a typical US jail has reduced its population by more than 30% since the onset of COVID-19, state prisons have been much slower to release incarcerated people. Because social distancing is extremely difficult in correctional facilities, incarcerated individuals come in close

---

[1] All individuals or parents/guardians where appropriate provided written consent for the inclusion of their narratives in this chapter.

contact with each other and with correctional staff – the latter of which serves as vectors to a variety of community settings where they may contract the disease – all of which contributes to higher rates of infection within the custodial setting. Contamination and viral spreading within custodial settings is exacerbated further by the overcrowding that is commonplace in custodial settings. Furthermore, the appalling conditions for solitary confinement add significant psychological stress to incarcerated individuals living with the pandemic.

As infection rates continue to rise, children report feeling "angry and scared" that their parent "is going to die" (Kaleah, age 12, personal interview). Numerous children have shared meaningful narratives in their therapeutic community-based settings that exemplify how they internalize their anxiety, worry, and depression:

> When the lockdown first started, I remember thinking I was going through what my daddy was going through. I felt like, 'I wonder if this is what he feels like every day.' When my mom told me that more people were getting Coronavirus in jail where my dad is, I was so scared because I know they don't have doctors there that care about them. I began to fear for my own life when I went outside and then couldn't stop thinking about if my dad was okay. I feel anxious all the time both for myself, my mom, my grandma, and my dad. I feel helpless. (Kaleah, age 12, personal interview)

The increased spread of COVID-19 in correctional facilities results in various operational changes that materially impact the day-to-day life of incarcerated parents and their children. To adhere to social distancing guidelines, most facilities have instituted a ban on physical visitation and have placed restrictions on the quantity and frequency of phone calls (Marshall Project, 2020) with loved ones, resulting in increased separation anxiety, grief, and loss for both children and caregivers. Arlene, an incarcerated mother at a correctional facility in New York, shares:

> The visits are all we have to look forward to, the only thing keeping us going some days are our children. So when this is taken away, we feel hopeless and fearful that our own mental health, along with the medical neglect we all receive, will only get worse and we'll have nothing to live for. (Arlene, age 33, personal interview)

Thus, children and parents now experience unprecedented threats from medical complications of disease contraction and greater separation as a result of social distancing, which compound the pre-pandemic social and emotional stress experienced by both incarcerated parent and child. The collateral consequences of both medical fear and social and emotional distress for children and parents separated by incarceration highlight the unique traumatic experiences and stressors facing families directly impacted by mass incarceration. Forms of attachment common for incarcerated individuals, such as phone calls, in-person visits, care packages, and letter writing, have now become compromised during COVID-19, and this poses additional barriers for the emotional security of the child.

Application of Relational-Cultural Theory in Treatment for Children of Incarcerated Parents

Constant and recurrent traumatic events that impact interpersonal security can lead to long-standing social and emotional consequences that affect various areas of individuals' health and well-being across their life span. Additionally, it is often understood that people who experience interpersonal traumas experience a sense of betrayal, powerlessness, and stigmatization (Deitz et al. 2015). When this impacts children, there is a likelihood that it can contribute to a distorted self-concept and worldview (Walsh et al. 2010).

Relational-cultural theory (RCT) employs a practice that allows for individuals to focus on connection with others throughout their life span, and by forming and maintaining healthy relationships, they can build a sense of safety and well-being (Jordan 2010). Moreover, RCT suggests that connecting with others and forming growth-fostering relationships serve as a healing mechanism (Jordan 2010). An RCT application can provide a framework and lens from which clinicians can partner with children on how to best recognize, form, and maintain healthy relationships during a time that can feel unsettling and ambiguous. Therefore, the use of RCT with children of incarcerated parents during COVID-19 is an approach that can be especially useful when naming the systems of oppression that have directly impacted the child's and parent's beliefs of safety and security in the world at large. Mental health providers working with individuals who have experienced trauma rooted in interpersonal victimization must consider all systems that traumatize the individual, family, and community and employ an anti-racist framework of safety within the therapeutic relationship that directly names those systems when addressing intergenerational systemic trauma. The emphasis RCT places on connection with oneself and others may help to diminish trauma symptoms and facilitate healthy functioning.

Application of Attachment Theory in Treatment for Children of Incarcerated Parents

The attachment theory literature highlights the importance of emotionally open communication in relationships. Telling children about difficult situations in honest, sensitive, and developmentally appropriate ways affirms their trust in caregivers. In contrast, when information is hidden, distorted in a manner that contradicts the child's experience, or includes details that frighten a child, distrust or mental health problems may ensue (Bowlby 1973). Attachment theory provides an intervention by which a child can address the stigmatization they experience as children of incarcerated parents and offers a clinical approach to help them heal from emotional, physical, and material consequences resulting from the traumatic loss of an incarcerated parent.

Barriers to Relational-Cultural and Attachment Theory Implementation and Fidelity

Therapists often struggle to identify and assess appropriate clients for treatment. While the model works most efficiently for children who present higher rates of depressive symptoms and have a willingness to engage in the therapeutic process, children who are experiencing stronger symptoms of trauma avoidance and mistrust in authoritative figures may struggle to initially connect to their therapists. This can cause critical delays in the application of therapeutic models such as RCT or attachment theory that may suggest a time-specific framework. In addition, one study found that symptom arousal and clinical withdrawal increased during the assessment period, suggesting that service initiation may increase symptom intensity, especially in cases where avoidance is common and where children may have difficulty tolerating these arousal symptoms early in the therapeutic process (Konanur et al. 2015). Therefore, adhering to the timetable in the model may prove to be difficult.

Advantages of Relational-Cultural and Attachment Theory Applications for Social Workers

Both relational-cultural and attachment theories recommend experience-dependent learning, which allows for the possibility that persistent, sensitive, and supportive parents may provide some corrective attachment-related experiences for the child. Both the incarcerated parent and the caregiver who may reside at home can offer a model of care and support that challenges the view that children may hold of caregivers as untrustworthy and of themselves as undeserving of attention and care. In addition, mental health practitioners can use the trusting and safe relationship employed throughout both models to help build the child's understanding of social interactions and provide a safe context in which new relational skills can be developed (Haight et al. 2003). It is important to note that all traumatic events occur within a sociocultural and historical context. More specifically, COVID-19 presently reinforces to children impacted by parental incarceration that several systems of oppression, including medical, mental health, and the injustice system, represent unsafe spaces that hinder healing and recovery. Therefore, even if another person does not acknowledge, address, or name the presence and power of that traumatic event, all traumatic experiences are embedded in a relational context, and it will be difficult for the therapist to undo in their rapport with the child and family. Each model is best understood in the context of relational movement, which is the process of individuals moving safely through connections and disconnections and back into newly defined and improved connections with others through their own narrative experiences (Comstock et al. 2008).

Shared Trauma and the Collective Experience of COVID-19

Tosone (2012) describes "shared trauma" as "affective, behavioral, cognitive, spiritual, and multimodal responses that mental health professionals experience as a result of primary and secondary exposure to the same collective trauma as their clients" (pg. 12). Transitions to virtual therapeutic care, or teletherapy, during the COVID-19 pandemic appear to be contributing to clinician burnout, as well. According to several clinicians interviewed as part of my research for this chapter, clinicians report teletherapy directly contributing to their feeling "overwhelmed, exhausted, and isolated." The barrier imposed by COVID-19 and the limits it places on clinicians' abilities to meet in person for therapeutic sessions impact the ability for the treated children to experience the security of the in-person attachment and consistency found within a safe therapeutic alliance achieved through in-person meetings. Therapists interviewed noted that children's trauma symptomatology has increased significantly and has been notably demonstrated by children impacted by parental incarceration through the narratives they share.

Simultaneously, therapists must navigate their own fears about virus contraction for themselves and their own loved ones, uncertainty about their security of employment and housing, and parallel feelings of worry and fear about how rapidly COVID-19 has changed their lives and disrupted daily routines that are necessary to one's own mental health. Tosone (2012) continues to explain that clinicians can experience shared trauma in ways that resemble compassion fatigue or secondary trauma in their own personal responses which can include feelings of exhaustion and depletion of empathy (pg. 3). In our collective clinical experiences, therapists have shared:

> It is hard to show up for clients when I'm struggling to know how to show up for myself. All of this feels so new. I don't feel like anyone has a blueprint to manage our own emotions of uncertainty during a pandemic, let alone our clients. Even our supervisors who we look to for answers are going through their own fear and discomfort. (Gen, LMSW, personal interview)

The Black Lives Matter uprising and protest events related to the unarmed killing of George Floyd by Minneapolis police officers have added additional challenges for clients in treatment. These protests and uprisings remind many clients of the legacy of systemic racism, inclusive of the lack of accountability for a brutal police force that disproportionately causes lethal harm to persons of color. Therapists working directly with Black clients explained how critical it has been for them to hold space for the increased fear, anger, and rage expressed by their clients through their narratives. The shared trauma of both client and clinician caused to them by the persistent lack of acknowledgment of police brutality and the impacts of systemic racism has opened up space for more vulnerable connections by both the client and clinician. The challenges of treating populations of color in the mid of these uprisings is particularly acute for therapists who are persons of color (POC). In one community-based setting in Brooklyn, New York, a POC therapist bravely noted:

> I had a hard time trusting my white colleagues and white supervisor which impacted my overall emotional well-being and safety, while being asked to still show up for my clients who were talking about how the injustice system was tearing apart their family. I felt my community and my own family were being torn apart and it was past time to acknowledge the level of systemic issues even within my own social service agency. (Sondra, LMSW, personal interview)

Examples of how to best address shared trauma for clinicians during this time are found within the "perceived level of support available to clinicians from their professional and educational organizations, agency-based work settings, supervisors, and colleagues" (Tosone 2012, p. 7). For clinical supervisors, encouraging supportive time off for mental health care, which normalizes the emotional and psychological implications of worry and fear related to the COVID-19 pandemic, has allowed staff to feel seen and heard during a time where they have to prioritize their own mental health alongside of the clients they work with. The utilization of supervisors and clinical staff of more expressive and humanizing language affirms the experience of both the client as well as the clinician who cannot be expected to be as productive during COVID-19 as they once may have been. By honoring the traumatic feelings and experiences of racism, combined with a global public health crisis and its associated medical traumas, clinicians have the opportunity to collectively take care of ourselves and one another. Clinicians must do this through constant validation of emotions and experiences that allow for clinicians to feel it is possible to move through fear while continuing to unpack the experiences shared by clients in all mental healthcare spaces.

Conclusion and Further Reflection

COVID-19 has underscored how significantly dangerous prisons and jails are during a viral outbreak. Public health professionals, correction officers, injustice reform advocates, politicians, and community organizers convey similar beliefs that decarceration will help protect both incarcerated people and the larger communities in which they live (Prison Policy Initiative 2020). Children with incarcerated parents, who are already predisposed to the development of trauma symptoms, face a new and additional risk to their emotional well-being as a result of their incarcerated parents facing a rising risk of infection and mortality due to the pandemic's widespread increase in the facilities where they must remain. Therefore, it is essential that mental health practitioners meaningfully and intentionally address the crisis and familial trauma experienced by the loved ones of those who remain the most at risk for infection.

By directly addressing and naming the racist implications of medical and mental health neglect in the correctional systems, clinicians will offer empathic recognition of how institutionalized racism and medical oppression have caused collateral psychological consequences for the children of incarcerated parents. Because attachment-based work and relational-cultural practices identify that isolation from others is a primary source of emotional suffering, clinicians can use their trusted relationship as the primary vehicle for therapeutic growth and change. In the reflective use of countertransference during the COVID-19 pandemic, clinicians should be encouraged to unpack their own shared trauma and feel safe to name their own feelings of exhaustion, pain, and anger related to the pandemic and the political uprising.

During a global pandemic and a time of impactful isolation, clinicians can address how essential connection is to address social withdrawal that prolongs and compounds trauma into emotional pain. Therefore, by prioritizing and centering the relationship of all family members through these practices and providing a non-pathologizing and culturally sensitive framework for therapists to use with children of incarcerated parents who have traumatic stress from systems of oppression, there will be increases to connection and self-worth by addressing and normalizing current conditions of connections and disconnections. Providing shared trauma psychoeducation may normalize clinician's, children's, and parent's symptoms; reduce distress related to symptoms (e.g., shame, excessive self-blame, fear of losing their loved ones); and assist in the development of adaptive coping skills (Kress and Paylo 2015). Strengthening therapeutic community and feelings of resiliency will be essential during uncertain times as we collectively continue to navigate all of our health and wellness during the global pandemic.

References

Bowlby, J. (1973). *Attachment and loss: Vol. 2. Separation: Anxiety and anger.* New York: Basic Books.

Comstock, D. L., Hammer, T. R., Strentzsch, K. C., Parsons, J., & Salazar, G., II. (2008). Relational-cultural theory: A framework for bridging relational, multicultural, and social justice competencies. *Journal of Counseling & Development, 86,* 279–287.

Covid-19's Impact on People in Prison. (2020, May 22). Retrieved July 22, 2020, from https://eji.org/news/covid-19s-impact-on-people-in-prison/

Deitz, M. F., Williams, S. L., Rife, S. C., & Cantrell, P. (2015). Examining cultural, social, and self-related aspects of stigma in relation to sexual assault and trauma symptoms. *Violence Against Women, 21,* 598–615.

Geller, A., Garfinkel, I., Cooper, C. E., & Mincy, R. B. (2009). Parental incarceration and child well-being: Implications for urban families. *Social Science Quarterly, 90*(5), 1186–1202.

Haight, W., Kagle, J., & Black, J. (2003). Understanding and supporting parent—Child relationships during foster care visits: Attachment theory and research. *Social Work, 48*(2), 195–207.

Jordan, J. V. (2010). *Relational-cultural therapy*. Washington, DC: American Psychological Association.

Kobak, R. (1999). The emotional dynamics of disruptions in attachment relationships: Implications for theory, research, and clinical intervention. In J. Cassidy & P. R. Shaver (Eds.), *Handbook of attachment: Theory, research, and clinical applications* (pp. 21–43). New York: The Guilford Press.

Konanur, S., Muller, R. T., Cinamon, J. S., Thornback, K., & Zorella, K. (2015). Effectiveness of trauma-focused cognitive behavioral therapy in a community-based program. *Child Abuse and Neglect: The International Journal, 50*, 259–170.

Kress, V. E., & Paylo, M. J. (2015). *Treating those who have mental disorders*. Columbus: Pearson.

Manning, R. (2011). Punishing the innocent: Children of incarcerated and detained parents. *Criminal Justice Ethics, 30*(3), 267–287.

The Marshall Project. (2020, July 16). A state-by-state look at coronavirus in prisons. Retrieved July 22, 2020, from https://www.themarshallproject.org/2020/05/01/a-state-by-state-look-at-coronavirus-in-prisons

Miller, A. L., Perryman, J., Markovitz, L., Franzen, S., Cochran, S., & Brown, S. (2013). Strengthening incarcerated families: Evaluating a pilot program for children of incarcerated parents and their caregivers. *Family Relations, 62*, 584–596.

Miller, H. V., & Barnes, J. C. (2015). The association between parental incarceration and health, education, and economic outcomes in young adulthood. *American Journal of Criminal Justice, 40*, 765–784.

Mumola, C. J. (2000). *Incarcerated parents and their children*. Washington, DC: U.S. Department of Justice, Office of Justice Programs, Bureau of Justice Statistics. August 2000.

Murray, J., & Farington, D. P. (2008). The effects of parental imprisonment on children. *Crime and Justice, 37*(1), 133–206.

Murray, J., Farrington, D. P., & Sekol, I. (2012). Children's antisocial behavior, mental health, drug use, and educational performance after parental incarceration: A systematic review and meta-analysis. *Psychological Bulletin, 138*(2), 175–210.

Phillips, S. D., Erkanki, A., Keeler, G. P., Costello, E. J., & Angold, A. (2006). Disentangling the risks: Parents' criminal justice involvement and children's exposure to family risks. *Criminology & Public Policy, 5*(4), 677–702.

Poehlmann, J. (2005). Representations of attachment relationships in children of incarcerated mothers. *Child Development, 76*(3), 679–696.

Tosone, C. (2012). Shared trauma. In C. Figley (Ed.), *Encyclopedia of trauma*. New York: Routledge.

Toth, S. L., Maughan, A., Manly, J. T., Spagnola, M., & Cicchetti, D. (2002). The relative efficacy of two interventions in altering maltreated preschool children's representational models: implications for attachment theory. *Development and Psychopathology, 14*(4), 877–908.

Turanovic, J. J., Rodriguez, N., & Pratt, T. C. (2012). The collateral consequences of incarceration revisited: A qualitative analysis of the effects on caregivers of children of incarcerated parents. *Criminology, 50*(4), 913–959.

Walsh, K., Fortier, M. A., & DiLillo, D. (2010). Adult coping with childhood sexual abuse: A theoretical and empirical review. *Aggression and Violent Behavior, 15*, 1–13.

Chapter 31
An Intimate Portrait of Shared Trauma Amid COVID-19 and Racial Unrest Between a Black Cisgender Femme Sex Worker and Her Black Cisgender Femme Therapist

Raashida M. Edwards

Introduction

The number of sex workers in the United States (US) is unknown. However, in the last three decades, increasing access to this knowledge through growing bodies of literature, research studies, first-hand narratives of sex workers, and social media has been contributing to the expanding academic discourse about the commercial sex industry. Overall, the consensual sex work market is divided into two main categories: indoor providers and outdoor providers (Flowers 2011). Each consists of multiple subgroups, which are influenced by the practitioner's race, age, perceived physical attractiveness, geographical location, and professional experience.

Indoor providers tend to be young, white, cisgender women. They often work with a third party, such as escort agency or brothel, which facilitates the financial and logistical transactions with the clients. Indoor work is significantly safer. Providers have access to better and consistent medical care, reputable work environments, and the continued emotional support of a reliable peer group, and their clients are routinely screened for psychological stability and physical health risks.

Outdoor providers comprise the bulk of the US-based sex worker demographic. The literature describes them as predominantly young cisgender women of color who originate from low-income urban communities. Yet, these statistics are somewhat inflated because Black cisgender female sex workers are arrested at higher rates than their white counterparts and have more contact with the legal system (Flowers 2011). The arrest records of the women, particularly when there is high recidivism, are conflated with estimations of the actual number of black cisgender

R. M. Edwards (✉)
Silver School of Social Work, New York University, New York, NY, USA
e-mail: re584@nyu.edu

© The Author(s), under exclusive license to Springer Nature Switzerland AG 2021
C. Tosone (ed.), *Shared Trauma, Shared Resilience During a Pandemic*,
Essential Clinical Social Work Series,
https://doi.org/10.1007/978-3-030-61442-3_31

women among outdoor providers. According to the US Bureau of Justice Statistics (2011) and the National Center for Victims of Crime (2013), in metropolitan areas, Black female sex workers comprise 40% of the street-level sex work demographic, and the proportion is probably lower in suburbs and nonurban communities. In fact, the largest outdoor US-based sex worker demographic is that of white adolescent cisgender women (Flowers 2011). Most are either runaways or "throwaways," referring to a minor who was forced to leave home. This statistic is supported by numerous studies that reflect the perspective of white female sex workers. In contrast to indoor providers, personal safety is not built into the outdoor provider's professional experience; and these women operate in unsafe working environments and are significantly more vulnerable to high-risk clients who are psychologically unstable and physically unhealthy (Blair 2010; Ditmore 2011, 2006; Flowers 2011; Krusi et al. 2012).

The Fight Against Sex Trafficking

The *Allow States and Victims to Fight Online Sex Trafficking Act* (FOSTA) and the *Stop Enabling Sex Traffickers Act* (SESTA), signed into law in April 2018, have significantly transformed the lives of sex workers across the United States. These laws are not new. They emerged out of Section 230 Amendment of the Communications Decency Act of 1996, which protects domain hosts from liability caused by user-generated content. In the late 1990s, the personal advertising sections of printed media moved online and free listing sites, such as Craigslist, rapidly became a new and safer means to negotiate with clients replacing transactions that theretofore had been taking place on the streets.

Originally, the intent of FOSTA/SESTA was to shut down websites that could potentially facilitate trafficking. However, the law also retracted all its previous protections for hosts. The result was the collapse of an online infrastructure that many sex workers relied heavily on. The sex worker community asserts that FOSTA/SESTA has put their lives in danger and in response they created grassroots movements to help vocalize their concerns. One such organization is Hacking/Hustling, a collective of sex workers, researchers, and computer technologists. Their focus is to discern the financial and psychological impacts of FOSTA/SESTA on diverse groups of US-based providers.

Pre- and Current COVID-19 Outdoor Sex Work

Social isolation is familiar to sex workers. It makes them vulnerable to many of the social ills that preclude personal safety and a sense of stable community support. COVID-19 mitigation by mandatory social distancing hit female providers the hardest across all demographics (Wenham et al. 2020; Walter and McGregor 2020). It follows that lower-income Black cisgender female providers may become more amenable to engaging in high-risk behavior to survive (Blair 2010; Gentile 2020; Tharoor 2020). Webcam, phone sex, and interactive porn offer opportunities for safer and paid contact, but Black street sex workers may not be able to take full advantage of these opportunities unless it had been a component of their work pre-COVID-19 (Naftulin 2020). Sex workers report that it is sometimes inconceivable to stop working, and the decision to stop is based on a host of external factors that influence daily behaviors, such as whether or not to travel to a reliable "big money" client or to an unsafe location chosen by a violent pimp (Gentile 2020; Holmes 2013). It is not surprising that Black cisgender female sex workers are among the most vulnerable groups during the pandemic. Anti-Black sentiment and the lack of access to crucial resources, including health care, support groups, and alternative financial opportunities, threaten the sex worker's ability to survive the global crisis.

Dana

Dana[1] is a 42-year-old Black cisgender femme sex worker (BCFSW). She was a "throwaway" when she began sex work at 14 years of age. Her biological father, who began molesting her when she was 3, demanded that she leave "his house" after she refused to submit to his sexual advances. She was homeless for a month until she met Damian rummaging through a trash bin on 33rd Street looking for food. He offered security. She eagerly accepted. It was at that time that she began her life as an outdoor sex provider.

Dana described her experiences during both pandemics, COVID-19, and racism. She anticipates that the industry will shift for the worse, now that many minority women will be forced further underground. Five years before COVID-19, Dana attended individual therapy sessions twice a week, ostensibly to explore safe ways to transition out of sex work. Our focus was the sustained physical toll of the work, coupled with the painful emotional ambivalence when articulating her personal needs in the face of the perceived expectations of her colleagues and friends. In mid-March, Dana asserted that leaving the work and her community were no longer realistic options. She requested that the treatment should instead focus on her health and physical safety.

---

[1] The patient's name and other personal identifiers have been changed to protect privacy and confidentiality.

Zoom

The initial transition of therapy into remote videoconferences using the Zoom platform was challenging for us both but in different ways. Our primary concerns were confidentiality and privacy. In-person sessions were emotionally intense. After 5 years of working together, we had crafted our own language. We were both US-born, first generation children of Black Panamanian working-class immigrants. Nonverbal communication was a crucial component of the treatment because she was a sex worker of color. The use of our bodies, specific facial expressions, and eye movements to convey delicate information is part of our cultural heritage. Implicitly, we both understood that certain things just cannot be said out loud, even when no one else was listening. The videoconference modality threatened that connection. Neither of us felt safe with the new platform. The popular Zoom videoconference computer program represented an oppressive entity, as we were forced to stop in-person sessions, at least temporarily. Dana was preoccupied about the duration of the online sessions. She foresaw that her resistance to attend remote sessions could have a negative impact on our new online relationship. I, on the other hand, was secretly pleased. I was facing the final presentation of my doctoral program, and she knew about it; but she did not know the urge I felt to cancel our sessions until I had completed my degree.

It was mid-March when we both agreed that the comfort of our respective apartments seemed a lot nicer than the twice-a-week, virally risky commute to my Manhattan office. We both preferred warmer weather, and pre-COVID-19 we often joked about working from home in the winter. Now the chance presented itself. Working from home also helped me avoid the concerns that the coronavirus pandemic presented for my own health and safety. Despite my initial reservations about remote therapy, I was ultimately content with the transition. It gave me more time to prepare for my graduation project. I expressed this to Dana during a FaceTime call. She shared her anger about what she interpreted as "my nonchalant attitude" towards her emotional struggle with our new arrangement.

Her disclosure made me aware of another feeling I noticed within myself but was ashamed to admit. I was near to the successful completion of my doctoral program, which filled me with a sense of enormous pride and even hubris. The closer I came to realizing this tremendous goal, the more disdain I felt towards Dana. I resented our sessions, especially as my deadline drew closer and the anxiety became harder to manage. Viewed from the perspective of shared trauma (Tosone 2011), I was dealing with my own reactions to the COVID-19 crisis, but was grateful that I did not share her predicament. Her situation was terrifying and exacerbated my own fears. Focusing on my impending graduation helped me to distance emotionally from Dana's experience and avoid the full impact of the COVID-19 crisis.

I explored my countertransference in supervision. My supervisor is a 78-year-old white woman from Alabama who asserted that I was struggling between seeing myself as superior to Dana and wanting to represent a positive, empathic role model.

Her observation was difficult to hear and made me defensive, but we continued to explore the idea for several weeks.

I began online sessions with Dana on March 25, as I had cancelled the previous week, letting her know that I was extremely fatigued. She appeared to understand, but she didn't. Her disappointment was apparent when we finally met. Dana was reliably effusive and gregarious in person. But on March 25, she had a flat affect and minimal body language and responded to my inquiries vaguely. The interaction felt as if we were slightly hostile acquaintances. Throughout the session she continued to sit quietly, looking down at what seemed to be the floor, occasionally glancing up at the camera, but her gaze never directly met mine. I thought "I could be using this time for my project." I resented this awkward exchange and ended the session prematurely, advising that it would be more productive if we spoke at a time that was better for her. In retrospect, I must have sounded condescending and patronizing. I justified my response, reasoning that social distancing significantly impacted her ability to work, affecting her mood. We concluded the session confirming that we would continue meeting but, at her suggestion, reducing the frequency to once a week until she felt more comfortable with the new format. I was not curious, nor did I inquire about her request. I was ecstatic. On April 1, Dana was 15 minutes late to our second online session. She spoke a bit more freely; however, she remained stoic and sullen. At her request, we ended 10 minutes before schedule. It was 2 days before my presentation. I was again grateful for the extra time.

On our meeting after my presentation, I was drained yet alert. My resentment towards her subsided. She commented that she entertained terminating therapy because of the palpable distance between us. I was unprepared to appropriately address the topic. However, I silently acknowledged her concern. Subsequent sessions continued to focus on financial anxieties and the anticipated loss of her fellow sex worker colleagues due to increased substance abuse and possible COVID-19-related illness and death. We also explored her "basic dread," which she described as a sense of severe hopelessness and constant presence in her life. To provide a more nuanced sense of our exchange and the feelings it evoked in me as we shifted to teletherapy, while we contended with the dual pandemics, I have included an excerpt from our 10th Zoom treatment session, a week after George Floyd's public assassination in Minneapolis. Dana provided a written consent for our conversations to be transcribed and published.

Transcript

Therapist: How do you think COVID will change traditional sex work?

Dana: The money. It will not be the same. We lost a lot of money. We stand to lose more. I have savings, but I have been up at night pacing around my apartment, my chest tight, pulling my hair, drinking, trying to figure out how I am going to manage after that runs out. I have been homeless a few times in my life when I was younger, but not now, not at 42 years old. I cannot imagine. I am estranged from my family members, and my sex work sisters are in the same predicament that I am, some worse.

Therapist: Before COVID, we were working on exploring possible alternative career paths. Is that still an option?

Dana: Part of me wants to say yes; part of me wants to say no. It is an extremely challenging question. We (sex workers) were already struggling with the FOSTA/SESTA reform.

It made sure that we cannot properly screen. That is scary! I know a lot of girls who continued to advertise off the radar at the increased risk of becoming another statistic. But COVID, completely unexpected, no time to plan, no time to think, I am in survival mode now. I am glad it is just me; if I had kids to worry about, I would be jumping off the walls right now. I thought about starting training or a job search from scratch. Truly daunting, what am I supposed to put on a cover letter or a resumé? What do I say when they ask what I have been doing for the last 27 years of my life? Smile nicely and say "Sir/Madam, I've been giving blow jobs." That will not be in my favor unless I have a pervert boss. For that I might as well stay on the street. Every girl I know is trying to figure side hustles right now, but that does not look like a "traditional job." Sex and sex work are my identity; that is all I know... at least for right now.

Therapist: I get it. There are a lot of difficult intersections between survival and identity and the choices one makes based on self-perception.

[*But I did not really get it. However, I do feel sad and connected to Dana. As a Black woman, I do instinctively understand what she meant: that her skin color marked her for life and she felt pigeonholed and boxed in, despite attempts to seize control of her internal narrative. I had struggled with the same issue quite often. However, I still could not fully engage or connect with Dana. I also felt quite entitled. I was thinking to myself: you should have gone to school, invested in yourself. Look at me: you could have done something different. It is your fault. I was also terrified about her choice to continue to work with clients who she did not know. Absolutely terrified about her health and safety. I was also preoccupied about liability that I may have in this situation. We discussed safety precautions; however, our conversations did not feel as if they were enough. So many people were dying daily. I am not sure that I did my best here and judged myself harshly for it. I had hopes of working with Dana on a transition plan and assisting her with creating a new identity; when I was sure that those hopes were no longer a priority to Dana, I became even more resentful. I felt immense shame for thinking this way, but the thoughts flooded me, and I did not have the control or perspective to stop them.*]

Dana: It is true. Look at everything that is happening now with the police. I am scared in a very different way than I have ever been. My life is at stake in a very different way. I sometimes feel a lack of inherent self-worth. I try, I really do, to feel good, to care for myself, and then I figure what is the point? When there is a loud voice telling you are nothing, you hear it; even when you try to tune it out, you hear it, and you believe it.

[*As she spoke, I felt more shame; I tried to ask myself what had shifted in me? I understand her. I knew her story all too well. Was my completion of a doctoral degree able to silence the voice of not good enough? Was I now able to have a better sense amid all the murders and the grief? Was my voice valid? Was I going to be able to write the articles, teach the classes, reform structural injustice in existing institutions, or create my own? Was I going to live up to the expectations of my family, friends, and professors who believed in me and dedicated their time to get me through this arduous journey? All I could feel as she continued to speak was a sense of embarrassment. I was ashamed that I represented a group who is disdained by white society. I was ashamed that I had worked so hard in my doctoral program to flee the common stereotypes, but that someone could still mistake me for a sex worker, a criminal instead of a doctor. I was angry at her for not being "a credit to her race"; I continued to listen as my stomach slowly churned.*]

Therapist: Tell me more about the "new" threats on your life.

Dana: I have always been under siege, in a sense. My father raped me. My first pimp/boyfriend raped me too and beat me. I am an intimate partner violence survivor, always have been. I experience very subtle forms of racism, so I am trying to put my finger on it. It is hard to identify; it kind of feels like I am slowly being erased. It is hard to describe. I am losing my community and my health. My resources are being threatened; it feels like we are slowly disappearing. It is strange to have this feeling amid protests, rallies, empowering social media posts where people are standing up and speaking out. I feel a sort of slippage though like I am going to wake up, be alive, but not exist. Cannot really explain it. This fuels my increased anxiety, panic, drinking, and hair-pulling. I do not have suicidal thoughts, but I sometimes think about the fine line between existing as a body and not as a person, remaining in a dissociative state so I can be just numb.

[*I recognized that I was also a new threat, in fact, more dangerous than the police. I was a black woman who had somehow lost touch with her and the sense of empathy that had previously provided Dana with a feeling of strength and empowerment, at a time she needed me the most. Moreover, how was I going to process these feelings with a white supervisor who, I knew, held implicit bias towards me and towards the patient despite our connection. My supervisor and I had also been working together for 5 years, and we got along very well, but she was an older white woman who grew up in the forties in Middle America where racist ideology was, and is, a part of her cultural perspective. I do not believe for a second that my inner turmoil was lost on Dana. Because of her history and sophisticated understanding of trauma, she is incredibly intuitive and hypervigilant. She also seeks my approval and wants me to be proud of her; my new doctoral degree is as much hers as it is mine. I know that her unspoken desire is to connect again. We both need mutual confirmation that our collective and individual contributions to life do matter. To assist my endeavor, I concluded supervision sessions and now seek the guidance of a Black woman to work through these issues. I cannot afford to let Dana down.*

I may look the part, but I do not have the stereotypical proletariat Black experience. My dual identity creates a multifaceted complexity to our interactions. On the one hand, my skin color, accent, and implicit cultural understanding deepen the bond between us. Dana often shares that our bond allows her to feel and articulate the most vulnerable parts of herself. She is a therapist's dream. Yet, the other identity, the one about which I am still not entirely certain, creates a divide between us and complicates the treatment. I feel a combination of negative judgment and shame towards her and towards myself. The fundamental challenge is to remain empathic, while still feeling that no matter how much professional success I have, I could still be mistaken for a sex worker.]

Final Thoughts

As the current societal discourse has unfolded, the Black experience in the United States can only be fully appreciated by fellow Blacks. For that reason, Black therapists are expected to have better outcomes with their Black patients. While it can be assumed that Dana and I share several collective traumas in common, namely, the COVID-19 crisis and the ongoing pandemic of racism, our reactions reflect our respective positions in society – me as a newly minted doctoral graduate and Dana as a sex worker trapped by her history and present circumstances due to COVID-19. Although we have demographics and potential exposure to COVID-19 in common, shared trauma does not imply that we "share" the same experience. Rather, the term acknowledges that I, as Dana's therapist, have reactions to her trauma history and discussion of COVID-19, while also contending with my own independent reactions to the convergence of the two pandemics. As a Black woman who has been chronically exposed to racism and now to the coronavirus pandemic, I have my own trauma narrative to tell. Paradoxically, our differences in background, family situations, professions, and societal positions need to be respected to more fully appreciate the trauma we share. To conclude, the complex empathy and rejection reactions experienced by a therapist who has endured similar lifelong societal abuse as their patient (as outlined here) need further exploration in the professional literature. This chapter is but a modest beginning step towards that end, as it is a nascent but essential step for Dana to enter the societal discourse on racism in America.

References

Blair, C. M. (2010). *I've got to make my livin': Black Women's sex work in turn-of-the-century Chicago*. Chicago: University of Chicago Press.

Bureau of Justice Statistics. (2011). Characteristics of suspected trafficking incidents, 2008–2010. Retrieved from https://www.bjs.gov/content/pub/pdf/cshti0810.pdf

Ditmore, M. H. (Ed.). (2006). *Encyclopedia of prostitution and sex work* (Vol. 1). Westport: Greenwood Press.

Ditmore, M. H. (2011). *Prostitution and sex work*. Santa Barbara: Greenwood Press.

Flowers, R. B. (2011). *Prostitution in the digital age: Selling sex from the suite to the street*. Santa Barbara: Praeger.

Gentile, D. (2020). SF sex workers forced to make tough and risky choices during pandemic. *SF Gate*. https://www.sfgate.com/offbeat/article/SF-sex-workers-weigh-in-on-working-through-the-15177239.php

Holmes, H. (2013). Fairfax prostitution sting nets 23 arrests. WJLA-ABC7 news. http://www.wjla.com/articles/2013/08/fairfax-prostitution-sting-nets-23-arrests-93028.html

Krüsi, A., Chettiar, J., Ridgway, A., Abbott, J., Strathdee, S. A., & Shannon, K. (2012). Negotiating safety and sexual risk reduction with clients in unsanctioned safer indoor sex work environments: a qualitative study. *American Journal of Public Health, 102*(6), 1154–1159.

Naftulin, J. (2020, April 2). Strippers, dominatrixes, and sex workers are being left out of a major US coronavirus relief package. Insider.com. Retrieved from: https://www.insider.com/sex-workers-are-ineligible-for-us-coronavirus-relief-package-2020-4

Tharoor, I. (2020). The pandemic is ravaging the world's poor, even if they're untouched by the virus. *Washington Post.* https://www.washingtonpost.com/world/2020/04/15/pandemic-is-ravaging-worlds-poor-even-if-theyre-untouched-by-virus/

The National Center for Victims of Crime, NCVRW Resource Guide. (2013). https://victimsofcrime.org/docs/ncvrw2013/2013ncvrw_stats_humantrafficking.pdf

Tosone, C. (2011). The legacy of September 11th: Shared trauma, therapeutic intimacy and professional posttraumatic growth. *Traumatology, 17*(3), 25–29.

Walter, L. A., & McGregor, A. J. (2020). Sex-and gender-specific observations and implications for COVID-19. *The Western Journal of Emergency Medicine, 21*(3), 507.

Wenham, C., Smith, J., & Morgan, R. (2020). COVID-19 is an opportunity for gender equality within the workplace and at home. *BMJ, 369*, m1546. https://www.bmj.com/content/369/bmj.m.1546.

Chapter 32
COVID-19 as Post-Migration Stress: Exploring the Impact of a Pandemic on Latinx Transgender Individuals in Immigration Detention

Diana Franco (ID)

Transgender asylum-seeking individuals are often exposed to traumatic events in their country of origin, during the migratory journey, and post-migration. Among the migrants forced to flee, lesbian, gay, transgender/two-spirited, queer, intersex, and asexual (LGBTQIA+) individuals are among the most vulnerable in the world (US Department of State n.d.). Latinx transgender individuals are frequently targeted by Latin America's persecutory and transphobic laws. These laws and policies often result in torture, human rights violations, forced human trafficking, and death (Reisner et al. 2016). These discriminatory conditions force these individuals to flee and seek asylum, citing credible fear for not being able to return to their countries of origin.

However, Latinx transgender migrants experience similar safety concerns upon arrival to the United States. The United States government increasingly relies on the use of detention centers, prison-like facilities where asylum seekers are locked up while they await a determination on their immigration cases (Human Rights First n.d.). Latinx transgender migrants in detention are at risk for psychological and physical health concerns, such as sexual assault by guards and other detainees, physical violence, and negligence resulting in death. Many transgender individuals in detention have unique medical needs, such as requiring hormone therapy (Evans 2020). This population is more likely to have underlying medical conditions which make them susceptible to diseases such as HIV, hepatitis C, and coronavirus (COVID-19) (Castro 2020; Fitzsimons 2020; Reisner et al. 2016). Transgender individuals in detention are also more likely to suffer from posttraumatic stress disorder, depression, and anxiety (Castro 2020). Detainment in these facilities has been

---

No potential conflict of interest was reported by the author.

D. Franco (✉)
School of Public Service Leadership, Department of Social Work, Capella University,
Minneapolis, MN, USA

© The Author(s), under exclusive license to Springer Nature Switzerland
AG 2021
C. Tosone (ed.), *Shared Trauma, Shared Resilience During a Pandemic*,
Essential Clinical Social Work Series,
https://doi.org/10.1007/978-3-030-61442-3_32

linked to an exacerbation in pre-existing trauma symptoms in transgender individuals (Castro 2020; Evans 2020; Human Rights First n.d.). Latinx transgender migrants need access to mental health treatment and other necessary health services, especially amid the current COVID-19 pandemic.

COVID-19 has had a substantial impact on the lives of Latinx transgender individuals in detention by exacerbating these pre-existing stressors. According to the World Health Organization (WHO) (2020), COVID-19 is an infectious, respiratory disease, now considered a pandemic affecting many countries in the world. Because of its high contagion factor, COVID-19 poses barriers in accessing mental health care to treat and assess histories of trauma, depression, and acute stress in credible fear asylum cases. In my role as a volunteer clinician, I conduct psychological evaluations in Spanish for Latinx transgender individuals in detention. As a result of COVID-19, this author and other clinicians have not been able to conduct psychological evaluations or have been limited to conducting these through a remote, virtual platform.

This chapter will focus on the unique needs of Latinx transgender individuals in detention and the challenges in service delivery imposed by COVID-19 restrictions. This pandemic barrier to mental health creates a multilevel problem in conducting psychological evaluations and delays and obstructs positive outcomes in pending asylum cases, which creates an indeterminate state in assessing credible fear and establishing a timely mental health diagnosis.

Lack of access to mental health also places transgender individuals in detention at risk of worsened psychiatric symptoms, including suicide (Reisner et al. 2016). This may also result in feelings of disempowerment and helplessness in the clinician. The resilience framework will be used to address shared trauma between Latinx transgender individuals in detention and clinicians in coping with COVID-19-related barriers to therapeutic services.

COVID-19 and Post-Migration Stress

Latinx Transgender Migrant Mental Health

Individuals forced to flee from their countries of origin are exposed to traumatic events throughout the three phases of migration: pre-migration, in-journey, and post-migration (Franco 2018). LGBTQIA+-identified migrants, specifically transgender migrants, are among the most vulnerable in the world (US Department of State n.d.). Latinx transgender migrants arrive to the United States with complex trauma histories, including significant symptoms of depression, anxiety, and post-traumatic stress disorder (Keller et al. 2003). Transgender individuals worldwide are displaced from their countries of origin due to persecutory laws based on their gender identity and expression. In keeping with this notion, Latinx transgender individuals around the globe face discrimination in obtaining employment, attending school, and engaging in day-to-day activities and, in many cases, are threatened by death and live in constant fear for their lives (Moloney 2019).

The journey to the United States, which seems a promising choice is, in reality, fraught with danger and threats. Throughout this perilous journey, human smugglers and gangs force Latinx transgender women into human trafficking, and they are often sexually abused and raped (Del Real 2018).

Once in the United States, Latinx transgender migrants are subjected to persecution based on gender identity, race, and immigration status (Klein 2020). If apprehended by Immigration and Customs Enforcement (ICE) or US Customs and Border Protection (CBP), Latinx transgender individuals are placed in immigration detention centers. Therefore, Keller and Wagner (2020) suggest that "for such traumatized individuals, immigration detention can cause severe psychological distress, including depression and post-traumatic stress disorder" (p. e245).

COVID-19 increases fear in transgender detainees, therefore functioning as a post-migration stressor that compounds pre-existing complex trauma. Hazardous conditions at immigration detention centers also pose threats to the psychological safety of these individuals. Klein (2020) suggests that COVID-19 disproportionately affects the mental health of LGBTQIA+-identified individuals because some members of this group may be at risk for substance use, depression, and other psychological sequelae (p. 240). Additionally, individuals with intersecting identities such as being a migrant and a sexual and gender minority, or "undocuqueer," may experience increased social marginalization during a pandemic (Klein 2020, p. 241). Social distancing may worsen symptoms of depression in non-detained LGBTQIA+-identified individuals (Klein 2020); therefore, migrants in detention may experience similar mental health outcomes. Similarly, Keller and Wagner (2020) suggest that "continued imprisonment during this pandemic could result in even more severe harm to the mental health of immigrant detainees" (p. e245).

Health Hazards in Detention Centers

Immigration detention centers have long been criticized for exposing detainees to a host of psychological and physical health hazards, including inhumane treatment, overcrowded conditions, inadequate and substandard medical care, and poor hygiene (Fitzsimons 2020; Montoya Galvez 2020; Vinson 2020). COVID-19 has exacerbated these pre-existing health conditions, revealing human rights violations and social justice concerns (Fitzsimons 2020).

To date, there are 22,835 detainees in ICE detention, of which 13,562 have been tested for COVID-19 and 3029 have tested positive for this virus (Detained in Danger 2020). These numbers indicate that COVID-19 is spreading rapidly in immigration detention centers. Transgender migrants in detention find it challenging to protect themselves from contagion. Some of these challenges include a disregard for Centers for Disease Control and Prevention (CDC) social distancing protocols by guards, tests administered solely to symptomatic detainees, insufficient access to testing, and a lack of access to personal protective equipment (PPE) (Chang 2020; Fitzsimons 2020; Kerwin 2020; Openshaw and Travassos 2020).

To illustrate, a 20-year-old Latinx transgender woman in immigration detention stated that guards often do not wear PPE, detainees are forced to share common areas with feverish individuals, and requests to see medical staff may take up to 4 days for symptomatic detainees (Vinson 2020). This individual reported that "being surrounded by men during the COVID-19 pandemic has been worse than the violence she fled in Mexico" and indicated feeling depressed and anxious (Vinson 2020, pp. 33–34).

Another Latinx transgender woman in detention reported feeling scared, vulnerable, and unprotected from COVID-19 (Fitzsimons, 2020). These physical and psychological safety concerns, aggravated by COVID-19, function as post-migration stressors and trauma triggers in Latinx transgender individuals in detention. Delays and denial of physical and psychological services serve to increase and compound fear in detainees, affirm their invisibility in society, and augment trauma symptoms.

The Psychological Evaluation and Shared Trauma

COVID-19 restrictions have forced clinicians to shift to virtual platforms, phone calls, or suspend in-person psychological evaluations altogether. As stated previously in this chapter, the psychological evaluation is an essential component in asylum cases. The psychological evaluation is a mechanism that allows for the provision of diagnostic information that may support the applicant's claims, determine credibility, elicit trauma narratives, and provide additional services to applicants who have been victims of torture (McKenzie et al. 2018; Meffert et al. 2010). Mental health professionals are essential in cases where torture has been alleged, since torture does not always leave physical scars but can manifest as posttraumatic stress, depression, anxiety, and other psychological sequelae (McKenzie et al. 2018). The evaluation consists of documenting forensic evidence in the form of a medicolegal affidavit, addressing a range of inflicted harms such as torture, rape, persecution, and other abuses – a process that can take anywhere from 3 to 6 h per case (McKenzie et al. 2018; Mishori et al. 2016). This evaluation process, while rewarding for the clinician, can also be concurrently physically and emotionally taxing.

Many clinicians who conduct asylum psychological evaluations do so as volunteer evaluators. Clinicians working with asylum cases report feeling motivated by "humanistic and moral values, noted personal and family experiences, having skills, expertise, and career interests as drivers" (Mishori et al. 2016, p. 210). However, while most clinicians have reported feeling positive about conducting these evaluations and find it personally and professionally rewarding (McKenzie et al. 2018, p. 137), some reported mixed feelings described as the "most horrible and most gratifying experience" and "harrowing, but rewarding" (Mishori et al. 2016, p. 214).

The content that emerges during asylum psychological evaluations – often intense trauma narratives – can be overwhelming for the clinician (Meffert et al.

2010). This may result in the clinician and the detainee experiencing "shared trauma," a term offered by Dr. Carol Tosone to explain when the therapist and the service user share collective trauma (Tosone 2020). As a result, the clinician may experience a countertransferential need to advocate for the detainee or bias the content of the evaluation (Meffert et al. 2010). "Countertransference" is used to describe the unconscious or conscious emotional or behavioral reactions of the clinician to the service user and is a process that may emerge in the therapeutic setting (Tosone et al. 2012, p. 232). Clinicians with similar backgrounds or trauma histories to the detainees may experience similar feelings.

This author is a Latinx first-generation migrant who grew up in a family with mixed migration statuses: lawful permanent residents, US citizens, and undocumented individuals who began their journey in South America and arrived in the United States via the US-Mexico border. The author and her family have experienced oppression, racism, and discrimination based on their ethnicity and immigration histories. Therefore, conducting evaluations with this vulnerable population has triggered her own grief, anger, powerlessness, and the shared trauma of oppression and racism, unbeknownst to the interviewee.

For clinicians motivated by altruistic and humanistic values, barriers posed by COVID-19 restrictions in conducting asylum evaluations may trigger feelings of hopelessness and immobilization as they are forced to socially isolate. Similarly, Latinx transgender individuals in detention also feel helpless, vulnerable, and powerless as their cases remain in legal limbo.

Practice Reflections and Recommendations

Resilience: A Framework for Understanding Shared Trauma

Literature (Tosone 2020; Brooks et al. 2015) suggests that shared trauma in crises and disasters can be understood through the resilience framework. Resilience has been linked to lower levels of stress and improved interpretation of the situation and response. Resilience, often defined in various ways within the literature, has been commonly defined as the ability to recover and bounce back from difficult events and then to integrate the disruptions and accommodate (Brooks et al. 2015; Pfefferbaum et al. 2017). Specifically, psychological resilience "relates to the adaptation of individuals after trauma, and that certain 'protective' factors may influence the extent to which individuals adapt" (Brooks et al. 2015, 386). However, some literature suggests that the resilience framework has shifted its focus from the experience of trauma to its role and application in managing difficult situations through emotion regulation and problem-solving (Bostelman 2020). For example, many clinicians have observed high levels of hope, courage, and resilience in asylees and in transgender women of color (Mishori et al. 2016; Ruff et al. 2019). Sexual- and gender-displaced minorities, such as Latinx transgender individuals in detention, promote resilience in their lives by staying hopeful and positive and relying on the legal services available to them (Alessi 2016). In this author's experience, many detainees develop supportive bonds with one another from where they draw hope and meaning in their lives. Nuttman-Shwartz (2014) refers to "shared resilience in a traumatic reality" as a way in which clients and clinicians can experience resilience as a result of exposure to the same communal disaster (p. 1).

To process shared trauma in a pandemic, clinicians may foster resilience in their lives by joining peer support groups, attending supervision sessions, and limiting media exposure (Meffert et al. 2010; Spiegel 2020; Tosone et al. 2012). Reaching out through virtual platforms to connect with other volunteer clinicians in asylum cases has been a source of support for the author, and communicating with immigration attorneys on upcoming plans to bridge gaps in services to Latinx transgender migrants in detention has reversed feelings of powerlessness and hopelessness.

Self-care is also an essential component to fostering resilience in a pandemic (Spiegel 2020). The author has found it beneficial to engage in more outdoor activities such as running and hiking, while adhering to social distancing protocols. COVID-19 affects us all, albeit in different ways. Being intentional in maintaining social support and personal self-care can be essential in developing resilience during such uncertain times.

References

Alessi, E. J. (2016). Resilience in sexual and gender minority forced migrants: A qualitative exploration. *Traumatology, 22*(3), 203–213. https://doi.org/10.1037/trm0000077.

Bostelman, C. (2020). Cultivating resilience in correction systems. *American Jails, 34*(2), 16–20.

Brooks, S. K., Dunn, R., Sage, C. M., Amlôt, R., Greenberg, N., & Rubin, G. J. (2015). Risk and resilience factors affecting the psychological wellbeing of individuals deployed in humanitarian relief roles after a disaster. *Journal of Mental Health, 24*(6), 385–413. https://doi.org/10.3 109/09638237.2015.1057334.

Castro, A. (2020, April 23). TLC, Ballard Spahr, & Rapid defense network announce class action lawsuit to free all transgender people in ICE custody. *Transgender Law Center.* https://transgenderlawcenter.org/archives/15791

Chang, W. (2020, June 11). Detained in danger: Database raises troubling questions about COVID-19 in ICE detention centers. *Human Rights First.* https://www.humanrightsfirst.org/press-release/detained-danger-database-raises-troubling-questions-about-covid-19-ice-detention

Del Real, J. A. (2018, July 11). 'They were abusing us the whole way': A tough path for gay and trans migrants. *The New York Times.* https://www.nytimes.com/2018/07/11/us/lgbt-migrants-abuse.html

Detained in Danger. (2020, July 13). Detained in danger: The COVID-19 pandemic inside ICE facilities. *Detained in Danger.* http://www.detainedindanger.org/

Evans, A. K. (2020, February 13). ICE detaining transgender individuals despite widespread calls for their release. *Boulder Weekly.* https://www.boulderweekly.com/news/ice-detaining-transgender-individuals/

Fitzsimons, T. (2020, April 29). Class action suit aims to free all transgender ICE detainees. *NBC News.* https://www.nbcnews.com/feature/nbc-out/class-action-suit-aims-free-all-transgender-ice-detainees-n1195556

Franco, D. (2018). Trauma without borders: The necessity for school-based interventions in treating unaccompanied refugee minors. *Child and Adolescent Social Work Journal, 35*(6), 551–565. https://doi.org/10.1007/s10560-018-0552-6.

Human Rights First. (n.d.). Immigration detention: We press the U.S. government to end harmful immigration detention centers. *Human Rights First.* https://www.humanrightsfirst.org/topics/immigration-detention

Keller, A. S., & Wagner, B. D. (2020). COVID-19 and immigration detention in the USA: Time to act. *The Lancet.* https://doi.org/10.1016/S2468-2667(20)30081-5.

Keller, A. S., Rosenfeld, B., Trinh-Shevrin, C., Meserve, C., Sachs, E., Leviss, J. A., Singer, E., Smith, H., Wilkinson, J., Kim, G., Allden, K., & Ford, D. (2003). Mental health of detained asylum-seekers. *The Lancet, 362*(9397), 1721–1723. https://doi.org/10.1016/S0140-6736(03)14846-5.

Kerwin, D. (2020). Immigration detention and COVID-19: How the US detention system became a vector for the spread of the pandemic. *Center for Migration Studies.* https://cmsny.org/publications/immigrant-detention-covid/

Klein, N. S. (2020). Rethinking COVID-19 vulnerability: A call for LGBT+ im/migrant health equity in the United States during and after a pandemic. *Health Equity, 4*(1), 239–242. https://doi.org/10.1089/heq.2020.0012.

McKenzie, K. C., Bauer, J., & Reynolds, P. P. (2018). Asylum seekers in a time of record forced global displacement: The role of physicians. *Journal of General Internal Medicine, 34*(1), 137–143. https://doi.org/10.1007/s11606-018-4524-5.

Meffert, S. M., Musalo, K., McNiel, D. E., & Binder, R. L. (2010). The role of mental health professionals in political asylum processing. *Journal of the American Academy of Psychiatry and the Law, 38*(4), 479–489.

Mishori, R., Hannaford, A., Mujawar, I., Ferdowsian, H., & Kureshi, S. (2016). "Their stories have changed my life": Clinicians' reflections on their experience with and their motivation to conduct asylum evaluations. *Journal of Immigrant and Minority Health, 18*, 210–218. https://doi.org/10.1007/s10903-014-0144-2.

Moloney, A. (2019, August 8). LGBT+ murders at 'alarming' levels in Latin America – Study. *Reuters.* https://www.reuters.com/article/us-latam-lgbt-killings/lgbt-murders-at-alarming-levels-in-latin-america-study-idUSKCN1UY2GM

Montoya Galvez, C. (2020, March 26). ICE resists calls to release immigrants as desperation mounts over coronavirus. *CBS News.* https://www.cbsnews.com/news/coronavirus-ice-detainees-immigrants-released-lawsuits/

Nuttman-Shwartz, O. (2014). Shared resilience in a traumatic reality: A new concept for trauma workers exposed personally and professionally to collective disaster. *Trauma, Violence, & Abuse,* 1–10. https://doi.org/10.1177/1524838014557287.

Openshaw, J. J., & Travassos, M. A. (2020). COVID-19 outbreaks in U. S. immigrant detention centers: The urgent need to adopt CDC guidelines for prevention and evaluation. *Clinical Infectious Diseases: An Official Publication of the Infectious Diseases Society of America,* ciaa692. Advance Online Publication. https://doi.org/10.1093/cid/ciaa692.

Pfefferbaum, B., Horn, R., & Pfefferbaum, R. (2017). A conceptual framework to enhance community resilience using social capital. *Clinical Social Work Journal, 45*(2), 102–110. https://doi.org/10.1007/s10615-015-0556-z.

Reisner, S. L., Poteat, T., Keatley, J., Cabral, M., Mothopeng, T., Dunham, E., Holland, C. E., Max, R., & Baral, S. D. (2016). Global health burden and needs of transgender populations: A review. *The Lancet, 388*(10042), 412–436. https://doi.org/10.1016/S0140-6736(16)00684-X.

Ruff, N., Smoyer, A. B., & Breny, J. (2019). Hope, courage, and resilience in the lives of transgender women of color. *The Qualitative Report, 24*(8), 1990–2008. https://nsuworks.nova.edu/tqr/vol24/iss8/11.

Tosone, C. (2020, April 6). Shared trauma during a pandemic. *Psychology Today.* https://www.psychologytoday.com/us/blog/traumatized/202004/shared-trauma-during-pandemic

Tosone, C., Nuttman-Shwartz, O., & Stephens, T. (2012). Shared trauma: When the professional is personal. *Clinical Social Work Journal, 40*(2), 231–239. https://doi.org/10.1007/s10615-012-0395-0.

United States Department of State. (n.d.). *At-risk populations: Bureau of populations, refugees, and migration.* https://www.state.gov/other-policy-issues/at-risk-populations/

Vinson, L. (2020). Transgender woman endures transphobic abuse in immigration prison during pandemic. *Southern Poverty Law Center.* https://www.splcenter.org/attention-on-detention/transgender-woman-endures-transphobic-abuse-immigrant-prison-during-pandemic

World Health Organization (WHO). (2020, April 17). *Q & A on coronaviruses (COVID-19).* World Health Organization. https://www.who.int/emergencies/diseases/novel-coronavirus-2019/question-and-answers-hub/q-a-detail/q-a-coronaviruses

Part V
Social Work Education

Chapter 33
Teaching Social Work Practice in the Shared Trauma of a Global Pandemic

Beth Sapiro

Shared Trauma

Unique clinical dynamics occur when both clinician and client are exposed to the same community trauma, whether a natural disaster or act of violence. These dynamics are referred to as *shared trauma* (Bell and Robinson 2013; Tosone 2011), defined as "the affective, behavioral, cognitive, spiritual, and multi-modal responses that clinicians experience as a result of dual exposure to the same collective trauma as their clients" (Tosone et al. 2012, p. 233). The term *shared traumatic reality* is also used, particularly by Israeli scholars, to describe ongoing experiences of collective terror with chronic effects on individuals and communities (Lavi et al. 2017). Many clinicians describe these experiences as "uncharted territory" (Boulanger 2013, p. 32). In a global pandemic, social work educators encounter similar uncharted territory; this reflection explores the relevance of the concept of shared trauma for the teaching relationship in a crisis.

Following a shared trauma, both clinician and client are involved in mourning the same loss at the same time (Bell and Robinson 2013), even as their experiences of the disaster may vary considerably (Dekel and Baum 2010; Tosone et al. 2012). Clinicians struggle to manage their own personal reactions of shock, worry, and sadness while continuing to work in a professional capacity (Boulanger 2013). Unique countertransference reactions are common, whether clients' anxieties mirror those of the clinician or diverge considerably (Boulanger 2013; Tosone et al. 2012). Experiencing a disaster and navigating its aftermath force clinicians to confront their own vulnerabilities, leading some clinicians to feel deskilled, ashamed, or unsure of their ability to help clients (Saakvitne 2002).

B. Sapiro (✉)
Montclair State University, Montclair, NJ, USA
e-mail: sapirob@montclair.edu

C. Tosone (ed.), *Shared Trauma, Shared Resilience During a Pandemic*,
Essential Clinical Social Work Series,
https://doi.org/10.1007/978-3-030-61442-3_33

Clinicians working in the context of shared trauma inevitably make changes to long-standing practice guidelines (Boulanger 2013; Rao and Mehra 2015). Following a traumatic event, clinicians may proactively contact vulnerable clients and inquire about their well-being, rather than wait for them to contact the therapist (Boulanger 2013; Tosone 2006). When the therapy office has been damaged or rendered inaccessible, clinicians find themselves working in temporary spaces or conducting teletherapy; this requires creativity and flexibility to create and maintain a holding environment in a temporary space (Boulanger 2013). Some clinicians report intensified emotional reactions in themselves, which may lead to increased self-disclosure and greater transparency in the clinical relationship (Boulanger 2013; Rao and Mehra 2015; Tosone 2006). For some, this increased therapeutic intimacy bolsters their sense of connection to clients and heightens their appreciation for the intersubjectivity of therapy (Rao and Mehra 2015; Tosone 2006); others may feel shame when their own emotional reactions are apparent to clients (Lavi et al. 2017). In either case, clinicians report a blurring or crossing of professional boundaries, as emotional distance becomes harder to justify (Bauwens and Tosone 2010; Bell and Robinson 2013; Rao and Mehra 2015). In the aftermath of a traumatic event, the traditional asymmetry of the clinical relationship becomes slightly more symmetrical (Boulanger 2013; Tosone 2006).

The impact of shared trauma on clinicians can be both negative and positive (Dekel and Baum 2010). Negative impacts include the challenges for clinicians of managing their own feelings of loss, fear, pain, sorrow, grief, and helplessness, alongside those of their clients (Dekel and Baum 2010). Symptoms of direct or vicarious trauma exposure can include difficulties with concentration, memory problems, dissociation, flooding, and numbing or avoidance (Bell and Robinson 2013). In some cases, clinicians may struggle to differentiate their own reactions from those of their clients (Day et al. 2017). Some clinicians report feeling a decrease in their sense of professional competence (Dekel and Baum 2010; Saakvitne 2002).

In addition, some also report positive impacts on their practice in the context of shared trauma. Nuttman-Shwartz (2015) coined the term "shared resilience in a traumatic reality" to describe the ways that both workers and clients can experience posttraumatic growth from this work. Clinicians report feeling deepened identification with clients as a result of working in a shared traumatic reality (Lavi et al. 2017). Others appreciate the possibility for mutual learning and mutual growth in the therapeutic relationship (Rao and Mehra 2015; Tosone 2006), when both clinician and client are open to being changed as a result of participating in the relationship (Miller and Stiver 1997). Some report that clinical work provides a sense of pride in professional purpose, a sense of meaning, and an antidote to feelings of helplessness following a traumatic event (Lavi et al. 2017; Saakvitne 2002).

Self-care and effective supervision are particularly essential for clinicians navigating shared trauma (Bell and Robinson 2013). Clinicians draw on their circles of support (Dekel and Baum 2010) from family, colleagues, supervisors, and the broader society. Lavi et al. (2017) found that clinicians who felt emotionally and instrumentally supported by supervisors and administrators reported a strong sense of group cohesion and resilience. In contrast, a lack of clear institutional support aggravates an already intensely challenging situation (Tosone et al. 2012).

Shared trauma also poses unique challenges for students and teachers (Tosone et al. 2003). Nuttman-Shwartz and Dekel (2009) note that students are uniquely vulnerable in shared trauma situations, because they are still learning the knowledge and skills to use in practice and are anxious about being evaluated in the classroom. Tosone (2011) described the challenges in staying committed to the course syllabus as she and her students struggled in the aftermath of 9/11. Her solution was to invite students to write reflections on their experiences and connect them to the literature on trauma and coping, which were ultimately compiled into an article (Tosone et al. 2003). Students may experience role ambiguity in a shared traumatic reality, since it can be challenging for students to maintain a clear perspective on their role as helpers when they are also affected by the situation (Nuttman-Shwartz and Dekel 2009). In these situations, the class must provide containment for students, so that they can maintain their roles as both helpers and students (Nuttman-Shwartz and Dekel 2009; Saakvitne 2002).

Teaching in a Pandemic

The COVID-19 global pandemic has affected nearly every aspect of life in the United States. The rapid spread of the virus in the northeast United States led to an abrupt lockdown and shelter-in-place orders for millions of residents in March 2020. Unemployment numbers skyrocketed, while those who were employed in essential positions struggled with a lack of access to protective gear and worries about contracting the illness and infecting loved ones. In March and April 2020, the death toll from the virus rose exponentially in the region. Institutions of higher education cancelled in-person classes and closed student residence halls, requiring students to move home and both students and faculty to make an emergency pivot to remote instruction. Worries about food shortages, sick loved ones, reduced income, and difficulties accessing unemployment benefits formed the backdrop for the second half of the spring 2020 semester. Similar to clinicians returning to work following a disaster, it was clear that teaching during a pandemic could never be "business as usual" (Boulanger 2013, p. 38).

Several aspects of my own experience teaching undergraduate and graduate social work students invite parallels with the conceptual framework of shared trauma. Perhaps most prominent were feelings of grief that both I and my students experienced in response to multiple dimensions of loss, including the loss of normalcy as a result of the closure of public life; loss of autonomy as a result of shelter-in-place regulations; loss of a predictable future; loss of connection with others in the classroom; loss of rituals to mark transitions, such as graduations; loss of work and predictable income; and loss of private space for living, working, or learning (Berinato 2020). The daily news reports of rapidly escalating death tallies left me feeling numb with grief. I also found that I was easily distracted and had difficulty concentrating on tasks. Finally, the news of the disproportionate toll the pandemic was taking on communities of color as a direct result of structural racism left me feeling furious, sad, and horrified.

In addition to mourning these losses, both faculty and students had to adapt to new technologies, unfamiliar ways of working, and lack of access to our familiar workspaces. The rapid spread of the virus meant that many of us were preoccupied with worry about loved ones who were ill or at risk, if we were lucky enough to be healthy ourselves. There was widespread concern about the economic fallout of the pandemic and immediate concern for everyone whose livelihoods disappeared in an instant. The collapse of distinctions between home and work led to a disorienting sense of time. The mandates to practice physical distancing and avoid contact with others created a profound sense of isolation, a source of considerable psychological distress (Miller and Stiver 1997).

Similar to clinicians and clients who experience a shared trauma, I found the mutuality of the teaching relationship heightened in the context of COVID-19. Intimacy in a teaching or therapeutic relationship involves exposing our imperfections (Tosone 2006). Self-disclosing to my students, I was honest about my unfamiliarity with online education for social work practice and that I was learning a new medium. I found that, like me, they were also anxious and disoriented by the sudden shift to remote instruction. In one of my first online classes, my computer kept freezing and crashing, interfering with my efforts to facilitate class effectively and leaving me frustrated and frazzled as a result. Later on, during small group discussions in this online class, a student offered me a compliment, saying "We were just saying what a great job you're doing." This graceful gesture initially caught me by surprise and made me self-consciously question my efforts to appear competent as a teacher. Had the student sensed that I was feeling vulnerable in an unfamiliar setting and needed a boost of encouragement? Ultimately, I saw this unsolicited compliment as one of the ways that relationships become more symmetrical in the aftermath of disaster. The professional distance that normally exists in the teaching relationship shrank as both teacher and students had to figure out how to navigate uncharted territory together. The boundaries of the teaching relationship, like other professional relationships, can sometimes be crossed in ways that facilitate connection and mutuality (Rao and Mehra 2015).

Both containment and validation are important in trauma treatment, as well as in classrooms following a shared trauma (Boulanger 2013; Nuttman-Shwartz and Dekel 2009). This is especially true when students and clients have encountered empathic failures elsewhere (Saakvitne 2002), as some of the students had. In all of my classes, I encouraged students to reflect on the challenges of this moment and connect their experiences and their clients in the pandemic to our course material. I noticed in myself a heightened emotional investment in my teaching, with stronger affective reactions on my part to student behavior in the online classroom. When students were honest about their struggles and able to reflect on their reactions either with peers in class or in written assignments, I felt strong waves of pride, admiration, and gratitude for their engagement and participation. At the same time, when students retreated into silence and participation was a struggle, I found myself feeling exhausted and frustrated. To me, my reaction felt like a response to the ongoing isolation imposed by the pandemic, even as I recognized the many valid reasons for silence in an online class.

After a traumatic event, some clinicians choose to reach out to clients rather than waiting for clients to contact them. I identified this dynamic in my teaching as well. When students referenced their own struggles with mental health challenges, I debated whether or not it was inappropriate to proactively reach out to students and ensure they had access to mental health support. I struggled with my own role clarity, aware of my role as a teacher and not a social worker for the students. At the same time, I felt it's necessary to acknowledge the emotional context of our learning during the pandemic and wanted to ensure that students with concerns knew how to access campus mental health support services. This gesture could be perceived as a boundary crossing but was also a form of affirming connection and care (Rao and Mehra 2015).

In spite of these numerous ways that my teaching experience reflected the concept of shared trauma, by the end of the semester, I recognized the many ways that my experience was not shared with the students. Compared to many of the students, I was lucky to retain employment and was able to work in a safe environment, protected from exposure to the virus. Shared traumatic realities take place in a political context (Nuttman-Shwartz and Dekel 2009); indeed, the impact of the COVID-19 pandemic is inextricable from the pandemic of anti-Black racism in the United States. The racial trauma and racial terror (Comas-Diaz 2007) resulting from police brutality and the weaponizing of White supremacy constitute a different kind of shared traumatic reality in this country. Trauma scholars describe how a traumatic event can shatter previously held assumptions that the world is a safe and benevolent place (Janoff-Bulman 1992; Saakvitne 2002). Experiencing unexpected and invisible threats to health and well-being, a loss of perceived safety, restricted freedom of movement, and in some cases loss of life are certainly destabilizing and disorienting in this moment, but they are sadly not new experiences for many people of color in the United States. The grossly unequal physical, emotional, and economic toll of these pandemics on communities of color in the United States means that it is disingenuous to describe the coronavirus pandemic simply as a shared or equalizing experience.

Implications for Educators

Experiencing a shared traumatic event changes the frame of the work (Saakvitne 2002). The literature on shared trauma has recommendations with relevant applicability for social work educators. Self-care is essential for both clinicians and educators who are struggling to regain a sense of equilibrium while maintaining a caring and responsive presence for clients or students (Bell and Robinson 2013). The reality of the pandemic continues to pose challenges to our physical, emotional, and social well-being, and living in a chronically stressful and isolating environment requires intentional efforts to stay healthy and nurture the self (Saakvitne 2002). Additionally, effective professional and administrative support of all kinds – technical, emotional, and informational – is necessary for teachers to adapt quickly to new and unfamiliar demands and avoid burnout.

Reflecting on the dynamics of shared trauma in the teaching relationship illustrates that teaching, like therapy, is ideally a growth-fostering relationship that leads to mutual empathy and mutual empowerment (Miller and Stiver 1997). In some cases, strategic self-disclosure can enhance mutuality in a relationship and reduce isolation (Rao and Mehra 2015). Feminist theorists have long observed the importance of authenticity and mutuality in healthy, growth-promoting relationships (Miller and Stiver 1997). In times of crisis, judicious boundary crossings can help foster connection between teacher and student, without leading to a dilution of the professional role (Rao and Mehra 2015). As educators, being authentic and empathic with our students can help us identify both the disproportionate vulnerabilities wrought by structural inequities, as well as our experiences of shared humanity.

References

Bauwens, J., & Tosone, C. (2010). Professional posttraumatic growth after a shared traumatic experience: Manhattan clinicians' perspectives on post-9/11 practice. *Journal of Loss & Trauma, 15*(6), 498–517. https://doi.org/10.1080/15325024.2010.519267.

Bell, C. H., & Robinson, E. H. (2013). Shared trauma in counseling: Information and implications for counselors. *Journal of Mental Health Counseling, 35*(4), 310–323. https://doi.org/10.17744/mehc.35.4.7v33258020948502.

Berinato, S. (2020). That discomfort you're feeling is grief. *Harvard Business Review*. Retrieved from https://hbr.org/2020/03/that-discomfort-youre-feeling-is-grief

Boulanger, G. (2013). Fearful symmetry: Shared trauma in New Orleans after Hurricane Katrina. *Psychoanalytic Dialogues, 23*(1), 31–44. https://doi.org/10.1080/10481885.2013.752700.

Comas-Diaz, L. (2007). Ethnopolitical psychology: Healing and transformation. In E. Aldarondo (Ed.), *Advancing social justice through clinical practice* (pp. 91–118). Mahwah: Lawrence Erlbaum Associates, Inc.

Day, K. W., Lawson, G., & Burge, P. (2017). Clinicians' experiences of shared trauma after the shootings at Virginia Tech. *Journal of Counseling & Development, 95*(3), 269–278. https://doi.org/10.1002/jcad.12141.

Dekel, R., & Baum, N. (2010). Intervention in a shared traumatic reality: A new challenge for social workers. *The British Journal of Social Work, 40*(6), 1927–1944. https://doi.org/10.1093/bjsw/bcp137.

Janoff-Bulman, R. (1992). *Shattered assumptions: Towards a new psychology of trauma.* New York: Free Press.

Lavi, T., Nuttman-Shwartz, O., & Dekel, R. (2017). Therapeutic intervention in a continuous shared traumatic reality: An example from the Israeli-Palestinian conflict. *British Journal of Social Work, 47*(3), 919–935. https://doi.org/10.1093/bjsw/bcv127.

Miller, J. B., & Stiver, I. P. (1997). *The healing connection: How women form relationships in therapy and in life.* Boston: Beacon Press.

Nuttman-Shwartz, O. (2015). Shared resilience in a traumatic reality: A new concept for trauma workers exposed personally and professionally to collective disaster. *Trauma, Violence & Abuse, 16*(4), 466.

Nuttman-Shwartz, O., & Dekel, R. (2009). Challenges for students working in a shared traumatic reality. *The British Journal of Social Work, 39*(3), 522. https://doi.org/10.1093/bjsw/bcm121.

Rao, N., & Mehra, A. (2015). Hurricane Sandy: Shared trauma and therapist self-disclosure. *Psychiatry: Interpersonal & Biological Processes, 78*(1), 65–74. https://doi.org/10.1080/003 32747.2015.1015881.

Saakvitne, K. W. (2002). Shared trauma: The therapist's increased vulnerability. *Psychoanalytic Dialogues, 12*(3), 443. https://doi.org/10.1080/10481881209348678.

Tosone, C. (2006). Therapeutic intimacy: A post-9/11 perspective. *Smith College Studies in Social Work, 76*(4), 89–98. https://doi.org/10.1300/J397v76n04_12.

Tosone, C. (2011). The legacy of September 11: Shared trauma, therapeutic intimacy, and professional posttraumatic growth. *Traumatology, 17*(3), 25–29. https://doi.org/10.1177/1534765611421963.

Tosone, C., Bialkin, L., Campbell, M., Charters, M., Gieri, K., Gross, S., et al. (2003). Shared trauma: Group reflections on the September 11th disaster. *Psychoanalytic Social Work, 10*(1), 57–77. https://doi.org/10.1300/J032v10n01_06.

Tosone, C., Nuttman-Shwartz, O., & Stephens, T. (2012). Shared trauma: When the professional is personal. *Clinical Social Work Journal, 40*(2), 231–239. https://doi.org/10.1007/s10615-012-0395-0.

Chapter 34
Reconceptualizing Service-Learning During the COVID-19 Pandemic: Reflections and Recommendations

Peggy Morton and Dina Rosenfeld

Introduction

"Service-learning" has been used to define a wide array of experiential educational experiences. Jacoby (1996) described it as containing three elements: students learn academic content while working in the community; reflection on their own experience in the community and how that informs the academic content; and consideration of how the academic content informs their community experience. Broadly defined, there is consensus that it is a pedagogy combining academic study with community service and reflection and fostering students' deeper understanding of subject matter and capacity for critical thinking. Especially relevant to our present moment, Sigmon (1994) noted that the "ideal" balance between service to community and academic learning varies and posited a typology, highlighting that service-learning may be more "SERVICE-learning" while at other times more appropriately denoted as "service-LEARNING," depending upon which goals are primary, with the hyphen symbolizing the process of reflection. Bringle and Hatcher (1996) focus on the transition from volunteering to participating in a credit bearing course where the needs of the community are served while enhancing "civic responsibility." Kaye (2010) highlighted the importance of service-learning, addressing real community needs; and Sandaran (2012) emphasized service-learning students having the opportunity to learn about communities other than their own and gaining insight into marginalized groups. Howard (1993) focused on students learning responsibility and addressing meaningful issues, while Speck and Hoppe (2004) made civic engagement and communitarian involvement primary. Studies have affirmed the

P. Morton (✉) · D. Rosenfeld
Silver School of Social Work, New York University, New York, NY, USA
e-mail: peggy.morton@nyu.edu

C. Tosone (ed.), *Shared Trauma, Shared Resilience During a Pandemic*,
Essential Clinical Social Work Series,
https://doi.org/10.1007/978-3-030-61442-3_34

331

long-term positive effects of service-learning programs for students' personal, academic, and moral development (Meyer et al. 2019).

Experiential learning in the curriculum area of field practice/internship has always been essential to social work education and in 2008, the Council on Social Work Education (CSWE) named field work its "signature pedagogy" (Boitel and Fromm 2014). In 2006, the dean of the college of arts and sciences and our dean agreed to collaborate on providing undergraduate students across campus with meaningful community engagement. Our School of Social Work, with its long-standing history in direct practice/experiential learning, would be an appropriate home for this approach to teaching and learning. In 2007, the first service-learning course was offered in partnership with a youth program housed at a settlement house, and our service-learning program has consistently evolved over the years, resulting in our current offering of seven different courses.

Service-Learning in the Time of COVID-19: When "Service-Learning Becomes Service-LEARNING"

When the emergence of the current health crisis necessitated a rapid pivot to remote learning, the service-learning instructors faced the unique challenges of transitioning courses that are experientially based to predominantly classroom-centered learning. How could courses with a significant service component be reconceptualized to remain meaningful and relevant during this time? How could our school retain a collaborative campus and community partnership, with an emphasis on reciprocity and mutual benefit? How could we deliver effective service-learning courses to our students in the virtual space? To address some of these concerns, the following service-learning courses were adapted: (1) *service-learning through youth and community engagement*, (2) *service-learning with immigrant youth*, (3) *service-learning with holocaust survivors*, and (4) *service-learning: Alzheimer's disease – sharing the lived experience*.

Service-Learning Through Youth and Community Engagement

In 2007, the school received a small "Learn and Serve" grant in partnership with a local community-based organization to create its first undergraduate service-learning course. For 2 hours weekly, students engage with middle school youth in academic tutoring, recreational activities, and cultural enrichment programs while attending a weekly class. The service-learning course is a collaborative effort, designed with an emphasis on reciprocity between partners. Through shared goals, interests, and commitment, students connect with youth by tutoring and providing mentorship, as well as helping to increase organizational capacity and learn about volunteerism with this unique age group. While many students have worked with other age groups, this is often their first exposure to middle school youth. The direct experience with the youth holds some surprises: it enhances their appreciation for the nuances of their behavior, strengths, and vulnerabilities and the challenges of negotiating a mentoring relationship with this age cohort. Through ongoing reflection, the course not only provides academic enhancement and civic engagement; it also offers a forum for students to identify their own values, assumptions, and biases throughout the service experience, a key objective of service-learning pedagogy.

With the onset of the pandemic, unfortunately, students working with the afterschool program were unable to remain directly involved with the youth for the duration of the semester. The site experienced challenges of its own in their efforts to move afterschool tutoring and recreational activities to an online format. Once accomplished, students had the opportunity to participate in activities albeit the primary obstacle: low youth attendance. Therefore, the focus of the class leaned toward the didactic content, and the key was to integrate the current situation into the existing material, making it as relevant and educational as possible; students maintained interest in the youth, and this was aided by remote involvement of the site director who provided continuous updates on the students and their families.

Coincidentally, and unfortunately, the middle school youths' situations highlighted the impact of the meso- and macro-level factors that had been the focus of discussions prior to the pandemic. The site director shared the challenges youth were having in participating remotely with both school and afterschool activities. Many are the result of the "digital divide"; they lack access to computers and the Internet, and if they reside in crowded quarters, they may not have a private/quiet space to complete their work. Their lack of attendance to afterschool remote activities was understandable, given their primary task of (and families' emphasis on) meeting the daily academic requirements of regular school subjects. Furthermore, as the middle school youth are largely of low-income backgrounds, many of their families were stressed with job loss and financial concerns. As the large majority are Chinese-American, residing on the Lower East Side and in Chinatown in New York City, they additionally faced a developing anti-Asian sentiment and bias erupting from the COVID-19 pandemic. The students noted how the current crisis had illuminated some of the meso-/macro-level factors' impact on the youths' situations in a "real-world" way, not just theoretically. The current situation presented an opportunity in real time to discuss major inequities in our systems; unequal access to income, health care, technology, housing, and employment was blatantly highlighted in the lives of these youth and their families. Additionally, as we had discussed the importance of peers and school in the "meso" worlds of middle school youth, the students considered how the rapid separation of students from their school and peer communities might impact their developmental needs and emotional well-being. On the macro-level, students were disappointed to learn that initial reports indicated that as a result of the city's financial losses due to the health crisis, the mayor's fiscal budget for 2021 includes a proposal to cut funding to afterschool programming, potentially negatively impacting 223,000 middle school youth who attend these programs.

Service-Learning with Immigrant Youth

Service-learning with immigrant youth focuses on students' understanding of the youth with whom they work and the contexts in which they live and learn. Students explore the processes of immigration and resettlement. The course touches on the fundamentals of engaging individuals in a helping situation, theories related to individual development, and implications of race, ethnicity, culture, and immigration. Students share their experiences, integrated with their readings through logs and class discussion.

Our students provide service through academic coaching and mentoring for refugees from such nations as Haiti, Honduras, Yemen, Bangladesh, Moldova, Uganda, and Sudan for a minimum of 2 hours weekly at an international high school. Students assist the classroom teachers by working with small groups of students, to help them understand the classroom lessons. Students are often placed in small groups where they share the students' native languages. The most useful languages our students speak are Arabic and Spanish. In addition to helping them with classwork and assignments, they also have the opportunity to get to know each other. The high school students often want to know about college life. They often talk about their country of origin and what life was like for them and the people they left behind.

Classroom content focuses on refugee and immigrant families, the countries they come from, and their experiences of arrival to the United States. Adolescent development is explored, as are the challenges and protective factors of being part of an immigrant group in New York City (NYC). The class also provides material on tutoring methods with immigrant adolescents.

When the pandemic forced the closure of both NYC public schools and our university, this service-learning course continued remotely. Students enrolled in the course returned to their homes in Texas, Tennessee, California, Egypt, Abu Dhabi, Hong Kong, Malaysia, and even, New York. They were eager to continue tutoring, and the international high school connected them to a tutoring lab. Though the high school students all received tablets, there were challenges: they did not have good internet connections and had to share small spaces with siblings and other family members, many of whom had jobs. In addition, the challenges of distance learning appeared to decrease their motivation. Finally, as time went on, given that these students were living within immigrant enclaves in communities of color, their families and neighbors were developing higher incidences of COVID-19 illness.

Classroom content increasingly focused on relevant weekly videos added to readings. These described life in refugee camps and adolescents' adjustment to American life both in New York City as well as in small towns throughout the United States. In the classroom, there was additional interest in exploring our students' immigration backgrounds, providing for a richer sense of community.

Service-Learning with Holocaust Survivors

This course, offered since 2010, is co-taught with a historian and provides psychosocial understanding of holocaust survivors within a historical perspective. It is offered in conjunction with students' participation in a weekly service experience, wherein they visit holocaust survivors who are clients of a community-based organization. The weekly class explores the historical/political backdrop of the holocaust in addition to the social and psychological effects of trauma on the lives of survivors. Emphasis is placed on resilience and the lives refashioned by immigration to the United States. The students' role is to form friendships with the survivors, so that they can learn about each other. A number of former students have stayed in touch with their "older friend" until the survivor died.

When in-person visits were suspended, our community partner was eager to have students continue either by phone or FaceTime. The elderly and often homebound survivors needed contact more than ever. Students were advised to adjust their phone calls to be shorter, increase their frequency, and make them more concrete in nature. They were surprised by their older friends' resilience in a time of such generalized anxiety and uncertainty. In class, the usual number of Yale archive testimonies listened to was increased to supplement the shorter conversations students were having with their "older friends." It is likely that students were able to successfully maintain their relationships because they had formed connections in person earlier in the semester. Class discussions reviewed testimonies they watched and presented the opportunity to discuss more generalized effects of long-term trauma both among holocaust survivors and survivors of torture from different parts of the world.

Service-Learning: Alzheimer's Disease – Sharing the Lived Experience

In 2019, the school partnered with the Family Support Program of the Alzheimer's and Dementia Center at a local medical center to initiate a service-learning course which added an academic component to an existing intergenerational program. Students (known as "buddies") provide companionship and activities to adults in the early stage of Alzheimer's disease (known as "mentors") and respite for their caregivers, while acquiring classroom knowledge about the disease and its impact on the adults and their caregivers. The direct experiences with program participants and their caregivers provide students the opportunity to challenge any preconceived ideas they may have had, especially the stigma that surrounds this population. As one student articulated, "The class helped me understand that people with dementia are capable of so much: what's considered an achievement or a good day might change as the disease progresses…but if people have the support they need they can still live a full and dignified life."

Given that most students were paired with older adults in this course, COVID-19 necessitated an immediate, precipitous end to the visiting experience, such that students were unable to say goodbye to their mentors in person. Some reverted to sporadic telephone "check-ins," but given the nature of the disease for some (memory loss/cognitive impairment) and the constant presence of the caregiver, these were challenging to maintain. Once again, remote learning became highly classroom focused and academic in nature, integrating time for reflection on the current situation and the relevant challenges it poses to this specific, already vulnerable population. A series of guest lectures had been scheduled prior to the disruption, and these proceeded smoothly on a remote basis.

The immediacy of the health crisis prompted discussion of what such an event means in the unique lives of people with Alzheimer's disease and their caregivers. How would this further the isolation, confinement, and stress of individuals who could not be oriented to the outside world and their caregivers who will find less time alone and opportunity for respite from their daily caretaking activities? What if their caregiver gets the coronavirus? And for those individuals who are institutionalized, how would this situation of separation from their loved ones affect their cognitive and emotional well-being? Finally, how would people with cognitive and recognition impairment react to caregivers wearing masks? Additionally, students reflected upon the experience of having to readily adapt to remote learning and the abrupt suspension of their in-person relationships.

Lessons Learned and Future Possibilities for Remote Service-Learning

With the future of in-person education uncertain, it is prudent to consider future possibilities for remote service-learning opportunities. Students should not be dissuaded from enrolling in such service-learning courses but rather should be encouraged and supported to participate in reimagining the design and implementation of volunteer activities to address community problems, especially at times of growing need. How can positive and productive college-community partnerships be continued, though reconceptualized?

First, service-learning courses must continue to provide mutual, reciprocal benefits for students' education while assisting community program participants. Therefore, community partners must be consulted and engaged in the process. How can the students best respond to their needs? In this past semester, as courses evolved remotely, instructors maintained open communication and ongoing evaluation with their partner organizations to ensure that all parties' goals were adequately and realistically met: students, community settings, and the individuals they serve. This effort will be ongoing as we resume remote service activities in the upcoming semester.

Second, alternative methods of service delivery should be population specific, and, where appropriate, "tried and true" approaches can be utilized. For example, in the case of older adults, when visiting was not feasible, students were encouraged to maintain contact with their partners, through technological means or through telephone "check-ins." Such "wellness calls" through computer or phone can decrease the social isolation of older adults. While it was not achieved this semester, with the advent of so many virtual activities developing, it may be possible for future students to join participants remotely in a group activity. For example, individuals with Alzheimer's disease have been engaging in remote art, music, exercise, and even museum trip programming. Students might join such activity efforts to observe participants and, where feasible, interact with them. Additionally, a platform like Zoom can ease the process of bringing "experts" into the classroom. For example, some holocaust survivors who would have been too frail to join the classroom in person to share their lived experience were now able to join more easily. Perhaps potential isolation of older adults can be decreased by connecting them to one another either by video platforms or, in the absence of Internet, by telephone.

With immigrant youth, tutors can potentially join classrooms and work with subgroups who need additional assistance in breakout rooms. With middle school youth in afterschool programs, innovative means of providing academic and social emotional learning can be further developed to include not only remote tutoring but also enriching arts, cultural, and recreational activities. Youth may enjoy interacting with peers, staff, and students through online games, whiteboard activities, contemporary music, etc. Students can provide interaction, structure, and consistency to support youth and promote their engagement; their creativity and knowledge of technology can facilitate the development of age-appropriate online programming activities that would improve attendance and enhance interest and further connection to their student-mentors. Perhaps our students can harness their intellectual interests and talents to offer basic lectures/presentations to youth/older adults in a remote, interactive environment. Of course, assuring equitable access to technology for all individuals would be essential for conducting successful remote involvement with any population served.

Third, didactic classroom material should be augmented with content relevant to the current situation including exploration of how various populations are attempting to adapt to the situation. In all likelihood, crises like COVID-19 may serve to underscore the unique histories and circumstances, underlying vulnerabilities, unmet needs, and strengths of the populations students work with.

Fourth, time must be spent on students' reflection on the redefinition of an experiential learning course. The precipitous nature of transitioning to remote instruction, the loss of the opportunity to "say goodbye" in person and concern about their partners' and their own well-being, cannot be overlooked. The opportunity for reflection on a shared experience, while challenging and/or disruptive, may serve to simultaneously highlight their strengths and underscore resilience and further a sense of community in the classroom.

Fifth, lessons learned during this time may have future implications for reconceptualization of service delivery as necessitated by situations that prohibit in-person contact. It is important to note that though the transition to remote learning was precipitous, the service-learning courses described benefited from a half semester completed with students in person, such that they were familiar with their instructors and their classmates. Should a situation arise wherein classes are remote from the onset, additional attention may need to be paid to reimagining service, developing a cohesive classroom environment and a feeling of community, while students similarly are working from the onset to develop relationships with their agency partners and constituents.

Conclusion

In conclusion, the COVID-19 pandemic has precipitated a plethora of changes in daily living, and the modalities of teaching and learning offered by educational settings are no exception. As institutions of higher education are currently positioned and required to further the promotion of remote education, so service-learning courses must keep pace by collaborating on the development of novel, innovative, and engaging methods of continuing service to organizations and their participants while enhancing college students' academic advancement and civic involvement. The past semester demonstrated a shared experience of severe disruption and even trauma for some elicited vulnerabilities and at the same time illuminated strengths of all parties involved: students, instructors, organizations, and their participants. Students and instructors successfully pivoted from traditional service-learning to more of a "service-LEARNING" model. As crisis may lead to opportunity, the continued need for remote learning can open new doors to innovative, creative, and valuable ways of integrating service with academic content, while adhering to the true mission and balance of service-learning.

References

Boitel, C. R., & Fromm, L. R. (2014). Defining signature pedagogy in social work education: Learning theory and the learning contract. *Journal of Social Work Education, 50*(4), 608–622.

Bringle, R. G., & Hatcher, J. A. (1996). Implementing service learning in higher education. *The Journal of Higher Education, 67*(2), 221–239.

Howard, J. (1993). *Praxis I: A faculty casebook on community service learning.* Ann Arbor: OCSL Press.

Jacoby, B. E. (1996). *Service-learning in higher education: Concepts and practices.* San Francisco: Jossey-Bass.

Kaye, C. B. (2010). *The complete guide to service learning: Proven, practical ways to engage students in civic responsibility, academic curriculum, & social action* (2nd ed.). Minneapolis: Free Spirit Publishing.

Meyer, M., Neumayr, M., & Rameder, P. (2019). Students' community service: Self-selection and the effects of participation. *Nonprofit & Voluntary Sector Quarterly, 48*(6), 1162–1185.

Sandaran, S. C. (2012). Service learning: Transforming students, communities and universities. *Procedia – Social and Behavioral Sciences, 66*, 380–390.

Sigmon, R. L. (1994). *Linking service with learning in liberal arts education*. https://eric.ed.gov/?id=ED446685

Speck, B. W., & Hoppe, S. L. (Eds.). (2004). *Service-learning: History, theory, and issues*. Westport: Praeger.

Chapter 35
Grief Lessons of the Apocalypse: Self-care Is a Joyful Jab in the Arm

Abigail Nathanson

"Your midterm papers are going to be returned to you a bit late," I wrote to my Master of Social Work (MSW) students, a few weeks into quarantine. "Unfortunately, I have coronavirus and am too sick to give them the attention they deserve right now." This was only half true; I did have coronavirus, and I was sleeping 14 h a day and coughing the rest. But really, I was just too sad and depleted to read their earnest papers about grief. It was hard enough to look into their deer-in-the-headlights faces over Zoom for class every week, trying to engage a sea of blank stares to talk about Grief, Loss, and Bereavement.

The irony of teaching a course on death and loss during a pandemic was not lost on any of us. By turns, it provided resonant material, and exhausted and drained us all. I teach my students to ask themselves, "Where is the suffering?", and to understand that it may not be where you expect. The students themselves were reeling from the last-minute cancellations of their field placements, having quickly fled the city for their childhood bedrooms to finish out graduate school online and wonder what kind of world they'd be graduating into. As a unique relational context drove new rules for self-disclosure, we mutually commiserated that our last semester in school—master's for them, doctorate for me—was not what we'd been imagining working toward all of these years.

I wrote to all of the students I'd had the past year on what would have been our graduation:

> To my newest colleagues: Happy graduation to those of you who are done! I hope you're looking back on everything you've done to get yourself to this place – all of the years of schooling, work, sacrifice, challenging yourself, taking the risk to go for what you want in the world – and that it brings you some measure of satisfaction and accomplishment. Much as we have discussed how your life is not defined and written by your last 10 minutes on

A. Nathanson (✉)
Silver School of Social Work, New York University, New York, NY, USA
e-mail: an768@nyu.edu

© The Author(s), under exclusive license to Springer Nature Switzerland AG 2021
C. Tosone (ed.), *Shared Trauma, Shared Resilience During a Pandemic*,
Essential Clinical Social Work Series,
https://doi.org/10.1007/978-3-030-61442-3_35

your deathbed, which you can't really control, your formal education is not defined solely by how it ends, either. The first year out is almost always a rough adjustment, and this year poses unique challenges for sure. This education is something you'll carry with you for the rest of your life, and will hopefully be a foundation for everything else you're going to learn.

I'm excited that you're the next generation of social workers and my newest colleagues. Welcome to the field! Stay in touch!

While many were touched to be remembered and have their experiences acknowledged, I asked myself how much was I creating a message that I needed to hear, too, creating a powerful transferential object that could save us both from the threat of anxious uncertainty (Liechty 2000). I wondered whether I was trying to shape their experience to protect myself from their reasonable disappointment and grief, because it hit so close to mine. The massive volume of death and illness of the pandemic was less shocking to me, after years of professional exposure and being kind of morbid at baseline, than the social isolation itself. That was rougher in ways that surprised and overwhelmed me.

"Where is the suffering?" I asked myself, too. When a friend at work asked how I was dealing with living alone during quarantine, my answer conveyed only what spin I could handle consciously acknowledging: "Well, after having coronavirus, going through a breakup in social isolation, and the apocalypse outside, the rest should be smooth sailing!". Briggs and Fronek's (2019) conceptualization of subjective incompetence in demoralization (as perceiving difficulty in expressing felt emotions when life seems overwhelming) was particularly apt.

While I didn't answer my friend with the full breadth of my emotional experience, I am not sure how much of their pain I could have been empathetically attuned to, either. Everyone around me was falling apart. There was emotional distance in places where there used to be a connection, and no time to try and make sense of it. Freud might have said that my libido had decathected from my friends and work, and had nowhere else to go, leaving me melancholic in my grief (Baker 2001). My friends, who largely work in trauma and hospice and hospitals, were reeling in their personal lives and exhausted by the emotional labor of their work during this uncertain, terrifying time. Those with partners, children, and families found their relationships being turned upside-down and quickly, aggressively renegotiated at a time when they already felt vulnerable and under-resourced. Our usual Bowlbyian attachment dance of mutual care-seeking and care-giving abruptly stopped (Baker 2001). The profound loss from our mutual distance, perhaps a reasonable response to our shared trauma (Tosone et al. 2012), functioned as both buffer and stressor at once.

Living alone while suffering relational losses without my usual distractions or the availability of healing connections, I became angry at my friends and coworkers, convinced they all had it easier than I did. After all, they were not sick, or they were living with other people, or had patients they were able to help; they were not, to my mind at the time, sitting at home feeling ineffectual and alone. They stopped being whole people with separate needs and just became a collective "bad breast"; I was regressing hard.

I was experiencing what Klein described as a reactivation of a depressive position from infancy; the loss of emotional connection to friends in the external world had me fantasizing that all of my good objects were gone, and the bad ones that left me feeling unsatisfied were now dominant. It led to the part of mourning involving intense, primitive feelings of guilt, persecution, and punishment, as well as projected feelings of hatred toward what I had lost (Baker 2001). Between ending my relationship and losing the hope for what it could have become, and the now-muted connections with my MSW students (and the sense of legacy it had given me), my doctoral cohort, my work, my friends—even just seeing another human being in person at all—I had lost so much of what energized and defined me, what had propelled me toward a future where I could see myself being happy and fulfilled. These connections usually served as a death-denying buffer from my own latent mortality anxiety (Liecthy 2000), now leaving me vulnerable to existential angst in all realms.

Eventually this anger turned inward, and I became withdrawn, grieving, and questioning my life choices. I felt guilty because I was safe, and judged myself because of how narcissistically the pain was landing for me; most of the time, I was more upset about being alone and unable to help anyone on the front lines than about the refrigerator trucks full of dead bodies up the road and the hospital tents in Central Park. I had the privilege of working from home, access to medical care and food, and no one else's care to manage; who was I to be this upset? I talked to my students about Maslow's Hierarchy of Needs, and how threats to your own safety and attachment come before anything else, reminding them that they should be gentle with themselves as they tried to meet the more self-actualized demands of school. I knew this, yet I could not offer myself the same grace.

The pain felt old, deep, and familiar. As I was unable to validate what I had lost, and lacked a foreseeable endpoint to the crises and a well-resourced social circle, my losses were psychologically ambiguous, a relational phenomenon that denied me resolution (Boss 2016). My grief festered, its tentacles extending to long-dormant pockets of depression and trauma. With those old pockets now at the forefront and energized with new grief and fear, my suffering felt global, internal, and permanent. I upped my now-Zoom therapy to twice a week—and worried about overwhelming my therapist with my pain when she surely must be reeling, too. My therapist, my friends, my students, their patients, and me—we were all experiencing a collective, shared trauma with no clear endpoint, and the usual protective boundaries that dictated our relationships became fluid. None of us likely had time to fully articulate our own traumas before returning to our respective work (Tosone 2020).

A month into quarantine, as I prepared to defend my doctoral work over Zoom, I worried that I would feel particularly alone, missing the connection of the cohort and friends and family with whom to share the experience. My colleagues who defended their work before I did had their loved ones present when they finished—partners and children and parents with whom they shared their daily lives, a stark contrast to the post-break-up loneliness and social isolation I was experiencing. It was hard not to compare myself to them; the destructive fantasies of my loss were overwhelming (Baker 2001). They posted pictures on Facebook of family celebrations and cute videos of people supporting them. I pictured giving my presentation, being anointed "doctor" by my beloved mentor, then shutting off my computer, continuing to sit alone in the room I had been sitting in for 2 months, and celebrating with my cats and some text messages.

I overcompensated for this fear of being alone, and ended up having 50 of my friends, former students, and colleagues joining my Zoom defense, far more than anyone else in my cohort. I leaned heavily into attempting to restore my internal relational object-states (Baker 2001; Stroebe and Schut 2010). On the day of my presentation, I looked out over the sea of faces of people who loved and supported me so deeply, enough to show up and listen to me talk for an hour about death anxiety during a pandemic. I became a doctor. And then I closed my laptop and cried, for hours, miserable and despondent (Briggs and Fronek 2019). And slept. The dissonance between what I saw onscreen and what I felt inside was too much to take in. I had gone through the motions of restoring coherence to my emotional connections, but was still protesting the reality of my losses and anxiously avoiding them (Strobe and Schut 2010).

With the end of school came the abrupt end of my purpose-driven forward momentum, at a time when my social connections were in flux. As the weeks went on, I realized how many of the things I was teaching my students about grief were resonating for me now. We talked about demoralization as the loss of purpose and meaning (Briggs and Fronek 2019), an evolutionary extension of the ways in which our social connections and accomplishments make us feel less vulnerable to inevitable annihilation (Liechty 2000). We discussed psychic numbing as a self-protective response to existential experiences of loss (among other things), and how it takes over your whole emotional being (Liechty 2000). "Humans find ways to cope with the pain of unmet needs and unprocessed feelings," I told them. "No one can hold on to that pain for very long before they turn it into something else."

I also shared with them what I had learned about self-care from my years working in hospice and palliative care, understanding it as an active practice to figure out what you need to do in order to both give and receive love, not just something nice you do for yourself after a long day. I talked to them about one of my favorite articles about self-care, which posits a need for playfulness, to go toward something solely for the joy of going toward it (Continuum Collective 2017). I explained to my students that even sharing funny memes on the Internet can be a legitimate form of self-care, an antidote to psychic numbing (Liechty 2000).

In that moment in class, talking to my students about their self-care and love, my own dissonance suddenly disappeared, and I realized: I could not take in love, not in the way I was used to. It was too painful to acknowledge a need for human connection, purpose, and social interaction; to tolerate my own projected rage at and jealousy of my friends; and to take in the loss of my relationship and sense of purpose as a student (Briggs and Fronek 2019). So, to keep my friends in my life and to keep myself going at all, I stopped feeling the full impact of it (Stroebe and Schut 2010). And then, when something wonderful did happen, and 50 people showed up to support me during the culmination of my years of doctoral training, the enormity of what I *wasn't* feeling weighed heavily.

I was still adjusting to that realization when I went for COVID-19 antibody testing about a month after my doctoral defense. When the phlebotomist was feeling around my arm for a suitable vein and tying a rubber tourniquet around my bicep, something else shifted inside. I found myself fighting the urge to hug her. Wishing I could prolong the physical encounter, I tried not to ask her to check my other arm for suitable veins, too. I was beginning to repair my lost good objects, seeking and wanting comfort and connection (Baker 2001). It was the closest I had been to another human being, and the most I had been touched, in over 2 months. I laughed at the absurdity of wanting another needle in my arm, and joked with my friends about whether I had to buy her a drink now, given our newfound physical intimacy. I was finally able, at least for a moment, to tolerate the uncertainty of my connections (Boss 2016) and abandon my infant depressive position, believing that my good, satisfying objects could be found again (Baker 2001).

It was in that moment of joking and laughter that I felt a spark of what I had been missing during those months; the edges of the numbing started to lift, just a little, and I went toward the joy (Continuum Collective 2017).

References

Baker, J. (2001). Mourning and the transformation of object relationships. *Psychoanalytic Psychology, 18*, 55–73.

Boss, P. (2016). The context and process of theory development: The story of ambiguous loss. *Journal of Family Theory and Review, 8*(3), 269–286. https://doi.org/10.1111/jftr.12152.

Briggs, L., & Fronek, P. (2019). Incorporating demoralization into social work practice. *Social Work, 64*(2), 157–164.

Continuum Collective. (2017). Retrieved from: https://www.continuumcollective.org/blog/2017/3/7/5-self-care-strategies-that-arent-fucking-mani-pedis.

Liechty, D. (2000). Touching mortality, touching strength: Clinical work with dying patients. *Journal of Religion and Health, 39*(3), 247–258.

Stroebe, M., & Schut, H. (2010). The dual process model of coping with bereavement: A decade on. *Omega-Journal of Death and Dying, 61*(4), 273–289.

Tosone, C. (2020). Shared trauma and social work practice in communal disasters. In J. Duffy, J. Campbell, & C. Tosone (Eds.), *International perspectives on social work and political conflict* (pp. 50–64). New York: Routledge.

Tosone, C., Nuttman-Shwartz, O., & Stephens, T. (2012). Shared trauma: When the professional is personal. *Clinical Social Work Journal, 40*(2), 231–239.

Chapter 36
Shared Trauma: Group Reflections on the COVID-19 Pandemic

Carol Tosone, Evelyn Solomon, Raquel Barry, Elisha Beinart, Kathryn K. Bellas, Emily Carlotte Blaker, Natalie Capasse, Moorea Diane Colby, Martha Corcoran, Amanda Delaney, Kylee Doyle, Stacie Elfo, Tyler-Ann Patricia Gilzene, Armina Kadriovski, Ray Kim, Madison Lavoie, Robin Lempel, Carly Iliza Linn, Catherine Yin Heung Liu, Kelly Felix Machado, Jennifer Maldonado, Alaphia Robinson, Alicia Denise Ross, Valerie Russell, Alexandra Skinder, and Zhaojie Wei

It's déjà vu. One year shy of two decades ago, my students and I were about to begin the first day of class when a plane hit the north tower of the World Trade Center. Needless to say, no class took place on that day, and no *normal* classes ensued for the remainder of the semester. Instead, as a class dedicated to group work intervention, we wrote about and processed our personal and professional reflections and had the opportunity to incorporate meaningful literature into the discourse, resulting in a published article, "Shared Trauma: Group Reflections on the September 11th Disaster" (Tosone et al. 2003). The experience was scholarly, therapeutic, and resilience-building, giving all involved the opportunity to consider the magnitude of the collective trauma that had just imploded on our lives. As the oft expression goes, "never forget 9/11," and we didn't; it was an indelible, defining moment in our individual and collective lives.

While catastrophic and having aftereffects to this day, 9/11 was a single traumatic event, witnessed directly by thousands, not millions or even billions. By contrast, the COVID-19 global pandemic has touched every country on the planet with the exception of Antarctica and a handful of little-known countries (World Health Organization 2020). Cases worldwide are 23 million and counting, with a staggering death rate of 3.5%; and at the time of this writing, the United States (US) accounts for approximately one quarter of the cases and deaths proportionally

C. Tosone (✉) · E. Solomon · R. Barry · E. Beinart · K. K. Bellas · E. C. Blaker · N. Capasse · M. D. Colby · M. Corcoran · A. Delaney · K. Doyle · S. Elfo · T.-A. P. Gilzene · A. Kadriovski · R. Kim · M. Lavoie · R. Lempel · C. I. Linn · C. Y. H. Liu · K. F. Machado · J. Maldonado · A. Robinson · A. D. Ross · V. Russell · A. Skinder · Z. Wei
Silver School of Social Work, New York University, New York, NY, USA
e-mail: ct2@nyu.edu

© The Author(s), under exclusive license to Springer Nature Switzerland AG 2021
C. Tosone (ed.), *Shared Trauma, Shared Resilience During a Pandemic*,
Essential Clinical Social Work Series,
https://doi.org/10.1007/978-3-030-61442-3_36

347

(World Health Organization 2020). Once again, I am teaching an MSW class when a collective trauma occurs, but this time it is midsemester and an elective course on trauma. This class experience is eerily similar to 9/11, yet the COVID-19 pandemic has no benchmark, no global reach from which to compare. I can state with confidence that no one reading this essay remembers the Spanish flu from direct experience.

Everyone has a 9/11 narrative; that is, we can all recite where we were and who we were with when we heard the news. Yet what is the defining moment of the coronavirus pandemic, an ongoing global trauma with negative societal and economic consequences, and, without a viable vaccine, no known cure or end date in sight? The trauma course is designed to have a strong experiential component in that students have the opportunity to learn directly from survivors of sexual abuse and mass violence and to visit the 9/11 memorial. When classes moved abruptly to a Zoom platform, the students and I were experiencing the uncertainty, fears, and trauma of the pandemic first hand, not as an academic exercise. Police and ambulance sirens could be heard in the background of every class. And as with the group class, students were given the option of writing a collaborative paper on their experiences and responded to questions they designed together with references to the professional literature. This paper describes the personal and professional reflections of MSW students about to graduate into a world of social distancing, face masks, and tenuous employment opportunities.

When describing their personal situations and living arrangements, some students remained in New York City alone, with families, or roommates, while others left the city to move back with their families of origin. A student who stayed in New York "developed a strange pride over not abandoning the city I love…my heart swells every night when I drop what I am doing at 7 PM to cheer for our essential workers. Seeing our city come together has been immeasurably rewarding." Other students described it as a "privilege" to be able to "escape" the city, and what was originally planned as a spring break visit for some became a semipermanent solution to the pandemic. Choosing to move back in with one's parents could be for comfort, practical advantages, or both as one student noted: "Mental illness played a role in my choice because I was worried about my symptoms increasing during this period of isolating. So to keep my mind in the present and safe, I decided to surround myself around people by staying with family." Another student recently moved in with her partner in an effort to be more independent from her family but acknowledged the ambivalence that this decision held: "Without this pandemic, I would not have felt as compelled to reach out to my parents as often, as I am working on co-dependence and setting boundaries… the fact that I am not able to see my parents has created more fear and dependence on them for that feeling of security."

The decision on whether to return home depended on financial necessity and the nature of existing family relationships. As one student acknowledged: "The most challenging part of going home was my personal regression to my teenage self as I navigated the new terrain of a post-COVID-19 world." Some students found it difficult to maintain an identity as a graduate student and intern when returning to their childhood home. As Nuttman-Shwartz and Dekel (2009) assert in their discussion of social work students' experience of shared traumatic reality, relocation, especially when forced by circumstances, can be stressful and traumatic in itself. Other students noted pre-existing anxiety and other issues that were exacerbated by the return to their childhood home: "We were unable to leave the house, use the car, and were rationing food. As someone with a history of body image difficulties and eating disorder tendencies, this was incredibly triggering for me." For students who lost part-time jobs due to the pandemic requiring a return home, they describe feelings of "loss of independence," "social deprivation," and the need to "create space" within the family home. Some, however, relished the opportunity to "reinvest" in family relationships that social quarantining demanded, even when it involved renegotiating parent-child and sibling relationships. Parenthetically, students did not report themselves or loved ones contracting COVID-19 but did know or hear of persons who developed or died of the virus.

Home held special meaning, whether as a haven for some or as a place no longer safe. As a student poignantly observed, "I have experienced a loss of safety. Nothing feels safe to touch anymore, even within your own home." Other unique challenges that the COVID-19 pandemic presented were not being able to rely on previous coping mechanisms, such as exercise and socialization, and as a result, experiencing "unmanageable levels of anxiety" and "struggling to complete simple tasks and maintain daily routines." Boredom was also considered problematic for some as it could lead to ruminations about the pandemic, a return to bad habits such as overeating and watching too much television.

While television and social media kept everyone updated and decreased isolation, it also served as a source of trauma, especially when someone was in the midst of other personal crises. One student articulated the experience as "The steady stream of images and news headlines capturing the frontline trauma and human loss – refrigerator trucks lined up outside of hospitals, the digging of a mass grave, screengrabs of final texts sent from those dying. Most challenging for me and for many others – that the pandemic isn't the only crisis in our lives." Another student cited the work of Bessel van der Kolk (2015), noting that we go through a fight, flight, or freeze reaction when in crisis or traumatic situations. When we freeze, we are immobilized, and our stress hormones remain high, allowing our fear, anxiety, depression, and anger to continue unmitigated, thereby increasing the likelihood of poor physical and mental health outcomes. In regard to the COVID-19 crisis, van der Kolk (2020) further observed that quarantining forces us to be somewhat immobilized. This student concluded her comments with "I think I froze hard."

Social media was described as both "a blessing and a curse" as it allows for connection but can also intensify negative emotions. In describing the coverage of COVID-19 on social media, one student acknowledged that it has "increased my distrust and anger towards people I don't even know personally." Another student observed "an abundance of fearful headlines, fearful images, panic, stress, and loneliness" on social media; she most feared the spread of false information. In fact, social media use has skyrocketed in recent months, with 55% of Americans polled reporting social media as their primary means for obtaining news (Eady 2020). Whereas social media was previously a source of "relaxation" and "escapism," it was now reported to be a source of "stress." One student adopted the approach of Tedeschi and Blevins (2015) by mindfully attending to the thoughts and emotions induced by traumatic exposure to social media content in order to reduce intrusive and negative thinking. Intentional reflection shifts unwanted negative thinking into a way to organize information and appraise the situation with some degree of emotional distance. She found that by exercising this skill, she was "able to stay informed with some control."

Social isolation has been a core challenge, even for those living with partners and parents. Students were mindful of the negative effects of isolation and loneliness, noting their correlation with depression, poor cognitive functioning, and worsened physical health (Smith and Victor 2018; Leigh-Hunt et al. 2017). The collective struggle of the pandemic and need to self-quarantine, along with the transition to remote learning and teletherapy shared with fellow students, has paradoxically helped to decrease individual feelings of isolation and loneliness. One student described isolation's silver lining: "Isolation is empowering in some ways, in that the more isolated I am, the more I know I am doing my part to help stop the spread [of COVID-19], which provides me with a small bit of agency in the overall situation." Others coped with isolation through spirituality, personal therapy, connection to loved ones via Zoom and other platforms, as well as engaging in established hobbies and learning new ones, such as cooking, art projects, and anything else deemed as "self-care." Pets, especially dogs, provided comfort and companionship for those living alone, an experience consistent with the literature on the importance of the human-animal bond for mental health (Compitus 2019).

School served as a stabilizing force for some, while for others, the loss of in-person connection to clients was a source of guilt and frustration. "It has been tough to cope with the knowledge that I broke my bond with my clients by leaving so abruptly," a sentiment echoed in the literature on forced termination (Siebold 1991). Other students emphasized the multiple losses – face-to-face client work, in-person classes, no graduation, and being "challenged by the unknown of tomorrow." During times of trauma, it is necessary to provide stability and normalcy to contend with the possible loss of hope and dreams (Walsh 2007; Straussner and Calnan 2014), so "maintaining personal routines and continuing with school work and internship feel like forms of self-care."

Indeed, helping others was viewed by some as a form of self-care: "I have found that the hours that I am in session with clients are those when I feel most centered." Citing the work of Pooler et al. 2013, one student spoke of the joy that social workers derive from relationships, both personal and professional: "I find that within the social work profession, my ability to help others and make a difference in others' lives gives me great joy and a sense of pride. Helping others helps me find purpose within my life as well. The belief that I may change somebody's life for the better inspires me, and I believe it also helps the greater society at large." Similarly, another student expressed the sentiment that it "grounded" her and gave her "purpose – the human connection and daily routine. Being of service helps me stay motivated and present in the world, attuned to others and myself. It's the purpose that gets me out of bed in the morning." Still, another student noted the opportunity for mutual reparation and shared resilience (Nuttman-Shwartz 2015) in the clinical encounter: "Helping others helps us gain connection in this time where everyone is struggling to feel connected to others. It shows us the strength of humanity through the strength shown by our clients." Therapeutic intimacy and increased self-disclosure are part of the experience for many and are consistent with other MSW student experiences of shared trauma, including 9/11 (Tosone 2006). Students reported using self-disclosure judiciously and mindfully. One student found self-disclosure essential during the pandemic, stating "I found myself showing my humanity, expressing statements such as, 'Things are extremely chaotic and I can relate with the struggle of adjusting to this new normal every day like you.' I was modeling how to lean into the range of feelings that have arisen and find coping strategies."

The intertwining of personal and professional boundaries was evident as some students noted the need to validate one's feelings first as an individual and then as a therapist; taking care of ourselves leaves us in a better position to help others. In fact, some students referred to it as a "responsibility" to take care of ourselves as we do our clients. Willis and Molina (2019) describe self-care as a way to show responsibility to clients, colleagues, and the broader society.

Making room for joy and sensory pleasure is an essential component of self-care (Knight 2013) as described vividly by one student: "When I went to walk on the beach… I imagined that I was stealing sunshine, absorbing the rays as they hit my face. I basked in what felt like novel luxuries of sun, fresh air, and sandy toes. It was a practice in not abandoning myself."

Altruism is inherent in the process of helping others and provides the giver with psychosocial benefits, including a sense of mattering to their community (Poulin et al. 2013). Although students were writing prior to the senseless and brutal murder of George Floyd and the Black Lives Matter response, the importance of community intervention and the discrimination faced by their Black and brown clients were emphasized by most students. The COVID-19 pandemic drew attention to the racism pandemic in that institutional racism and the disparities in health care for Blacks and Latinxs were near impossible to ignore. Students wrote passionately about the need for systemic change: "It is essential to take this crisis and use it to change the systems that oppress the people of color within our country. Systemic racism and bias against people of color have been an issue within the healthcare system far prior to the COVID-19 pandemic… COVID-19 has only shined a light on a blip of time." Another student writing about essential workers made similar observations: "The current public health crisis has only shone a light on these problems that were already there, including the fact that many of our underpaid and undervalued essential workers, who are putting their lives on the line, are low income and people of color… Poverty and racism are creating disparities between who works and stays home and who lives and who dies. We see how little we value essential workers rather than treating them with dignity." Students also observed the significant impact on the homeless and incarcerated, many of whom are persons of color.

Students of color reported experiencing discrimination and had concerns about securing employment in the near future, as did many students. For them, the coronavirus pandemic brought into sharp relief the deep-rooted institutional racism and the need for social workers to focus on remedying social injustice and fostering permanent social change. "The social work role as gatekeeper will be transformed" asserted one student, adding that "activism is needed to challenge these systemic issues." Students also addressed the need for changes in social work education, including the need for awareness of culturally informed interventions that facilitate community connectedness to heal from collective trauma (Schultz et al. 2016). Students also recognized the need for cultural humility (Fisher-Borne et al. 2015), that is, the need to accept that there is no way to fully understand the culture of another and the need to be mindful of the biases that affect our work with clients.

In conclusion, we are learning valuable lessons from the COVID-19 pandemic. It has underscored the importance of relationships, both personal and professional. It has taught us the value of self-care and how our own emotional responses impact our work with clients. COVID-19 has the potential to prepare us to live in a "world of shared trauma." It has reminded us to not lose sight of social work's core values and illuminated the continued need for social workers to be on the front lines of the fight for social justice and equality. The COVID-19 pandemic reminds us that we are all connected as individuals and as communities and that the reactions and emotions we see in clients may be reflected in ourselves. Lastly, it invites us to "show ourselves the same level of compassion and grace we show our clients."

References

Compitus, K. (2019). Traumatic pet loss and the integration of attachment-based animal assisted therapy. *Journal of Psychotherapy Integration, 29*(2), 119–131.

Eady, L. (2020, April 8). COVID-19's effects on social media. *The Horizon.* https://horizon.westmont.edu/1971/news/covid-19s-effects-on-social-media/

Fisher-Borne, M., Cain, J. M., & Martin, S. L. (2015). From mastery to accountability: Cultural humility as an alternative to cultural competence. *Social Work Education, 34*(2), 165–181.

Knight, C. (2013). Indirect trauma: Implications for self-care, supervision, the organization, and the academic institution. *The Clinical Supervisor, 32*(2), 224–243.

Leigh-Hunt, N., Bagguley, D., Bash, K., Turner, V., Turnbull, S., Valtorta, N., & Caan, W. (2017). An overview of systematic reviews on the public health consequences of social isolation and loneliness. *Public Health, 152,* 157–171.

Nuttman-Shwartz, O. (2015). Shared resilience in a traumatic reality: A new concept for trauma workers exposed personally and professionally to collective disaster. *Trauma, Violence, & Abuse, 16*(4), 466–475.

Nuttman-Shwartz, O., & Dekel, R. (2009). Challenges for students working in a shared traumatic reality. *British Journal of Social Work, 39*(3), 522–538.

Pooler, D., Wolfer, T., & Freeman, M. (2013). Finding joy in social work: Intrapersonal sources. *Families in Society: The Journal of Contemporary Social Services, 95*(1), 34–42.

Poulin, M. J., Brown, S. L., Dillard, A. J., & Smith, D. M. (2013). Giving to others and the association between stress and mortality. *American Journal of Public Health, 103*(9), 1649–1655.

Schultz, K., Cattaneo, L. B., Sabina, C., Brunner, L., Jackson, S., & Serrata, J. V. (2016). Key roles of community connectedness in healing from trauma. *Psychology of Violence, 6*(1), 42.

Siebold, C. (1991). Termination: When the therapist leaves. *Clinical Social Work Journal, 19*(2), 191–204.

Smith, K. J., & Victor, C. (2018). Typologies of loneliness, living alone and social isolation, and their associations with physical and mental health. *Ageing and Society, 39*(8), 1709–1730.

Straussner, S. L. A., & Calnan, A. (2014). Trauma through the life cycle: A review of current literature. *Clinical Social Work Journal, 42*(4), 323–335.

Tedeschi, R. G., & Blevins, C. L. (2015). From mindfulness to meaning: Implications for the theory of posttraumatic growth. *Psychological Inquiry, 26*(4), 373–376.

Tosone, C. (2006). Therapeutic intimacy: A post-9/11 perspective. *Smith College Studies in Social Work, 76*(4), 89–98.

Tosone, C., Lee, M., Bialkin, L., Martinez, A., Campbell, M., Martinez, M. M., et al. (2003). Shared trauma: Group reflections on the September 11th disaster. *Psychoanalytic Social Work, 10*(1), 57–77.

Van der Kolk, B. A. (2015). *The body keeps the score: Brain, mind, and body in the healing of trauma.* Penguin Books.

Van der Kolk, B. A. (2020). *Steering ourselves through new and developing traumas* [Livestream webcast]. Retrieved from https://catalog.pesi.com/sq/bh_001345_body_keeps_the_score_free-video_email_sq-119908?utm_medium=email&utm_source=sp&utm_campaign=040320_bh_c_rt_Bessel_BodyKeepsScore_FREEWebcast_9am_throttled&spMailingID=32100886&spUserID=MzA2MjMzMTY2ODM3S0&spJobID=1683104686&spReportId=MTY4MzEwNDY4NgS2

Walsh, F. (2007). Traumatic loss and major disasters: Strengthening family and community resilience. *Family Process, 46*(2), 207–227.

Willis, N. G., & Molina, V. (2019). Self-care and the social worker: Taking our place in the code. *Social Work, 64*(1), 83–86.

World Health Organization. (2020, August 24). *WHO COVID-19 global data [Data set].* WHO Coronavirus Disease (COVID-19) Dashboard. https://covid19.who.int/table

Part VI
Clinician Self-Care During the COVID-19 Pandemic

Chapter 37
The COVID-19 Self-Care Survival Guide: A Framework for Clinicians to Categorize and Utilize Self-Care Strategies and Practices

Julian Cohen-Serrins

The COVID-19 pandemic has created a crisis that is unprecedented in both presentation and spread. It has created a global tragedy perpetuating illness, death, and economic disarray. Currently, the pandemic has killed over 800,000 people worldwide (Johns Hopkins University Coronavirus Resource Center 2020) while millions more are hospitalized and suffering (COVID-19 Hospitalizations 2020). Clinicians on the front line treating those affected by COVID-19 are battling the virus's lethal effects on their clients and themselves. They confront daily their clients' suffering and death (along with their own fears of contracting the virus and spreading it to loved ones) in a work environment profoundly affected by limited revenue and resources. The overwhelming needs for services caused by this catastrophe renders it near impossible to initiate the vital process of creating organizationally rooted infrastructure needed to mentally and physically support their workers.

Instead, the best option is to create a guide for those who have limited resources to mitigate the profound occupational stress incurred from the COVID-19 pandemic, thereby benefitting from the implementation of their own self-care practices and strategies. Self-care is a flexible term used in a multitude of contexts. It is fundamentally a deliberate personal or professional action or strategy undertaken by an individual to reduce stress (Lee and Miller 2013). This guide seeks to provide self-care resources that are specifically actionable to individual clinicians affected by the pandemic. It excludes practices that conflict with CDC recommendations to avoid and prevent COVID-19 exposure and spread, such as those where maintaining social distance is not possible and those involving contact with frequently touched surfaces, indoor areas, and large crowds (implementing safety practices for critical infrastructure 2020). This guide cannot treat or eliminate the immense stress

J. Cohen-Serrins (✉)
Silver School of Social Work, New York University, New York, NY, USA
e-mail: jcs891@nyu.edu

© The Author(s), under exclusive license to Springer Nature Switzerland AG 2021
C. Tosone (ed.), *Shared Trauma, Shared Resilience During a Pandemic*,
Essential Clinical Social Work Series,
https://doi.org/10.1007/978-3-030-61442-3_37

incurred by the pandemic, nor is it meant to replace robust preventative and responsive organizational procedures to support workers (see Cohen-Serrins, Chap. 27, this volume). Instead, it represents a tertiary effort to categorize and define self-care strategies and practices for those in immediate need. The guide aims to be an accessible organized framework of self-care resources to be creatively and individually applied within the workplace by clinicians during the COVID-19 pandemic.

Prior to implementing these self-care measures, clinicians should assume a mindset focused on recognizing the sources and potential easing of their occupational stress. Clinicians, along with their administrators, need to critically examine their specific working conditions in order to combat its detrimental psychosocial and physical effects. This recognition may be a catalyst to help administration view employees not as capital or labor power, needing subsistence resources and maintenance to continue functioning, but with a humanistic lens valuing their need to be secure and supported in the workplace. The predominant view of clinicians is that they live to serve, requiring only enough gratitude to endure the shared traumatic effects of COVID-19 without additional resources (Palmieri 2017). However, clinicians need both structures and resources to persevere.

The application of self-care to meet such profound needs requires practice. While each of the techniques and strategies described may offer some immediate mitigating effects, research has shown that their continued use and refinement lead to a more significant and positive effect (Jha et al. 2010). This may be due to the effectiveness of self-care practices themselves, along with prioritizing self-care. Since adequate research regarding the optimal synthesis of these self-care concepts does not yet exist, it is recommended that this guide should be understood as a reference resource for clinicians to individually sample and thus refine, to meet their specific occupational circumstances and needs.

Areas of Self-Care

The structure of this guide intends to make self-care intuitive for clinicians practicing during the COVID-19 pandemic. There are three main self-care categories in this guide: mindfulness, setting boundaries, and finding enjoyable activities outside of work. The exploration of mindfulness contains three main sections: meditation, applied mindfulness practices, and the intersection of mindfulness and technology. The section on meditation aims to define meditation along with its benefits. Under the topic of applied mindfulness, this guide provides an exploration of mindful eating and mindfulness practices using one's surroundings. The three areas that encompass the intersection of mindfulness and technology are mindfulness applications (or apps), mindfulness on social media, and live virtual mindfulness groups. Following the discussion on mindfulness, this guide examines two structurally focused self-care practices that clinicians can establish individually that support their physical and psychological health: setting boundaries to promote self-care and allowing time for enjoyable activities outside of work. This guide provides a layout of useful self-care practices within the context of the COVID-19 pandemic and prioritizes a conceptual understanding of the resources available for clinicians.

Mindfulness Techniques

The most researched self-care practices are mindfulness techniques. Mindfulness is the practice of being authentically present and aware of the current moment (Spickard et al. 2002; Krasner et al. 2009). This awareness may include one's momentary surroundings, emotions, or physiology and endeavors to create a disposition less fixated on aspects of life that are unchangeable, specifically those in the past or future (Epstein 1999). Mindful actions represent the most direct and individualistic interventions for self-care as they rely upon reflective actions.

Additionally, their fit with the individualistic norms of capitalist-driven societies has allowed mindfulness techniques to become increasingly numerous and innovative (see Cohen-Serrins, Chap. 27, this volume). Today, mindfulness practices are used as an intervention for a myriad of psychosocial conditions, including occupational stress and combatting some elements in the sequelae of trauma (Muir and Keim-Malpass 2019; Ortiz and Sibinga 2017). The following mindfulness techniques are included based on their utility for clinicians specifically within the workplace.

Meditation

Meditation is considered the oldest spiritually rooted form of self-care with historical estimates suggesting that it may have emerged among Hindus as early as 1500 BCE and integrated into Buddhist practices in the eleventh century (Everly and Lating 2002). However, meditation does not require a religious affiliation, historical knowledge, or even a distinct philosophy. Rather, it requires four conditions: (1) a relatively quiet space; (2) a consistent and calming thought or sound; (3) a comfortable position; and (4) a passive mindset (Everly and Lating 2002). Once such conditions are satisfied, meditation requires one to sit still, think calming thoughts or listen to calming sounds, and take slow relaxing breaths.

Clinicians can be flexible in establishing these conditions. For example, a quiet space can be any space where the clinician will not be interrupted by loud noises. The consistent sound can simply be one's own breathing, and the comfortable position is entirely subjective (one can stand, sit, lean, lie down, or even walk). Therefore, meditation is a mindfulness strategy that can be practiced in most workplaces including a community clinic or hospital and be applied during one's personal life outside of the workplace. The straightforwardness and flexibility of meditation make it a tested and evidence-based stress reduction practice for clinicians (Burke and Hassett 2020). While meditation can be difficult to sustain, the benefits are numerous, extending beyond stress reduction to brain health and neuroplasticity

(Yang et al. 2019; Tang et al. 2019; Adluru et al. 2020). There is established and ongoing research in the neuroscience fields that explore the benefits of sustained meditation practice (Yang et al. 2019; Tang et al. 2019; Adluru et al. 2020). Additionally, as meditation has become highly popular, it also has the benefit of being a socially recognizable and accepted practice. The sight of one meditating is likely to be synonymous with clinicians coping rather than projecting their COVID-19-related work stress, allowing meditation to be a stigma-free self-care practice.

Applied Mindfulness Practices

Despite its reputation, mindfulness is not relegated to meditation, and as mindfulness has had a resurgence in popularity over the last 20 years (O'Donnell 2015), it has been applied in a plethora of creative ways, adapting to distinct environments and populations. As such, specific mindfulness practices have shown efficacy in the workplace, especially for mitigating occupational stress (Guidetti et al. 2019). As clinicians in the field today face the pandemic in both their personal and professional lives, it is necessary to emphasize some applied mindfulness practices that offer utility for practicing clinicians and have undergone peer review.

Mindful Eating One such practice is mindful eating or when one focuses their undivided attention to the process and sensations of what they are eating (Lyzwinski et al. 2019). This can include the texture, taste, smell, and the effect of the food on the body over time as one eats (Lyzwinski et al. 2019). Mindful eating is a slower process in order to provide an adequate time to gain a frame of mind conducive to mindful awareness. Additionally, it may be helpful to take small bites of food so as not to overwhelm one's senses or interfere with bodily responses. If done properly, mindful eating should provide an immersive and mindful experience to accompany nourishment.

Because eating engages all of our senses, it is an ideal activity to achieve the goal of mindfulness: the awareness of and focus on the present. Mindful eating exemplifies the type of practice beneficial to clinicians as it highlights that many do not take time during their workday to eat sufficiently. Since the COVID-19 pandemic has permeated and compromised all aspects of normal life, building these practices into something as basic as eating may be a feasible and intuitive method.

Mindfulness of Surroundings An equally accessible practice for clinicians involves using our surroundings as a vehicle to mindfulness. Using the perception of our surroundings as a mindfulness technique requires selecting an aspect of our environment that is largely static, such as an object or physical structure in the workplace, to perform a sensory- and detail-oriented examination of that object. For example, a hospital social worker could choose a noticeable part of their surroundings such as an emergency exit sign or a desk lamp. Once an object is selected, the clinician would deeply explore the object, including the colors of the object, its size, construction materials, illumination, sounds emitted, and moving parts. The goal of this exercise is to temporarily turn one's focus on to something in the current environment and away from past, current, and future sources of stress. During COVID-19 it is essential to perform this mindfulness exercise without engaging the sensation of touch. Although touch is crucial for our connection to the world, it is ill-advised to touch the object as public health agencies caution the avoidance of frequently touched surfaces (implementing safety practices for critical infrastructure 2020).

Mindfulness and Technology

The intersection of technology and mindfulness has been building in popularity well before the COVID-19 pandemic (Van Emmerik et al. 2020). Due to our increased reliance on technology during the pandemic, mindfulness technology has become an indispensable area for clinician-focused self-care practices. Using technological resources to facilitate mindfulness, such as mindfulness apps on a phone or tablet, pre-recorded YouTube videos, or live mindfulness classes on Zoom, that guide users through a variety of mindfulness practices may, on a surface level, seem counterintuitive because the use of technology is not consistently associated with health or wellness. However, when applied properly, technological innovations related to mindfulness provide the ability for clinicians to harness the expertise and wisdom of experts who otherwise would be inaccessible due to travel and in-person gathering restrictions during the pandemic. It also allows for such expertise and wisdom to be accessed immediately when needed and privately. Clinicians should use mindfulness technology in a space and time with an attitude that prioritizes self-care purposes.

Mindfulness Apps Perhaps the most researched mindfulness intervention is the use of mindfulness applications (or apps) due to their accessibility (Van Emmerik et al. 2020). Mindfulness apps can be accessed on several devices including a cell phone, computer, or a tablet and provide a guided practice or sequence of exercises to a consumer (Van Emmerik et al. 2020). These apps can provide guidance on meditation techniques and applied mindfulness practices with content tailored to the specific user. Typically, the apps involve audio guidance but may also include written instructions and imagery or be entirely text-based. Additionally, because these apps are delivered without the use of printed material, they provide both new and improved mindfulness practices.

A vast array of choices for mindfulness apps exists. While there are organizations providing mindfulness apps for a fee, such as the "Head Space" app, there are also a multitude of free apps available, including YouTube channels providing content. Although there is no preferred or optimal app for mindfulness, what should be sought is an app that facilitates an authentic experience. It is important to consider the type of mindfulness exercise employed, the length of time required, and its compatibility to a specific work environment. For example, while a spoken-guided 20-minute meditation accompanied by music may be enticing, it may not be feasible in a busy hospital ICU environment, whereas a 60-second meditative breathing exercise without audio is a more feasible option.

Mindfulness and Social Media Another venue to both practice and learn more about mindfulness is social media. There is, again, a vast amount of social media posts, accessible through nearly every social media platform. One can learn about mindfulness apps, new applied practices, theories, and even live events with experts. The only challenge to optimally harnessing social media is to ascertain what is beneficial for one's specific needs. For example, a Google search of the term "mindfulness practices at work" generates over 44 million results, an incomprehensible amount of information (Google's Mindfulness Practices at Work 2020a). The same search on LinkedIn yields 231000 results, still an enormous amount (LinkedIn Mindfulness at Work 2020b). Therefore, it may be advantageous to first develop a specific question regarding mindfulness and search for results on the social media platform that one is most comfortable using.

Another way to use this resource is to learn through social media who is producing app-based or virtual mindfulness content and what kinds of mindfulness content is available for specific audiences. Various platforms provide users with apps to consume or information to make them better consumers of mindfulness practices. According to the PEW Research Center, in 2019, 72% of adults in the United States use some type of social media (Demographics of Social Media Users and Adoption in the United States 2020). As mindfulness has grown in popularity, its overlap with the global pandemic will include a growing collection of resources for those interested in learning more about applying mindfulness and those seeking to add to their established routines.

Virtual Mindfulness Groups Although mindfulness is an individually facilitated practice, there are communities and organizations providing self-care resources in live virtual meetings. While social media can facilitate communication about mindfulness practices, due to face-to-face meeting restrictions from COVID-19, some venues and organizations may offer similar virtual classes online accessed globally. In fact, the pandemic may have accelerated the availability of virtual mindfulness groups and classes. These resources tend to require at least 30 min of undivided attention and access to an uninterrupted space. Clinicians who are isolated from their families and friends due to pandemic-related work, and who may be seeking a health-focused community experience, may benefit from this resource.

Setting Boundaries for Self-Care

Establishing proper boundaries may be a difficult endeavor during pandemic conditions, but its importance to clinicians cannot be overstated. The overwhelming number of people and communities afflicted may cause one's work to become relentless, complex, dangerous, and debilitating. These realities make boundary setting a potentially dystonic but indispensable step for clinicians to establish. Prior research indicates that all professionals require a balance between workplace autonomy and structure to thrive. In 1979, Dr. Robert Karasek's demand and control model sought specifically to define the proper qualities and amounts of autonomy and structure in order to facilitate employee wellness and success. Recent scholarship applying his model has emphasized the importance of moderating job demands such as clinician caseload (Jalilian et al. 2019; Brandtzæg et al. 2018). Adherence to Karasek's model is challenging under COVID-19 conditions. In the absence of organizationally produced infrastructure, establishing manageable boundaries such as a self-care practice to reduce the demands of and increase control over one's work is necessary.

The establishment of workplace boundaries can be segmented into two areas: working hours and post-working hours. During working hours for clinicians in certain environments, such as large clinics or hospitals, it becomes impossible to tightly regulate caseloads. Since COVID-19 has caused a dramatic spike in service needs, clinicians cannot be expected to limit their caseloads. However, there is legal precedent and established norms relating to taking breaks during the workday (Tippett 2018; Lim et al. 2016). During this time of acute stress, every clinician needs to establish a routine of taking a break, ideally a full reprieve from the work environment, in order to rejuvenate themselves psychologically (Sos and Melton 2020). Such breaks may be the best opportunity for clinicians to practice the self-care practices previously described. If enough clinicians were to establish this self-care practice as a part of their professional values, it may incentivize and normalize breaks for their co-workers and provide the foundation for future organizational policy discussions on promoting breaks during the workday.

Once a shift is complete, clinicians should ideally disengage from all workplace communications (Aranda and Baig 2018). This is especially pertinent during the pandemic. Disengagement requires that clinicians establish an emergency communication policy at their workplace and then actively choose not to engage with workplace activities including emails, contact from clients, and calls or texts from co-workers about work-related topics. Such stringent measures are an opportunity for clinicians to have enough physical and psychological rest to work though the exorbitantly stressful current working conditions. Clearly some clinicians may not fully have this ability, as they may be "on-call" or covering several roles outside of their job title. Nevertheless, it is still essential to emphasize the value of establishing individual workplace boundaries delineating time at work from time outside of the work environment.

Notably, the establishment of boundaries is the only self-care procedure that requires communication with other people. Clinicians should have the ability to frequently and easily communicate with co-workers. Although communication about boundaries with management and leadership are necessary to ensure that breaks are fully respected, it is also important to inform co-workers and supervisees about communication boundaries. Having these conversations at any level of an organization helps co-workers respect self-care practices and also may ease the initiation of other self-care practices and strategies.

Making Time for Self-Care

The final area of self-care for clinicians during the COVID-19 pandemic builds on the establishment of boundaries and involves finding safe and accessible outlets to release the physical and emotional energy caused by prolonged work in the current environment and renewal of energy for the next day. Such stress, if unmitigated, has been linked with increased emotional regulation issues, sleep disturbances, depression, and anxiety (Van der Klink et al. 2001). While the aforementioned self-care practices and strategies are in place to relieve stress, they are not meant to replace meaningful hobbies or activities that bring joy to an individual. Although some hobbies and activities are impossible due to restrictions during the pandemic, the foundation and enactment of enjoyable nonwork activities can be developed and can help to shift one's attention away from a stressful workplace and in turn elevate one's mood.

Included in the category of creating time for enjoyable and meaningful activities is allowing time for rest, as adequate sleep is a causal factor for replenishment of one's body and mind (James et al. 2017). Contemporary research on the area of workforce well-being among nurses places proper sleep hygiene and the allocation of adequate sleeping time as a principal element of any successful self-care routine (Allison 2007; Denyes et al. 2001). Indeed, without the balance of both engaging in pleasurable activities outside of work and an ample sleep schedule, self-care practices cannot meet the monumental challenges posed by the pandemic.

Although making time for hobbies and enjoyable activities is obviously a subjective task, there are two elements most likely to be beneficial. The first is to find activities or hobbies that are expressive, meaning, any activity where one feels that they can fully release their authentic cognitions and emotions. When in the workplace, clinicians are not often provided a time and space to be expressive and authentic. Seeking expressive activities provides a way to release the cognitive and emotional impacts of experiencing a shared trauma while simultaneously being required to perform a caretaking role with confidence and precision. Contemporaneous research undertaken during the COVID-19 pandemic has suggested that clinicians participating in expressive activities has a therapeutic effect, specifically in relation to elucidating the processing of and coping with traumatic events in the workplace (Reed et al. 2020).

The second element of a successful self-care-oriented hobby or meaningful activity is physical activity. Aside from the known benefits of physical activity, such as cardiovascular health, physical exercise is an excellent and important method for reducing the psychological aspects of stress (De Vries et al. 2017). Before the COVID-19 pandemic, the range of physical activities for clinicians were numerous. However, the pandemic necessitated that gyms, team sports, and any indoor activities be closed. Instead, self-care-focused physical activities include at-home workouts with an app or YouTube channel or outdoor activities that one can do individually such as running, biking, hiking, or swimming. While the chosen method of physical activity is variable, undertaking sustained physical exercise represents an ideal self-care activity for clinicians during their free time.

Conclusion

This guide defines categories of self-care practices and strategies (Table 37.1) pertinent for clinicians operating during the COVID-19 pandemic. While the range of resources listed are not exhaustive, the conceptual dissection of each type allows readers to understand the core elements of each category and apply them toward creating their own individually customized self-care routine. The execution of many detailed elements of each self-care action outlined depends on the clinician's individual occupational environment and resources. For example, if a clinician is deciding between performing a mindful eating exercise and an observational self-care exercise, the clinician's work environment and allocated free time during the workday will impact their decision. Rather than describing a strategy for each clinical environment, this guide challenges readers to commit to internalizing an awareness of self-care in their professional life and provides them with the logical tools to adapt accessible practices.

Although this guide presents preeminent and, hopefully, effective self-care resources to alleviate occupational stress on clinicians, they should not be adopted in lieu of organizationally structured approaches for mitigating the effects of shared trauma, occupational stress, and burnout. Indeed, the creation of this guide should be considered in the context that during the COVID-19 pandemic, it is unreasonable to expect historically overwhelmed organizations to adopt innovative and effective

Table 37.1 Summary of self-care categories

Mindfulness	Setting boundaries	Finding enjoyable activities outside of work
Meditation	Delineating time at work from time outside of the work environment	Making time for self-care
Applied mindfulness practices	Working hours	Enjoyable and meaningful activities
Mindful eating	Taking breaks	Expressive activities or hobbies
Mindfulness of one's surroundings		Physical activity
Mindfulness and technology	Post-working hours	Allowing time for rest
Mindfulness apps	Disengaging from all workplace communications	Proper sleep hygiene
Mindfulness and social media		Adequate sleep time
Virtual mindfulness groups		

organizational policies and practices to assuage occupationally induced mental health issues. Thus, providing a guide that can support clinicians during this time is both practical and ethical.

References

Adluru, N., Korponay, C. H., Norton, D. L., Goldman, R. I., & Davidson, R. J. (2020). BrainAGE and regional volumetric analysis of a Buddhist monk: A longitudinal MRI case study. *Neurocase, 26*(2), 79–90.

Allison, S. E. (2007). Self-care requirements for activity and rest: An Orem nursing focus. *Nursing Science Quarterly, 20*(1), 68–76.

Aranda, J. H., & Baig, S. (2018). Toward "JOMO" the joy of missing out and the freedom of disconnecting. In Proceedings of the 20th international conference on human-computer interaction with mobile devices and services. *Digital Memories and Emotions*, pp. 1–8.

Brandtzæg, P. B., Følstad, A., & Heim, J. (2018). Enjoyment: Lessons from Karasek. *Funology, 2*, 331–341. Springer.

Burke, A., & Hassett, S. (2020). Evaluating an instructional resource used for teaching and learning meditation: A pilot study. *Journal of Cognitive Enhancement*, 1–10.

CDC COVID-NET. (2020, August 15). *COVID-19 hospitalizations.* https://gis.cdc.gov/grasp/COVIDNet/COVID19_5.html

Centers for Disease Control and Prevention. (2020). *Implementing safety practices for critical infrastructure workers who may have had exposure to a person with suspected or confirmed COVID-19.* https://www.cdc.gov/coronavirus/2019-ncov/community/critical-workers/implementing-safety-practices.html

De Vries, J. D., Van Hooff, M. L., Geurts, S. A., & Kompier, M. A. (2017). Exercise to reduce work-related fatigue among employees: A randomized controlled trial. *Scandinavian Journal of Work, Environment & Health*, 337–349.

Denyes, M. J., Orem, D. E., & Bekel, G. (2001). Self-care: A foundational science. *Nursing Science Quarterly, 14*(1), 48–54.

Epstein, R. M. (1999). Mindful practice. *JAMA, 282*(9), 833–839.

Everly, G. S., & Lating, J. M. (2002). *A clinical guide to the treatment of the human stress response* (p. 131). New York: Kluwer Academic/Plenum.

Google Web Search. (2020a). *Google's mindfulness practices at work.* Retrieved August 26, 2020, from https://www.google.com/search?q="mindfulness practices at work"

Google Web Search. (2020b). *LinkedIn mindfulness practices at work.* Retrieved August 26, 2020, from https://www.google.com/search?q="LinkedIn mindfulness practices at work"

Guidetti, G., Viotti, S., Badagliacca, R., Colombo, L., & Converso, D. (2019). Can mindfulness mitigate the energy-depleting process and increase job resources to prevent burnout? A study on the mindfulness trait in the school context. *PLoS One, 14*(4), e0214935.

Jalilian, H., Shouroki, F. K., Azmoon, H., Rostamabadi, A., & Choobineh, A. (2019). Relationship between job stress and fatigue based on job demand-control-support model in hospital nurses. *International Journal of Preventive Medicine, 10.*

James, S. M., Honn, K. A., Gaddameedhi, S., & Van Dongen, H. P. (2017). Shift work: Disrupted circadian rhythms and sleep – Implications for health and well-being. *Current Sleep Medicine Reports, 3*(2), 104–112.

Jha, A. P., Stanley, E. A., Kiyonaga, A., Wong, L., & Gelfand, L. (2010). Examining the protective effects of mindfulness training on working memory capacity and affective experience. *Emotion, 10*(1), 54.

Johns Hopkins University. (2020). *Johns Hopkins University Coronavirus Resource Center.* Retrieved August 26, 2020 from https://coronavirus.jhu.edu/

Krasner, M. S., Epstein, R. M., Beckman, H., Suchman, A. L., Chapman, B., Mooney, C. J., & Quill, T. E. (2009). Association of an educational program in mindful communication with burnout, empathy, and attitudes among primary care physicians. *JAMA, 302*(12), 1284–1293.

Lee, J. J., & Miller, S. E. (2013). A self-care framework for social workers: Building a strong foundation for practice. *Families in Society, 94*(2), 96–103.

Lim, G. J., Mobasher, A., Bard, J. F., & Najjarbashi, A. (2016). Nurse scheduling with lunch break assignments in operating suites. *Operations Research for Health Care, 10*, 35–48.

Lyzwinski, L. N., Edirippulige, S., Caffery, L., & Bambling, M. (2019). Mindful eating mobile health apps: Review and appraisal. *JMIR Mental Health, 6*(8), e12820.

Muir, K. J., & Keim-Malpass, J. (2019). The emergency resiliency initiative: A pilot mindfulness intervention program. *Journal of Holistic Nursing*, 0898010119874971.

O'Donnell, A. (2015). Contemplative pedagogy and mindfulness: Developing creative attention in an age of distraction. *Journal of Philosophy of Education, 49*(2), 187–202.

Ortiz, R., & Sibinga, E. M. (2017). The role of mindfulness in reducing the adverse effects of childhood stress and trauma. *Children, 4*(3), 16.

Palmieri, E. T. (2017). *Safeguarding the counselor heart: Exploring the relationship between burnout, resilience and gratitude in clinical counselors*. Doctoral dissertation, The University of North Carolina at Charlotte.

PEW Research Center. (2020, June 5). *Demographics of social media users and adoption in the United States*. https://www.pewresearch.org/internet/fact-sheet/social-media/

Reed, K., Cochran, K. L., Edelblute, A., Manzanares, D., Sinn, H., Henry, M., & Moss, M. (2020). Creative arts therapy as a potential intervention to prevent burnout and build resilience in health care professionals. *AACN Advanced Critical Care, 31*(2), 179–190.

Sos, T., & Melton, B. (2020). Incorporating mindfulness into occupational stress management programming for nursing staff. *Workplace Health & Safety, 68*(4), 203–203.

Spickard, A., Jr., Gabbe, S. G., & Christensen, J. F. (2002). Mid-career burnout in generalist and specialist physicians. *JAMA, 288*(12), 1447–1450.

Tang, Y. Y., Tang, R., Rothbart, M. K., & Posner, M. I. (2019). Frontal theta activity and white matter plasticity following mindfulness meditation. *Current Opinion in Psychology, 28*, 294–297.

Tippett, E. C. (2018). How employers profit from digital wage theft under the FLSA. *American Business Law Journal, 55*(2), 315–401.

Van der Klink, J. J., Blonk, R. W., Schene, A. H., & Van Dijk, F. J. (2001). The benefits of interventions for work-related stress. *American Journal of Public Health, 91*(2), 270.

Van Emmerik, A. A., Keijzer, R., & Schoenmakers, T. M. (2020). Integrating mindfulness into a routine schedule: The role of Mobile-health mindfulness applications. In *Nutrition, fitness, and mindfulness* (pp. 217–222). Humana.

Yang, C. C., Barrós-Loscertales, A., Li, M., Pinazo, D., Borchardt, V., Ávila, C., & Walter, M. (2019). Alterations in brain structure and amplitude of low-frequency after 8 weeks of mindfulness meditation training in meditation-naïve subjects. *Scientific Reports, 9*(1), 1–10.

Index

A

Ableism, 157, 158, 160, 162, 207
Abolition social work
  praxis, 288
  values, 287
Absent without leave (AWOL), 251
Acceptance and Commitment Therapy
    (ACT), 99
Accomplishments, 111
Accountability, 62, 67
Achilles' heel, 43
Acknowledging trauma and loss
  ASAN, 160
  behavioral mechanisms, 160
  identity-affirmative coping strategies, 160
  importance, 160
  intersectional aspects, 160
  normality, 160
  SAMHSA, 160
  social and emotional experiences, 160
Acknowledgment, 159
Actual presence, 171
Adaptive coping skills, 119
Adaptive information processing (AIP), 238
Addiction, 103–105
Administration for Children and Families, 254
Administration for Children's Services
    (ACS), 249
Adolescents, 147, 149, 155
Advanced directives, 45
Adverse childhood experiences (ACEs), 282
Adverse mental health consequences, 158
Advocacy, 196

Ageism, 207, 209
Agency-based social workers, 139, 140
Agendas/schedules, 111
Age-related self-consciousness, 168
AIDS Coalition to Unleash Power
    (ACT UP), 128
Alcoholics Anonymous (AA), 18
Alienating parent (AP), 82, 84
Alienation, 34, 181
Altruism, 351
Alzheimer's and Dementia Center, 335
Alzheimer's disease, 335–337
American Psychiatric Association (APA), 282
American public, 167
American Red Cross disaster mental health
    team, 16
American social fabric, 158
Animal-assisted education, 216
Animal-assisted interventions, 195, 201
Animal-assisted therapy (AAT), 8
  educators and clinicians, 213
  health restrictions, 216
  micro-farm sanctuary, 214
  species, 214
  therapy animal, 215
  treatment modality, 215
  virtual environment, 215
  virtual format, 214
  virtual model, 216
Anorexia nervosa (AN), 94, 95
Anti-Blackness, 284, 286
Anticipatory anxiety, 72, 76
Anti-oppressive practices, 55

© The Author(s), under exclusive license to Springer Nature
Switzerland AG 2021
C. Tosone (ed.), *Shared Trauma, Shared Resilience During a Pandemic*,
Essential Clinical Social Work Series,
https://doi.org/10.1007/978-3-030-61442-3

Anti-oppressive social work practitioners, 157
Anxiety, 61, 168
Applied mindfulness practices
    mindful eating, 360
    occupational stress mitigation, 360
    surroundings perception, 360, 361
Asylum psychological evaluations, 316
Attachment, 216, 217
Attachment-based work, 300
Attachment-focused interventions, 292
Attachment theory, 296, 297
Auditory bilateral stimulation, 245
Autism spectrum disorder (ASD), 158, 159
Autistic people
    behavioral interventions, 160
    COVID-19 impacts, 158, 160, 161
    mental health needs, 158
    resilience, 161
    sense of loss, 160
    shared sense of humanity, 159
    social distancing, 159
    supports, 159
    trauma-informed clinical care, 160
    unconscious bias, 159
Autistic Self Advocacy Network (ASAN), 160
Auto-emancipation, 262

B
Basic anxiety
    definition, 181
    loneliness, 182
    shared trauma, 180
    vulnerability, 183
    wholeheartedness, 183
Basic wishes, 199
Bereavement, 341
Binge eating disorder (BED), 94, 97
Biophilia, 195, 198, 201
Biophilic design, 201
Black and Brown individuals, 168, 175
Black boys, 175
Black cisgender femme sex worker (BCFSW)
    arrests, 303
    fight against sex trafficking (see Fight
        against sex trafficking)
    outdoor providers, 304
    personal safety, 304
    street-level sex work demographic, 304
Black codes, 284
Black criminality post-chattel slavery, 283
Black experience, 281
Black female sex providers, 305
Black labor exploitation, 284

Black Lives Matter (BLM) movement, 154
    Black people, 282
    brutality, 283
    carceral systems, 284
    Civil Rights Act of 1965, 284
    education, 284
    former slaves, 283
    media, 283
    poverty, 284
    public torture, 283
    social work, 281
    trauma African people, 283
    white supremacy, 283
Black therapists, 310
Black trauma, 283
Body language, 171
Borderline personality disorder (BPD),
        220, 221
Boston Change Project, 171
Brief Resilient Coping Scale, 161
Bulimia nervosa (BN), 94
Bureau of Justice Statistics, 291
Burial arrangements, 199
Burnout
    awareness, 266
    designing and implementing reduction
        strategies, 264
    interventions, 264, 265
    organizational procedures, 265
    precipitators, 264
    pressing and detrimental issue, 260
    prevalence, 260
    psychosocial effects, 260
    reduction measures, 265, 266
    remedial approaches, 259
    self-care, 261
    social workers, 262
    supervisors, 265
Business associate agreement (BAA), 240

C
Cancer, 34
Carceral apparatus, 284
Carceral systems, 282
CARES Act, 254
Catharsis, 286
CBO school social work, 139
Center to Advance Palliative Care (CAPC), 28
Centers for Disease Control and Prevention
        (CDC), 6, 70, 129, 137, 315
Charter Management Network (CMO), 137
Charter schools, 136–138, 140, 142
Chattel slavery, 283, 289

Chief operating room (OR), 15
Child maltreatment, 83
Child protection policies, 251
Child welfare, 249–251
Children's trauma symptomatology, 298
Children–body relationship, 172
Chronic traumatization, 246
Circumvent anxiety, 182
Cisheteropatriarchy, 287
City Council of Minneapolis, 274
Civic engagement, 206
Civil Rights Act of 1965, 284
Clients uncertainties, 54
Climate insomuch, 46
Clinical social work, 167, 176
Clinical supervisors, 299
Clinical treatment models, 158
Clinicians
    clinical dynamics, 323
    and educators, 327
    frontline treating, 357
    group cohesion and resilience, 325
    personal reactions, 323
    professional boundaries, 324
    relationship, 324
    self-care/effective supervision, 324
    shared trauma, 324
    social work practice, 326
    support circles, 324
    teletherapy, 324
    traumatic event, 327
    uncharted territory, 323
Co-created therapeutic space, 191
Coercive control, 72
    abuser, 87
    acknowledge, 86
    aspects, 81
    constraint, 85
    COVID-19, 86–88
    definition, 80
    dominant pattern, 85
    impact on children, 79, 83
    IPV, 80
    PA (see Parental alienation (PA))
    PSA, 81, 88
    psychological and emotional abuse, 80
    witnesses and victims, 79
Collective trauma, 17, 34, 245
    characteristics, 168
    COVID-19, 72, 219
    definition, 72
    practice issues, 167
    shared trauma, 74
College-community partnerships, 336

Combat veterans
    activities of daily life, 115
    adaptive coping skills, 119
    biographical information, 115
    clinical self-disclosure, 122, 123
    disasters, 116
    maladaptive skills, 119
    moral injury, 121, 122
    organizational pressures, 123, 124
    pandemic crisis, 115
    posttraumatic growth, 116, 117
    posttraumatic stress disorder, 118, 119
    public health safety, 116
    resilience, 116, 117
    survivor guilt, 120, 121
    threat at home, 117, 118
    US veterans, 115
Communication skills, 66
Community-based organizations
        (CBOs), 136
Community-based programs, 65
Community connectedness, 352
Community gardening, 196, 198
Community organizations, 196
Community school model, 136, 142
Community trauma, 26, 141
Compassion fatigue, 40
Competence, 57
Complacency, 157
Complex posttraumatic stress disorder
        (C-PTSD)
    complex relationships, 237
    diagnostic nomenclature, 235
    EMDR, 235
    psychopathological symptoms, 235
    PTSD elements, 236
    relational trauma, 235
    risks, 240
    technological malfunctions, 246
    trauma-related symptoms, 236
Complex post-traumatic stress disorder
        (C-PTSD), 86, 88
Confidentiality violations, 64
Conscious behaviors, 42
Consensual sex work market, 303
Consultation team model, 230
Contemporaneous research, 364
Controlling behavior, 80
Conversations, 198
Convict leasing system, 283
Coping mechanisms, 349
Coronavirus, 5, 7–9, 341, 342
Council on Social Work Education (CSWE),
        196, 332

Counseling
  friendship, 190
  illness with COVID-19, 188
  motivation, 189
  sessions, 189
  therapeutic goals, 188
  therapeutic intimacy, 190
  therapeutic value, 190
  therapy, 188, 190
Countertransference reactions, 180, 323
COVID-19, 345
  acceptance, 103–105
  adaptive coping strategies, 103
  behavior, 102
  complex and multilayered response, 101
  coping mechanisms, 104
  crisis intervention, 142
  experience, 101
  harm reduction, 103, 105
  HIV/AIDS, 128, 131
  identical process, 101
  individual experience, 141
  maladaptive coping mechanisms, 103
  New York City, 127
  policies and practices, 103
  PTSD, 141
  public health approach, 103
  quarantine, 101, 102
  self-destructive behavior, 102, 104
  self-destructive compulsions, 103
  self-disclosure, 102, 105
  self-regulate and process emotions, 102
  shared trauma, 101
  sleep patterns, 101
  social media, 102
  treatment, 101, 104
  vulnerability, 104
Crisis intervention, 135, 136
Crisis management, 222
Critical care nurse, 16
Critical care units, 15
Culmination, 35, 36
Cultural dissonance, 16
Cultural humility, 352
Custodial commissary, 293
Cyber-Seniors, 209

D
DBT practitioner, 221
DBT treatment during COVID-19
  collaborative experience, 224
  consultation team, 230, 231
  HIPAA-compliant video platform, 224

  individual therapy, 224–226
  phone coaching, 228, 229
  skills training group, 226, 227
Dead on arrival (DOA), 17
Death, 341, 342, 344
Deathbed scene, 187
Debilitation, 44
Debrief, 18
Deep ecology, 195, 198, 201
Deep justice, 195
Deep-rooted institutional racism, 351
De-escalation tools, 62
Delineation, 189
Demoralization, 109
Department of Education (DOE), 136
Depersonalization, 260
Derealization, 213
Destabilization, 44
Diabetes, 55
Diagnostic and Statistical Manual of Mental
       Disorders (DSM-III), 282
Dialectical behavior therapy (DBT)
  aim/purpose, 220
  BPD, 220
  clinicians, 220, 231
  Cochrane Collaboration Review, 221
  consultation team, 223
  COVID-19, 220
  definition, 220
  individual therapy, 221, 222
  phone coaching, 223
  providers and patients, 231
  psychiatric community, 221
  skills training group, 222
  therapists, 232
  treatment during COVID-19 (see DBT
         treatment during COVID-19)
Didactic classroom material, 337
Direct approach, 28
Direct care workers, 252
Disaster 9/11, 347, 348, 351
Diseases, 55
Disorientation, 109
Disparities, 54
Disproportionate risk, 252, 253
Distress, 34
Distress tolerance, 222
DOE-based social workers, 139
DOE social workers, 137
Doffing, 16
Domestic violence, 87
  calls, 61
  COVID-19, 66
  organizations, 65

shelters, 64
supporting survivors, 61, 64
Domestic violence (DV)
feminist perspective, 70
homicides, 71
LGBTQ+ relationships, 70
psychological trauma, 72
recognized theories, 70
re-endanger, 72
reported incidents, 71
seeking help, 71
stay-at-home orders, 71
victims, 69
Domestic violence homicides, 81
Donning, 16
Dorm-style shelter arrangements, 54
Dorm-style shelter environments, 55
Doxy sessions, 168
DSM-5 definition, 40
Dysthymia, 215

E
Eating disorders (EDs)
ACT, 99
BED, 94
BN, 94
brain based, 94
CBT, 98
characterological traits, 96
clinical resiliency, 94
clinicians, 96–98
countertransference, 98
COVID-19, 93
diagnostic criteria, 96
eating-in-secret, 97
experiences, 98
physical diseases, 95
preliminary research, 97
professionals, 99
psychiatric comorbidity, 95
shared resiliency, 98
stocked cabinets, 97
suffering, 93
symptom-use, 95–96
therapeutic routes, 97
Ecological justice, 194
Ecological social work, 193
Ecological systems, 260
Ecosocial approach, 193
Ecosocial work
biophilia, 195
characteristics, 194
COVID-19 pandemic, 198–200

deep ecology, 195
facets, 194
nature connections, 197, 198
practices, 195–197
Educational programs, 29
Embodiment, 167, 171
EMDR sessions, 241
EMDRIA report, 244
EMDRIA task group, 244
EMDR-oriented therapy, 241
EMDR-RDI
affect tolerance, 239
aim, 238
clients access, 238
COVID-19, 239
definition, 238
interventions and exercises, 239
resources and protocols, 239
teletherapy, 236
treatment efficacy, 239
EMDR-trained therapists, 240, 241
Emotion regulation skills, 222
Emotional connection, 343
Emotional maltreatment, 86
Emotional reactivity, 237
Emotional responses, 62
Engagement, 56
Environmental justice, 194, 201
Environmental social work, 193
Erroneous assumption, 265
Essential workers, 54, 348
Etiological catalyst, 282, 285
Evidence-supported frameworks, 160
Experiential learning course, 337
External stressors, 292
External validation, 113
Eye movement desensitization and
reprocessing (EMDR)
AIP model, 238
C-PTSD, 235
mHealth applications, 239, 240
phases, 238
protocol centers, 238
psychotherapy modality, 236
RDI (see EMDR-RDI)
relational process, 240
resource development strategies, 238
technology, 239
TF-CBT, 237
trauma resolution approach, 237–238
traumatic experiences processing
tools, 237
V-EMDR (see Virtual EMDR (V-EMDR)
therapy)

Eye Movement Desensitization and
        Reprocessing (EMDR), 8
Eye on Ethics, 189

F
FaceTime calls, 168
Face-to-face encounters, 199
Faculty housing
    administrators, 206
    CDC guidelines, 207
    dry goods and toiletries, 208
    members, 205
    mental wellness, 208
    Volunteers and clients, 206
Fear of death, 190
Federal Communications Commission
        (FCC), 240
Federal programs, 205
Fight against sex trafficking
    Communications Decency Act of
        1996, 304
    pre-and current COVID-19, 304, 305
    Zoom platform, 306–307
Fight Online Sex Trafficking Act
        (FOSTA), 304
Financial necessity, 348
Financial stressors, 75
Flexibility, 47
Food and Drug Administration (FDA), 240
Food delivery, 97
Forest bathing, 196
Fresh air, 198
Friendship, 190, 191

G
Gas masks, 17
Gay Men's Health Crisis (GMHC), 128
Gay Related Immunodeficiency
        (GRID), 127
Gender-based violence, 71
General approaches, 28
George Floyd by Minneapolis police
        officers, 298
Gibbs' reflective cycle, 29
Global public health crisis, 299
Google forms, 139
Grade 12 education, 206
Green policies, 196
Green social work, 193
Grief, 341–344
Grocery workers, 19
Group meetings, 47

H
Hacking/hustling, 304
Hallway consultation, 230
Hand-delivered recruitment, 207
Harm reduction, 103
Health care and housing, 284
Healthcare professionals experience, 266
Healthcare sectors, 259
Healthcare workers, 18, 19, 260
    acute care, 21, 29
    agonizing situations, 28
    certainty and regularity, 25
    communication, 28
    compassion and distress, 25
    COVID-19, 21, 26
    high-stress environment works, 22
    interdisciplinary team, 23
    job satisfaction loss, 22
    MDA, 22 (*see also* Moral distress and
        moral anguish (MDA))
    mental health, 22
    mission-driven organizations, 25
    recovery and maintaining personal
        wellness, 28
    reflective model, 27
    self-care, 29
    self-determination, 28
    shared trauma, 26, 27
    struggles, 24
    virus pandemic, 28
Health Insurance Portability and
        Accountability Act
        (HIPAA), 240
Helplessness, 109
Hidden curriculum, 161
Hierarchical approach, 188
Higher education institutions, 325
HIPAA compliance, 58
HIPAA-compliant telecommunications, 240
HIV/AIDS
    anxiety, 131
    COVID lockdown, 131
    COVID-19 pandemics, 128, 129
    gay men, 127, 128
    history, 132
    LGBTQ community, 131
    memories, 131
    resilience, 130
    self-worth and helplessness, 131
    shared trauma, 131, 132
    violation of expectations, 129, 130
Holding environment approach
    actual and virtual, 172, 173
    archetype, 170

best practices, 146, 155
case of Alex, 148, 149
case of Jane, 147, 148
change and adaptation, 170
clinical staff, 145
consistency, 149, 150
educational instruction, 145
face-to-face treatment interventions, 146
feelings, 145, 146
flexibility and humor, 170
maternal preoccupation, 147
opportunities, 147
presence, 151, 152
psychodynamic approach, 146
psychological defense mechanism, 146
psychological dimension, 170
qualities, 147
reliability, 150
remote therapy, 152, 153
residential treatment settings, 145
rituals, 169
school social workers, 146
shared trauma, 153, 154, 170
social workers, 145
technological issues, 146
telehealth platform, 179
treatment approach, 146, 149
vocal matching, 151
Holding environment telehealth, 175
Holocaust survivor, 35, 335, 337
Hopelessness, 109
Hospital culture, 16
Hospital social work terminology, 187
Housing, 54, 55
Human-animal bond
brainstorming, 215
COVID-19, 214
powerful relational tool, 214
therapeutic benefits, 213, 214
Human-animal interactions, 216
Human-animal relationships, 195
Human commonality, 276
Human feelings and emotions, 276
Human spirituality
acknowledgment, 275
COVID-19 pandemic, 276
culture and traditions, 274
external recognition, 275
rationalizing thoughts and beliefs, 275
spiritual approach, 275
spiritual level, 275
spiritually oriented therapist, 275
traumatic events, 275
Hyper-incarceration, 291, 292

Hypertension, 55
Hypervigilance, 72, 237

I
ICE detention, 315
Illnesses, 69
Immigrant youth, 334
Immigration
asylum seekers, 313
attorneys, 318
detention centers, 315, 316
ethnicity, 317
Immigration and Customs Enforcement
(ICE), 315
Impaired social communication, 159
Impaired social interaction, 159
Implicit bias, 159
Imposter, 17, 113
Indirect approach, 28
Individual DBT therapy
apply and generalize skills, 221
assumptions, 221
goal, 221
pathology, 222
Individual's cultural environment, 180
Individualized Education Plans (IEPs), 136
Indoor sex providers, 303
Influencers, 19
Inner-city violence, 288
Innovative biophilic designs, 198
In-person connection loss, 350
In-person counseling, 192
In-person EMDR therapy, 245, 246
In-person sessions, 96
Insight-oriented psychotherapy, 43
Intensive care unit (ICU), 15, 23
Interactive environment, 337
International Association of Human-Animal
Interaction Organizations, 195
International consulting, 113
International Federation of Social Workers
(IFSW), 196
International medical graduates (IMGs), 42
Interpersonal effectiveness, 222
Intimate partner abuse, 61
Intimate partner violence (IPV), 70
attachment insecurity, 83
COVID-19, 85
delinquency, 83
experiences, 84
geography, 87
homicides, 81
impact, 79

Intimate partner violence (IPV) (*cont.*)
  isolation and quarantine, 85
  and mental health issues, 84
  physical and emotional, 84
  psychological abuse, 80
  rates and nature, 88
  situations, 80
  suicidal ideation, 84
  trauma, 86
  victims, 81, 87
Intimate terrorism, 72, 80
Intimate therapeutics, 174
Intrusive thoughts, 44
Isolation, 61, 198
Israeli bomb shelter, 17

J
Job losses, 75
  COVID-19 pandemic, 113
  fear/anxiety and trauma, 107
  impact, 107
  relationship loss, 109
Job offer, 113
Job placement assistance, 107
Job satisfaction, 255
Job-seeking, 108, 109, 112
Joy and sensory pleasure, 351
Judgmental support, 216

K
Karasek's model, 363
Karen Horney
  alienation, 182
  COVID-19 pandemic, 182
  defensive and unconscious solutions, 182
  person's development, 181
  relational theory and constructs, 180
  social work community, 180
  theory and ideas, 180
  wholeheartedness, 180
  Zen Buddhism principles, 183
Knowledge, 45

L
Laptop distribution program, 139
Latinx transgender individuals
  detention, 314, 317
  discrimination, 314
  immigration detention centers, 315
  Latin America's persecutory, 313
  minorities, 317

post-migration stressors, 316
  psychiatric symptoms, 314
  psychological evaluations, 314
  service delivery challenges, 314
Latinx transgender migrants
  contagion, 315
  mental health treatment, 314
  migration statuses, 317
  persecution, 315
  powerlessness and hopelessness, 318
  psychological/physical health
      concerns, 313
  safety concerns, 313
  sexual and gender minorities, 315
  trauma histories, 314
Latinx transgender women, 315, 317
Legislative barriers, 58
Lesbian, gay, bisexual, transgender, and queer
      (LGBTQ), 128
Lesbian, gay, transgender/two-spirited, queer,
      intersex, and asexual
      (LGBTQIA+), 313
LGBTQIA+-identified individuals, 315
LGBTQIA+-identified migrants, 314
Liberty crime, 80
Liceu Opera Barcelona, 197
Lockdown, 15, 66
Loneliness, 190, 213
Low-tech handholding, 18

M
Mail deliverers, 19
Maintaining contact, 66
Maladaptive skills, 119
Manhattan clinicians post-9/11, 75
Manipulation, 61
Man-made catastrophes, 69
Marginalization, 157
Marginalized communities, 194
Marginalized people, 281
Mass incarceration, 288
  jails and prisons, 285
  misnomer, 288
  prison industrial complex, 285
  racialized oppression, 285
  research and interventions center, 285
  social work, 285
  traumatic stress, 285
Maternal feeling, 47
Mayoral initiative, 55
MDA challenges
  caring human connection, 24
  feelings of isolation, 24

hospitalization, 25
medical team, 25
self-care, 25
self-determination and autonomy, 24
video discussions, 24
visitation policy, 24
Meaning-making
cliché, 35
clinical social worker, 34
distress and search, 35
inquiries, 34
life suffering and loss, 35
pandemic crisis, 35
resilience and sources, 33
Meditation, 359, 360
Mental health breakdown, 286
Mental health clinicians, 219
Mental health crisis, 158
Mental health practitioners, 299
Mental health professionals, 58, 196
Mental health symptoms, 139, 213
Mental illness, 348
Mental wellness, 208
Mezirow's transformative learning, 29
Micro-farm sanctuary, 214
Migration phases, 314
Military analogies, 17
Military culture, 16
Mind-body attunement, 245
Mindful eating, 360, 365
Mindfulness
applied mindfulness practices, 360–361
apps, 361, 362
awareness, 359
capitalist-driven societies, 359
intervention, 359
meditation, 359, 360
social media, 362
technology, 361
virtual groups, 362
Miss Fine philosophy, 29
Modifications, 44
Monitoring, 61
Moral distress and moral anguish (MDA)
COVID-19, 22–24
emotional responses, 22
health professions, 23
HWs, 21
value-laden standards, 22
Moral Distress Scale-Revised (MDS-R), 23
Moral injury, 45, 121, 122
Mortality and physical vulnerability, 168
Motion sickness, 200
Motivation, 189, 191

MSW students, 348
Multi-bed hospital rooms, 198
Multidimensional response, 219
Mutuality, 326, 328
My Next Guest (Book), 252

N
NASW Code of Ethics, 53, 58
National Association of Social Workers
(NASW), 53, 196
National Institute of Allergy and Infectious
Diseases, 129
National Network to End Domestic
Violence, 64
Natural world
artist's inspiration, 197
biophilia, 195
environmental issues, 198
green policies, 196
impacts, 194
intuition and spiritual experiences, 194
mental health professionals, 196
personal and professional growth, 201
physical environment, 193
social workers, 197
urban planners, 198
Neighbor to Neighbor Volunteer Corps (N2N)
conceptual framework, 206
Faculty Housing, 207
food resources, 208
goal, 206
health care, 207
mental wellness, 208
outcome and critique, 209
productive aging, 211
shared trauma/resilience, 210, 211
technology assistance, 208, 209
volunteer, 207
Neoliberalism, 262
Neophyte, 42
Neurobiological basis, 171
Neurodiversity, 158, 159
New Jersey Coalition to End Domestic
Violence, 71
New York City, 45, 136, 199, 209, 334
Non-ICU workers, 23
Noninstitutional and nonsectarian
organizations, 65
Nontraumatic memory, 190
Normalcy, 159, 215
Novel coronavirus (COVID-19)
death rate, 347
societal and economic consequences, 348

Novel coronavirus disease (COVID-19), 21
No-visitor policies, 26
NYC hospital, 17, 33
NYC public schools, 334

O
Oasis rooms, 18
Object relations, 344
Occupational stress
   clinicians, 365
   COVID-19, 259, 357
   depersonalization, 260
   forms, 261
   healthcare workers, 260
   interventions, 264, 265
   laissez faire approach, 263
   management, 263
   meditation, 261
   organizational changes, 264
   organizational resource deficiencies, 263
   resilience, 265
   self-care, 262, 266
Olson's Hospital Ethical Climate Survey
   (HECS-S), 23
Oncology, 33, 34
Online programming activities, 337
Oppression structures, 157
Organizational policy, 26
Organizational pressures, 123, 124
Outdoor sex providers, 303
Overstimulation, 159
Oxytocin, 215

P
Pain management medications, 27
Palliative care, 34
Palliative Care Network (SWHPN), 28
Pandemic, 19, 33, 141
Paper-based CBT self-monitoring forms, 98
Parallel processes, 45, 213
Parental alienation (PA)
   children, 82
   coercive control, 83
   correlation, 83
   IPV, 83
   monitoring behaviors, 82
   narratives, 82
   PAS, 82
   perpetrator, 82
   psychological abuse, 79
   psychological associations, 83
   psychological foundation, 82
   psychological maltreating, 83

Parental alienation syndrome (PAS), 82
Parental incarceration
   attachment theory, 292, 296, 297
   children's attachment disruptions,
      293, 294
   children's trauma symptomatology, 298
   COVID-19, 297
   effects, 291
   empirical investigation, 292
   healing spaces, 293
   in-person attachment/consistency, 298
   material and emotional insecurity, 292
   mental health crisis, 294
   racialized systemic oppression, 292
   RCT, 292, 296
   shared trauma, 298, 299
   trauma symptoms development, 299
Parent-child and sibling relationships, 349
Patients' subjective realities, 183
Patient-therapist dyads, 174
PCW agencies, 254
PCW workers
   conversations, 250
   fiscal problems, 254
   jobs, 254
   leadership needs, 250
   managing and supporting
      practices, 255
   organizational strategies, 255
   pain and conflict, 252
   safety concerns, 252
   SdTS, 250, 253
   social distancing advisories, 253
   social stressors, 254
   traumatic stories, 251
   vulnerable populations, 254
People Living with AIDS (PLA), 128
Perfect storm, 86
Perpetrators, 71
Personal and professional boundaries, 351
Personal and professional relationships, 352
Personal narratives, 160
Personal protective equipment (PPE), 16, 55,
      130, 254
Person-in-environment, 194, 196
Persons of color (POC), 299
Pets, 350
   animal-assisted therapists, 215
   care, 214
   companions, 216
   mindful and joyous living, 216
   older adults with dementia, 214
   oxytocin, 214, 215
   shelter-in-place orders, 215
   virus spreading, 216

Phone coaching
  DBT patients, 223
  function, 228
  patient and therapist, 223
  rules, 228
  secondary effect, 223
  skills generalization, 223
Physical boundaries, 73
Physical violence, 61
Physician and emergency responder, 45
Pleasure reading, 201
Police brutality
  Black and brown communities, 273
  COVID-19 crisis, 273
  death factor, 273
  Minneapolis, 273
  nationwide protests, 271
  racial profiling, 273
  racism, 271, 273
  second-class citizenship, 274
Positionality, 158
Positive consequences, 75
Positive psychological change, 27, 28
*Post Hurricane Katrina Quality of
    Professional Practice Survey*
    (PKQPPS), 4
Post-migration stress
  health hazards, detention centers, 315, 316
  Latinx transgender migrants, 314–315
Post-Separation Abuse (PSA)
  children and alienation, 87
  coercive control, 81
  definition, 81
  domestic violence, 81
  experience, 83
  hopelessness, 86
  IPV incidences, 84, 85
  pawns, 81
Posttraumatic growth, 27, 28, 75, 189
Posttraumatic stress disorder (PTSD), 22, 118,
    119, 253, 282
Poverty and racism, 351
PPE-clad nurses, 18
Pre-COVID treatment interventions, 95
Pre-pandemic, 172
Primary person model, 139
Priorities, 199
Prison Policy Initiative, 294
Privacy illusion, 287
Procrastination, 189
Professional advocacy, 252
Professional growth, 196, 201
Professional posttraumatic growth, 75, 76
Professionalism, 190
Prone patients, 18

Provider-patient interactions, 26
Psychiatric emergency/and inpatient
    psychiatry units, 16
Psychiatric pandemic, 158
Psychiatry training, 41
Psychic death, 182
Psychoanalytic psychotherapy, 41
Psychoanalytic tradition, 189
Psychoanalytic training, 44, 47
Psychodynamic psychotherapy, 46
Psychological abuse, 86
Psychological and emotional distress, 34
Psychological distress, 190
Psychological evaluations
  asylum, 316
  in-person, 316
  mechanism, 316
  mental health professionals, 316
  shared trauma, 317
  therapeutic setting, 317
Psychological maltreatment, 84
Psychological narratives, 17
Psychological resilience, 317
Psychological subjective responses, 27
Psychological trauma, 44, 72
Psychological violence, 80
Psychosocial and medical implications,
    COVID-19, 294, 295
Psychotherapy, 46, 48, 108, 179
Public child welfare (PCW)
  challenges, 249
  human services workforces, 250
  organizational culture shifts, 255
  out-of-home placements, 249
Public health, 129, 168, 183, 351
Public schools, 136, 142

Q
Quarantine, 342, 343

R
*Race Traits and Tendencies of the American
    Negro* (Book), 283
Racial and ethnic minority, 54
Racial inequity, 277
Racial injustice, 274
Racial trauma and error, 327
Racism, 6, 8, 305
Racists, 282
Rational self-interest, 262
Recognition, 191
Reconceptualization, 337
Recovery-oriented principles, 56

Recovery Record, 98
Reflective learning cycle, 27
Registered nurse (RN), 27
Relational components, 169
Relational-cultural and attachment theories,
    297, 298
Relational-cultural practices, 300
Relational-cultural theory (RCT), 296
Relational Resource, 239
Relational therapy, 191
Relational trauma, 241
Remote counseling
    curated therapeutic space, 191
    potentials, 192
    research and literature, 191
    therapeutic approach and expertise, 191
    therapeutic benefits, 191
    transition loss, 191
Remote learning, 137, 138, 140
Remote therapy, 152, 153
Replacement behaviors, 222
Resident, 42
Residential treatment, 145, 146
Resilience, 28, 130
    asylees, 317
    clinical social work, 157
    community requirement, 158
    coping, 161 (*see also* Resilient coping)
    COVID-19 pandemic, 157
    definition, 157
    field, 161
    impacts, 158
    social workers, 157
    stress levels, 317
Resilient coping
    ASD, 161
    Brief Resilient Coping Scale, 161
    social workers, 161
Resource development and installation
    (RDI), 238
Responsibility, 276, 351
Retraumatization, 246
Road-mapping, 99

S
Safe "pod", 62
Safe and secure holding environment, 35
Safe communication, 64
Safe technology access, 64
Safety tools, 64
Sankofa, 281
Scholarship, 205
School of Social Work, 332

School social workers
    agency-based, 139
    cash grants and gift cards, 140
    CDC, 137
    charter schools, 136–138, 140, 142
    communication, 137
    community school model, 136, 142
    community school staff, 138
    COVID-19, 135–137, 142
    crisis intervention, 136, 142
    DOE school, 137
    families, 139
    Google forms, 139
    health crisis, 140
    high school, 135, 136, 140
    historical events, 135
    IEP evaluation, 136
    laptop distribution program, 139
    mental health challenges, 142
    mental health needs
        families, 140
        staff, 140, 141
        students, 140, 141
    mental health symptoms, 139
    non-profit, 138
    NYC, 136, 142
    population, 135
    primary person model, 139
    public schools, 136, 142
    remote learning, 137, 138
    resource response, 139
    school-based counseling program, 136
    school-based staff, 137
    settings, 135
    students, 139
Schwartz Center Rounds, 28
Second law of thermodynamics, 275
Secondary traumatic responses, 255
Secondary traumatic stress, 40
Self-awareness, 179
Self-care, 200, 344, 350
    advantages, 261, 262
    application, 358
    boundaries setting, 362, 363
    comprehensive guide, 261
    COVID-19 pandemic, 263
    definition, 261
    guides, 358
    identify, 261
    individually initiated strategies/rituals, 261
    making time, 364
    measures implementation, 358
    mindfulness (*see* Mindfulness)
    neoliberalism, 262, 263

occupational stress, 262
practices, 287, 365
resilience, 318
resources, 357
rudimentary elements, 262
social work education, 262
strategies and practices, 358
theoretical foundations, 262
Self-care-focused physical activities, 364
Self-care-oriented hobby, 364
Self-compassion, 99
Self-defense empowerment training, 65
Self-destruction, 43
Self-determination, 56
Self-directed EMDR, 240
Self-disclosure, 48, 132, 245, 341, 351
Self-efficacy, 215
Self-esteem, 112, 158
Self-guided grounding techniques, 244
Self-hatred, 96
Self-less self, 183
Self-loathing, 96
Self-proclaimed hoarder, 73
Self-protection, 65
Self-quarantine, 168, 350
Self-regulation, 94
Semipermanent solution, 348
Sense of control, 110
Sense of friendship, 192
Sense of integrity, 57
Sense of safety, 181
Sensory-and detail-oriented examination, 360
Sensory-based stimulus, 240
Service-learning
    Alzheimer's disease, 335, 336
    community program participants, 336
    course, 332, 338
    COVID-19 crisis, 332
    elements, 331
    holocaust survivors, 335
    immigrant youth, 334
    importance, 331
    in-person education, 336
    long-term positive effects, 332
    youth and community engagement,
        332, 333
Service-LEARNING model, 331, 338
Sex workers
    Black street, 305
    FOSTA/SESTA, 304
    hacking/hustling, 304
    social isolation, 304
    US, 303
Shared embodiment, 171, 172

Shared reality, 26
Shared resilience, 27, 318
Shared therapeutic space, 191
Shared trauma, 17, 131, 132, 140, 153, 154,
        342, 343
    AAT, 8
    children and adolescents, 8
    civic engagement program, 8
    client and clinician, 5
    clinical distance, 2
    clinician-based trauma, 2
    collective disaster, 4, 5
    collective trauma, 2
    compassion fatigue, 3
    compassion satisfaction, 5
    conflicts, 7
    coping and managing, 36
    coronavirus pandemic, 5
    COVID-19, 29
    definition, 2, 41, 74
    disaster, 3, 4
    domestic violence, 6
    emotional contagion, 2
    existential distress, 33
    experience, 5, 37, 46
    fears, 7
    HWs, 21, 26
    influence, 3
    intimate interaction, 6
    intimate partner, 6
    learning, 9
    macro-level issues, 9
    mindfulness-based practices, 9
    mobile health applications, 8
    moral distress, 6
    multiple levels, 2
    pain and uncertainty, 33
    pandemic-specific stressors, 8
    person-in-environment perspective, 7
    populations, 6
    post-separation abuse, 6
    posttraumatic stress, 3
    PQPPS, 3
    professional posttraumatic growth, 3
    psychoanalysts, 2
    racial and economic inequality, 9
    risk factors, 3
    secondary trauma constructs, 3
    secure attachment, 3
    self-care and reflective practice, 7
    self-disclosure, 4
    sex industry, 8
    shared reality, 2
    shared traumatic reality, 2

Shared trauma (*cont.*)
   social distancing, 6
   social norms, 7
   social service agencies, 9
   social work educators, 2, 6
   social work health care, 6
   spiritual framework, 8
   STPPG, 4
   stress, 3
   supervisors, 48
   vicarious resilience, 5
   virtual space, 7
   virtual speaking engagements, 5
Shared trauma psychoeducation, 300
Shared Traumatic and Professional
      Posttraumatic Growth Inventory
      (STPPG), 4
Shared traumatic experiences, 159
Shared traumatic reality, 75, 168, 189, 323
Shared traumatic stress (SdTS), 250, 253, 255
Shell shock, 282
Sheltering, 86
Signature pedagogy, 332
Skills training group, 222
Social and economic injustices, 54
Social communication, 161
Social deprivation, 349
Social distancing, 55, 58, 161, 205, 307
Social emotional learning, 337
Social injustice, 55
Social isolation, 57, 215, 342, 343, 350
Social justice, 54, 55
Social media, 95, 349
Social/political climate, 183
Social work education, 342
Social work educators, 327
Social workers
   clients' and patients' experiences, 36
   competence, 57, 58
   complexity and challenge, 33
   dignity and worth, 55, 56
   essential workers, 259
   front lines, 36
   housing programs, 54
   human relationships, 56, 57
   integrity, 57
   macro-level navigating complex
      systems, 259
   mental health services, 58
   mental health treatment, 54
   New York City, 53
   NYC hospital system, 33
   primary goal, 53
   responding and supporting people, 37

   shared connection and understanding, 34
   social justice, 54, 55
   support complex trauma, 33
   tasks, 35
   themes, 36
   training, 47
   values, 36
Social Work Hospice, 28
Social work practice history, 194
Social work practitioners, 196, 197
Social work students, 260, 349
Societal abuse, 310
Socioeconomic status, 36
Socioeconomic systemic oppression, 292
Somatized symptoms, 242
Spiritual and metaphysical approach, 277
Spirituality-based approach, 275, 276
Splitting, 82
Sporadic telephone check-ins, 336
Stabilization resourcing, 245
Stance/emotional distance, 74
Stay-at-home orders, 69, 72, 95, 168, 179
Stereotypical proletariat Black experience, 309
Stigma, 159
Stop Enabling Sex Traffickers Act
      (SESTA), 304
Strengthening therapeutic community, 300
Stress and conflict management, 62
Stress hormones, 349
Stress management workshops, 110
Stress symptoms, 110
Stressors, 220
Stress-reducing companionship, 216
Strict no-visitation policy, 200
Student's educational status, 46
Submissive states, 70
Substance Abuse and Mental Health Services
      Administration's (SAMHSA), 160
Suffering, 35
Suicidal and self-injurious urges, 222
Supervisee, 40, 43, 48
Supervising psychiatry residents
   anxiety, 42
   competition and potential belittlement, 44
   COVID-19, 39, 41
   disease contacting, 39
   dynamic approach, 42
   guidance and instruction, 41
   IMGs, 42
   intrusive thoughts, 44
   mental health care, 40
   overidentification, 42
   personal difficulties, 43
   psychiatry training, 41

psychodynamic works, 44
resemblances, 40
shared trauma, 39, 42
supervisee, 40
supervisors, 40
teletherapy, 43
transient identification, 40
trauma-informed care, 41
trauma-informed supervision, 46
veiled charges, 44
Supervision
complements, 47
complexities, 46
medical workers, 45
patients, 48
principal program, 41
psychoanalytic training, 44
self-disclosure, 48
structure and mission, 43
supervisee, 40
supervisor, 39
unconscious expression, 47
Supervisors, 40, 47
Supervisory situation stability, 48
Survivor-centered advocacy, 63
Survivor-focused advocacy, 66
Survivor-focused safety planning, 63, 64
Sustainable social work, 193
Symptom-use, 94
Systemic racism, 291, 299, 351

T
Targeted parent (TP), 82
Teaching relationship
boundaries, 326
COVID-19 pandemic, 325
gestures, 326
higher education institutions, 325
mutuality, 326
professional distance, 326
shared trauma, 323, 328
undergraduate/graduate social work
students, 325
Team meeting, 230
Telehealth, 73, 95
Telehealth platform, 69, 73
Telehealth sessions, 73
Telepresence, 171
Telepsychotherapy, 242, 246
Teletherapy, 5–8, 96, 145, 146, 150, 152,
153, 237
Television and social media, 349
Theory of mind, 47
Therapeutic approaches, 29

Therapeutic attitudes, 169
Therapeutic dyad, 169
Therapeutic exchanges, 189
Therapeutic frame
conceptualization, 169
elements, 169
importance, 169
psychotherapeutic works shifts, 170, 176
structural and relational components, 169
structural dimension, 170
Therapeutic intimacy, 190, 351
Therapeutic relationship, 74
clinical experience post-9/11, 170
collective trauma, 174
holding environment, 170
psychotherapy differing delivery, 172
safety, 184
shared trauma experience, 167
Therapy animals, 217
Therapy-interfering behavior, 225
Traditional masculinity/control paradigms, 66
Trainee's insecurities and inexperience, 44–45
Training supervisors, 46
Transcendence, 37
Transformative learning, 27
Transgender asylum-seeking individuals, 313
Trauma, 40
ACEs, 282
awareness, 286
biological research, 282
conceptual framework, 282
definition, 282
genesis, 282
PTSD, 282
shell shock, 282
Trauma-focused cognitive behavioral therapy
(TF-CBT), 237
Trauma-informed care, 41
Trauma-informed supervision, 46
Trauma-laden environment, 140
Trauma scholars, 327
Trauma survivors, 75
Traumatic impact of 9/11, 188
Traumatization, 176
Traumatogenic context, 167
Treatment modality, 221–222
TV personalities, 19

U
U-Haul rental, 199
Uncertainty, 76, 187
climate, 179
helplessness, 182
vulnerability, 182

Uncharted territory, 323
Unconscious bias, 159
Unemployment
    clinician/coach, 109
    COVID-19, 107, 108
    disorientation, 113
    frustration, 109
    getting job, 108
    pressures, 108
    shocks, 110
    U.S., 109
    worthlessness feelings, 107
University-wide policy, 205
Unmetabolized memories, 238
Urban planners, 198
US-based sex worker demographic, 304
US Customs and Border Protection
        (CBP), 315
US jails and prisons, COVID-19, 294
US prison system, 294
User-friendly safety skills manual, 66

V
V-EMDR-specific training and education, 246
Vicarious trauma, 40
Video platform, 171
Violation of expectations, 129, 130
Violence against women, 70
Violent incident model, 80
Viral pandemic, 16
Virtual AA meetings, 19
Virtual EMDR (V-EMDR) therapy
    appropriate and regulated environment, 240
    BAA, 240
    confidential therapeutic environment, 241
    practices, 240
    tele-mental health certification, 241
    therapists, 240
Virtual meeting, 216
Virtual mindfulness, 362
Virtual schooling, 74
Volunteer community, 211
Volunteering, 47
Volunteer-Neighbor pairs, 207
Volunteers, 209

W
WE WORK organizations, 19
WE WORK situation at home, 15
Well-being, 19, 159

Wellness calls, 337
White supremacists, 282
White supremacy
    anti-Blackness, 286
    Black lives, 284
    colonization, 283
    omnipresence, 289
    oppression and trauma, 288
    trauma, 281
Whiteboard activities, 337
Wholeheartedness
    analyst's attention, 181
    aspects, 180
    basic anxiety, 181
    experiential, 180
    healing splits process, 183
    ideas, 183
    intuitive assessment, 181
    shared trauma, 180
    significance, 182
    therapeutic state, 181
    traumatized people, 181
Work absenteeism, 260
Work Life office, 205, 206
Work-life balance, 363
World Trade Center, 347

Y
Youth and community engagement
    appreciation, 333
    digital divide, 333
    experienced challenges, 333
    meso-and macro-level factors, 333
    programming, 333

Z
Zoom and GoToMeetings, 57
Zoom group, 226
Zoom invasion, 286
Zoom meetings, 168
Zoom platform
    interaction, 307
    presentation, 307
    remote videoconferences, 306
    teletherapy, 307
    treatment session, 307
    videoconference computer program, 306
Zoom platforms, 350
Zoom therapy, 343
Zoom/GoToMeeting platform, 58

Printed by Printforce, the Netherlands